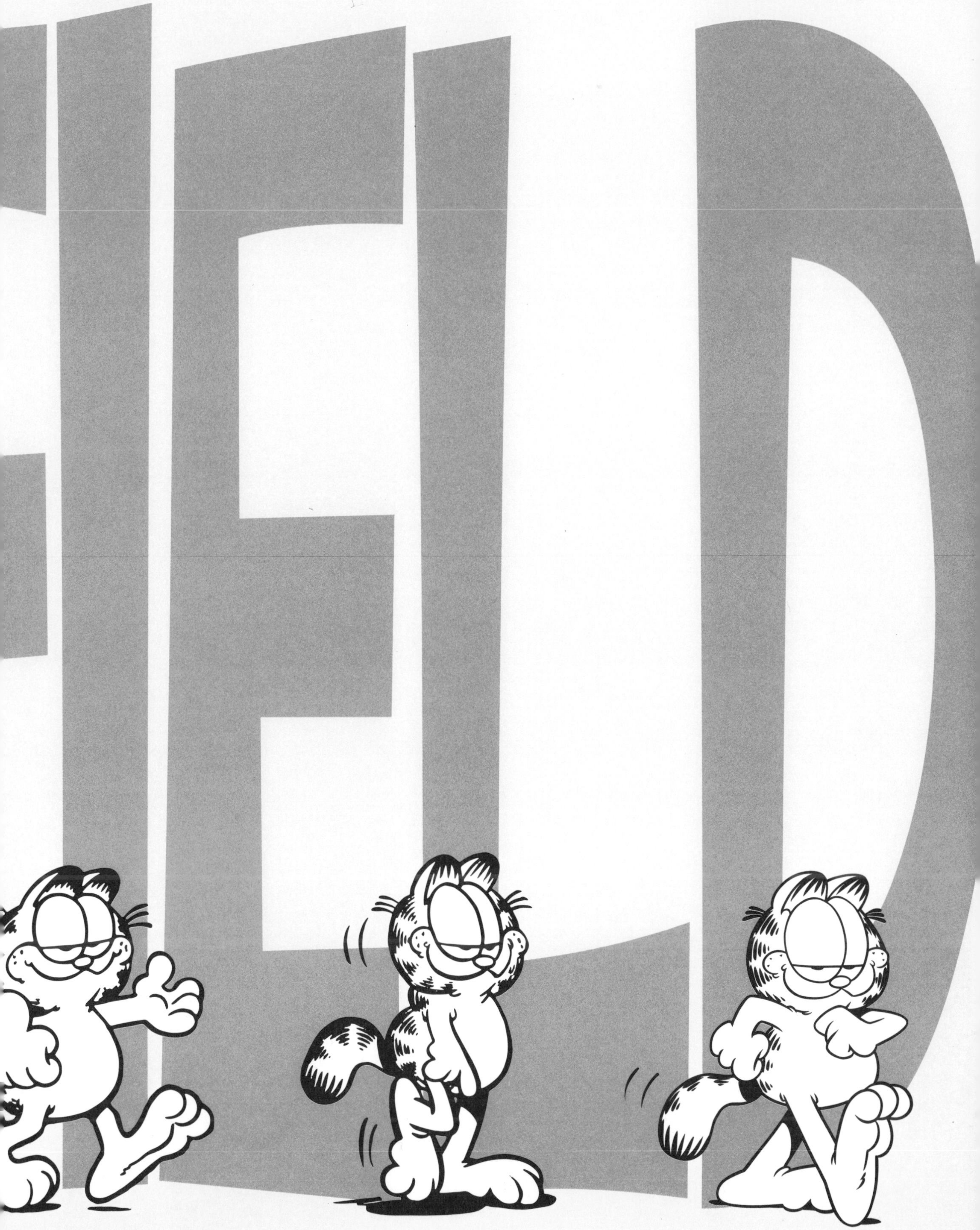

AGE HAPPENS

Garfield

HITS THE BIG 4-0

AGE HAPPENS

Garfield
HITS THE BIG 4-0

BY
JIM DAVIS

Ballantine Books • New York

Published in the United States by Ballantine Books, an imprint of Random House, a division of Penguin Random House LLC, New York.

BALLANTINE and the HOUSE colophon are registered trademarks of Penguin Random House LLC.

Hardback ISBN 978-0-345-52609-0
Ebook ISBN 978-0-525-61878-2

Printed in China on acid-free paper

randomhousebooks.com

987654321

First Edition

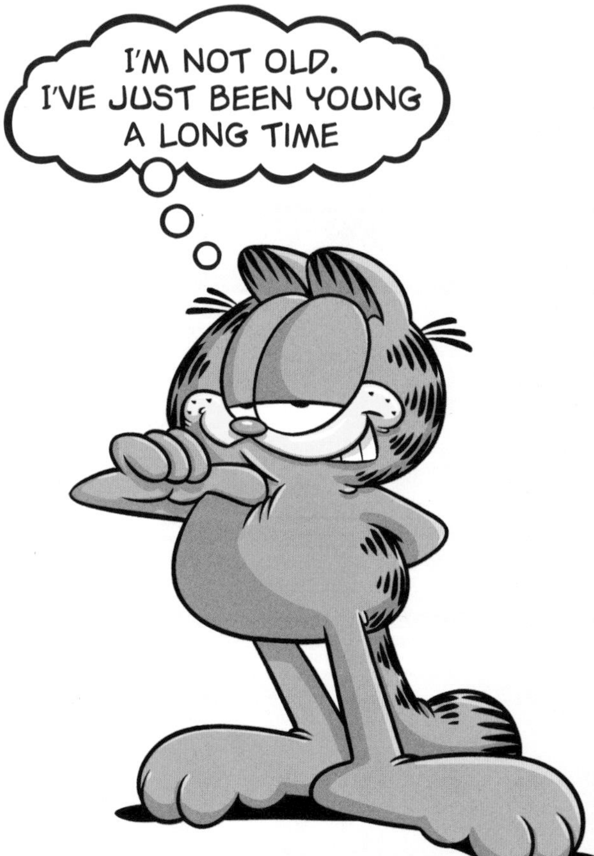
I'M NOT OLD. I'VE JUST BEEN YOUNG A LONG TIME

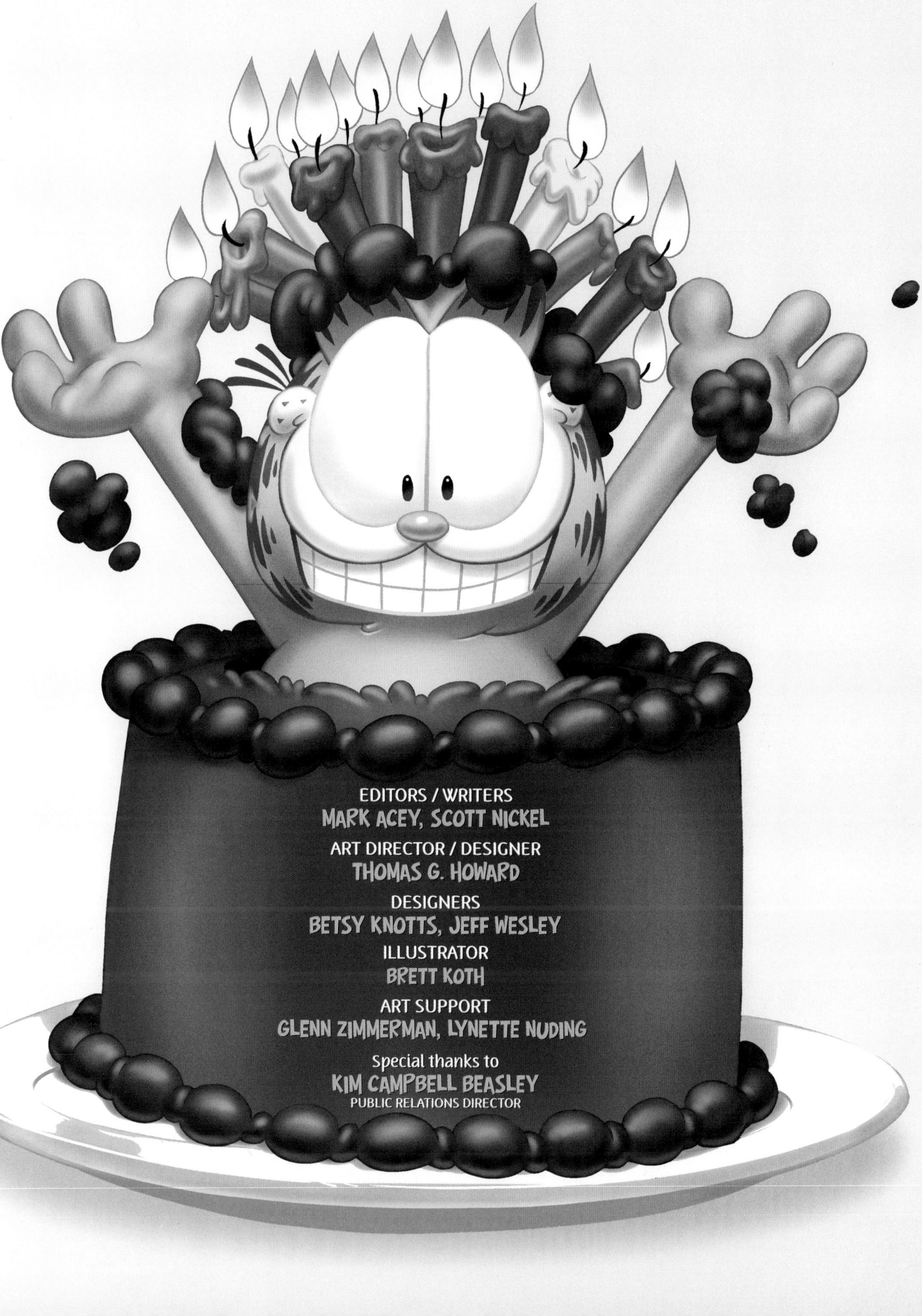

EDITORS / WRITERS
MARK ACEY, SCOTT NICKEL

ART DIRECTOR / DESIGNER
THOMAS G. HOWARD

DESIGNERS
BETSY KNOTTS, JEFF WESLEY

ILLUSTRATOR
BRETT KOTH

ART SUPPORT
GLENN ZIMMERMAN, LYNETTE NUDING

Special thanks to
KIM CAMPBELL BEASLEY
PUBLIC RELATIONS DIRECTOR

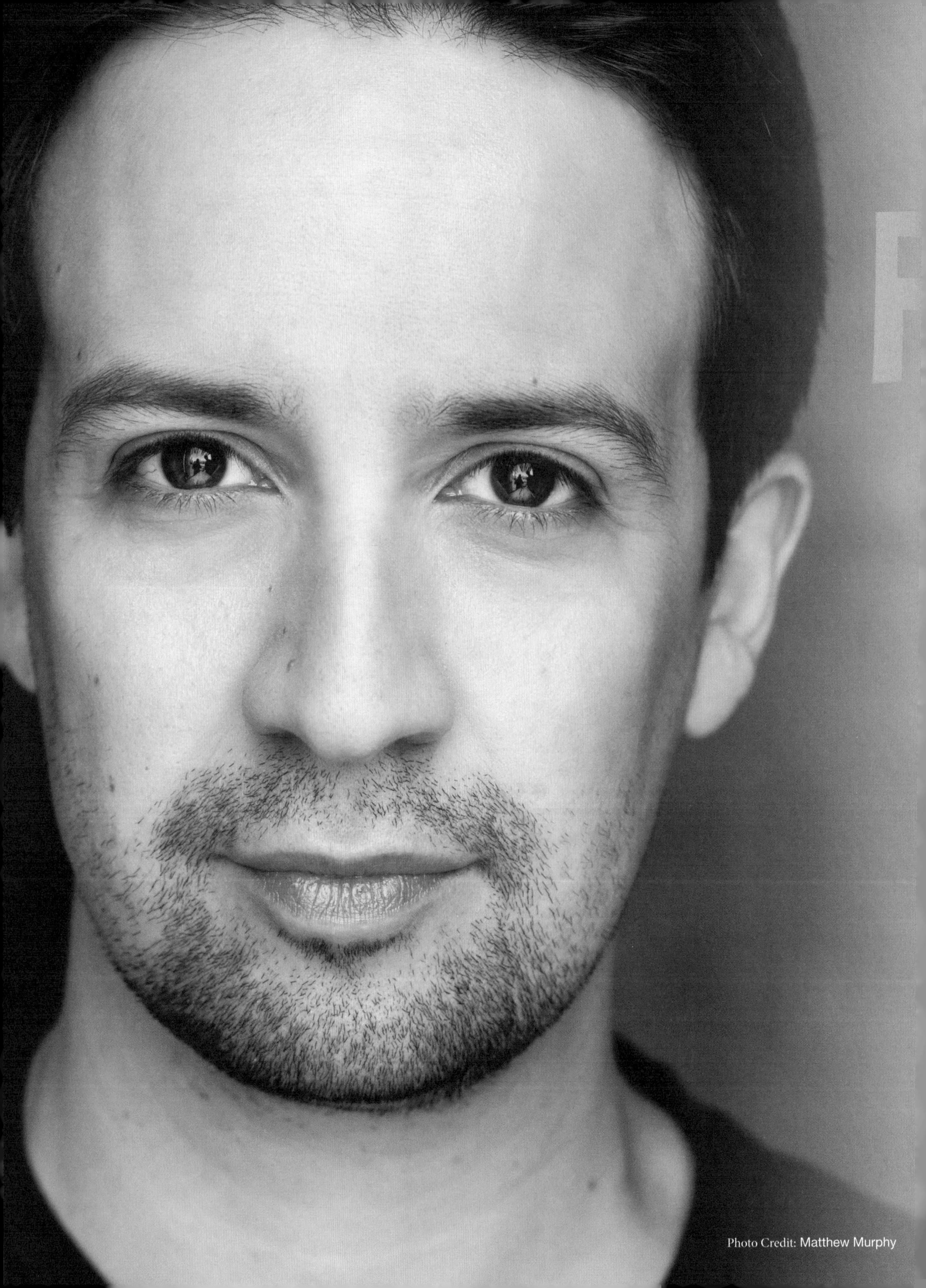

Photo Credit: Matthew Murphy

OREWORD

by Lin-Manuel Miranda

I suppose it began with the book order form.

Do you remember the book order form? They came to your elementary school classroom? Order three or more books and get a poster of a basket of puppies or a dangling kitten with the words "Hang in There, Baby"?

This is how Garfield's fifteenth collection, *Garfield Worldwide*, ended up in my hands. It was a gray cover (Nermal color) and differently shaped than any other book I'd ever seen. Garfield was on the cover, a globe of Earth on his stomach, and the thought bubble over his head read, "Your hemisphere or mine?"

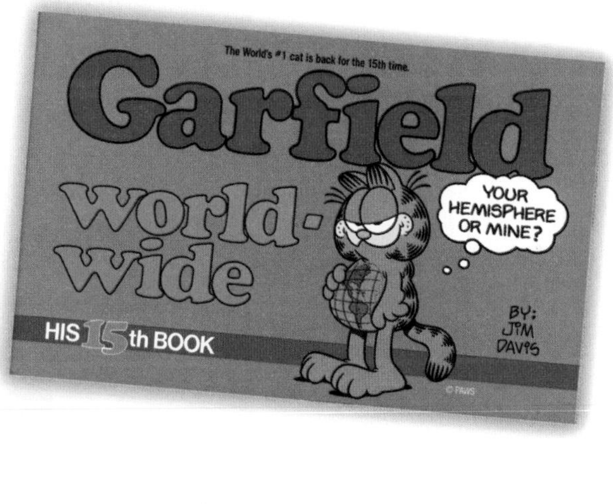
The World's #1 cat is back for the 15th time.
Garfield
world-wide
YOUR HEMISPHERE OR MINE?
HIS 15th BOOK
BY: JIM DAVIS

I opened the book and started laughing. My world was never the same.

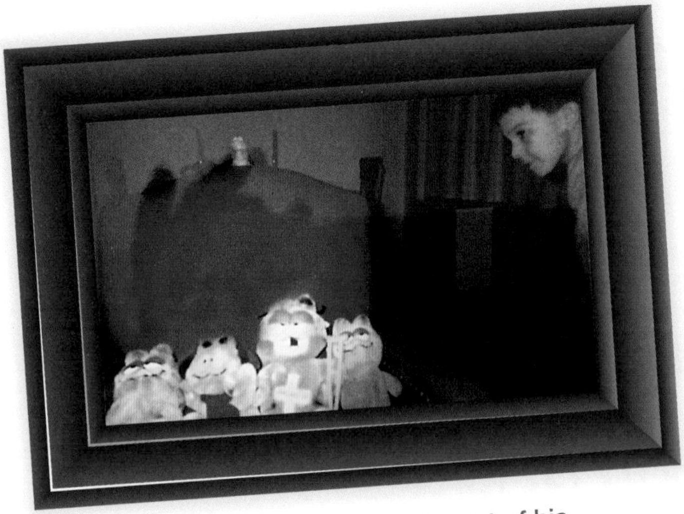

A young Lin-Manuel with part of his prized Garfield collection.

By the end of the year, I'd have ALL the books and dozens of Garfield and Odie dolls. I'd bring a Garfield-shaped cake into school on Garfield's birthday, June 19, only to burst into tears when I realized I'd have to cut the cake into pieces. I'd name my sister's kitten Nermal. I'd wait every Saturday morning for 11 a.m. when *Garfield & Friends* would air.

Garfield was my first full-blown pop-culture obsession. Why?

It begins with the strip. *Garfield* was the first comic strip to make me laugh out loud. Jim Davis's gags are such a heady mix of verbal and visual humor—he can make you laugh with a patented Garfield one-liner, or a pie in the face from an unexpected location (WHO IS THROWING THOSE SPLUTS?). Garfield's universe felt like a place where anything could happen—and as long as it was funny, everything would be okay the next day.

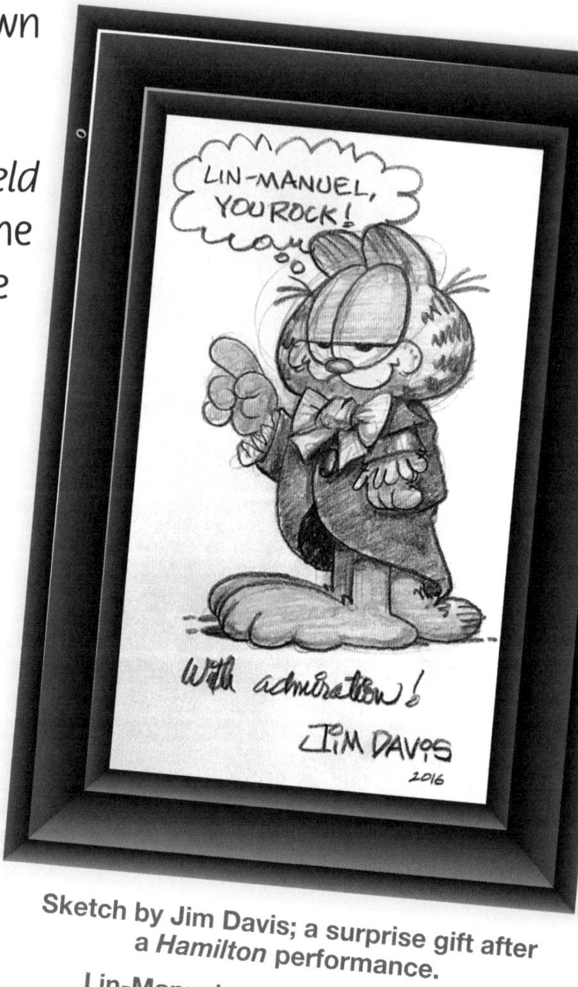
LIN-MANUEL, YOU ROCK!
With admiration!
JIM DAVIS
2016

Sketch by Jim Davis; a surprise gift after a *Hamilton* performance.

Lin-Manuel: "It makes me cry.... It's my Rosebud sled."

Then there's the character of Garfield himself, an ironic, detached cat who is mean to everyone and somehow all the more lovable for it. When I was a child, he was the closest thing I had to an id—able to poke fun at everyone around him, the coolest person in the room at all times, yet just as often be the butt of the joke, the victim of the universe. There was no question that he ran Jon Arbuckle's household in that way real cats do. Poor, meek Jon—hapless in every way, downright tragic if you remove Garfield from the equation (as anyone who has read *Garfield Minus Garfield* can tell you).

When I was in third grade, we all had to write "novels" for school—I turned in an eight-chapter odyssey about Garfield traveling to the past, present, and future in a time machine. This novel is now lost to time, but the entire thing was in rhyming couplets—my first lyric writing. I'm not saying Garfield is responsible for *Hamilton*, but Garfield himself would probably take credit.

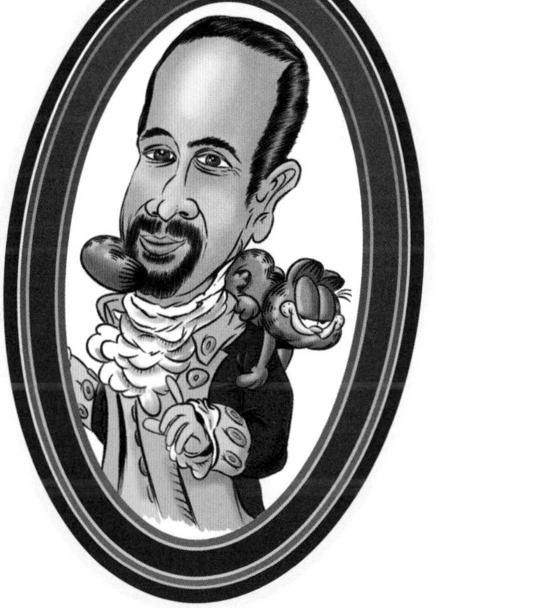

And now you hold in your hands a Garfield fortieth-anniversary collection. I hope you enjoy it. And if this is your FIRST Garfield collection—maybe you've ordered it on a book order form to get a free poster—get ready, kid. Your world will never be the same.

Siempre,

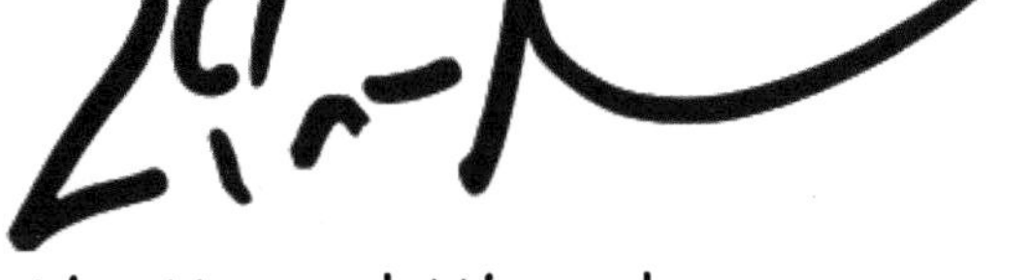

Lin-Manuel Miranda

40 YEARS OF GETTING DOWN WITH MY BAD SELF

MADE IN 1978
6-19-78

AGE HAPPENS
Garfield Hits the Big 4-0

A ★ IS BORN! JUNE 19, 1978

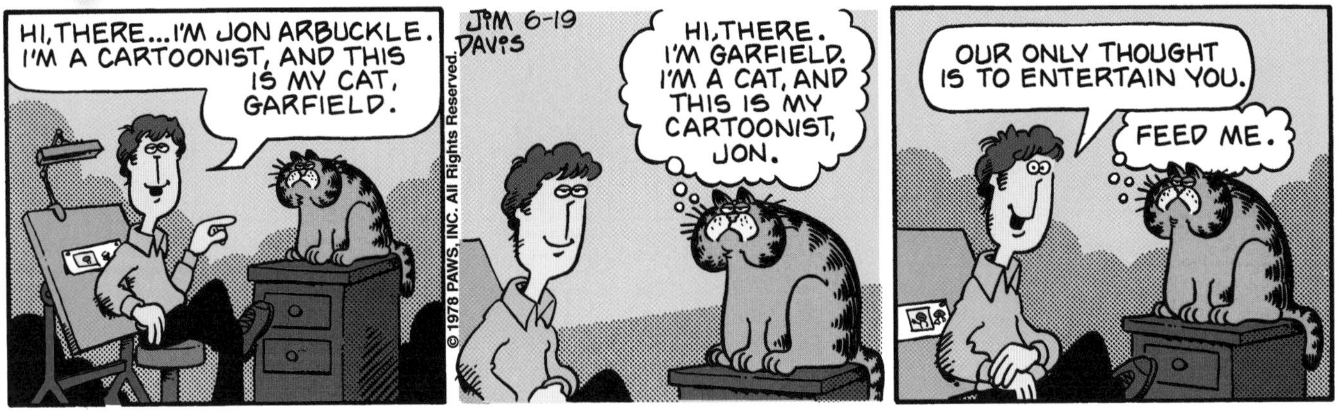
HI, THERE...I'M JON ARBUCKLE. I'M A CARTOONIST, AND THIS IS MY CAT, GARFIELD.
JIM DAVIS 6-19
© 1978 PAWS, INC. All Rights Reserved.
HI, THERE. I'M GARFIELD. I'M A CAT, AND THIS IS MY CARTOONIST, JON.
OUR ONLY THOUGHT IS TO ENTERTAIN YOU.
FEED ME.

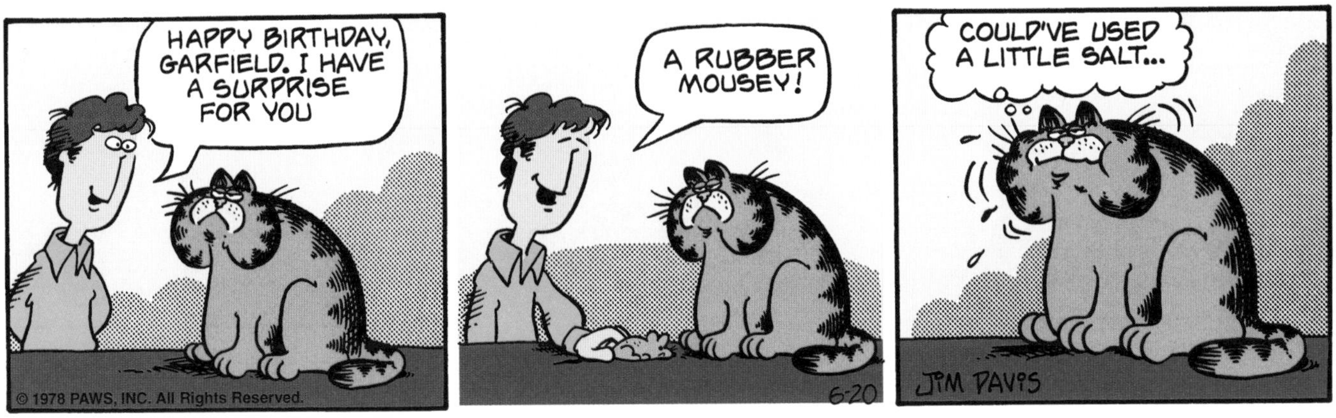
HAPPY BIRTHDAY, GARFIELD. I HAVE A SURPRISE FOR YOU
© 1978 PAWS, INC. All Rights Reserved.
A RUBBER MOUSEY!
6-20
COULD'VE USED A LITTLE SALT...
JIM DAVIS

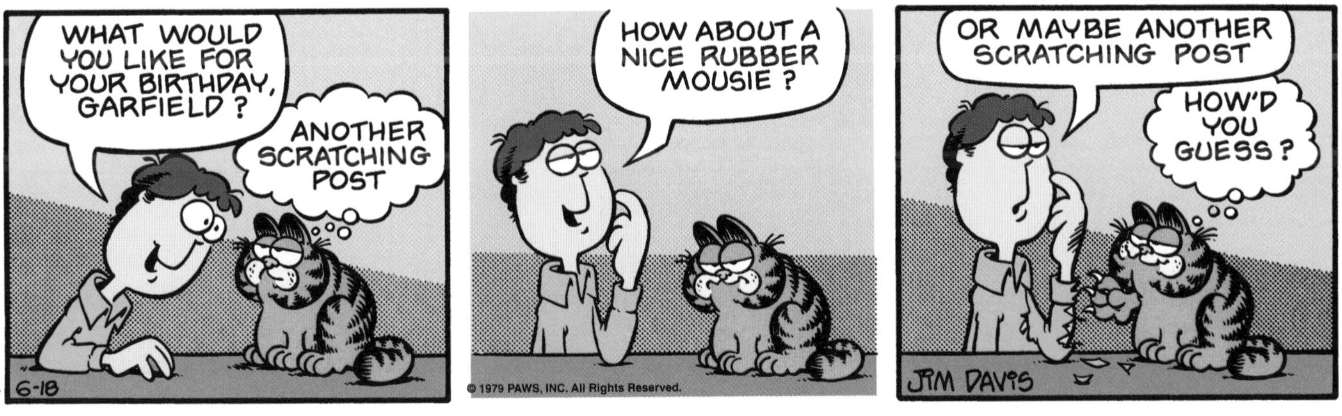
WHAT WOULD YOU LIKE FOR YOUR BIRTHDAY, GARFIELD?
ANOTHER SCRATCHING POST
6-18
HOW ABOUT A NICE RUBBER MOUSIE?
© 1979 PAWS, INC. All Rights Reserved.
OR MAYBE ANOTHER SCRATCHING POST
HOW'D YOU GUESS?
JIM DAVIS

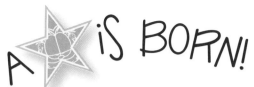

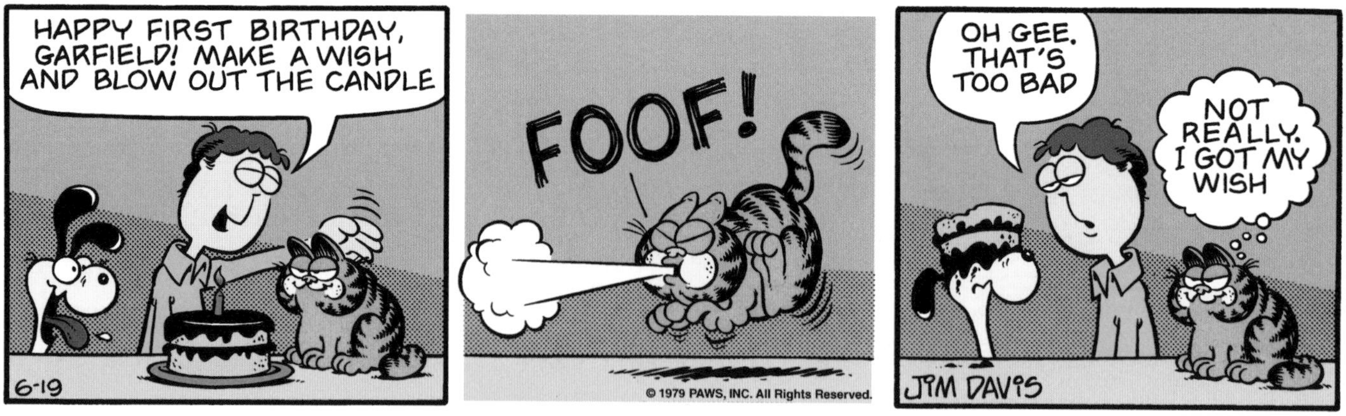
HAPPY FIRST BIRTHDAY, GARFIELD! MAKE A WISH AND BLOW OUT THE CANDLE
6-19
FOOF!
© 1979 PAWS, INC. All Rights Reserved.
OH GEE. THAT'S TOO BAD
NOT REALLY. I GOT MY WISH
JIM DAVIS

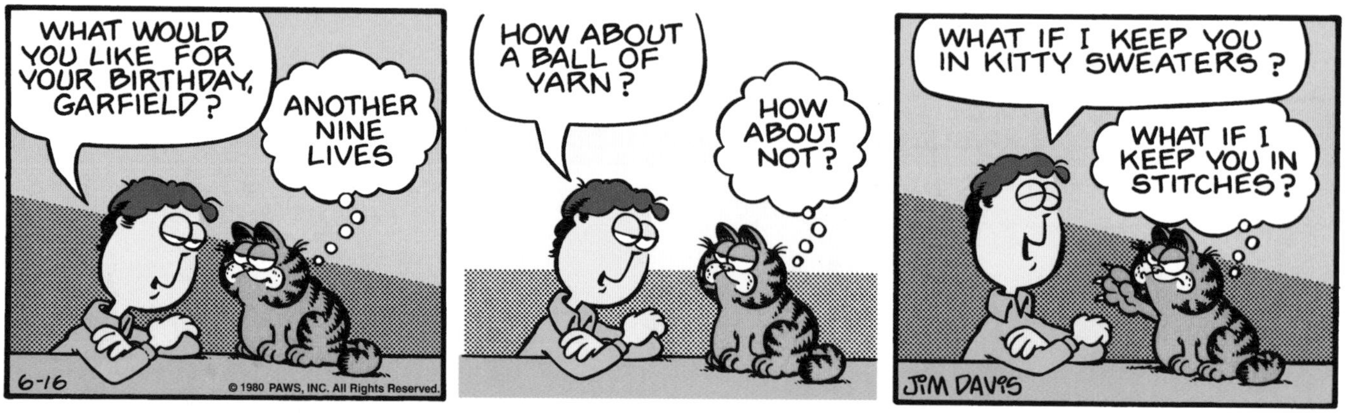
WHAT WOULD YOU LIKE FOR YOUR BIRTHDAY, GARFIELD?
ANOTHER NINE LIVES
6-16
© 1980 PAWS, INC. All Rights Reserved.
HOW ABOUT A BALL OF YARN?
HOW ABOUT NOT?
WHAT IF I KEEP YOU IN KITTY SWEATERS?
WHAT IF I KEEP YOU IN STITCHES?
JIM DAVIS

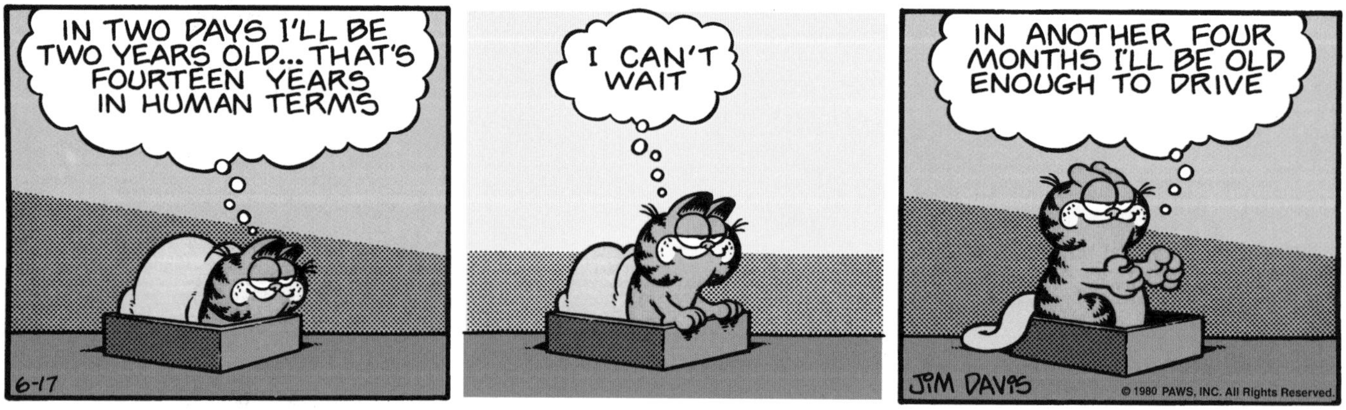
IN TWO DAYS I'LL BE TWO YEARS OLD... THAT'S FOURTEEN YEARS IN HUMAN TERMS
6-17
I CAN'T WAIT
IN ANOTHER FOUR MONTHS I'LL BE OLD ENOUGH TO DRIVE
JIM DAVIS
© 1980 PAWS, INC. All Rights Reserved.

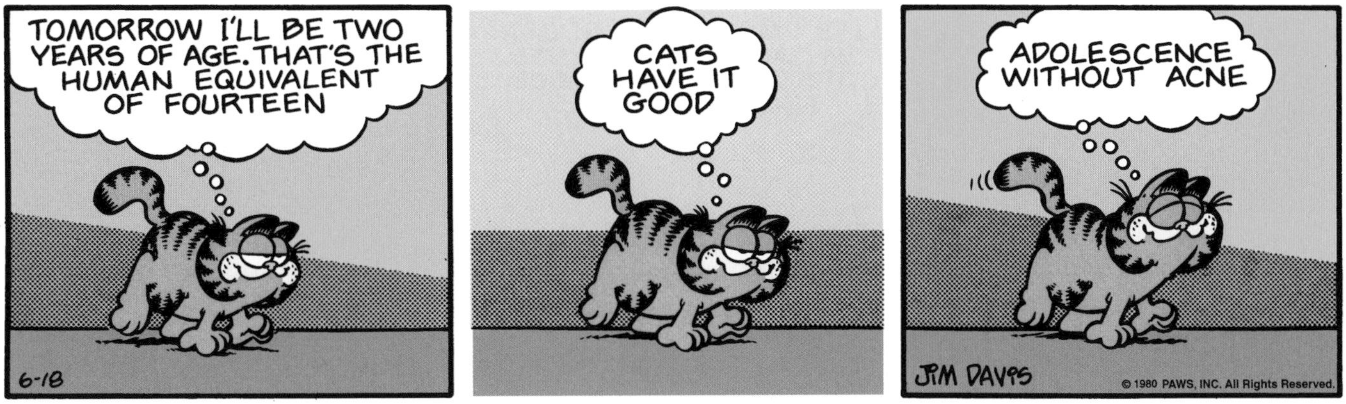
TOMORROW I'LL BE TWO YEARS OF AGE. THAT'S THE HUMAN EQUIVALENT OF FOURTEEN
6-18
CATS HAVE IT GOOD
ADOLESCENCE WITHOUT ACNE
JIM DAVIS
© 1980 PAWS, INC. All Rights Reserved.

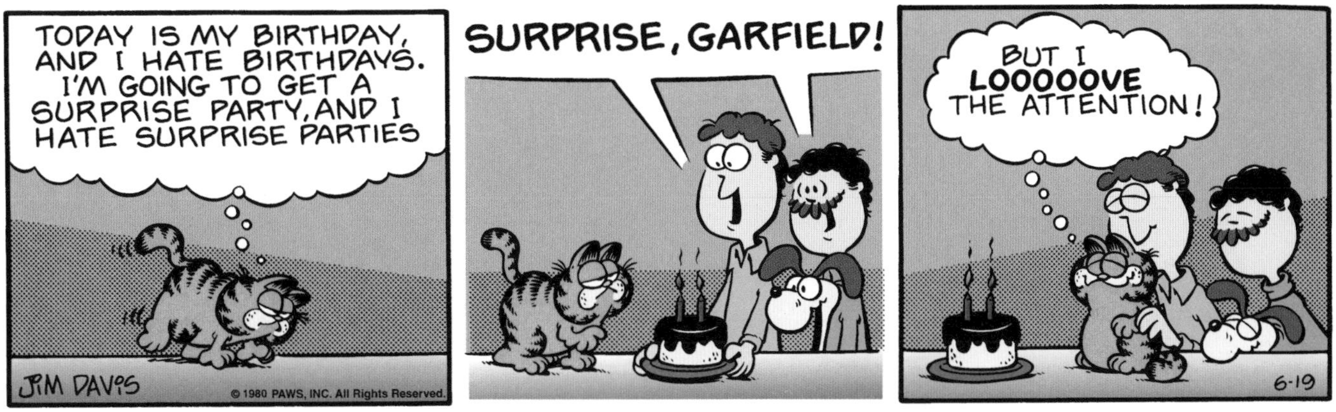
TODAY IS MY BIRTHDAY, AND I HATE BIRTHDAYS. I'M GOING TO GET A SURPRISE PARTY, AND I HATE SURPRISE PARTIES
JIM DAVIS
© 1980 PAWS, INC. All Rights Reserved.
SURPRISE, GARFIELD!
BUT I LOOOOOVE THE ATTENTION!
6-19

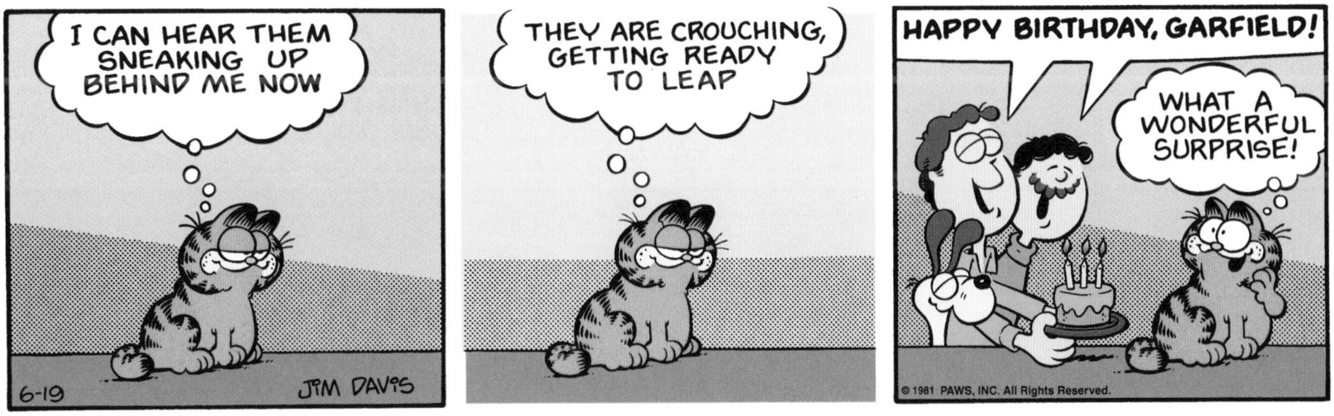
I CAN HEAR THEM SNEAKING UP BEHIND ME NOW
6-19
JIM DAVIS
THEY ARE CROUCHING, GETTING READY TO LEAP
HAPPY BIRTHDAY, GARFIELD!
WHAT A WONDERFUL SURPRISE!
© 1981 PAWS, INC. All Rights Reserved.

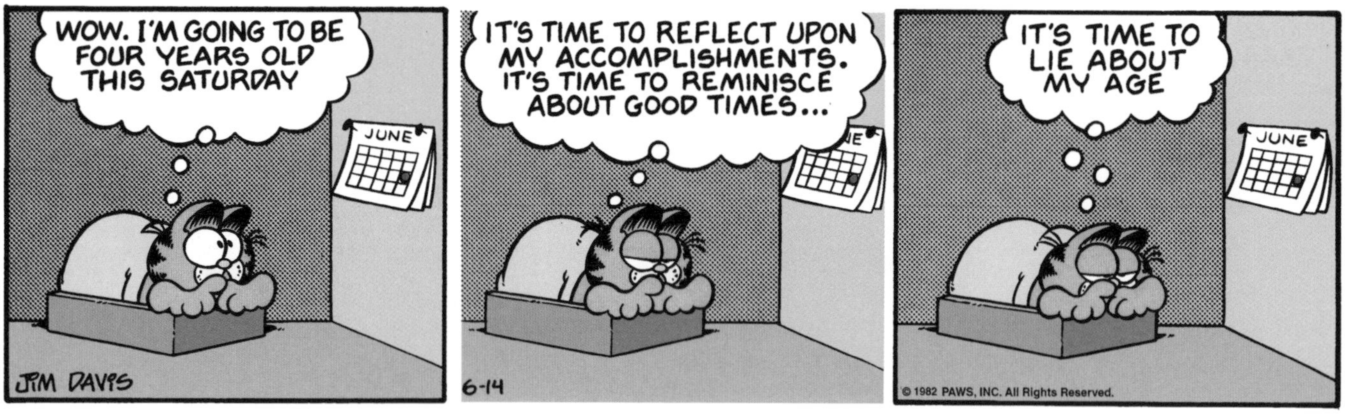
WOW. I'M GOING TO BE FOUR YEARS OLD THIS SATURDAY
JIM DAVIS
IT'S TIME TO REFLECT UPON MY ACCOMPLISHMENTS. IT'S TIME TO REMINISCE ABOUT GOOD TIMES...
6-14
IT'S TIME TO LIE ABOUT MY AGE
JUNE
© 1982 PAWS, INC. All Rights Reserved.

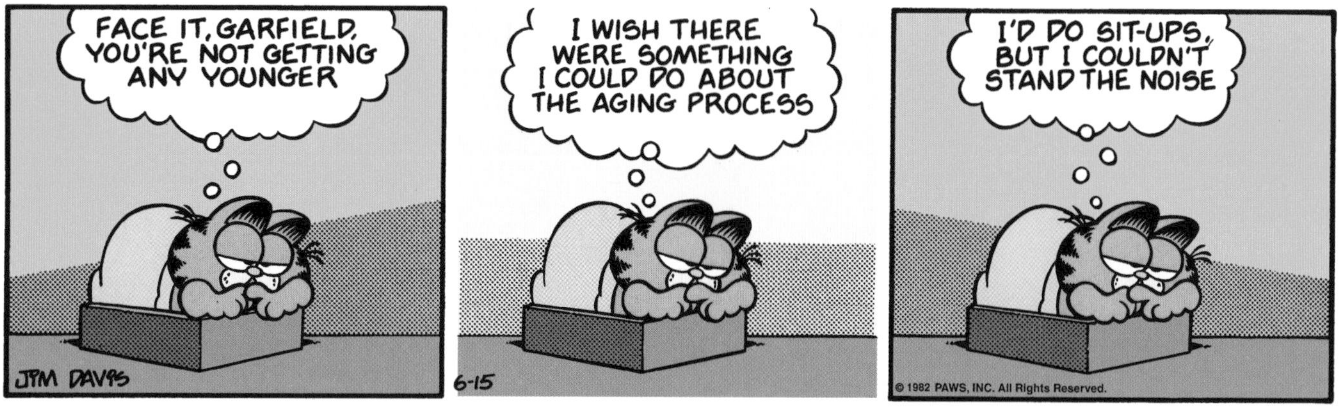
FACE IT, GARFIELD, YOU'RE NOT GETTING ANY YOUNGER
JIM DAVIS
I WISH THERE WERE SOMETHING I COULD DO ABOUT THE AGING PROCESS
6-15
I'D DO SIT-UPS, BUT I COULDN'T STAND THE NOISE
© 1982 PAWS, INC. All Rights Reserved.

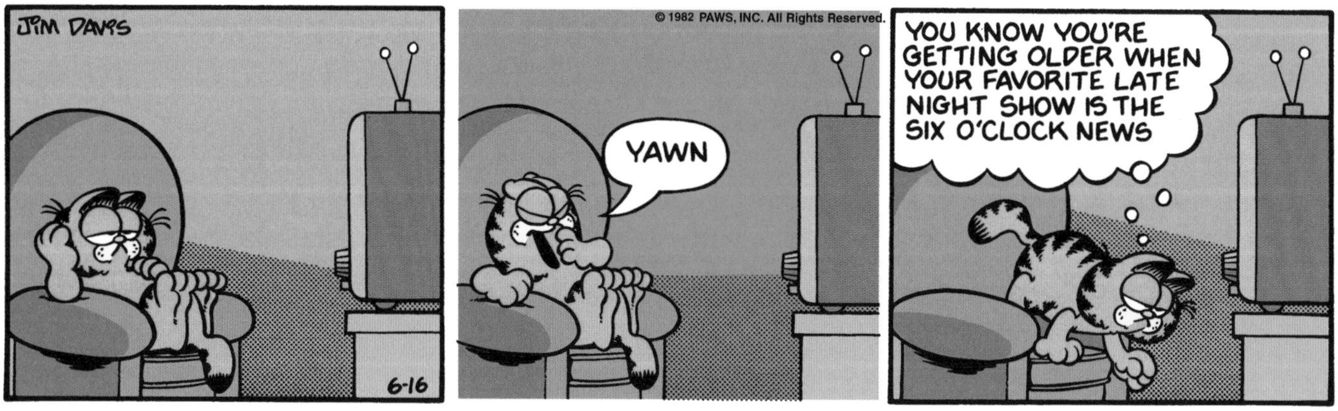
JIM DAVIS
6-16
© 1982 PAWS, INC. All Rights Reserved.
YAWN
YOU KNOW YOU'RE GETTING OLDER WHEN YOUR FAVORITE LATE NIGHT SHOW IS THE SIX O'CLOCK NEWS

IT HARDLY SEEMS POSSIBLE I'M CELEBRATING MY FOURTH BIRTHDAY TOMORROW
JIM DAVIS
6-18
BARK!
SPLAT!
TIME FLIES WHEN YOU'RE HAVING FUN
© 1982 PAWS, INC. All Rights Reserved.

5 FUN FACTS ABOUT GARFIELD

READING THE NEWSPAPER AGAIN?
WHY? THERE'S NOTHING IN THERE ABOUT ME
EXCEPT FOR THAT ARTICLE ABOUT THE CANDY STORE RIOT

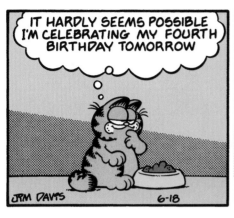

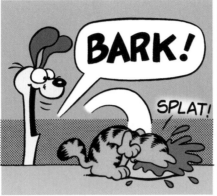

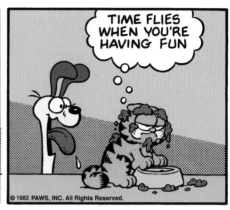

GARFIELD holds the Guinness World Record as the most widely syndicated comic strip in the world.

Garfield has 17 million Facebook fans. And several stalkers!

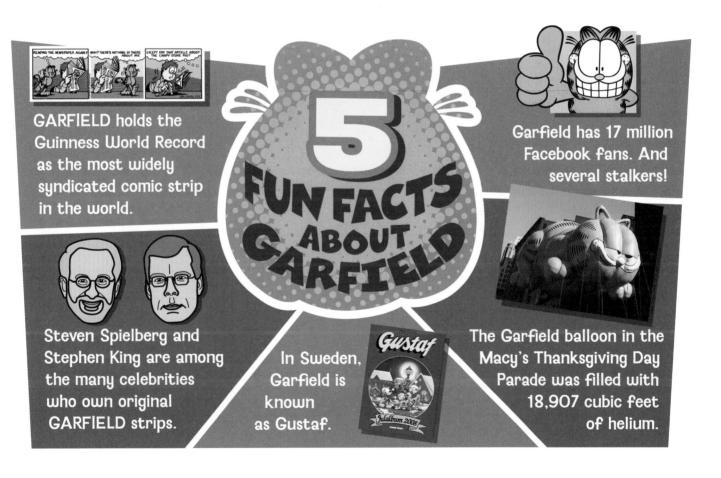

Steven Spielberg and Stephen King are among the many celebrities who own original GARFIELD strips.

Gustaf
Julalbum 2008

In Sweden, Garfield is known as Gustaf.

The Garfield balloon in the Macy's Thanksgiving Day Parade was filled with 18,907 cubic feet of helium.

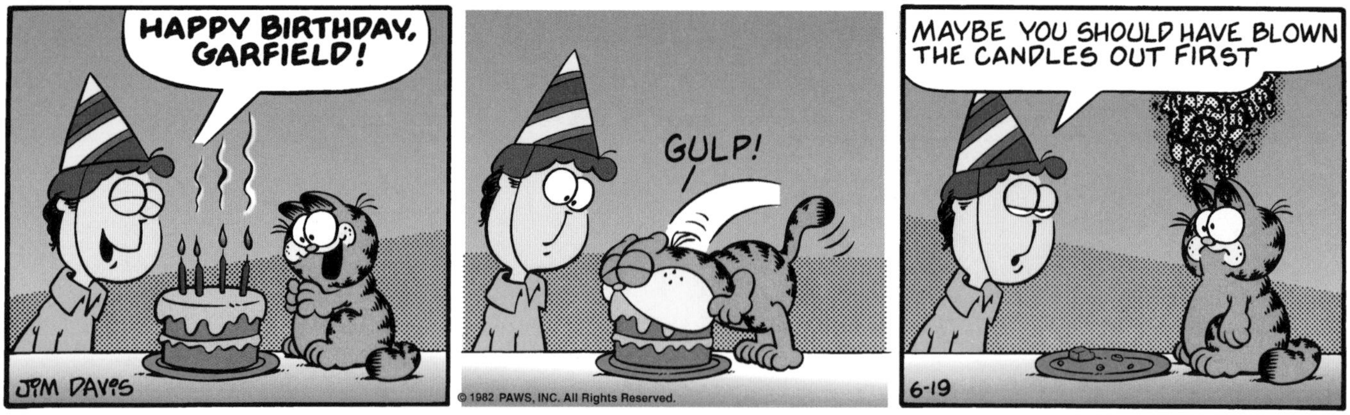
HAPPY BIRTHDAY, GARFIELD!
JIM DAVIS
GULP!
© 1982 PAWS, INC. All Rights Reserved.
MAYBE YOU SHOULD HAVE BLOWN THE CANDLES OUT FIRST
6-19

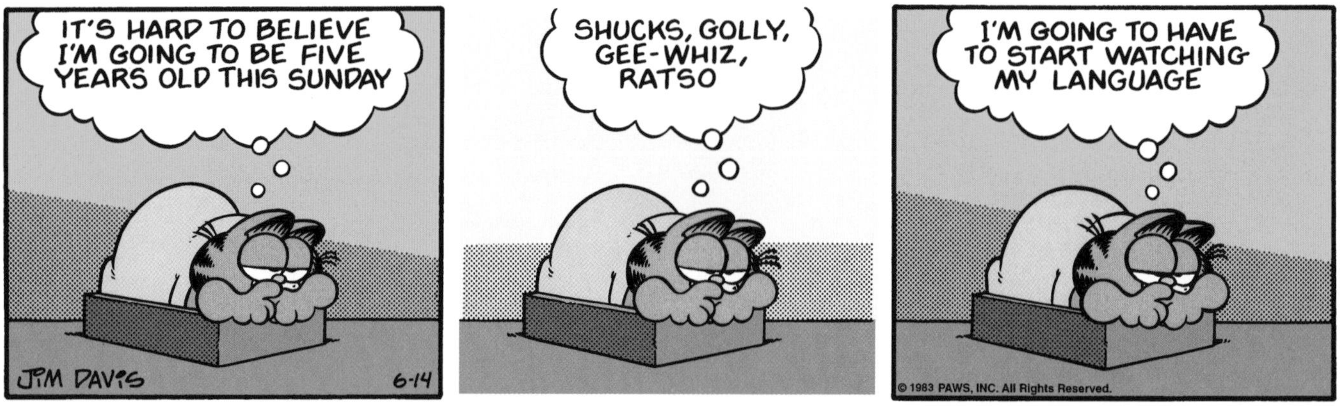
IT'S HARD TO BELIEVE I'M GOING TO BE FIVE YEARS OLD THIS SUNDAY
JIM DAVIS
6-14
SHUCKS, GOLLY, GEE-WHIZ, RATSO
I'M GOING TO HAVE TO START WATCHING MY LANGUAGE
© 1983 PAWS, INC. All Rights Reserved.

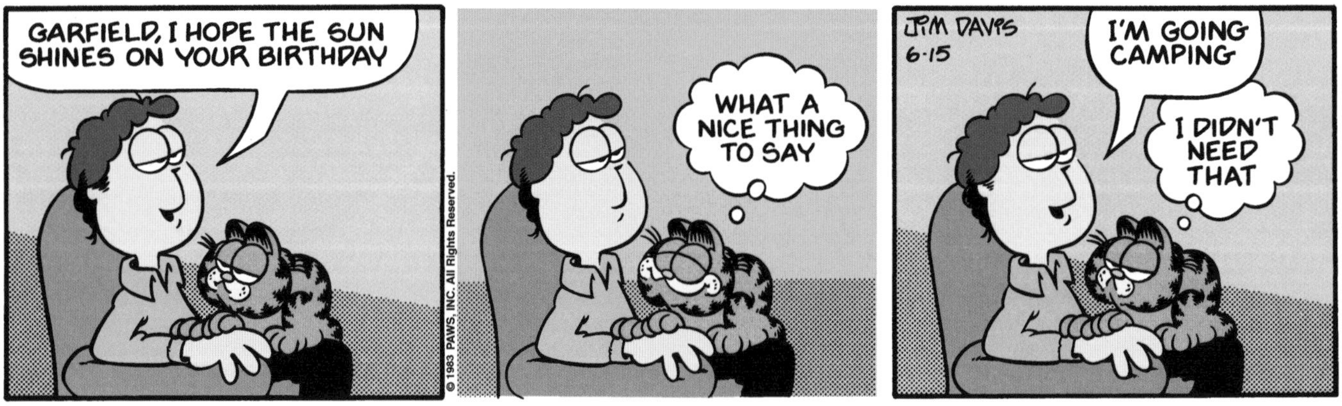
GARFIELD, I HOPE THE SUN SHINES ON YOUR BIRTHDAY
© 1983 PAWS, INC. All Rights Reserved.
WHAT A NICE THING TO SAY
JIM DAVIS
6-15
I'M GOING CAMPING
I DIDN'T NEED THAT

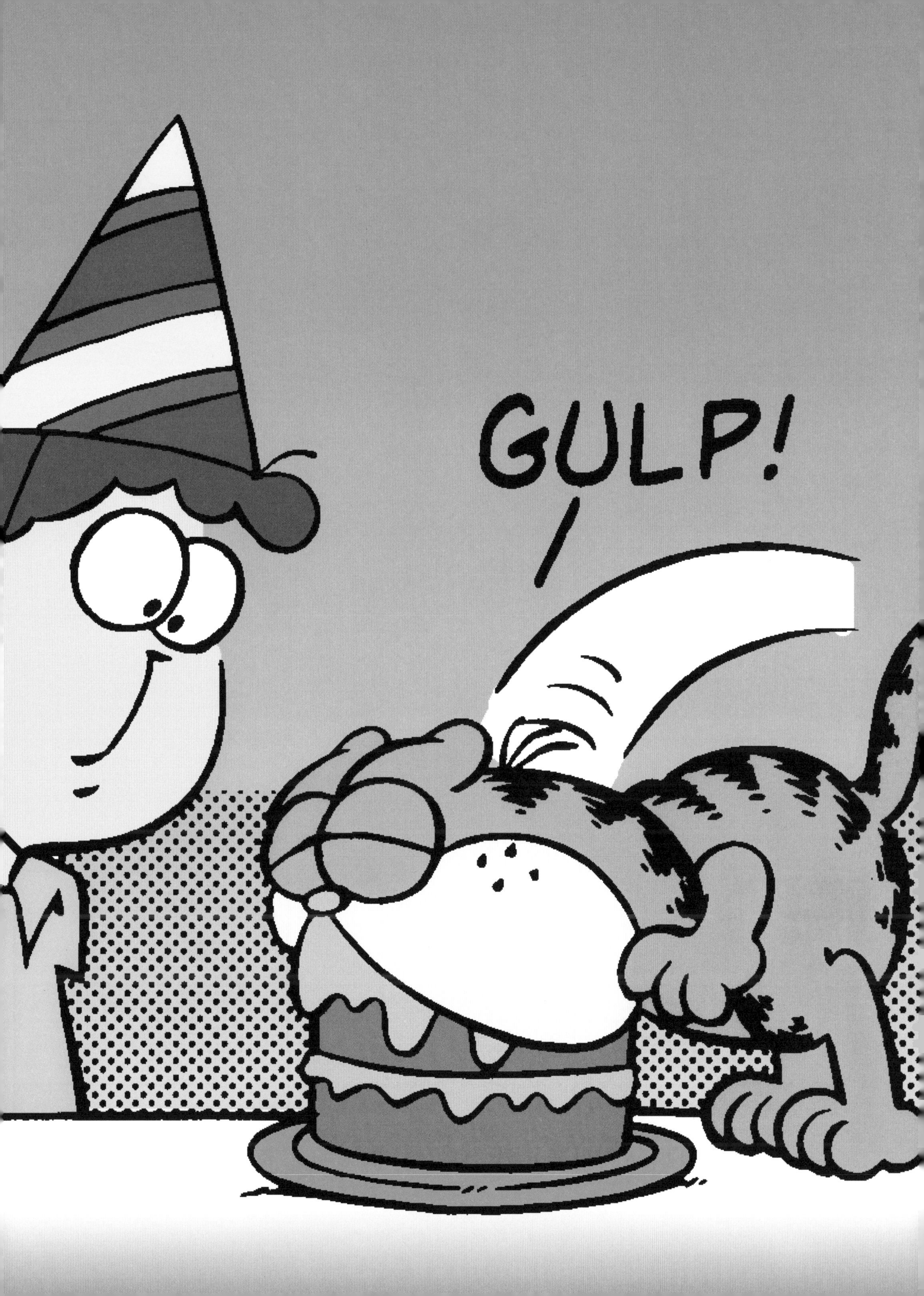
GULP!

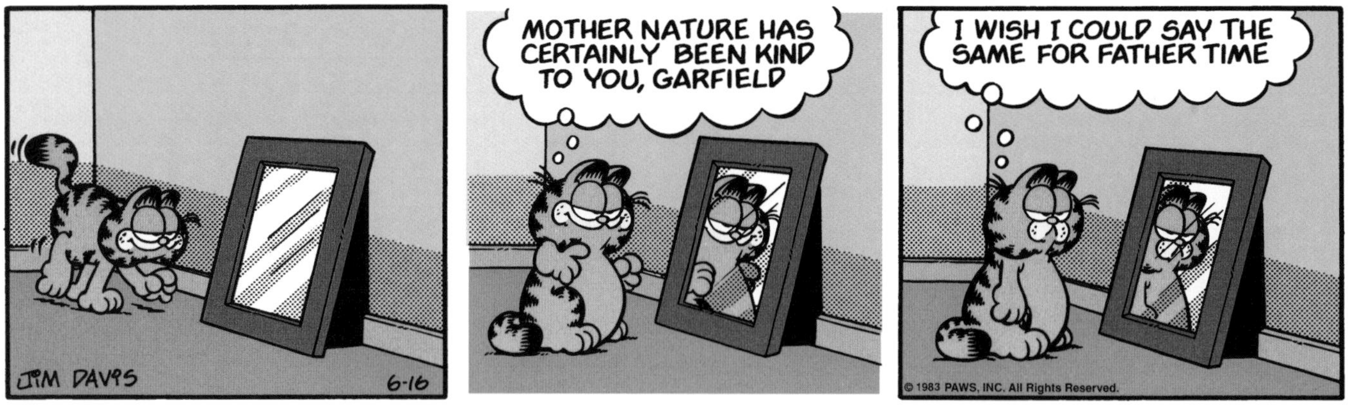
JIM DAVIS
6-16
MOTHER NATURE HAS CERTAINLY BEEN KIND TO YOU, GARFIELD
I WISH I COULD SAY THE SAME FOR FATHER TIME
© 1983 PAWS, INC. All Rights Reserved.

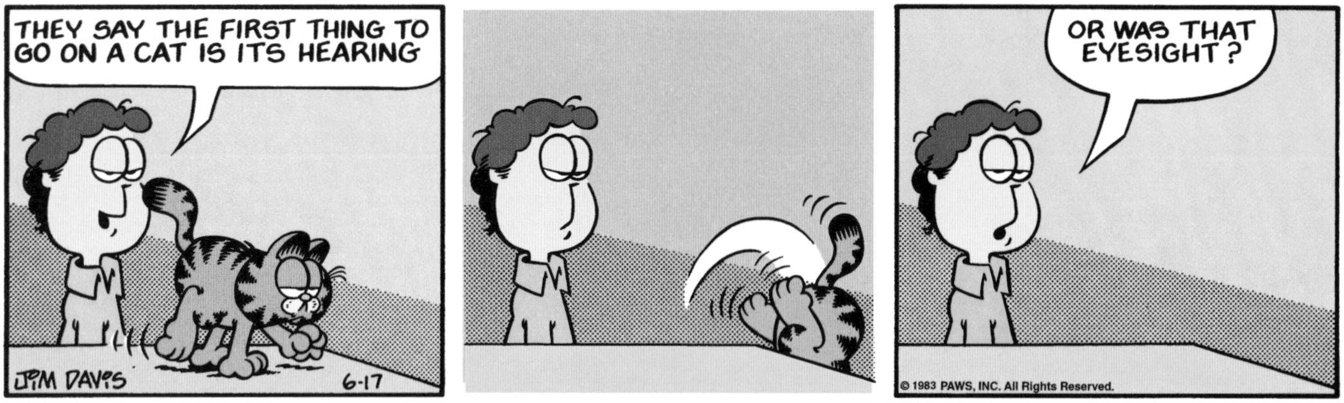
THEY SAY THE FIRST THING TO GO ON A CAT IS ITS HEARING
JIM DAVIS
6-17
OR WAS THAT EYESIGHT ?
© 1983 PAWS, INC. All Rights Reserved.

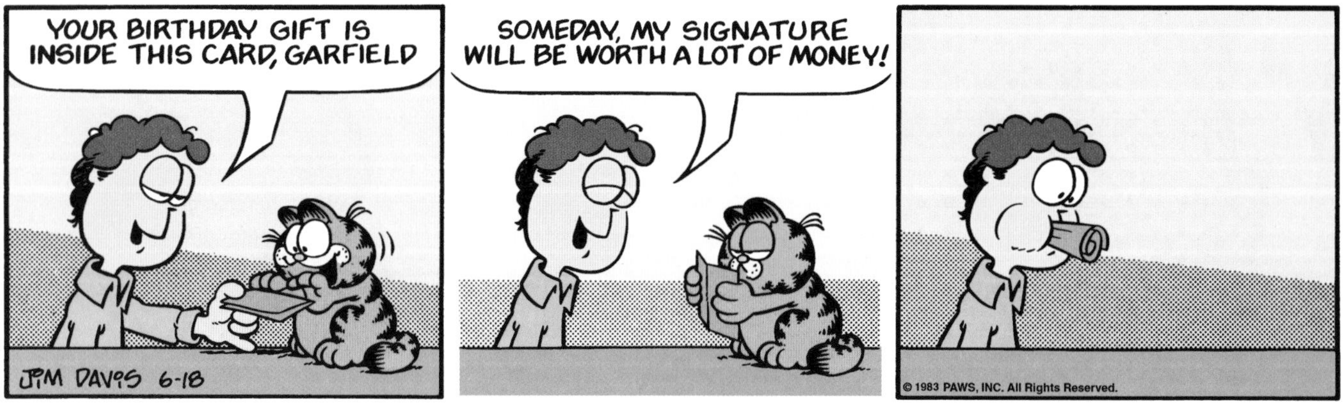
YOUR BIRTHDAY GIFT IS INSIDE THIS CARD, GARFIELD
JIM DAVIS 6-18
SOMEDAY, MY SIGNATURE WILL BE WORTH A LOT OF MONEY!
© 1983 PAWS, INC. All Rights Reserved.

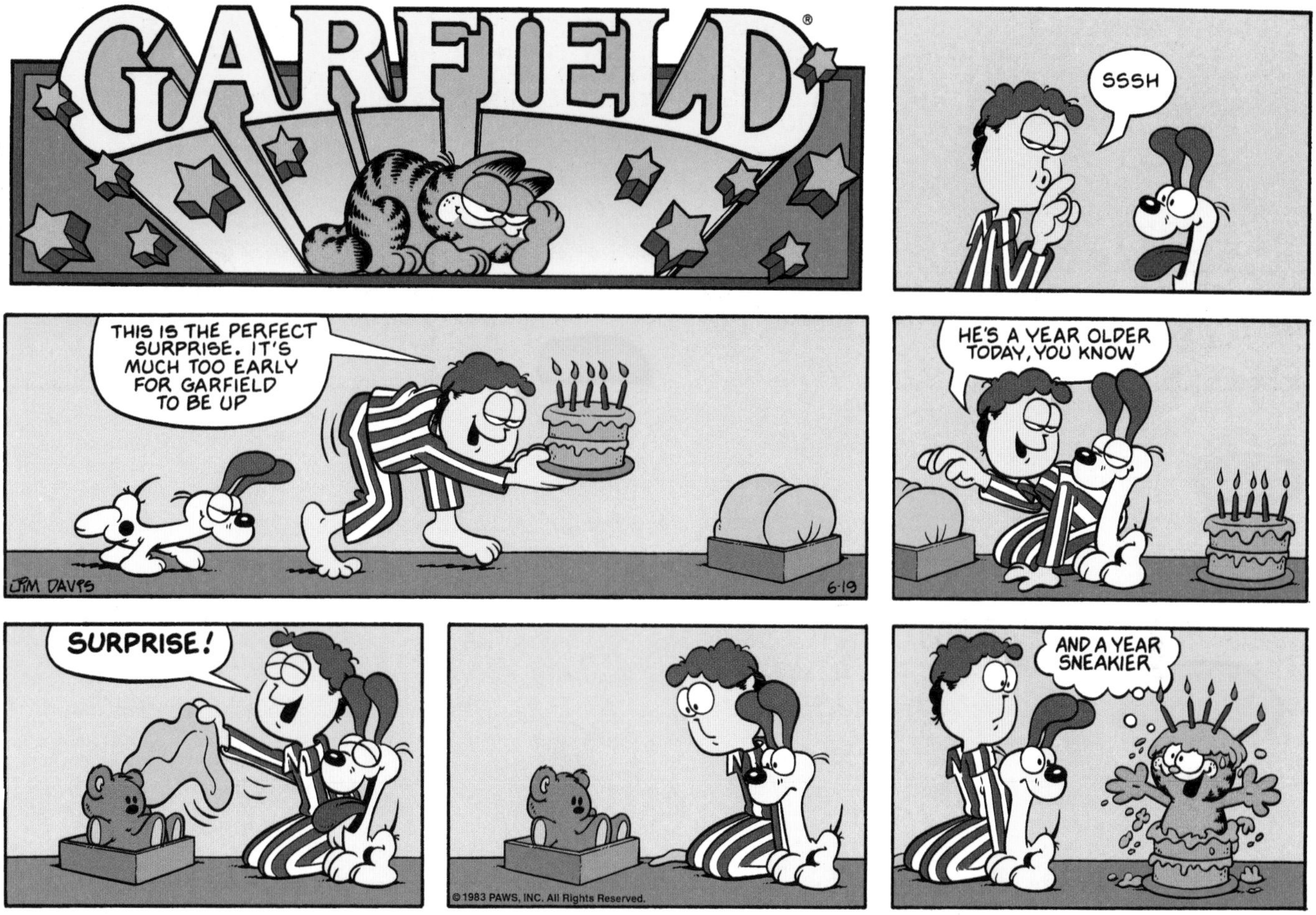
GARFIELD
SSSH
THIS IS THE PERFECT SURPRISE. IT'S MUCH TOO EARLY FOR GARFIELD TO BE UP
JIM DAVIS
6-19
HE'S A YEAR OLDER TODAY, YOU KNOW
SURPRISE!
© 1983 PAWS, INC. All Rights Reserved.
AND A YEAR SNEAKIER

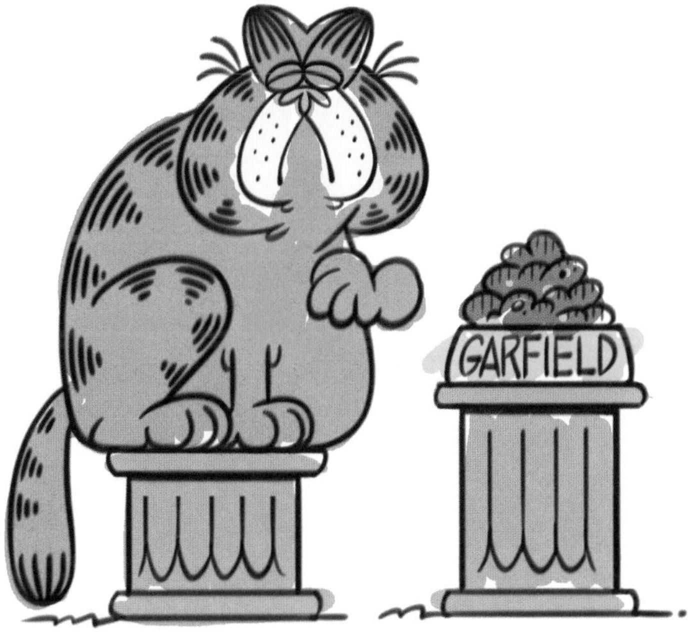
GARFIELD

I'm not old...

I'm a

classic

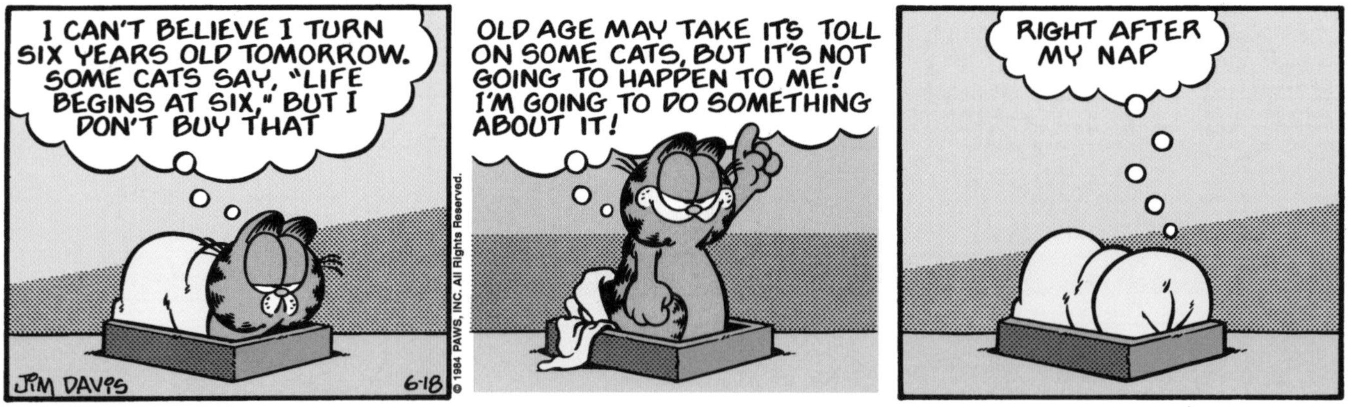
I CAN'T BELIEVE I TURN SIX YEARS OLD TOMORROW. SOME CATS SAY, "LIFE BEGINS AT SIX," BUT I DON'T BUY THAT
JIM DAVIS
6-18
© 1984 PAWS, INC. All Rights Reserved.
OLD AGE MAY TAKE ITS TOLL ON SOME CATS, BUT IT'S NOT GOING TO HAPPEN TO ME! I'M GOING TO DO SOMETHING ABOUT IT!
RIGHT AFTER MY NAP

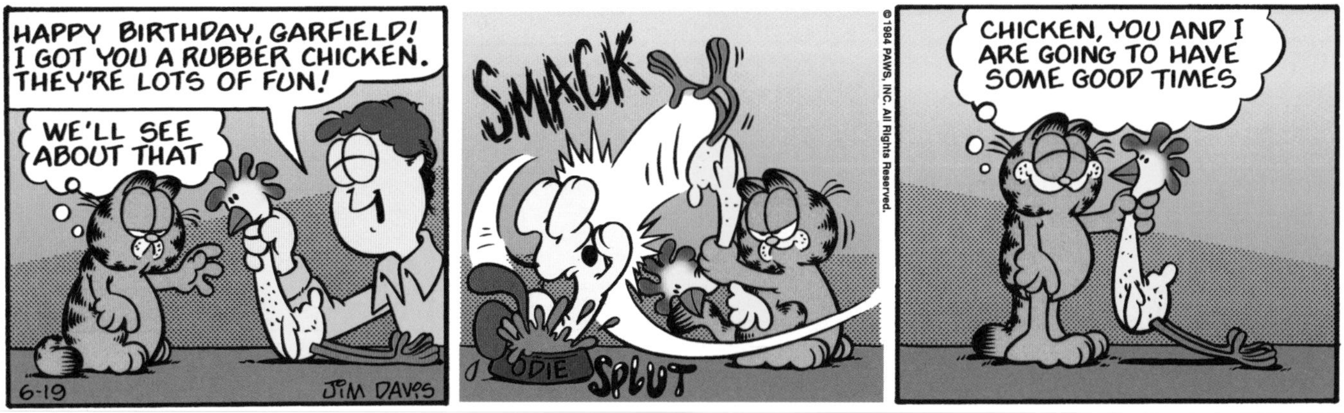
HAPPY BIRTHDAY, GARFIELD! I GOT YOU A RUBBER CHICKEN. THEY'RE LOTS OF FUN!
WE'LL SEE ABOUT THAT
6-19
JIM DAVIS
SMACK
ODIE
SPLUT
© 1984 PAWS, INC. All Rights Reserved.
CHICKEN, YOU AND I ARE GOING TO HAVE SOME GOOD TIMES

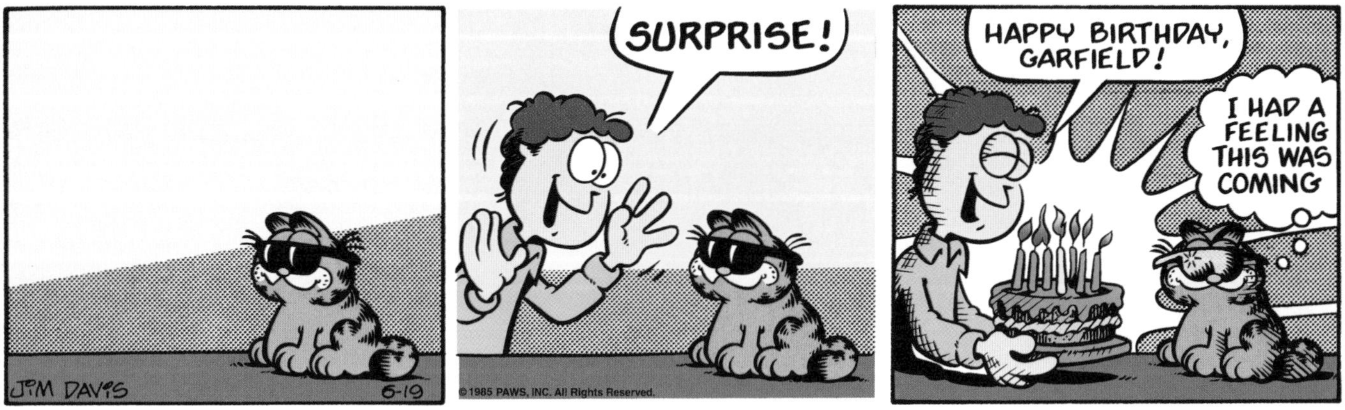
JIM DAVIS
6-19
SURPRISE!
© 1985 PAWS, INC. All Rights Reserved.
HAPPY BIRTHDAY, GARFIELD!
I HAD A FEELING THIS WAS COMING

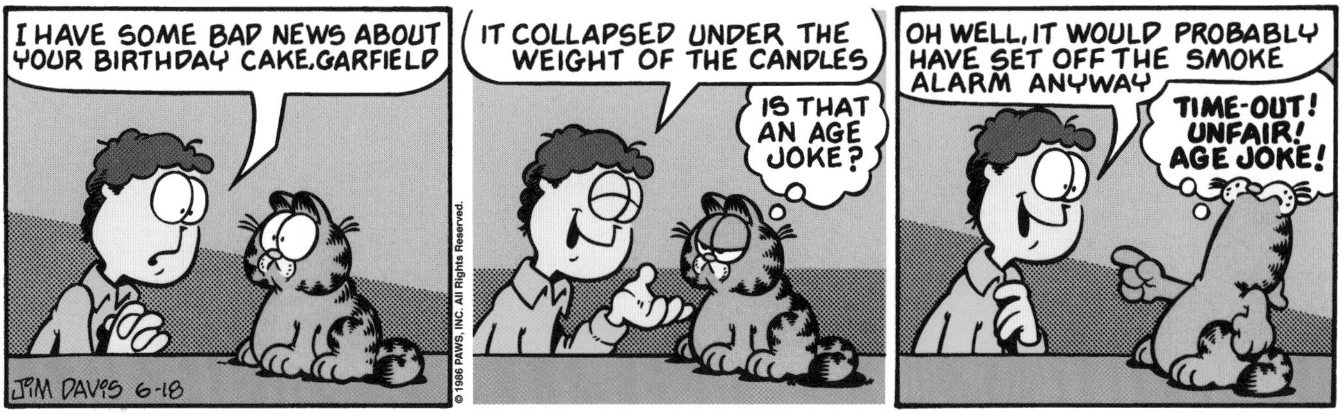
I HAVE SOME BAD NEWS ABOUT YOUR BIRTHDAY CAKE, GARFIELD
JIM DAVIS 6-18
© 1986 PAWS, INC. All Rights Reserved.
IT COLLAPSED UNDER THE WEIGHT OF THE CANDLES
IS THAT AN AGE JOKE?
OH WELL, IT WOULD PROBABLY HAVE SET OFF THE SMOKE ALARM ANYWAY
TIME-OUT! UNFAIR! AGE JOKE!

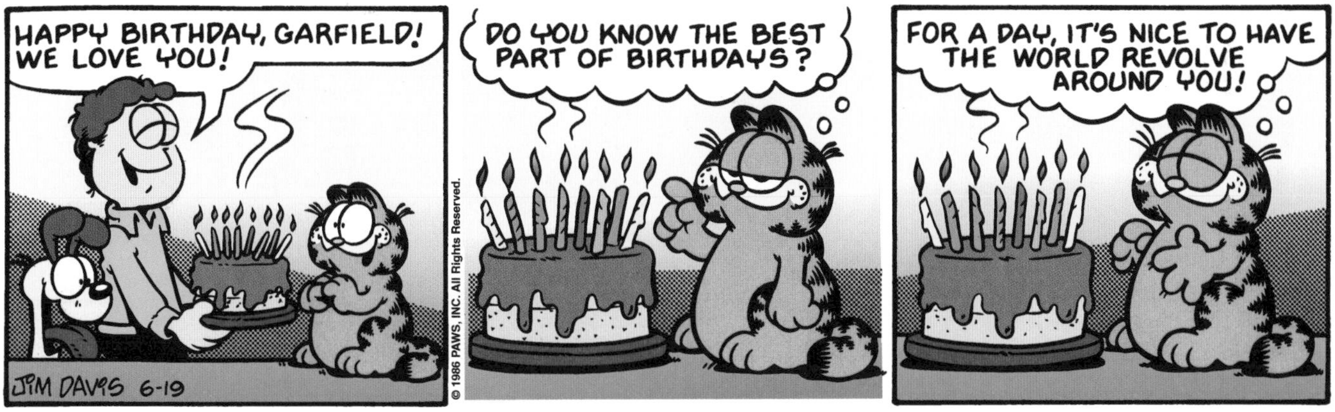
HAPPY BIRTHDAY, GARFIELD! WE LOVE YOU!
JIM DAVIS 6-19
© 1986 PAWS, INC. All Rights Reserved.
DO YOU KNOW THE BEST PART OF BIRTHDAYS?
FOR A DAY, IT'S NICE TO HAVE THE WORLD REVOLVE AROUND YOU!

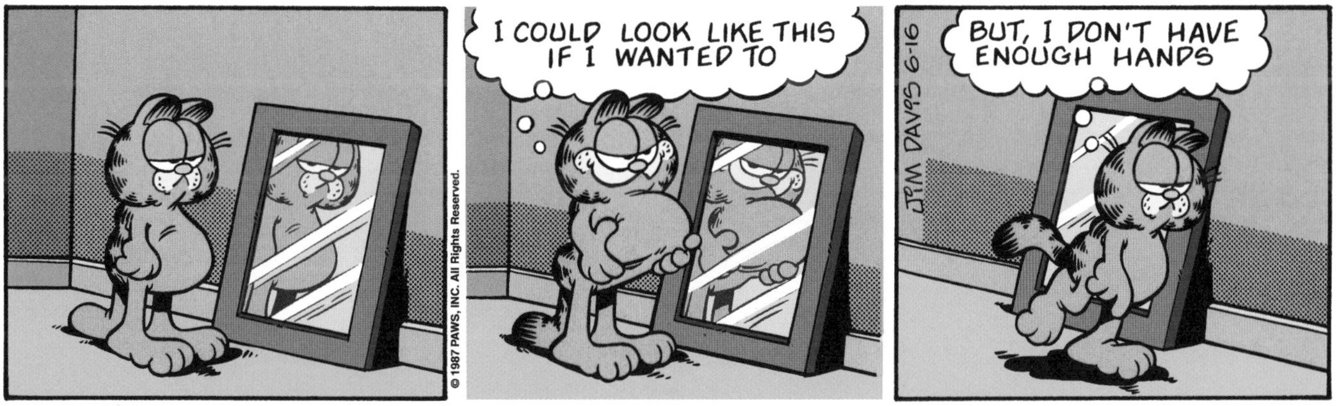
© 1987 PAWS, INC. All Rights Reserved.
I COULD LOOK LIKE THIS IF I WANTED TO
JIM DAVIS 6-16
BUT, I DON'T HAVE ENOUGH HANDS

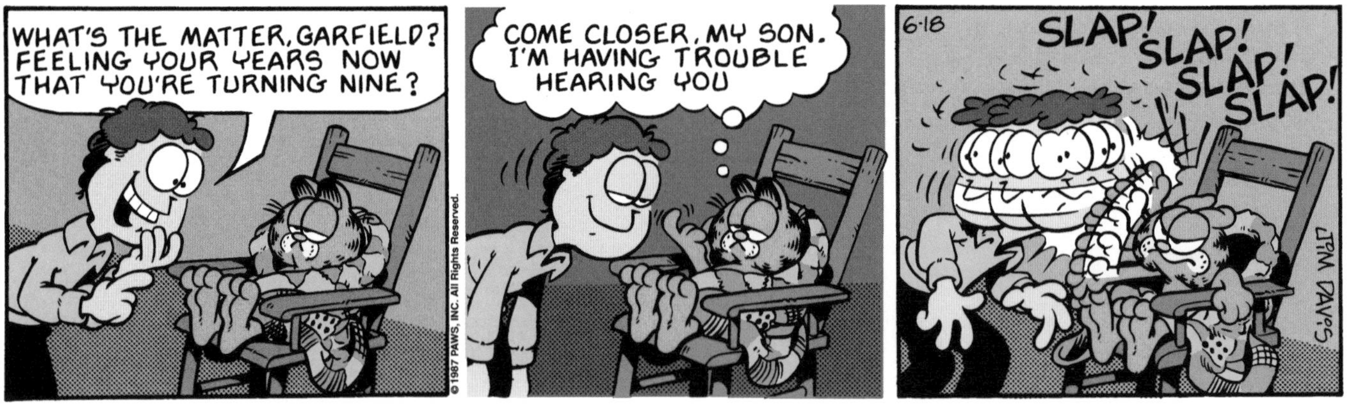
WHAT'S THE MATTER, GARFIELD? FEELING YOUR YEARS NOW THAT YOU'RE TURNING NINE?
COME CLOSER, MY SON. I'M HAVING TROUBLE HEARING YOU
6-18
SLAP! SLAP! SLAP! SLAP!
JIM DAVIS
© 1987 PAWS, INC. All Rights Reserved.

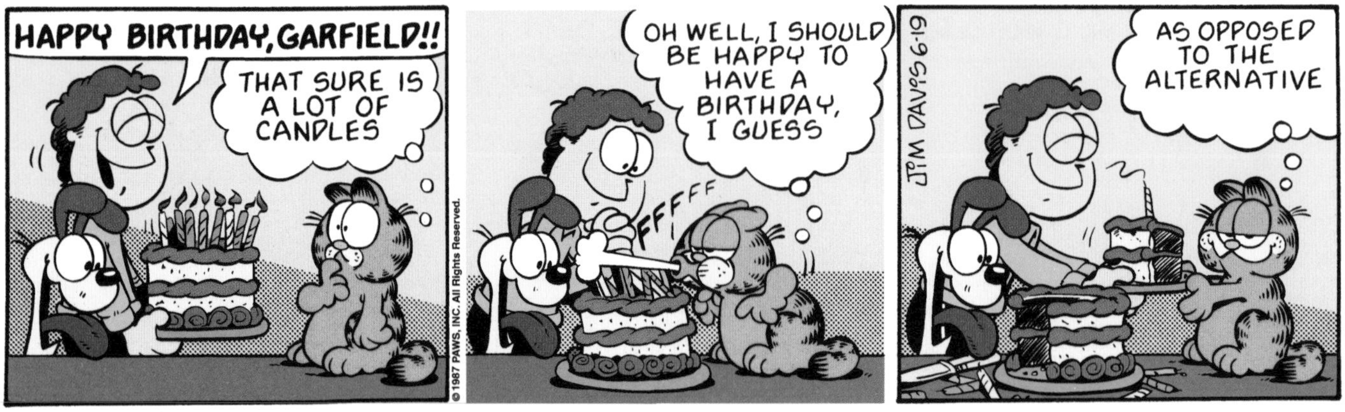
HAPPY BIRTHDAY, GARFIELD!!
THAT SURE IS A LOT OF CANDLES
FFFFF
OH WELL, I SHOULD BE HAPPY TO HAVE A BIRTHDAY, I GUESS
JIM DAVIS 6-19
AS OPPOSED TO THE ALTERNATIVE
© 1987 PAWS, INC. All Rights Reserved.

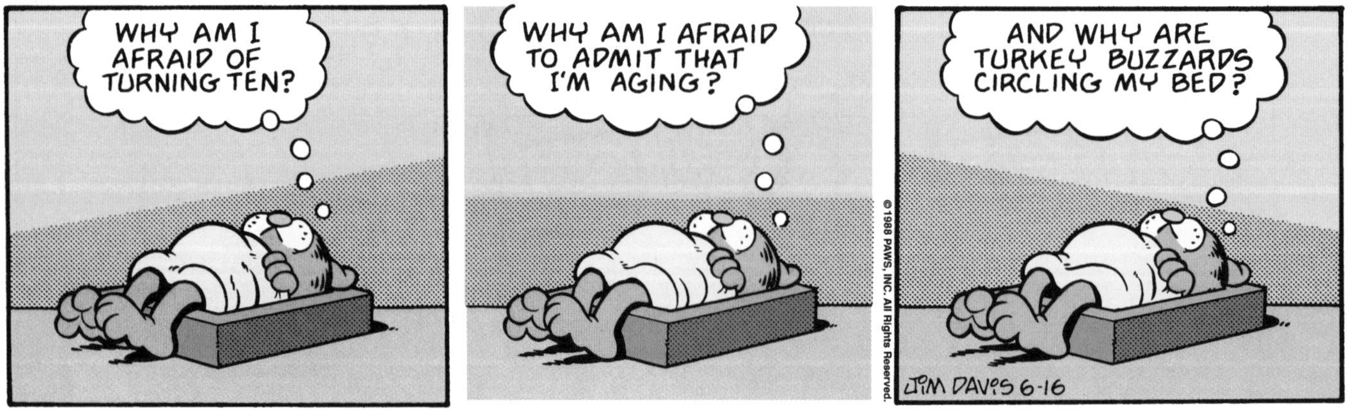
WHY AM I AFRAID OF TURNING TEN?
WHY AM I AFRAID TO ADMIT THAT I'M AGING?
AND WHY ARE TURKEY BUZZARDS CIRCLING MY BED?
JIM DAVIS 6-16
© 1988 PAWS, INC. All Rights Reserved.

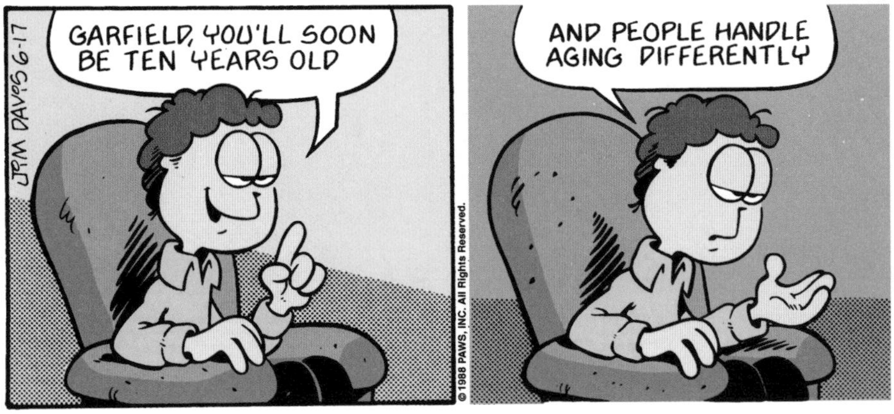
GARFIELD, YOU'LL SOON BE TEN YEARS OLD
AND PEOPLE HANDLE AGING DIFFERENTLY
HAVE YOU CONSIDERED AGING GRACEFULLY?
JPM DAVIS 6-17
© 1988 PAWS, INC. All Rights Reserved.

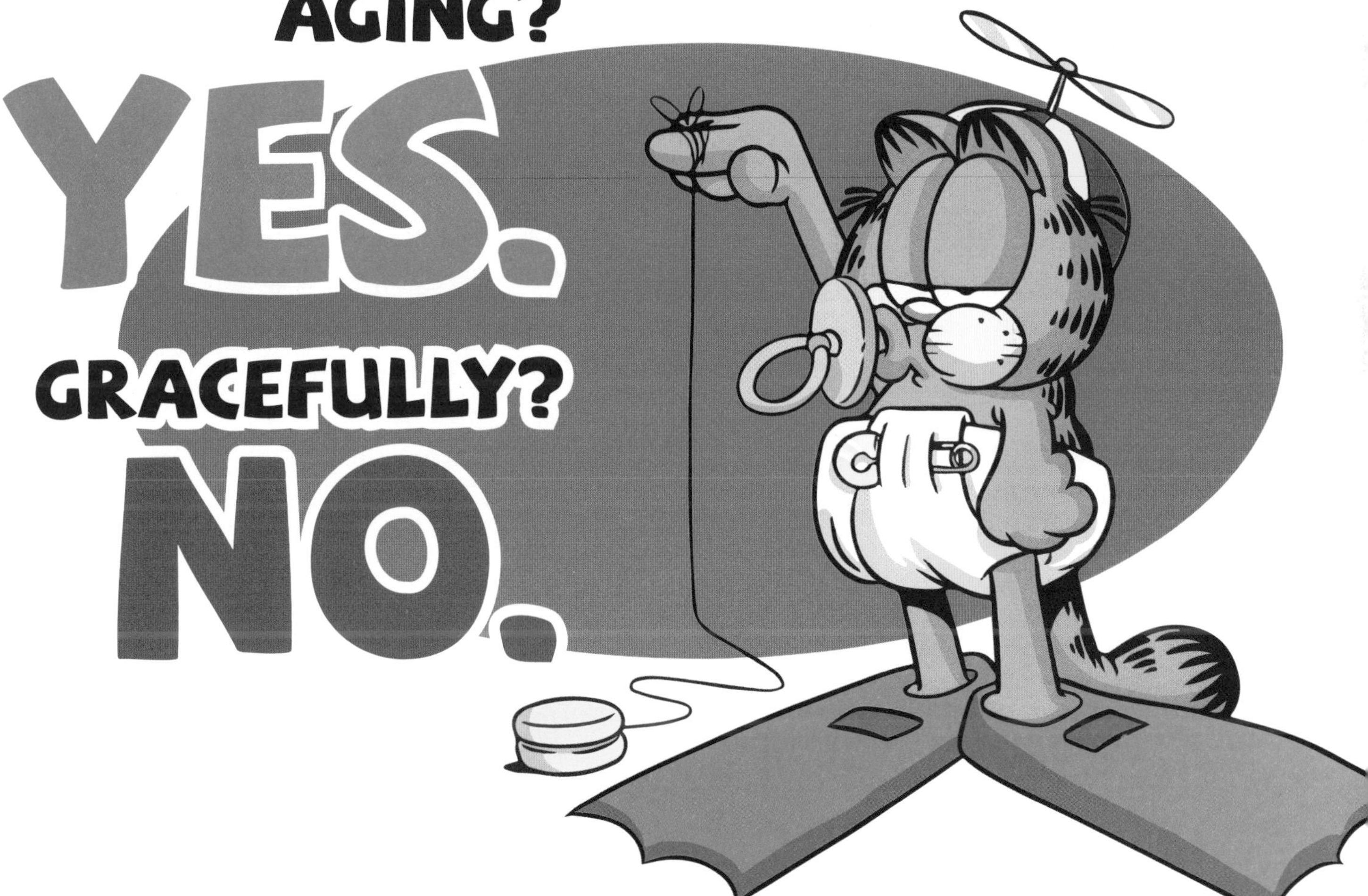
AGING?
YES.
GRACEFULLY?
NO.

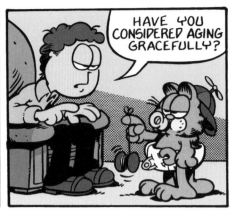

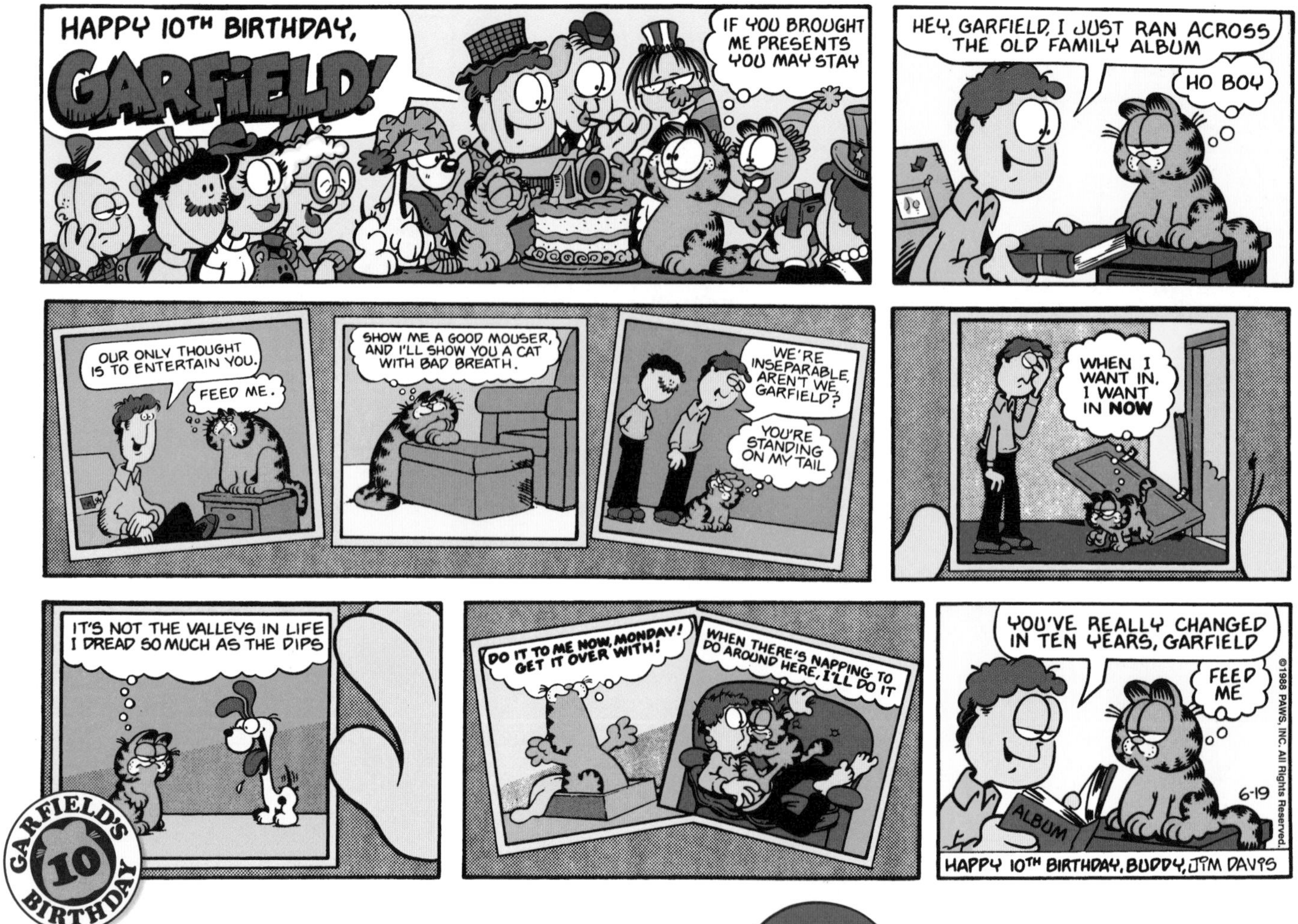
HAPPY 10TH BIRTHDAY, GARFIELD!
IF YOU BROUGHT ME PRESENTS YOU MAY STAY
HEY, GARFIELD, I JUST RAN ACROSS THE OLD FAMILY ALBUM
HO BOY
OUR ONLY THOUGHT IS TO ENTERTAIN YOU.
FEED ME.
SHOW ME A GOOD MOUSER, AND I'LL SHOW YOU A CAT WITH BAD BREATH.
WE'RE INSEPARABLE, AREN'T WE, GARFIELD?
YOU'RE STANDING ON MY TAIL
WHEN I WANT IN, I WANT IN NOW
IT'S NOT THE VALLEYS IN LIFE I DREAD SO MUCH AS THE DIPS
DO IT TO ME NOW, MONDAY! GET IT OVER WITH!
WHEN THERE'S NAPPING TO DO AROUND HERE, I'LL DO IT
YOU'VE REALLY CHANGED IN TEN YEARS, GARFIELD
FEED ME
ALBUM
6-19
HAPPY 10TH BIRTHDAY, BUDDY, JIM DAVIS
GARFIELD'S 10 BIRTHDAY
©1988 PAWS, INC. All Rights Reserved.

YOU HAVE THE RIGHT TO PARTY.

If you don't have a party, one will be provided for you...

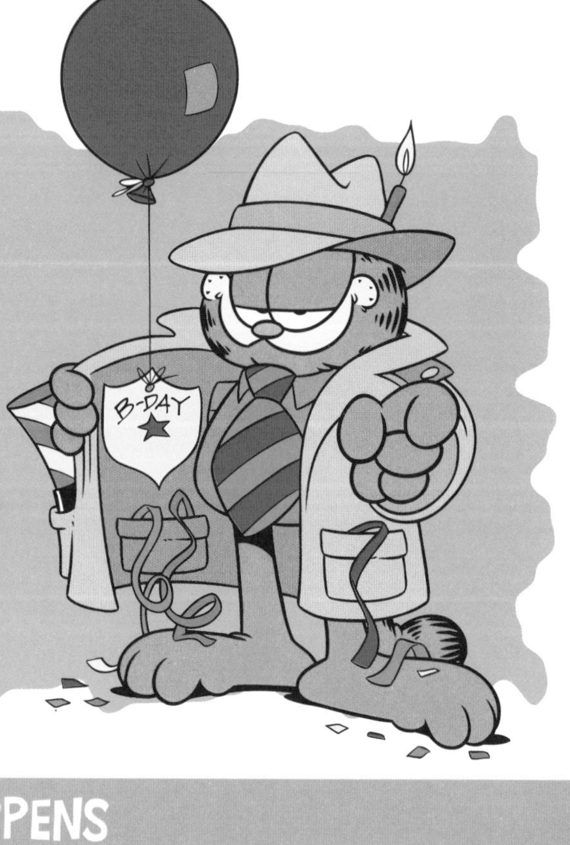
B-DAY

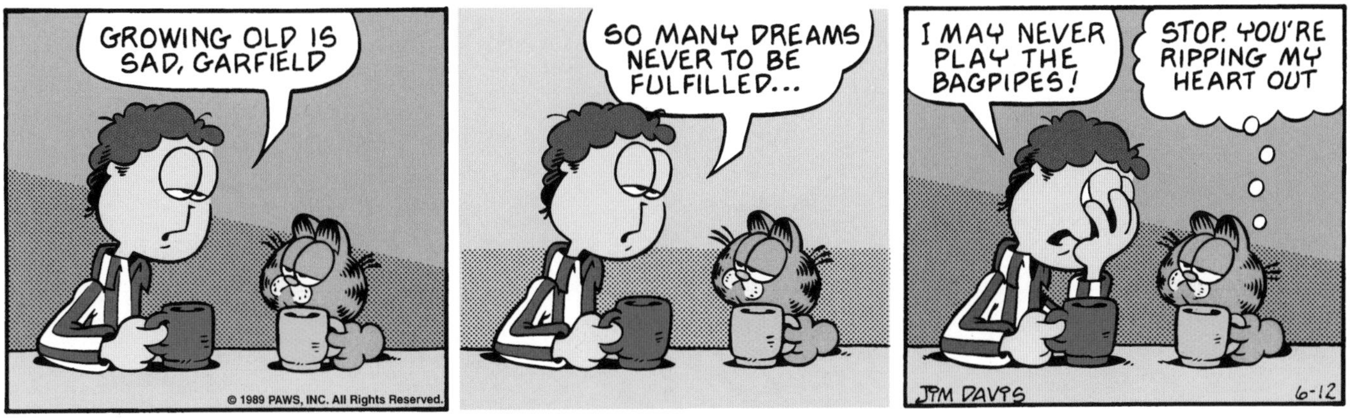
GROWING OLD IS SAD, GARFIELD
SO MANY DREAMS NEVER TO BE FULFILLED...
I MAY NEVER PLAY THE BAGPIPES!
STOP. YOU'RE RIPPING MY HEART OUT
© 1989 PAWS, INC. All Rights Reserved.
JIM DAVIS
6-12

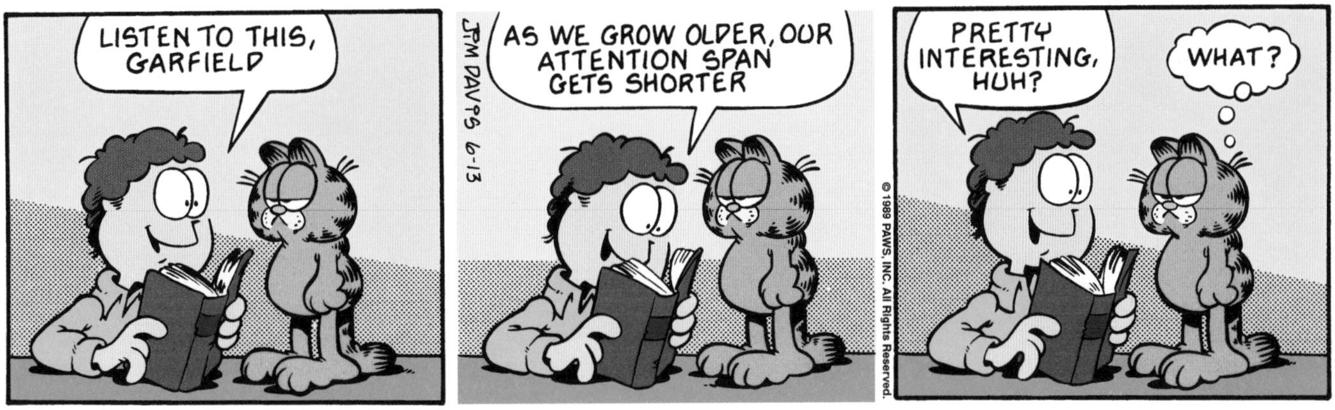
LISTEN TO THIS, GARFIELD
JIM DAVIS 6-13
AS WE GROW OLDER, OUR ATTENTION SPAN GETS SHORTER
© 1989 PAWS, INC. All Rights Reserved.
PRETTY INTERESTING, HUH?
WHAT?

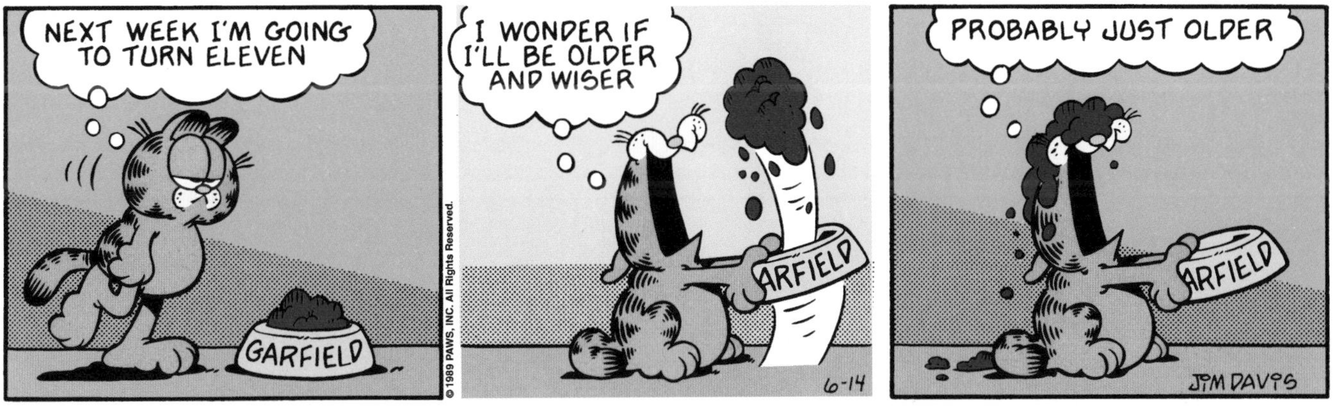
NEXT WEEK I'M GOING TO TURN ELEVEN
GARFIELD
© 1989 PAWS, INC. All Rights Reserved.
I WONDER IF I'LL BE OLDER AND WISER
ARFIELD
6-14
PROBABLY JUST OLDER
ARFIELD
JIM DAVIS

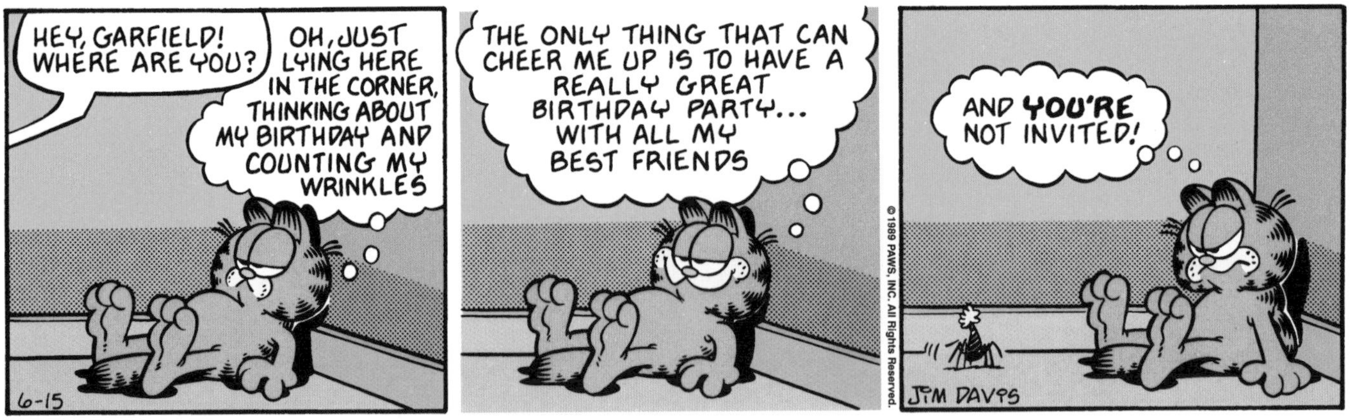
HEY, GARFIELD! WHERE ARE YOU?
OH, JUST LYING HERE IN THE CORNER, THINKING ABOUT MY BIRTHDAY AND COUNTING MY WRINKLES
6-15
THE ONLY THING THAT CAN CHEER ME UP IS TO HAVE A REALLY GREAT BIRTHDAY PARTY... WITH ALL MY BEST FRIENDS
© 1989 PAWS, INC. All Rights Reserved.
AND YOU'RE NOT INVITED!
JIM DAVIS

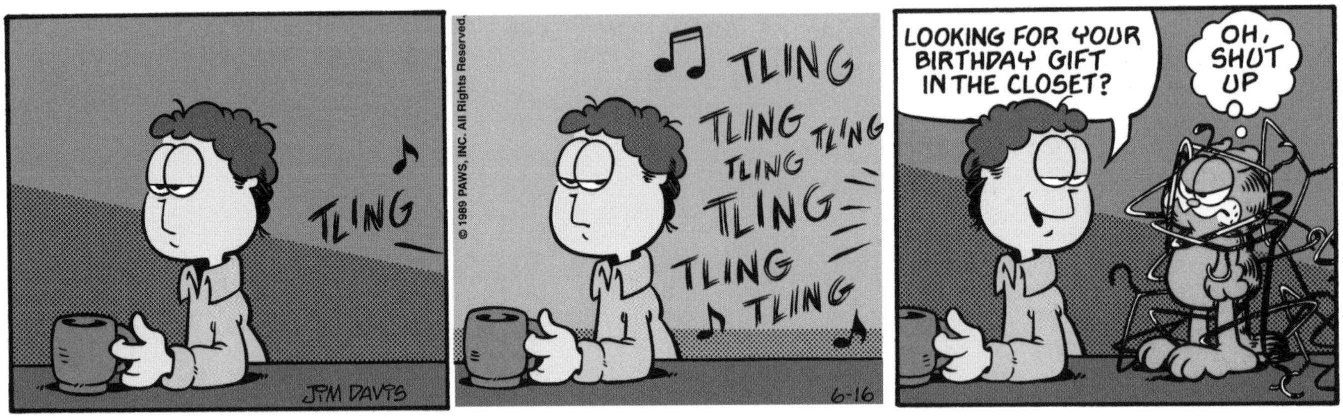
TLING
JIM DAVIS
© 1989 PAWS, INC. All Rights Reserved.
TLING TLING TLING TLING TLING TLING TLING
6-16
LOOKING FOR YOUR BIRTHDAY GIFT IN THE CLOSET?
OH, SHUT UP

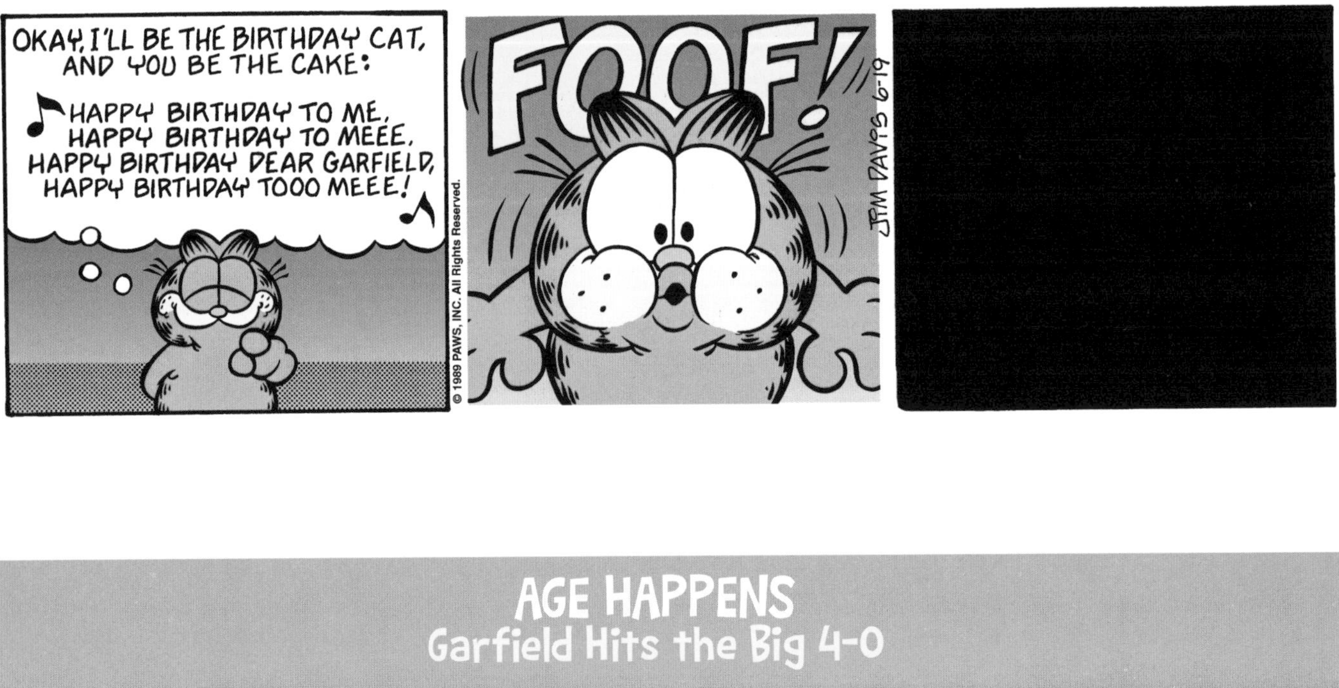
OKAY, I'LL BE THE BIRTHDAY CAT, AND YOU BE THE CAKE:
HAPPY BIRTHDAY TO ME, HAPPY BIRTHDAY TO MEEE, HAPPY BIRTHDAY DEAR GARFIELD, HAPPY BIRTHDAY TOOO MEEE!
© 1989 PAWS, INC. All Rights Reserved.
FOOF!
JIM DAVIS 6-19

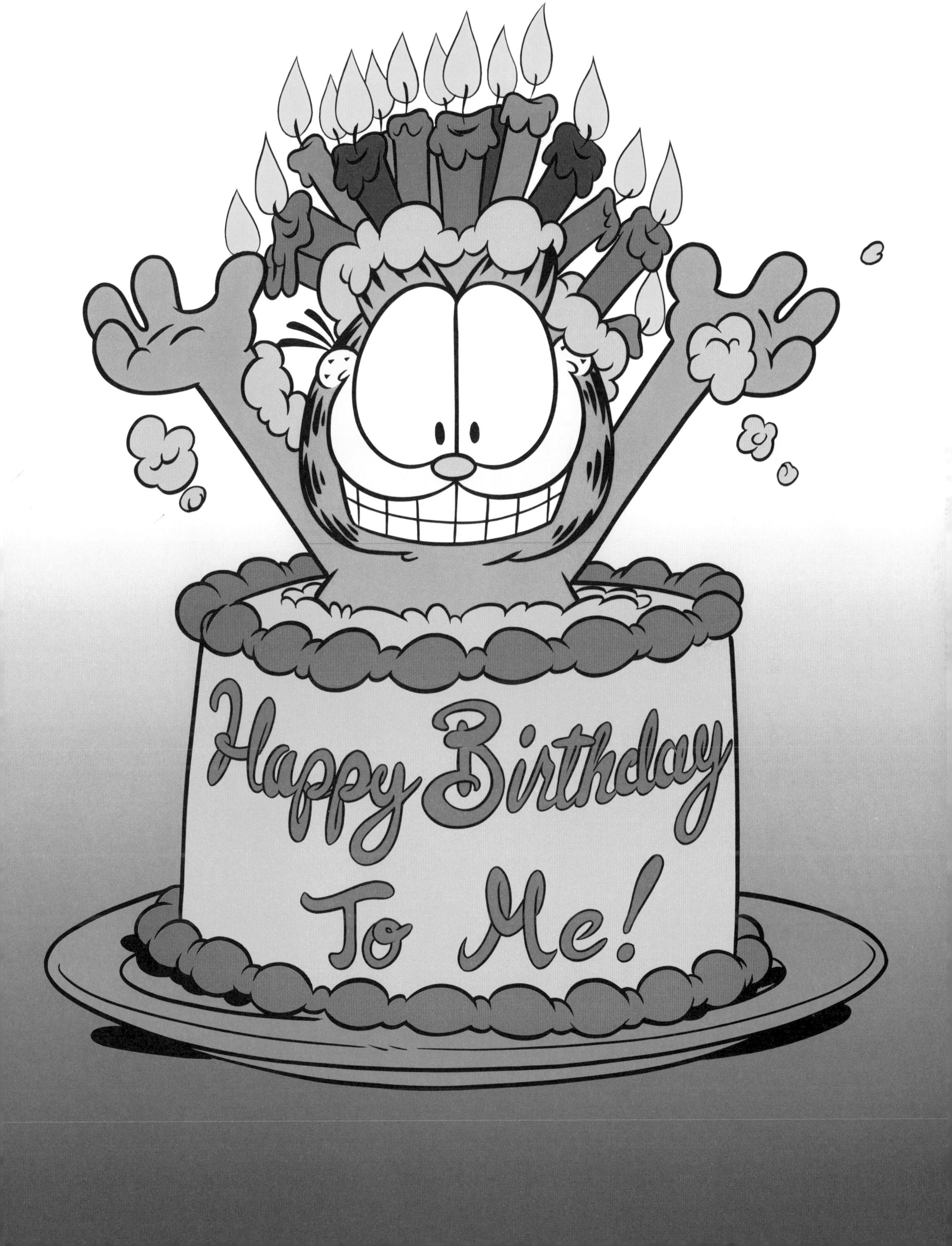
Happy Birthday
To Me!

CARTOONISTS' CLUB

The gang's all here! Birthday greetings from Jim Davis's fellow comic-strip creators.

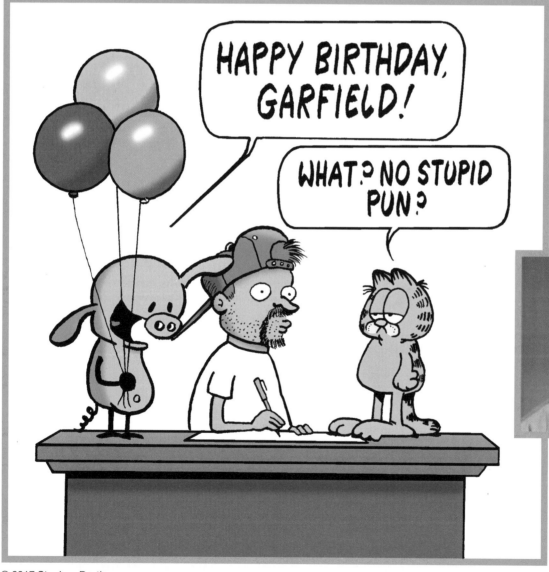

Stephan Pastis
PEARLS BEFORE SWINE

AGE HAPPENS
Garfield Hits the Big 4-0

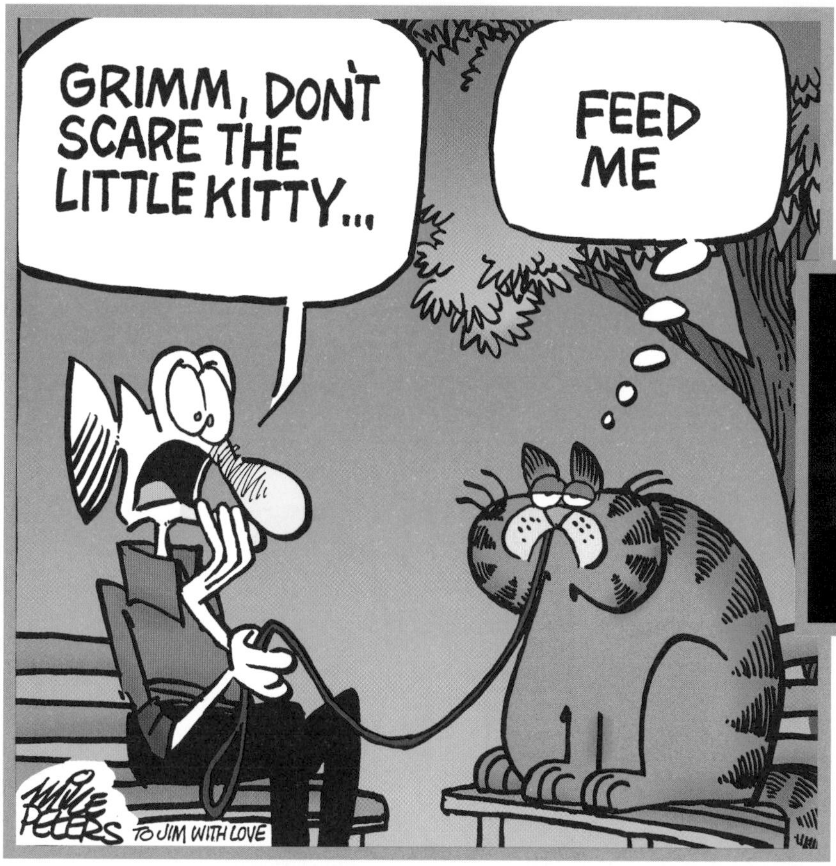
GRIMM, DON'T SCARE THE LITTLE KITTY...
FEED ME
MIKE PETERS TO JIM WITH LOVE

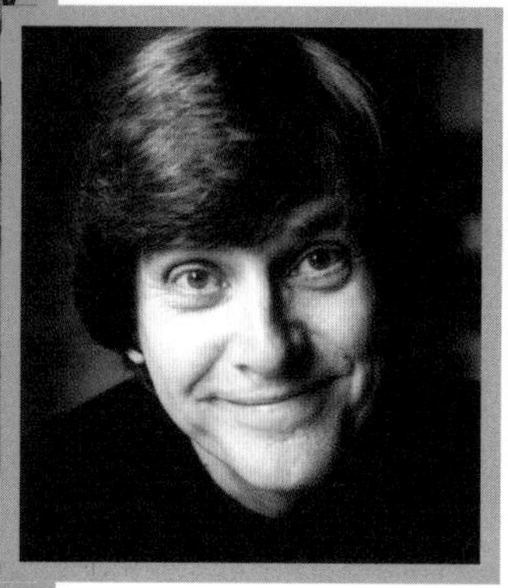

Mike Peters
MOTHER GOOSE AND GRIMM

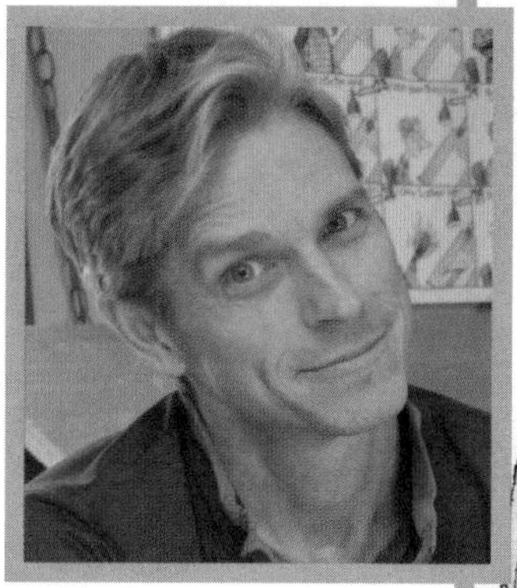

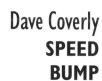

Dave Coverly
SPEED BUMP

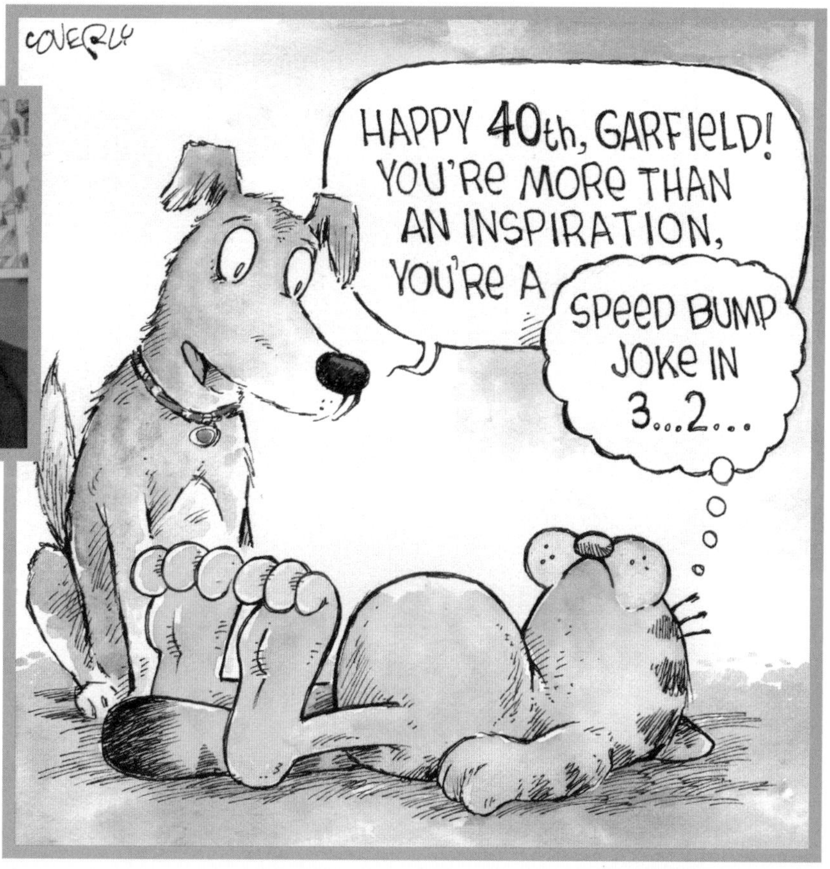
COVERLY
HAPPY 40th, GARFIELD! YOU'RE MORE THAN AN INSPIRATION, YOU'RE A
SPEED BUMP JOKE IN 3...2...

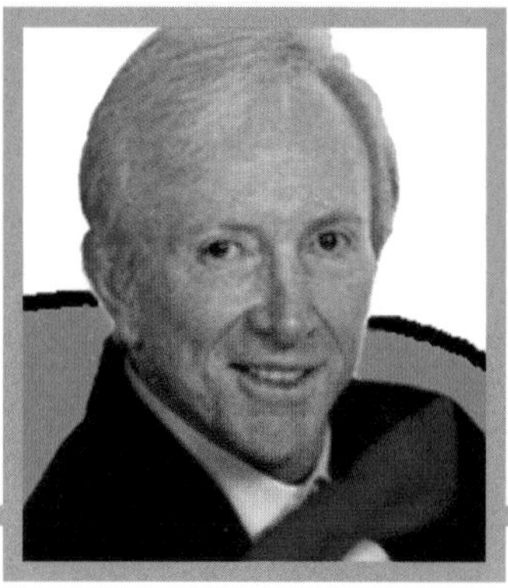

Dean Young
BLONDIE

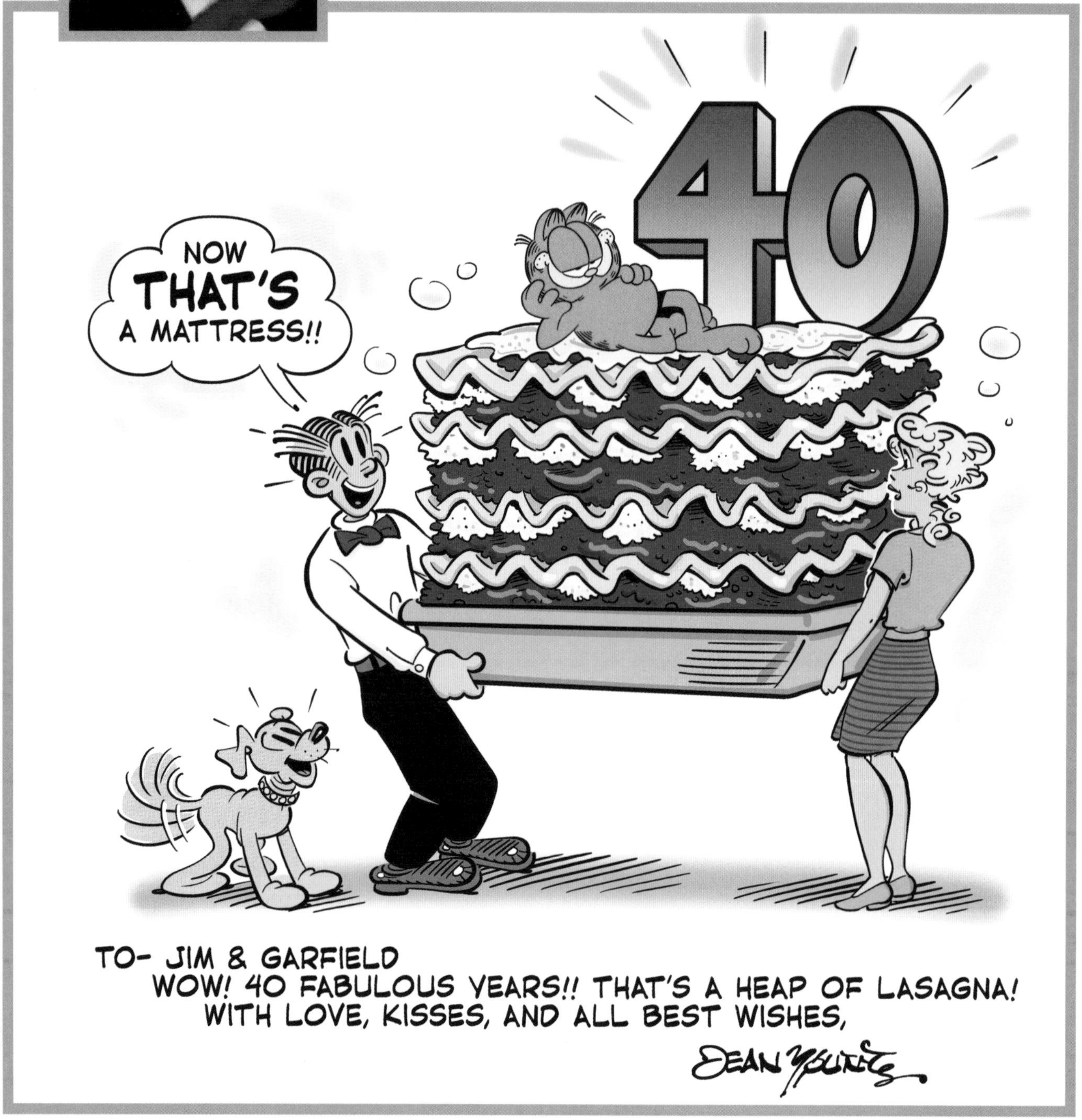
NOW THAT'S A MATTRESS!!
40
TO- JIM & GARFIELD
WOW! 40 FABULOUS YEARS!! THAT'S A HEAP OF LASAGNA!
WITH LOVE, KISSES, AND ALL BEST WISHES,
DEAN YOUNG

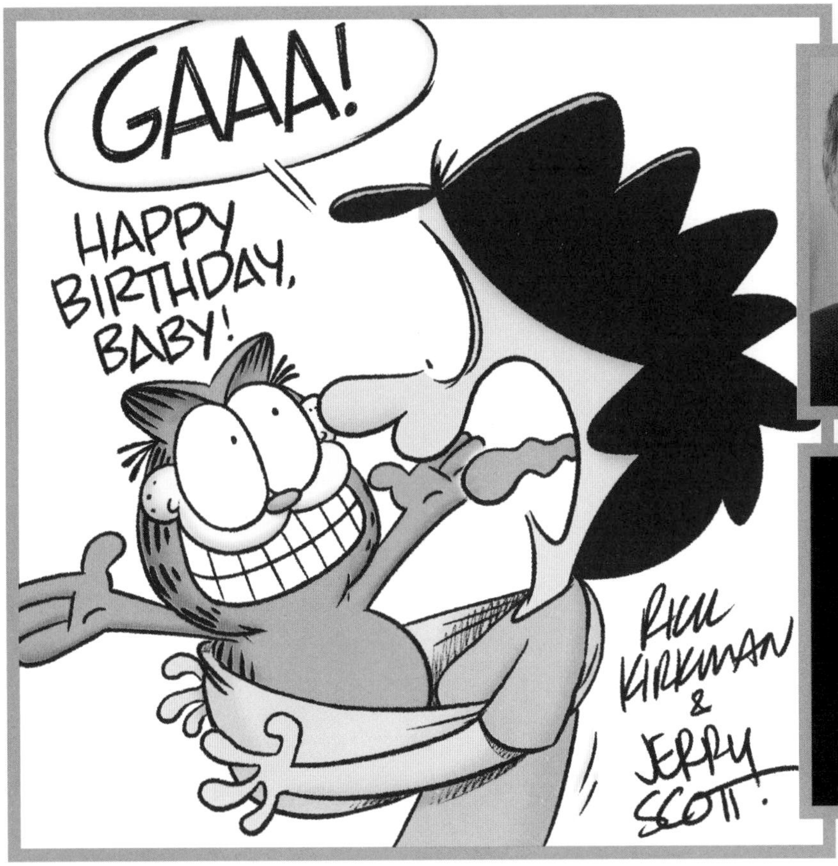
GAAA!
HAPPY BIRTHDAY, BABY!
RICK KIRKMAN & JERRY SCOTT!

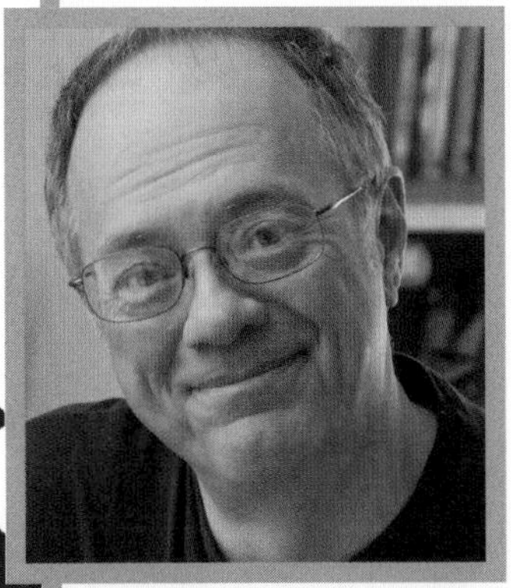

Rick Kirkman

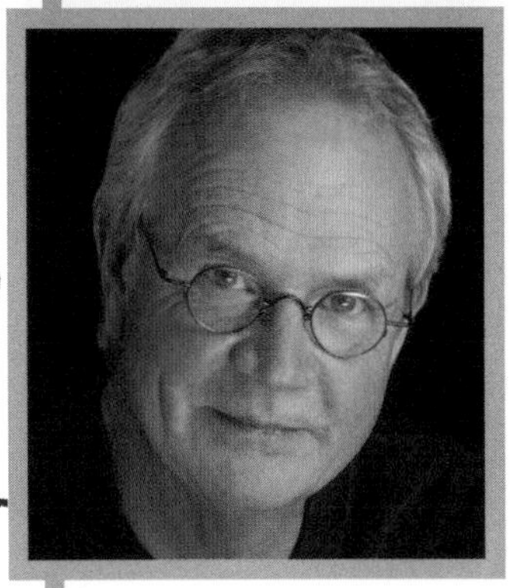

Jerry Scott

BABY BLUES

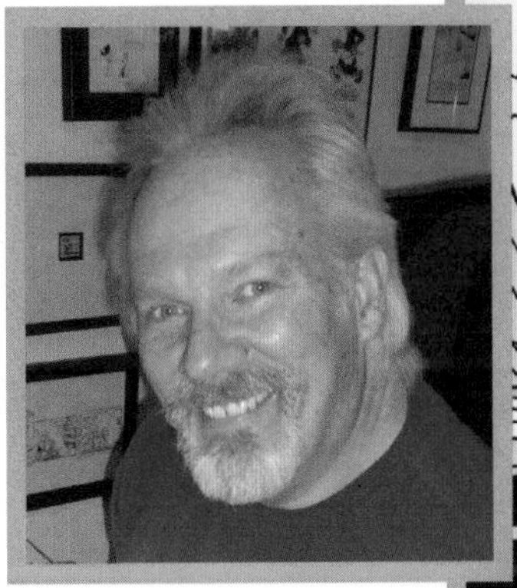

John Rose
SNUFFY SMITH

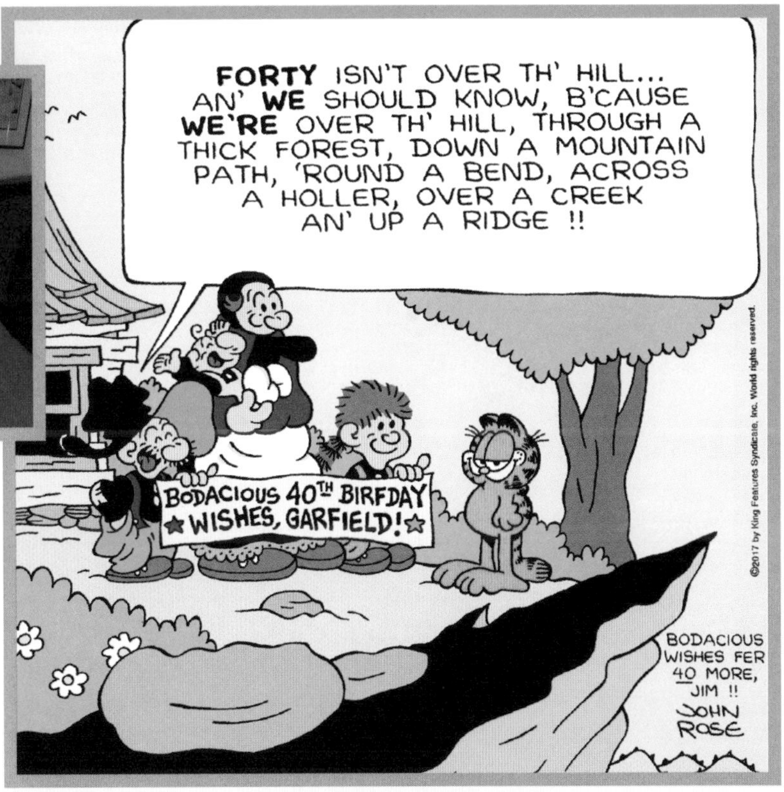
FORTY ISN'T OVER TH' HILL... AN' **WE** SHOULD KNOW, B'CAUSE **WE'RE** OVER TH' HILL, THROUGH A THICK FOREST, DOWN A MOUNTAIN PATH, 'ROUND A BEND, ACROSS A HOLLER, OVER A CREEK AN' UP A RIDGE !!
BODACIOUS 40TH BIRFDAY WISHES, GARFIELD!
BODACIOUS WISHES FER 40 MORE, JIM !! JOHN ROSE
©2017 by King Features Syndicate, Inc. World rights reserved.

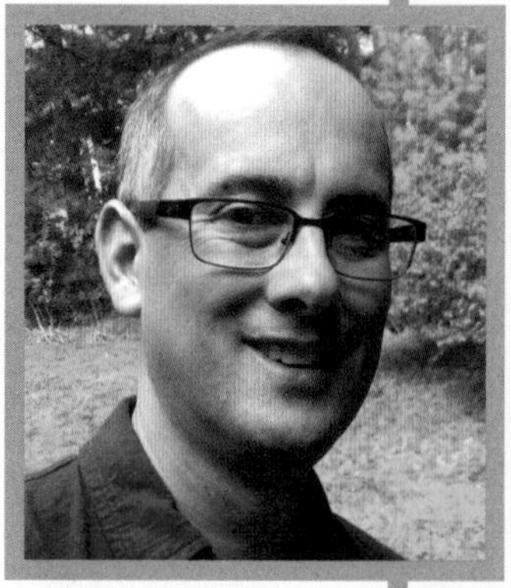

Norm Feuti
RETAIL

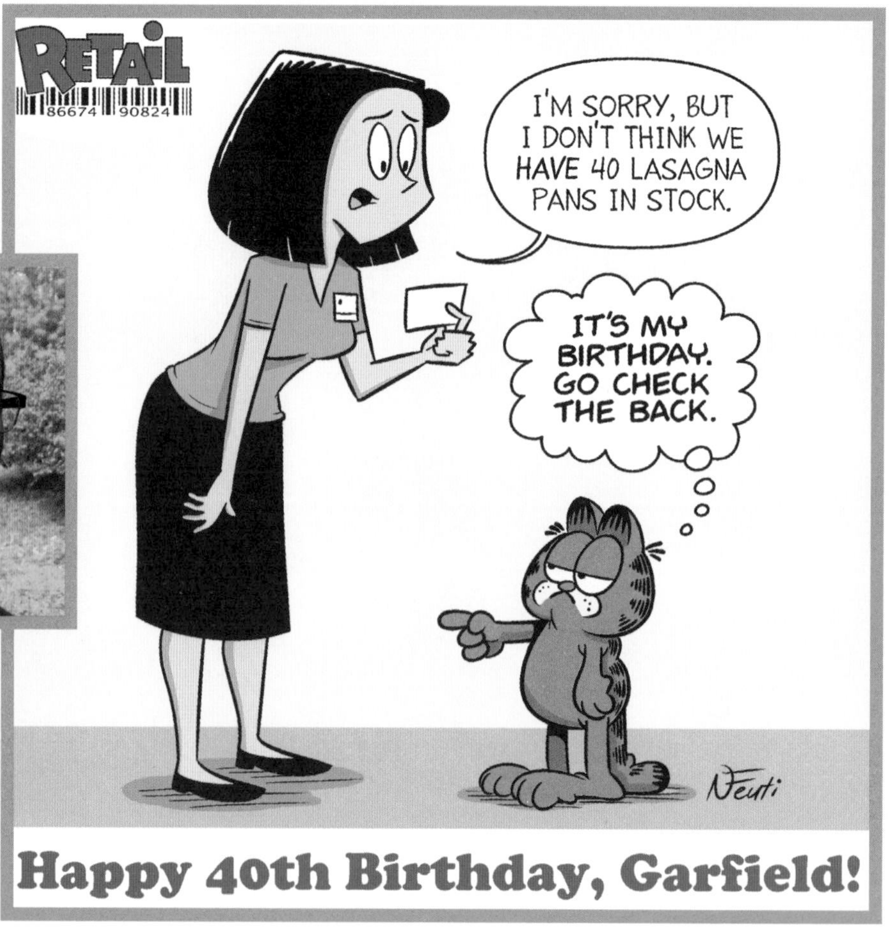
RETAIL
I'M SORRY, BUT I DON'T THINK WE HAVE 40 LASAGNA PANS IN STOCK.
IT'S MY BIRTHDAY. GO CHECK THE BACK.
NFeuti
Happy 40th Birthday, Garfield!

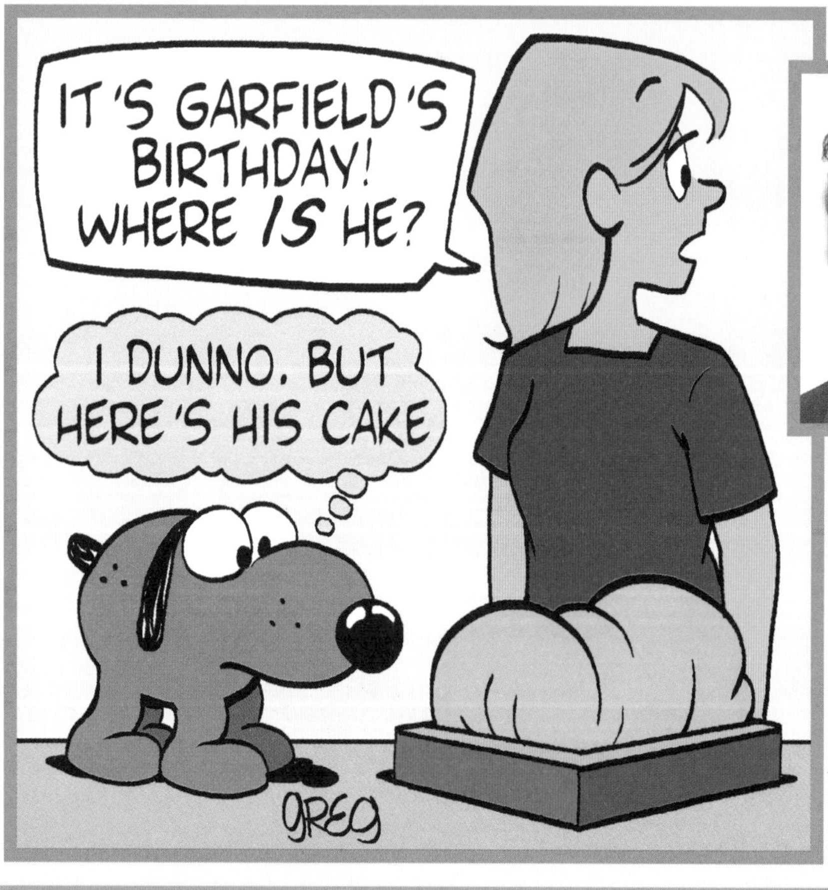
IT'S GARFIELD'S BIRTHDAY! WHERE *IS* HE?
I DUNNO. BUT HERE'S HIS CAKE
GREG

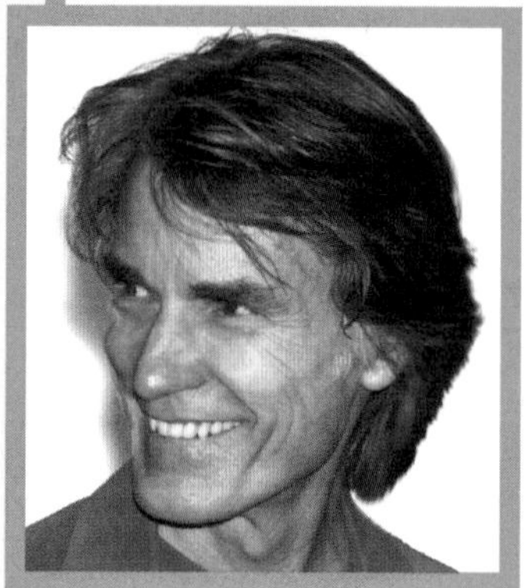

Greg Evans
LUANN

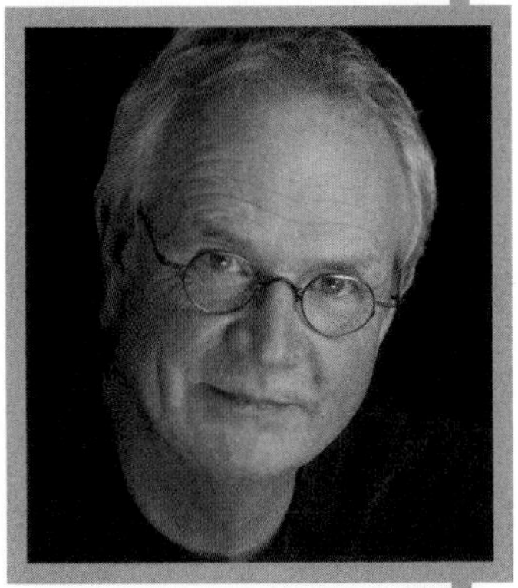

Jerry Scott

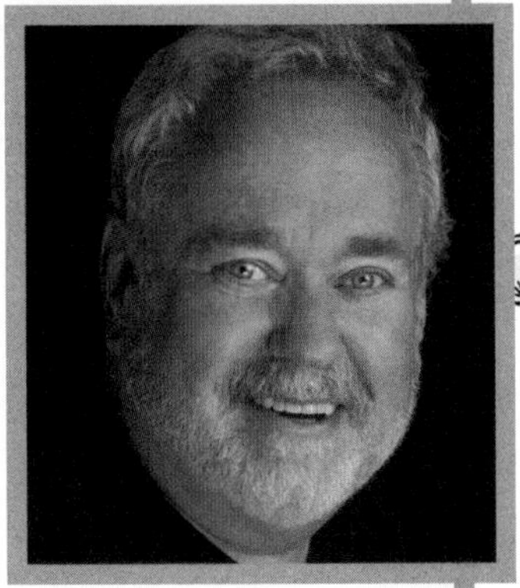

Jim Borgman

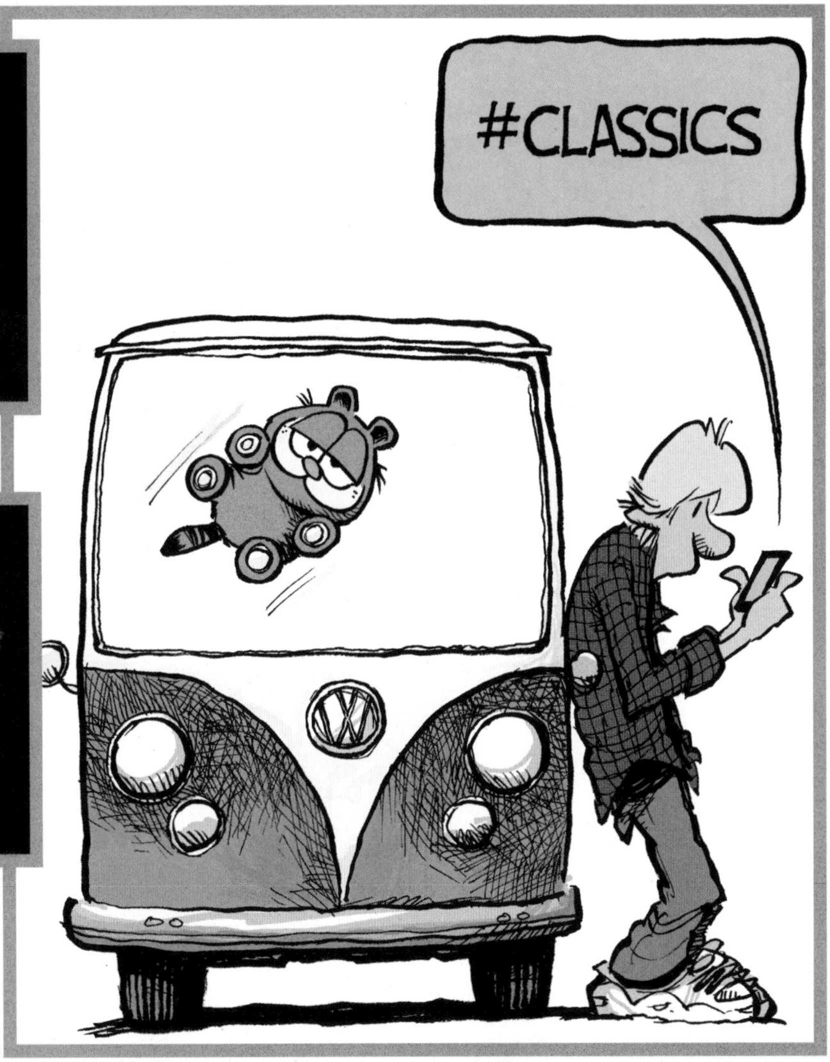
#CLASSICS

ZITS

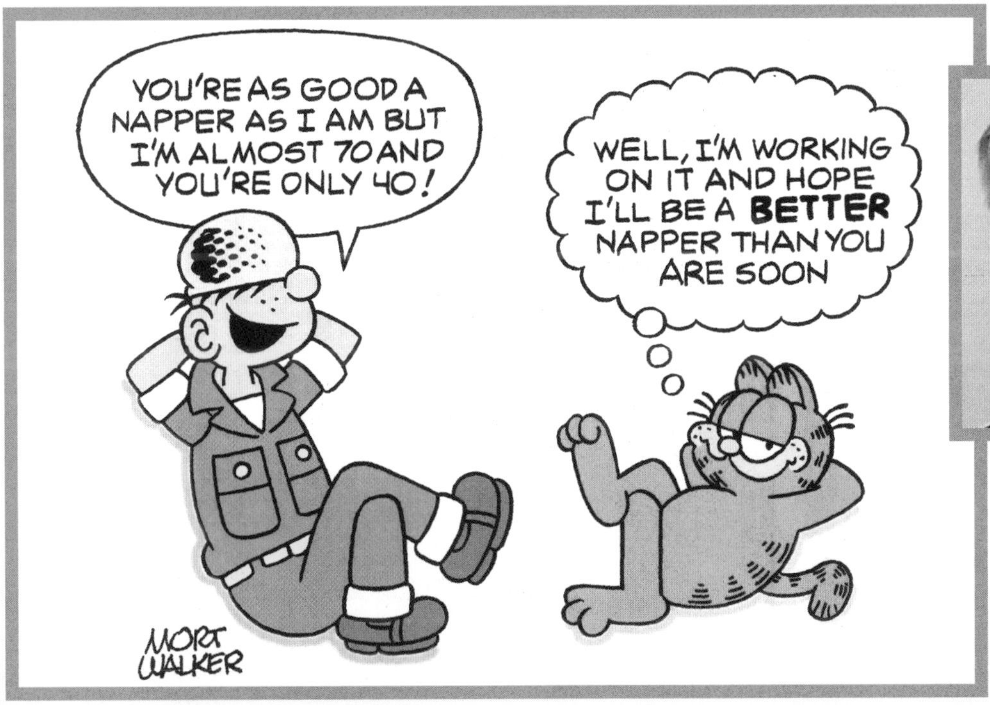
YOU'RE AS GOOD A NAPPER AS I AM BUT I'M ALMOST 70 AND YOU'RE ONLY 40!
WELL, I'M WORKING ON IT AND HOPE I'LL BE A **BETTER** NAPPER THAN YOU ARE SOON
MORT WALKER

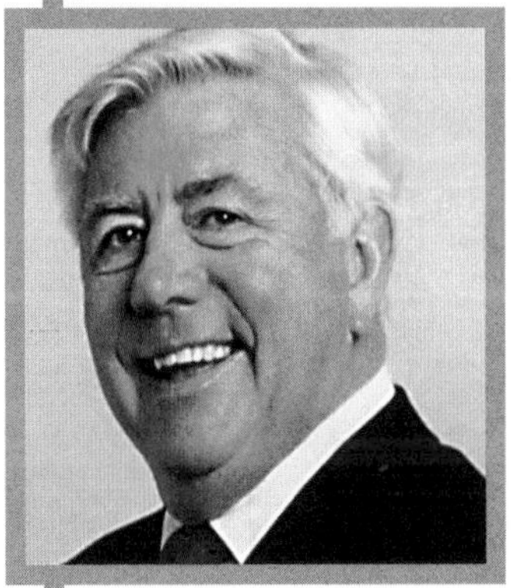

Mort Walker

BEETLE BAILEY

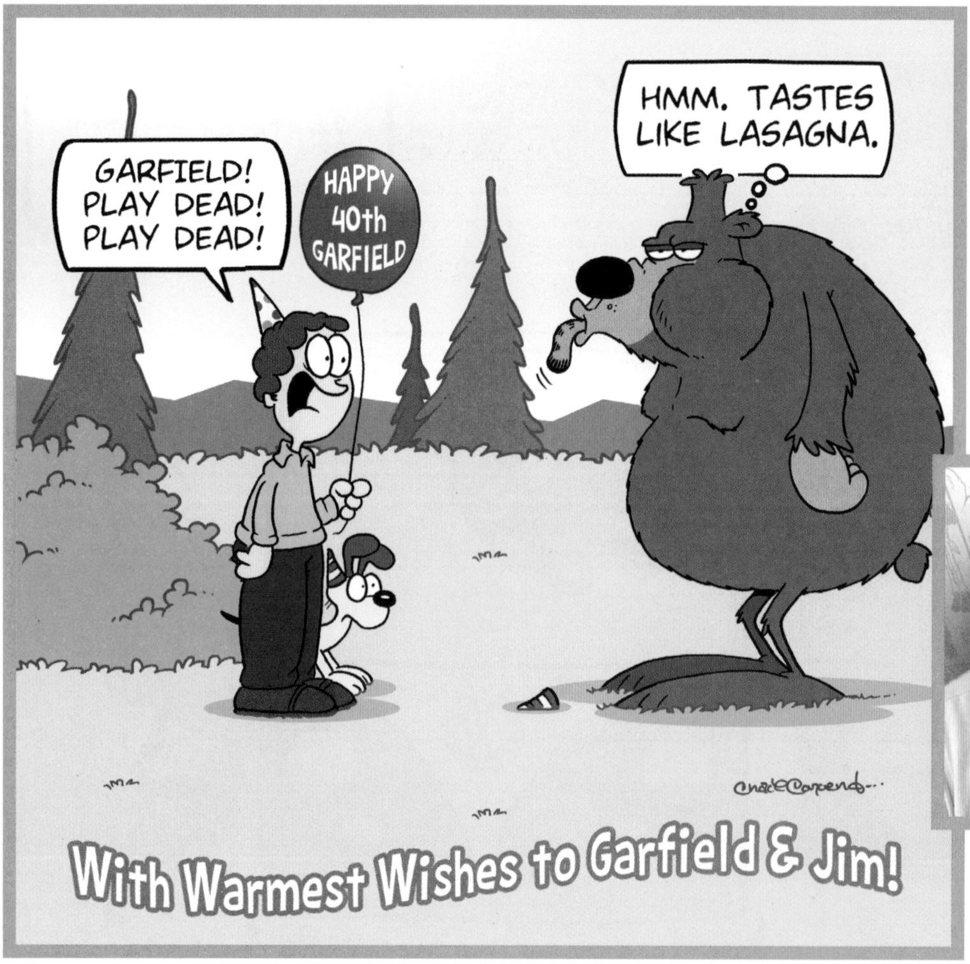
GARFIELD! PLAY DEAD! PLAY DEAD!
HAPPY 40th GARFIELD
HMM. TASTES LIKE LASAGNA.
With Warmest Wishes to Garfield & Jim!

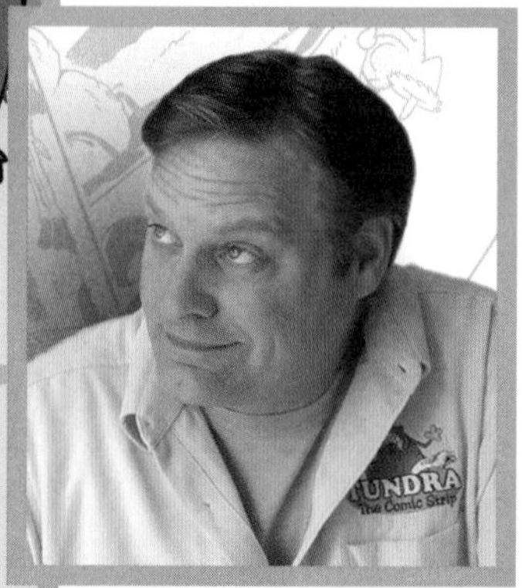

Chad Carpenter
TUNDRA

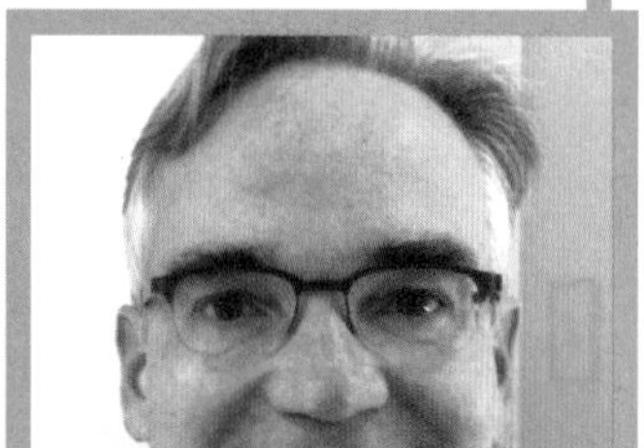

Bob Scott
BEAR WITH ME

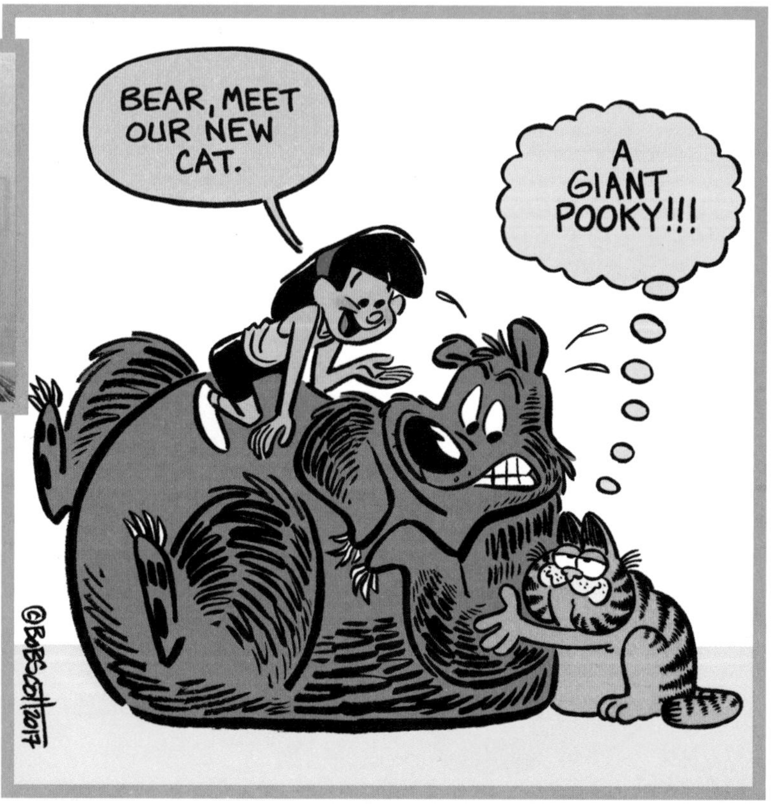
BEAR, MEET OUR NEW CAT.
A GIANT POOKY!!!

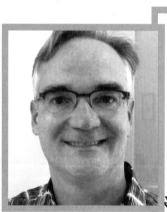

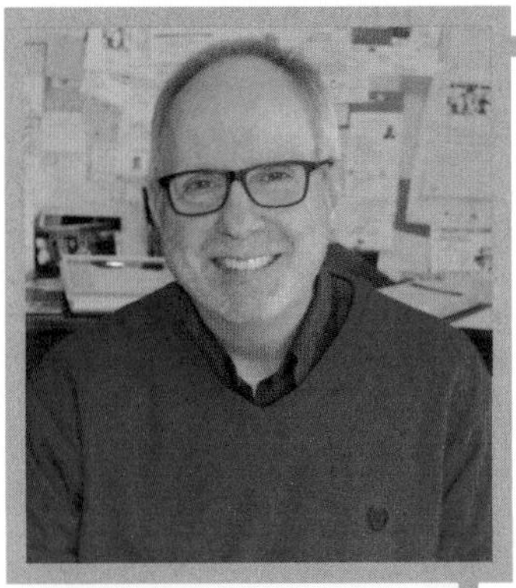

Chuck Batiuk

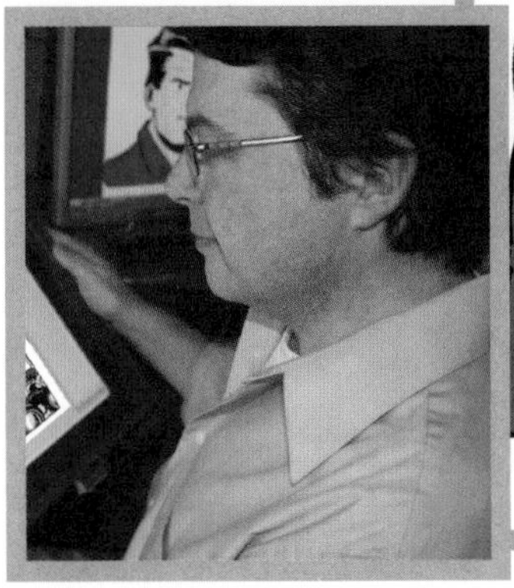

Dan Davis

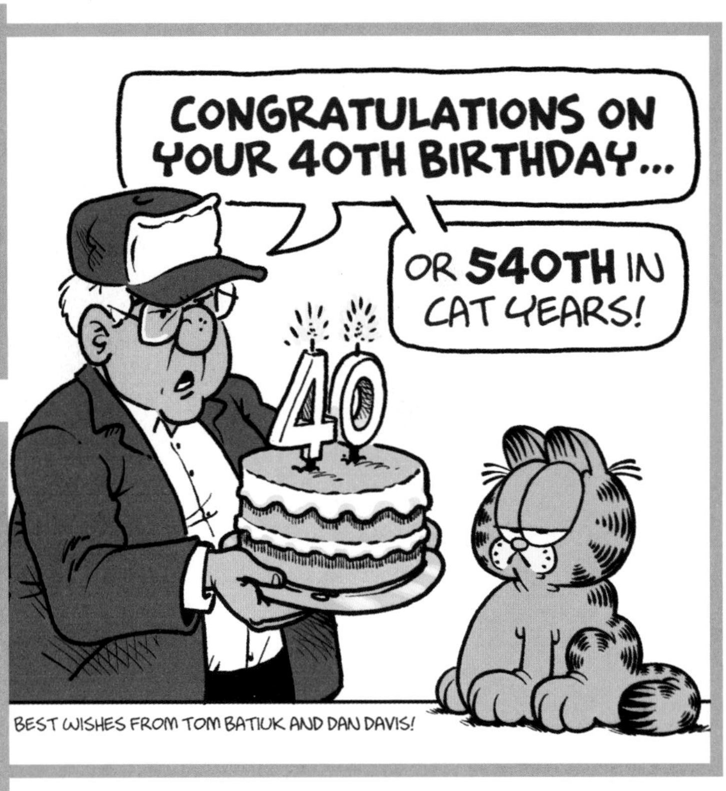

CONGRATULATIONS ON YOUR 40TH BIRTHDAY...
OR 540TH IN CAT YEARS!
40
BEST WISHES FROM TOM BATIUK AND DAN DAVIS!

CRANKSHAFT

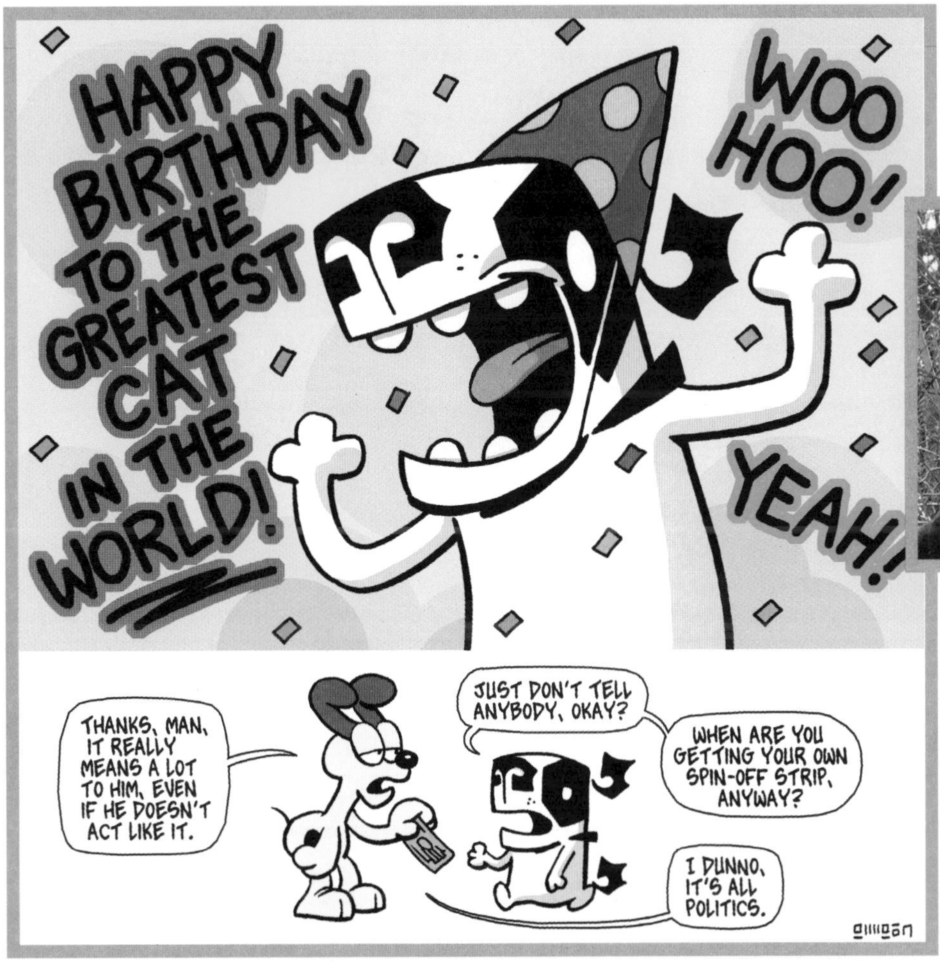

HAPPY BIRTHDAY TO THE GREATEST CAT IN THE WORLD!
WOO HOO!
YEAH!
THANKS, MAN, IT REALLY MEANS A LOT TO HIM, EVEN IF HE DOESN'T ACT LIKE IT.
JUST DON'T TELL ANYBODY, OKAY?
WHEN ARE YOU GETTING YOUR OWN SPIN-OFF STRIP, ANYWAY?
I DUNNO, IT'S ALL POLITICS.
gilligan

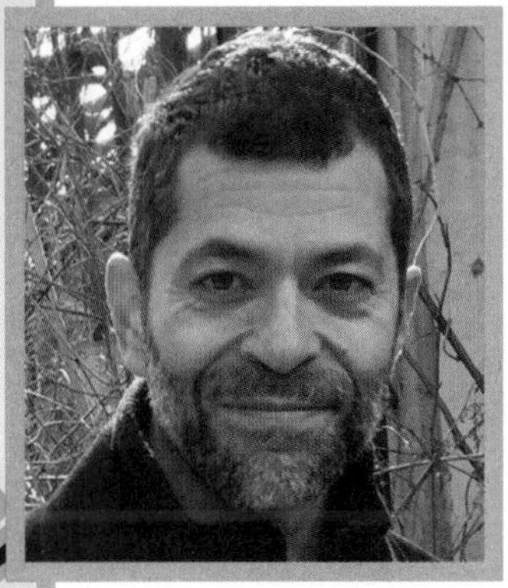

Paul Gilligan

POOCH CAFE

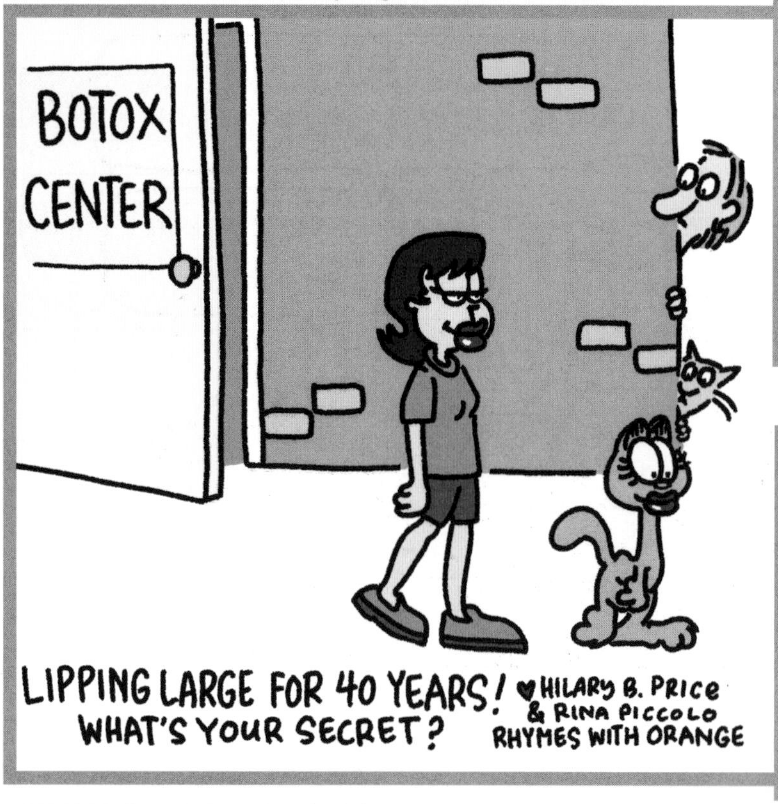
BOTOX CENTER
LIPPING LARGE FOR 40 YEARS! WHAT'S YOUR SECRET?
♥HILARY B. PRICE & RINA PICCOLO RHYMES WITH ORANGE

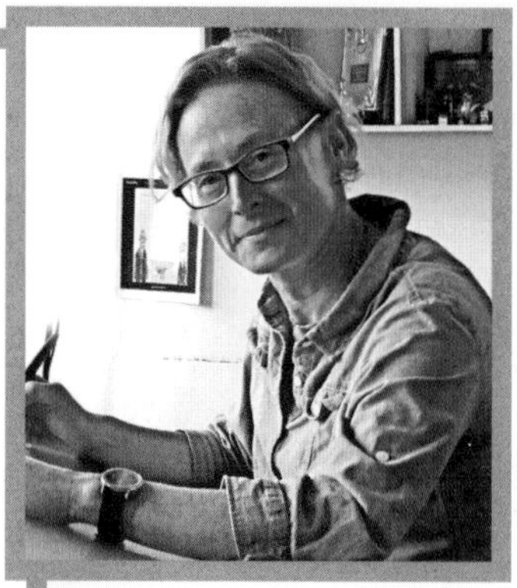

Hilary Price

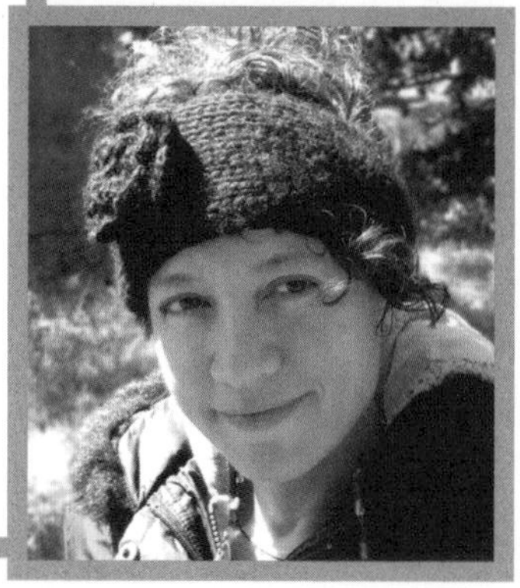

Rina Piccolo

RHYMES WITH ORANGE

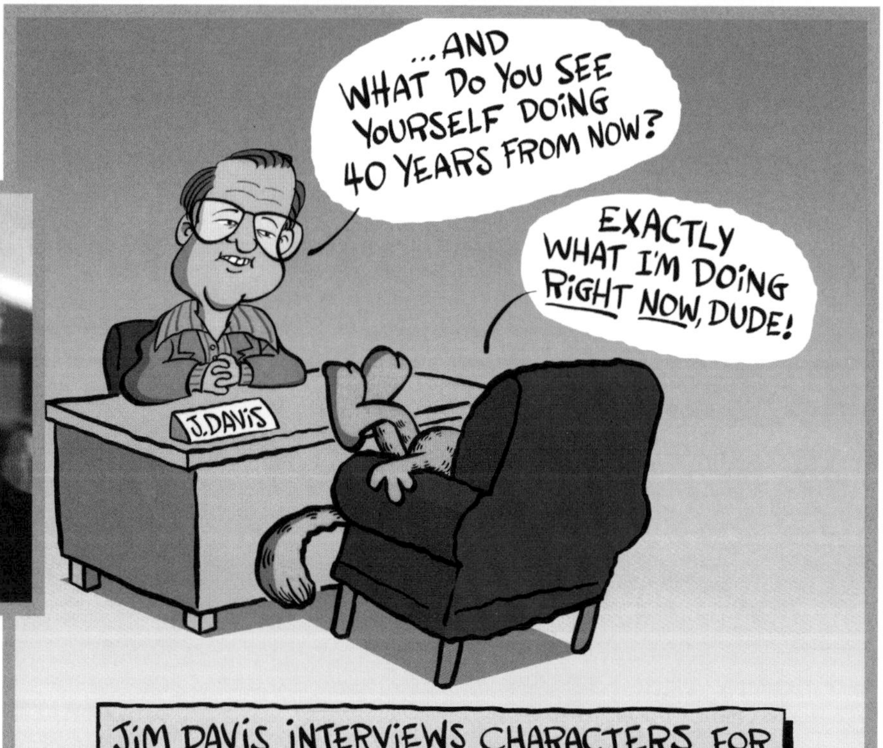
...AND WHAT DO YOU SEE YOURSELF DOING 40 YEARS FROM NOW?
EXACTLY WHAT I'M DOING RIGHT NOW, DUDE!
J. DAVIS
JIM DAVIS INTERVIEWS CHARACTERS FOR HIS NEW COMIC STRIP, CIRCA THE 1970s
HAPPY 40TH, GARFIELD! -BILL WHITEHEAD

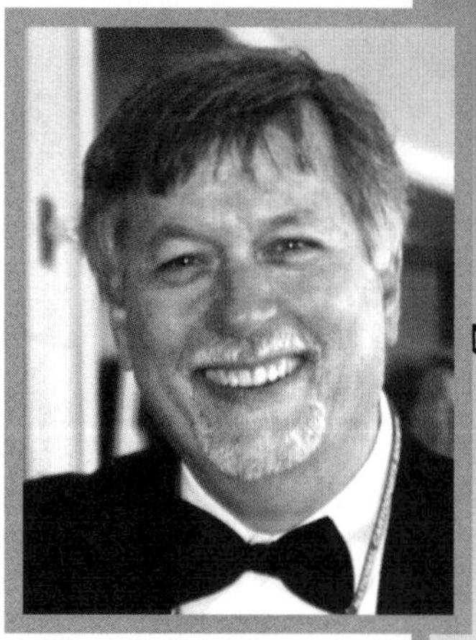

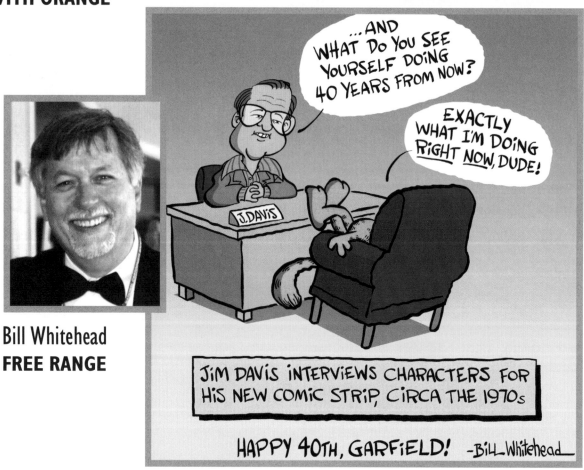

Bill Whitehead
FREE RANGE

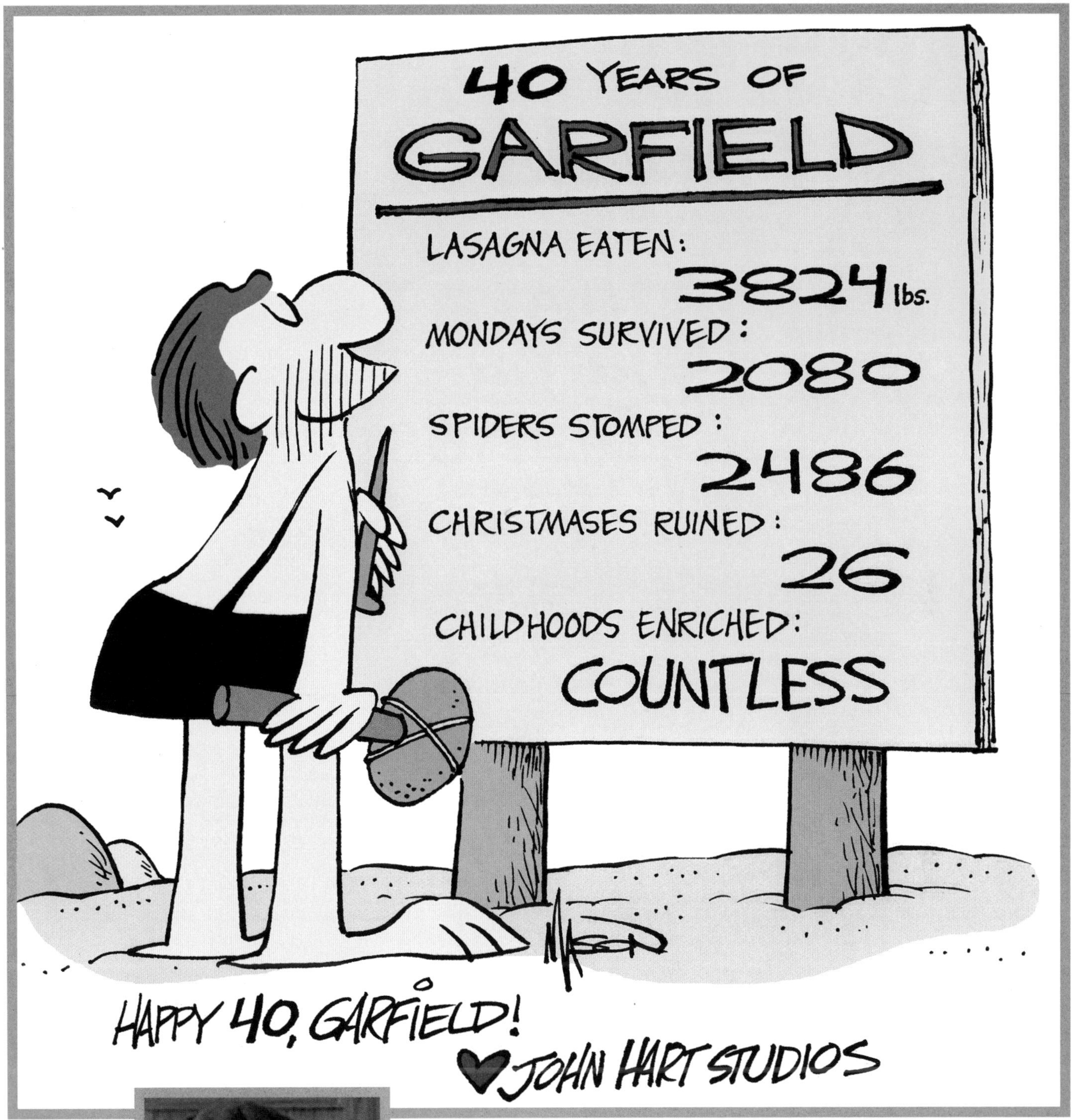
40 YEARS OF
GARFIELD
LASAGNA EATEN:
3824 lbs.
MONDAYS SURVIVED:
2080
SPIDERS STOMPED:
2486
CHRISTMASES RUINED:
26
CHILDHOODS ENRICHED:
COUNTLESS
MASON
HAPPY 40, GARFIELD!
♥ JOHN HART STUDIOS

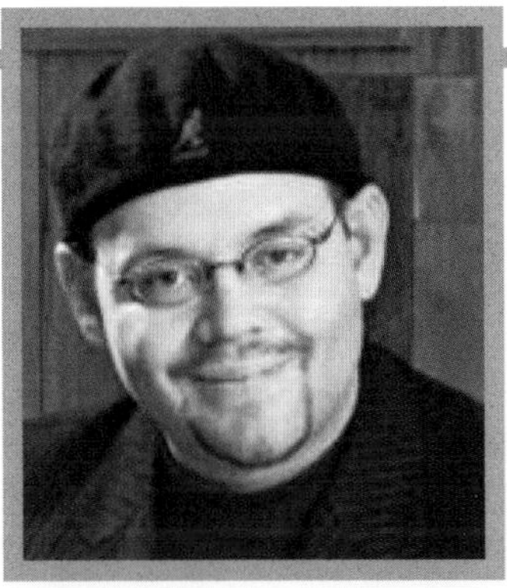

Mason Mastroianni
BC

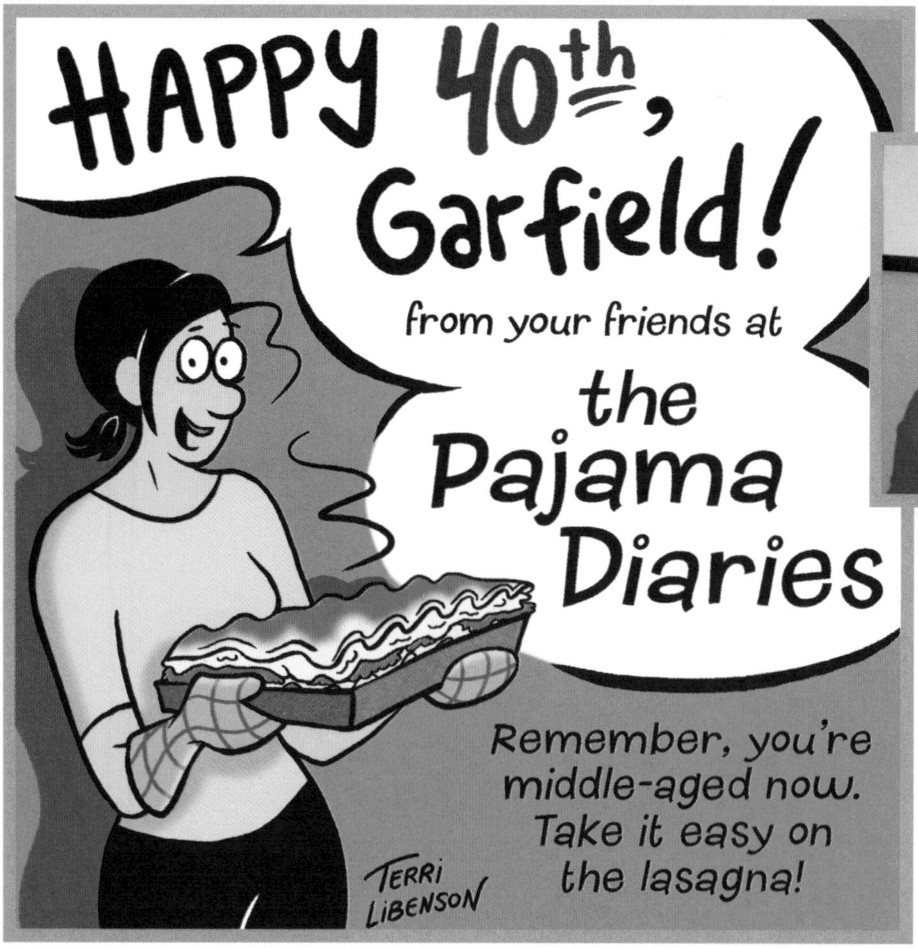
HAPPY 40th, Garfield!
from your friends at
the Pajama Diaries
Remember, you're middle-aged now. Take it easy on the lasagna!
TERRI LIBENSON

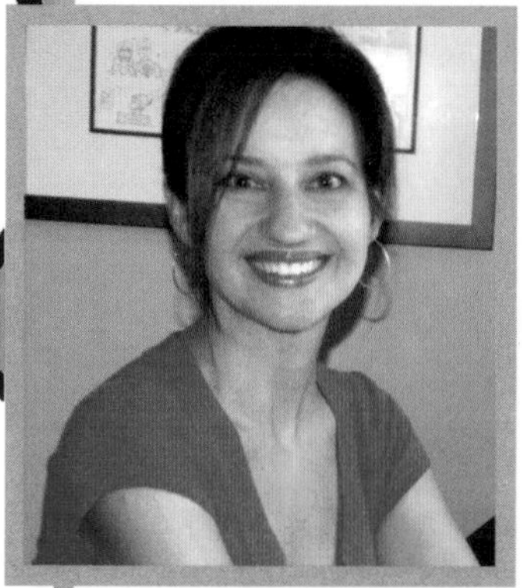

Terri Libenson
THE PAJAMA DIARIES

Lincoln Peirce
BIG NATE

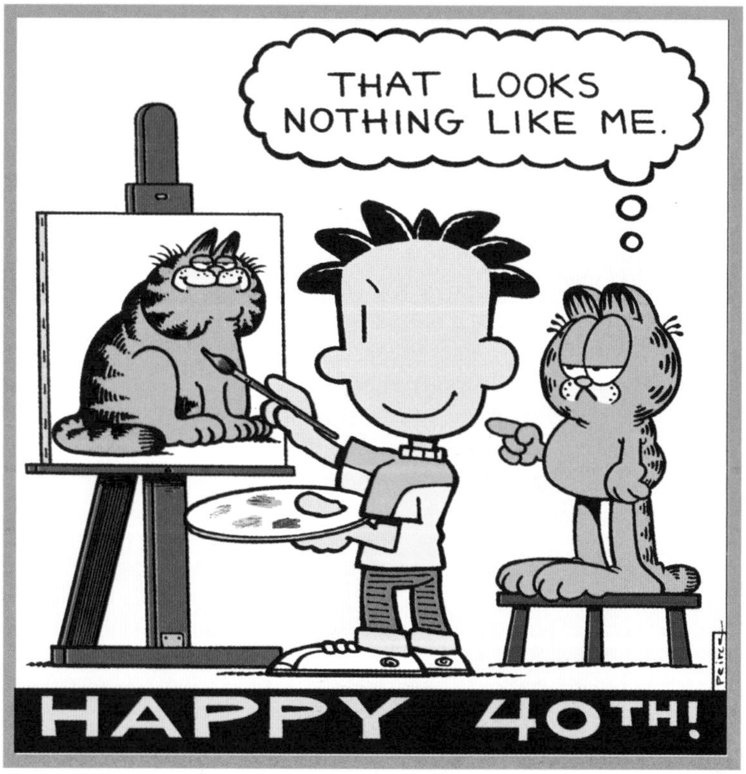
THAT LOOKS NOTHING LIKE ME.
HAPPY 40TH!

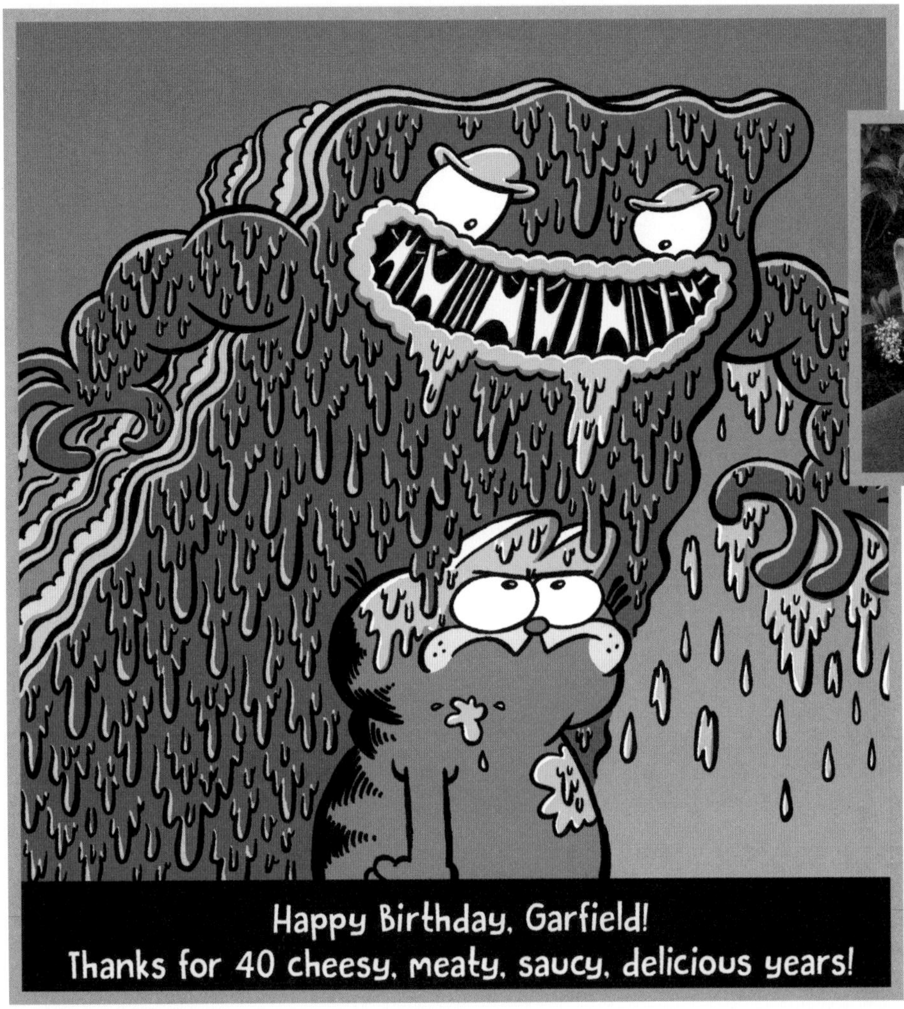
Happy Birthday, Garfield!
Thanks for 40 cheesy, meaty, saucy, delicious years!

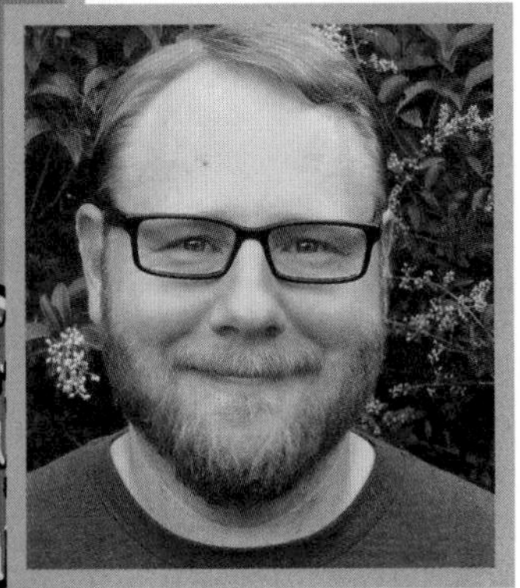

David DeGrand
BOOM! COMICS

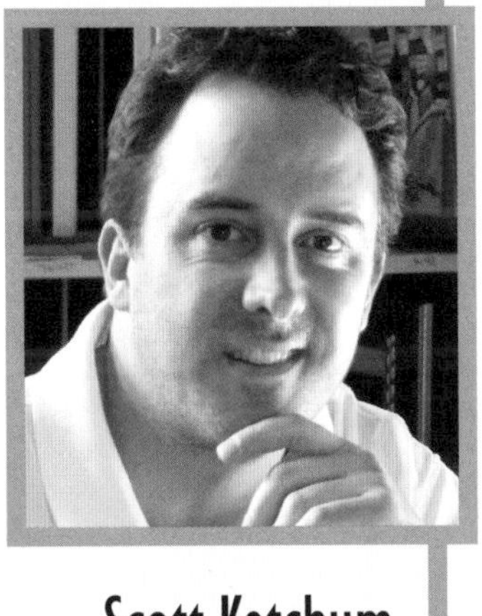

Scott Ketchum
DENNIS THE MENACE

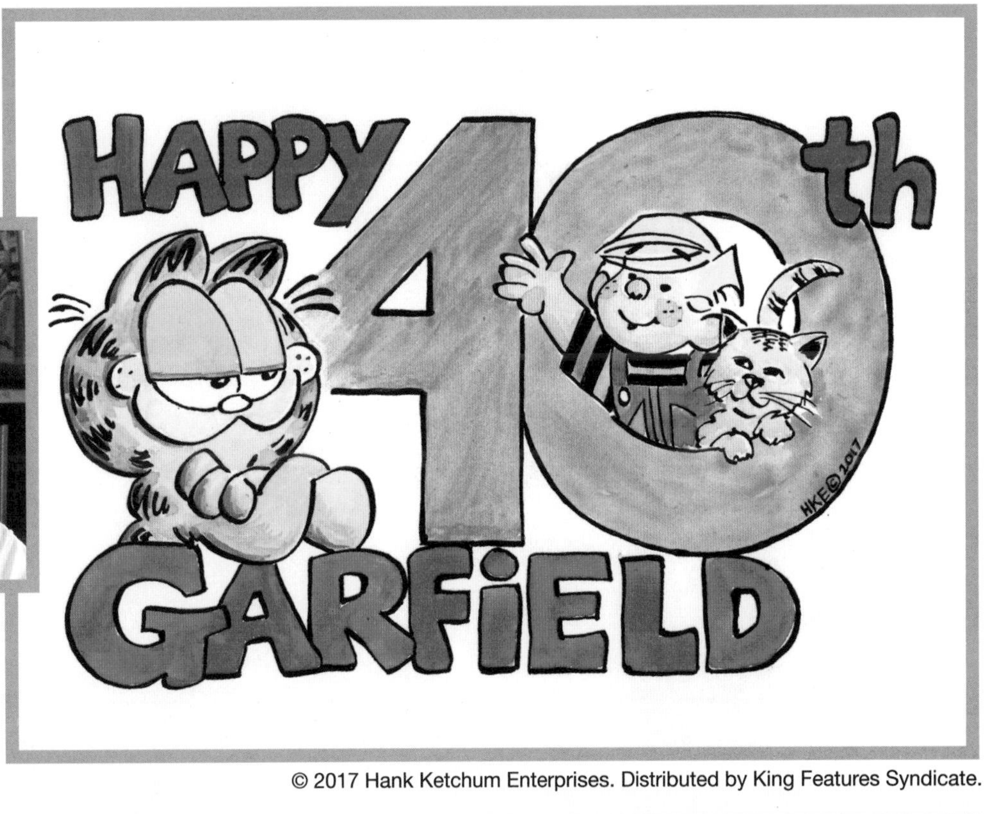
HAPPY 40th
GARFiELD
HKE© 2017

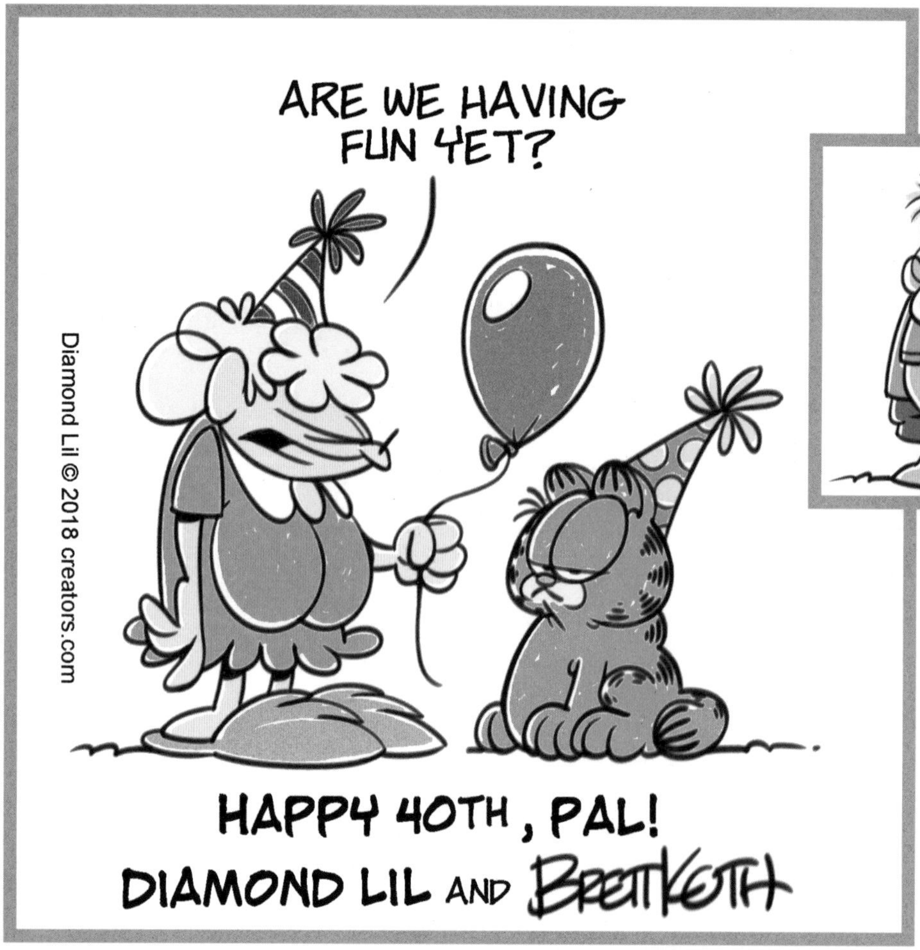
ARE WE HAVING FUN YET?
Diamond Lil © 2018 creators.com
HAPPY 40TH, PAL!
DIAMOND LIL AND BRETT KOTH

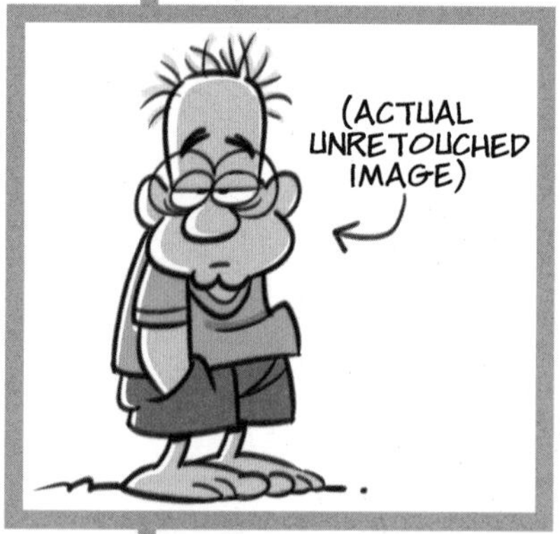
(ACTUAL UNRETOUCHED IMAGE)

Brett Koth
DIAMOND LIL

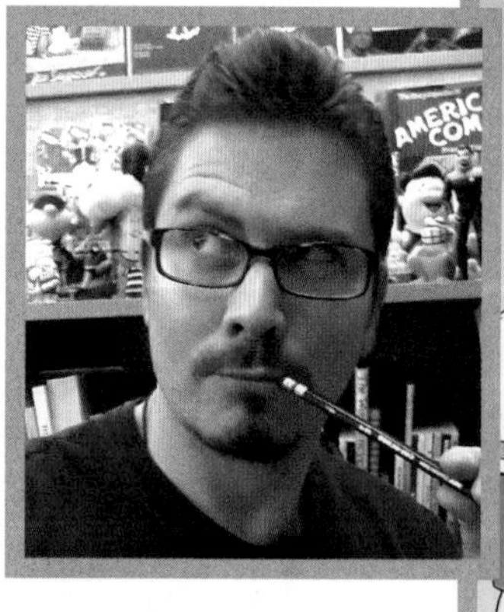

David Reddick
INTELLIGENT LIFE

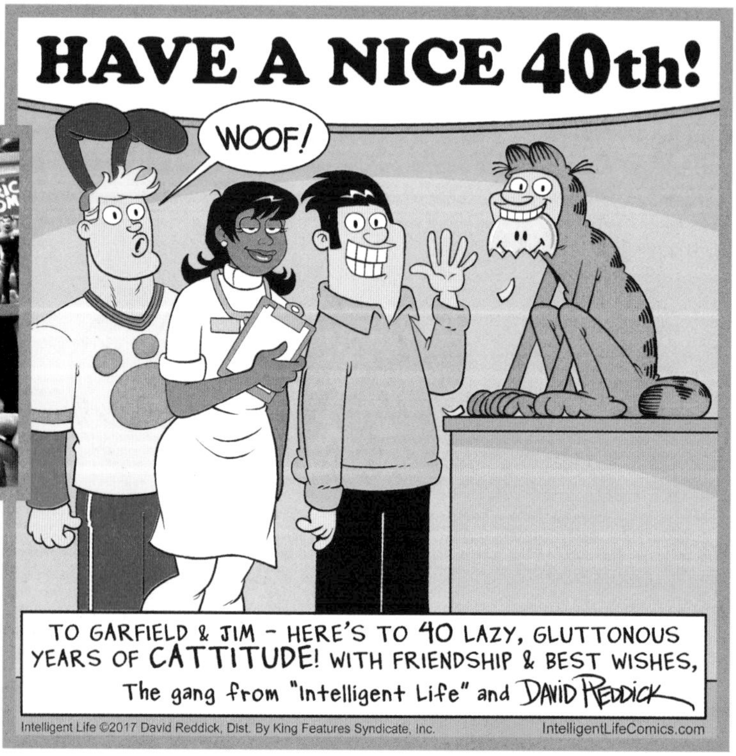
HAVE A NICE 40th!
WOOF!
TO GARFIELD & JIM – HERE'S TO 40 LAZY, GLUTTONOUS YEARS OF CATTITUDE! WITH FRIENDSHIP & BEST WISHES,
The gang from "Intelligent Life" and DAVID REDDICK
Intelligent Life ©2017 David Reddick, Dist. By King Features Syndicate, Inc.
IntelligentLifeComics.com

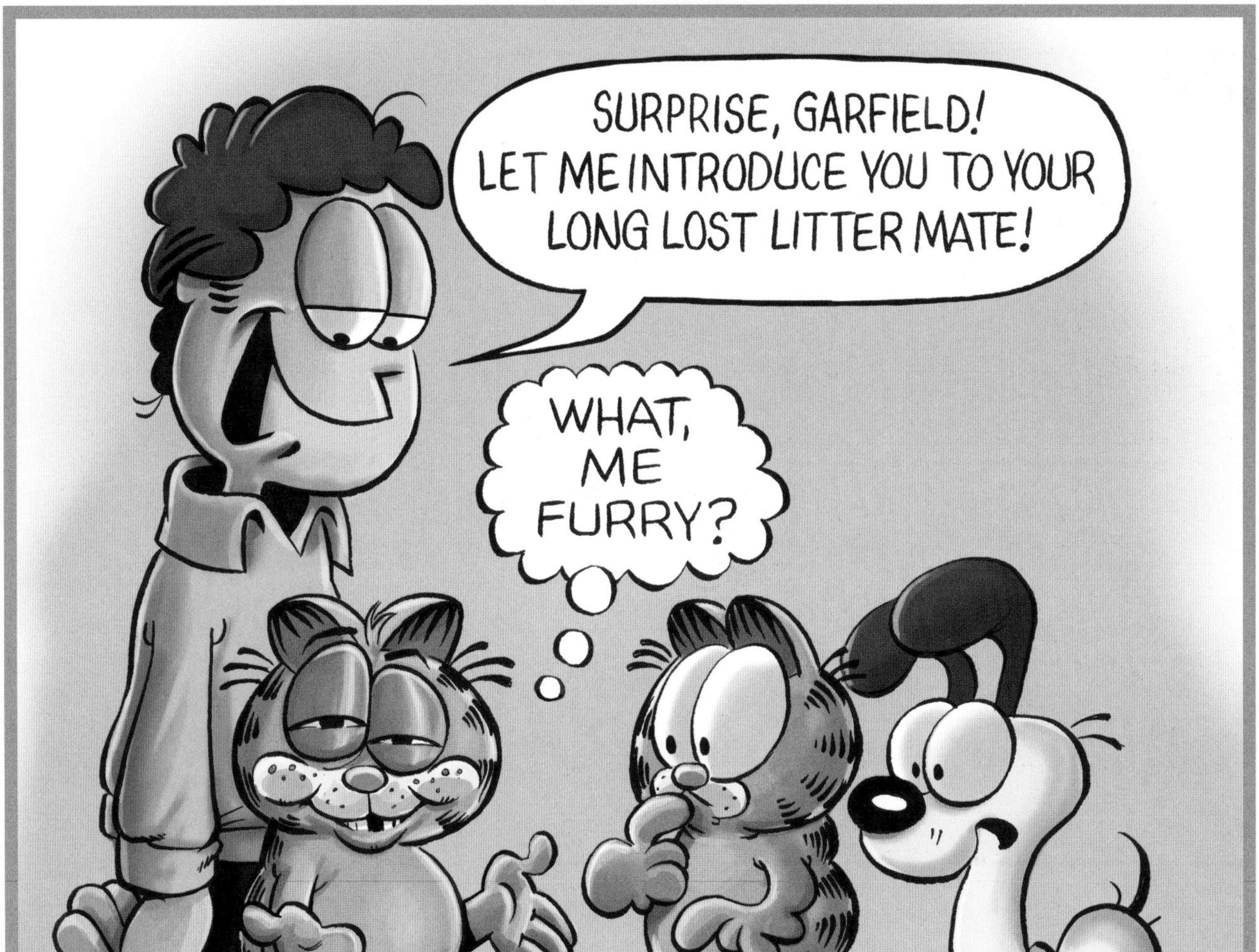
SURPRISE, GARFIELD! LET ME INTRODUCE YOU TO YOUR LONG LOST LITTER MATE!
WHAT, ME FURRY?
HAPPY 40th BIRTHDAY, GARFIELD!
MADLY—

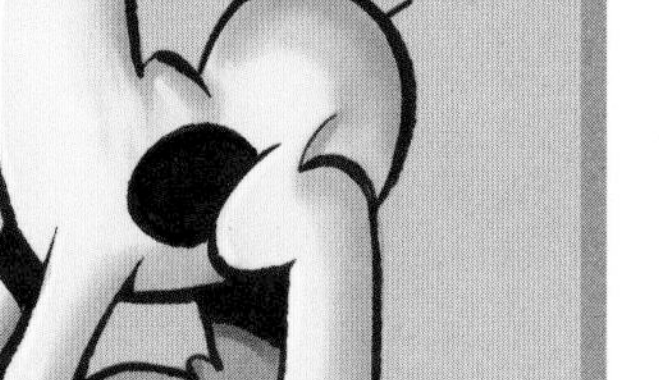

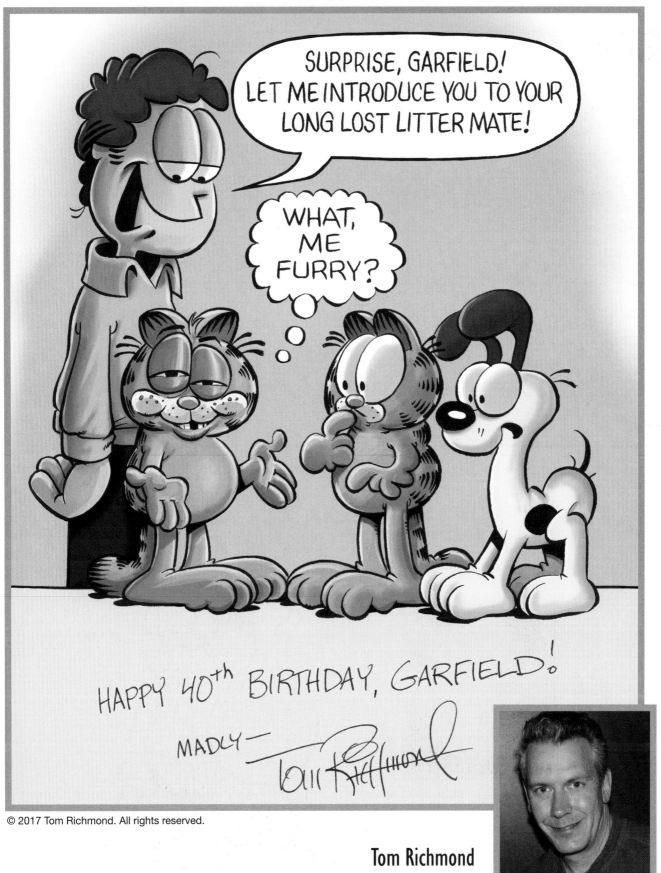

Tom Richmond
MAD MAGAZINE

Scott Kurtz
PvP

HAPPY BIRTHDAY GARFIELD!

KURTZ

Chris Browne
HAGAR THE HORRIBLE

YOU LOOK LIKE A GUY WHO ALWAYS KNOWS HOW TO FIND FOOD.

CHRIS BROWNE

AGE HAPPENS
Garfield Hits the Big 4-0

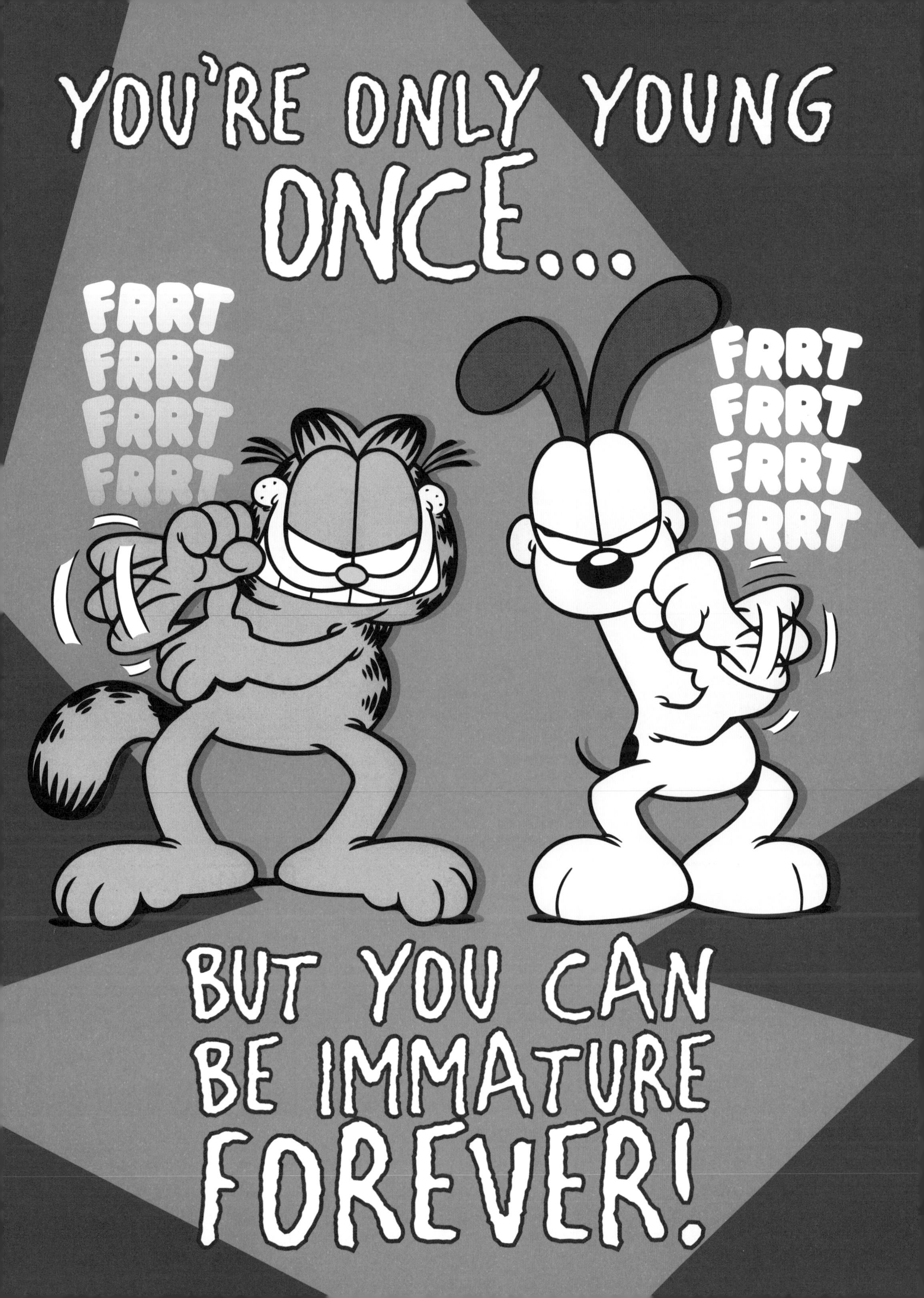
YOU'RE ONLY YOUNG
ONCE...
FRRT
FRRT
FRRT
FRRT
FRRT
FRRT
FRRT
FRRT
BUT YOU CAN
BE IMMATURE
FOREVER!

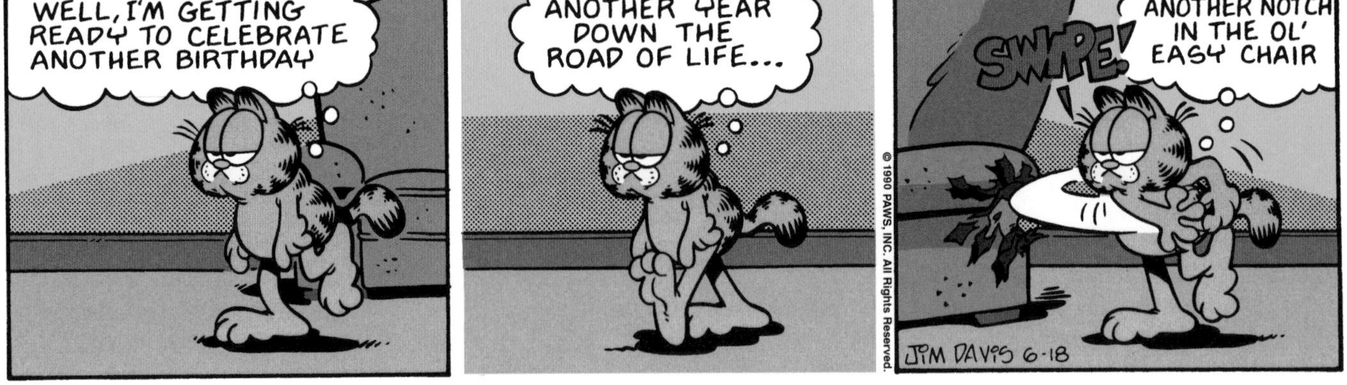
WELL, I'M GETTING READY TO CELEBRATE ANOTHER BIRTHDAY
ANOTHER YEAR DOWN THE ROAD OF LIFE...
SWIPE!
ANOTHER NOTCH IN THE OL' EASY CHAIR
© 1990 PAWS, INC. All Rights Reserved.
JIM DAVIS 6-18

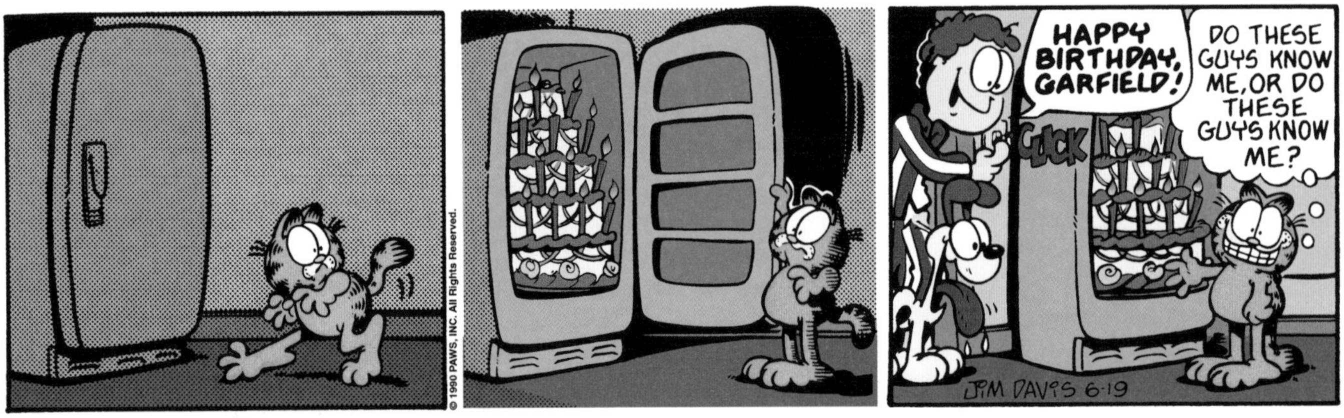
© 1990 PAWS, INC. All Rights Reserved.
HAPPY BIRTHDAY, GARFIELD!
DO THESE GUYS KNOW ME, OR DO THESE GUYS KNOW ME?
JIM DAVIS 6-19

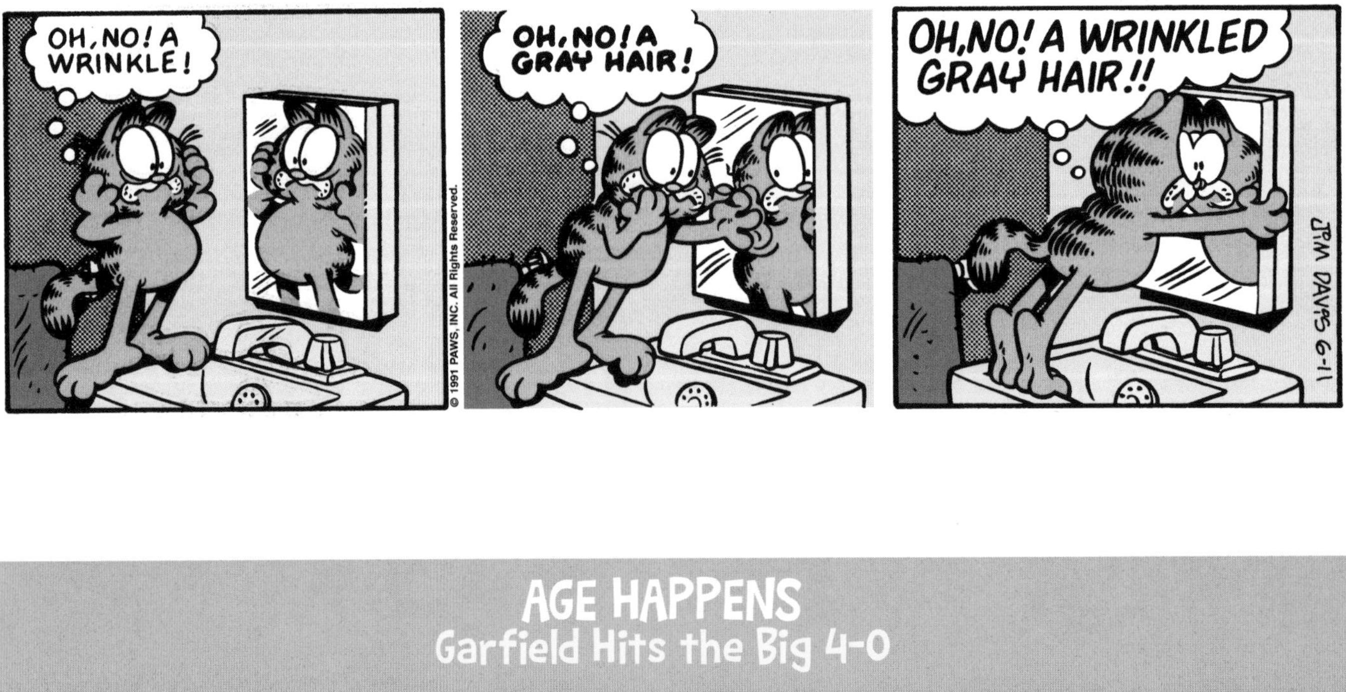
OH, NO! A WRINKLE!
OH, NO! A GRAY HAIR!
© 1991 PAWS, INC. All Rights Reserved.
OH, NO! A WRINKLED GRAY HAIR!!
JIM DAVIS 6-11

AAAAAHHHHHH!!
YAAAHHHHHHH!
AARRRRRRGGGHH!
FOUND HIS FIRST GRAY HAIR
JIM DAVIS 6-12
© 1991 PAWS, INC. All Rights Reserved.

RATS! ANOTHER GRAY HAIR!
MAYBE HAIR DYE WILL HELP
NAAAH
JIM DAVIS 6-13
© 1991 PAWS, INC. All Rights Reserved.

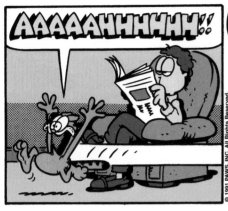

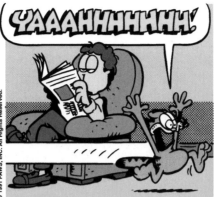

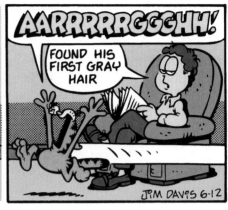

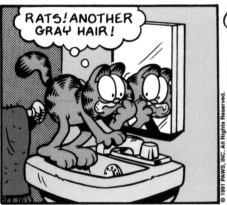

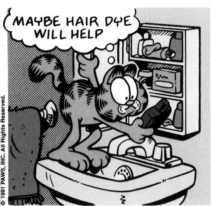

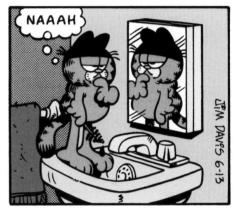

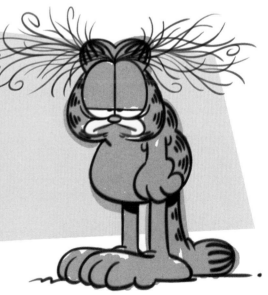

You know you're old when:

The only hair you can grow is in your ears

WOW! WHAT HAPPENED TO YOU?!
I FOUND A GRAY HAIR AND USED HAIR DYE, OKAY?
THAT LOOKS WEIRD
I KNOW
YOU LOOK LIKE MICKEY MOUSE!
I KNOW!
© 1991 PAWS, INC. All Rights Reserved.
JIM DAVIS 6-14

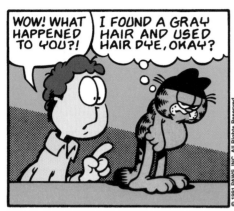

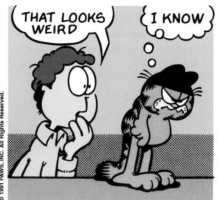

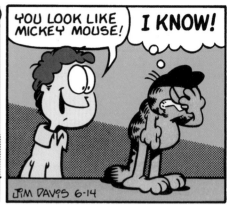

Party till the cows come home...

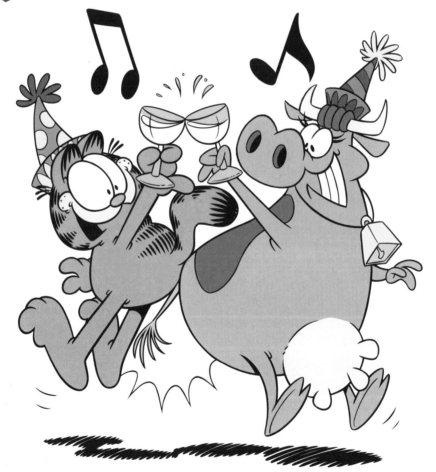

then party with the cows!

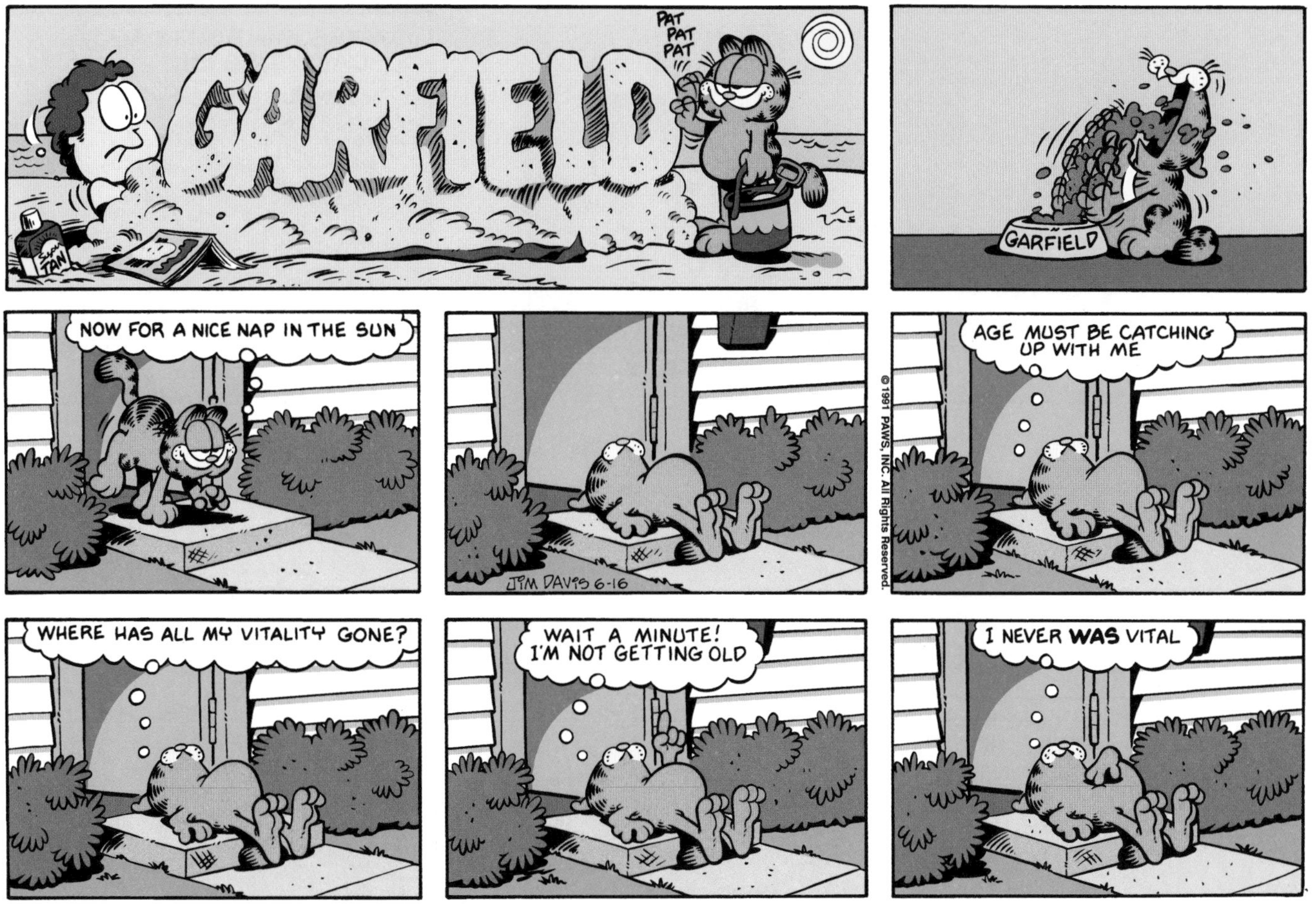
PAT PAT PAT
GARFIELD
Super TAN
GARFIELD
NOW FOR A NICE NAP IN THE SUN
JIM DAVIS 6-16
© 1991 PAWS, INC. All Rights Reserved.
AGE MUST BE CATCHING UP WITH ME
WHERE HAS ALL MY VITALITY GONE?
WAIT A MINUTE! I'M NOT GETTING OLD
I NEVER **WAS** VITAL

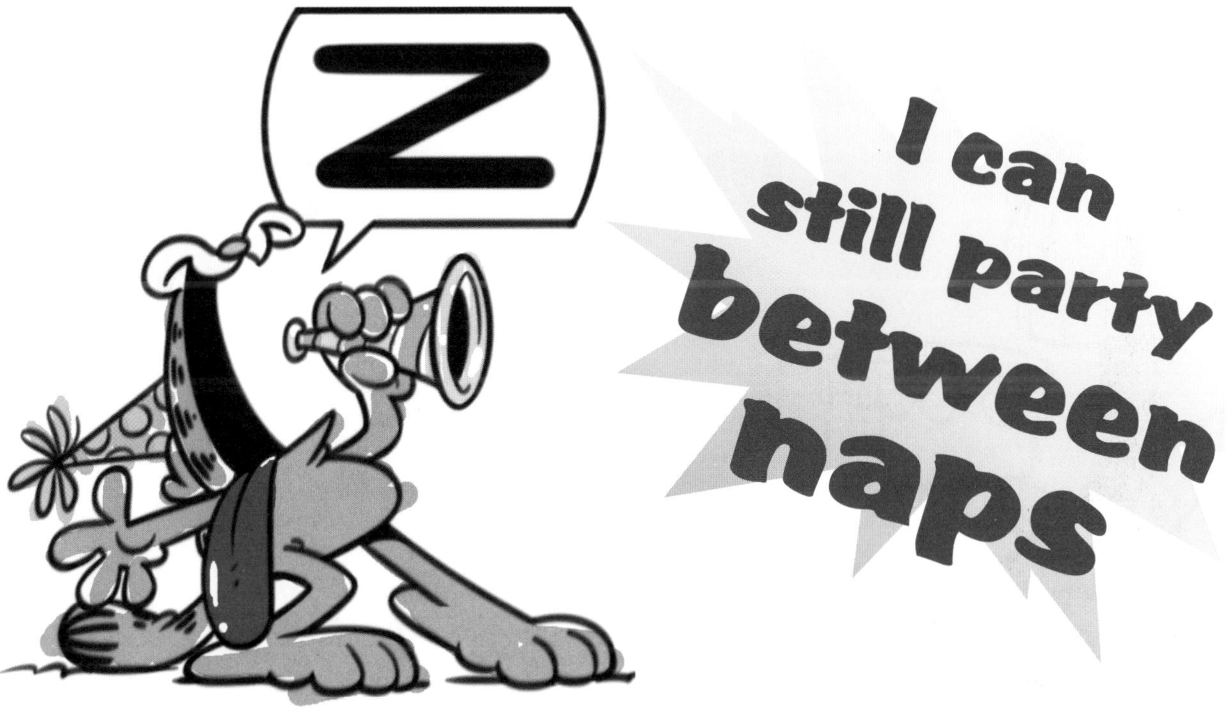
Z
I can still party between naps

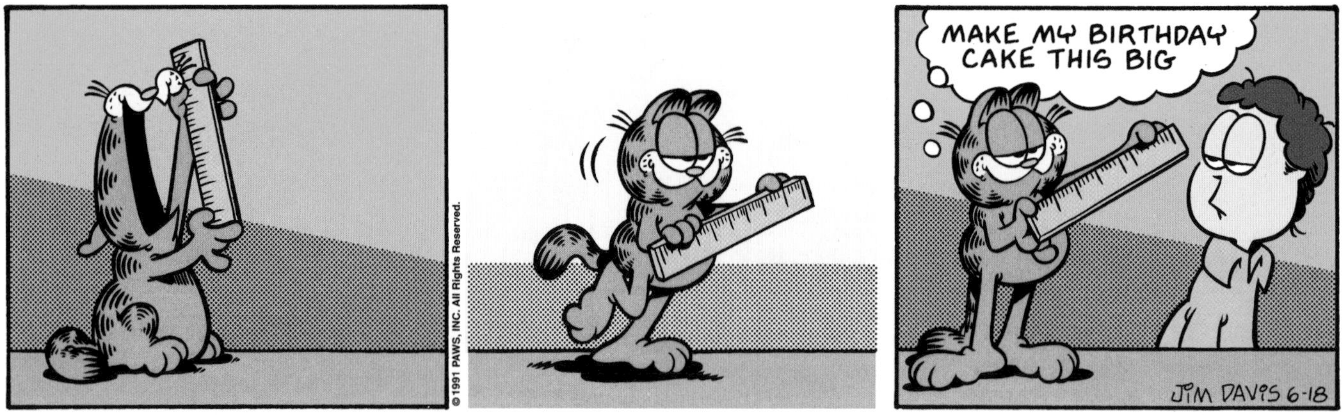
© 1991 PAWS, INC. All Rights Reserved.
MAKE MY BIRTHDAY CAKE THIS BIG
JIM DAVIS 6-18

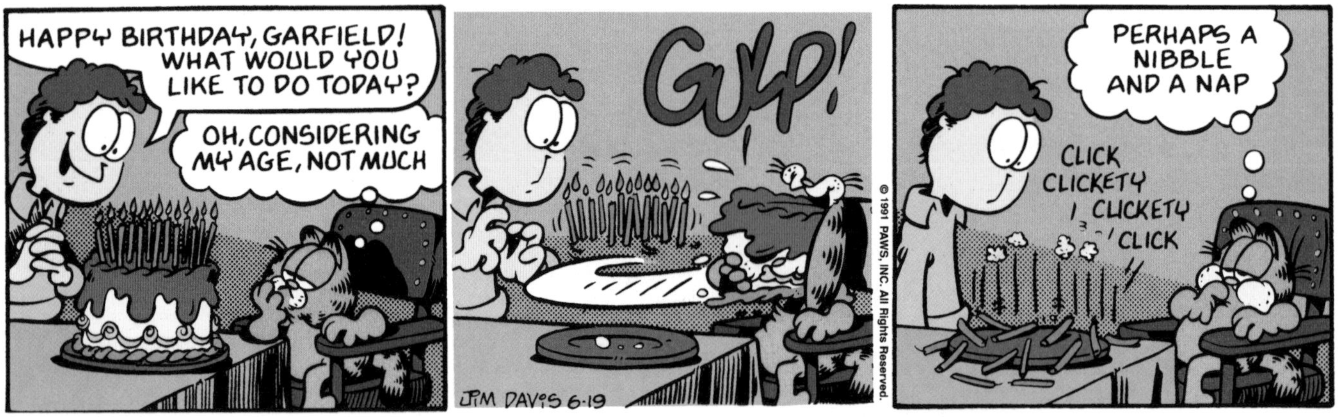
HAPPY BIRTHDAY, GARFIELD! WHAT WOULD YOU LIKE TO DO TODAY?
OH, CONSIDERING MY AGE, NOT MUCH
GULP!
JIM DAVIS 6-19
© 1991 PAWS, INC. All Rights Reserved.
PERHAPS A NIBBLE AND A NAP
CLICK CLICKETY CLICKETY CLICK

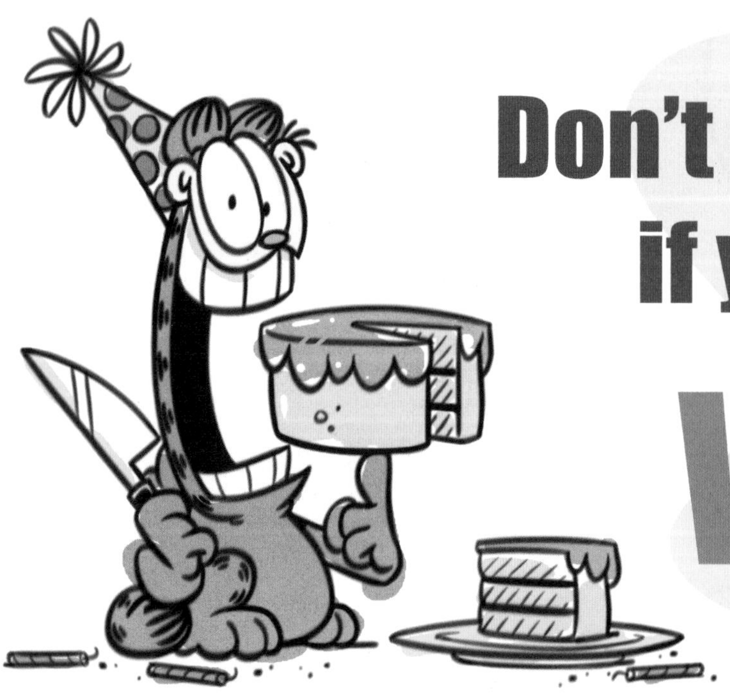

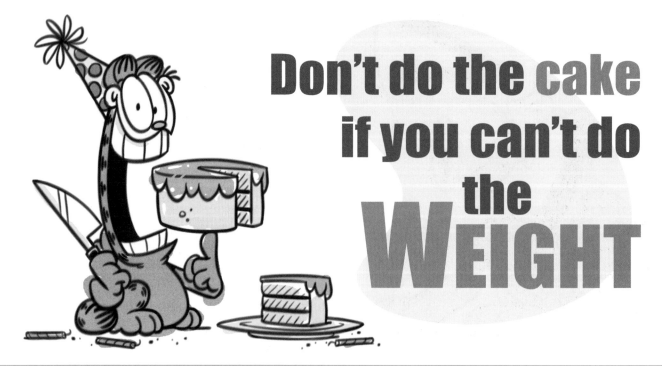

Don't do the cake if you can't do the WEIGHT

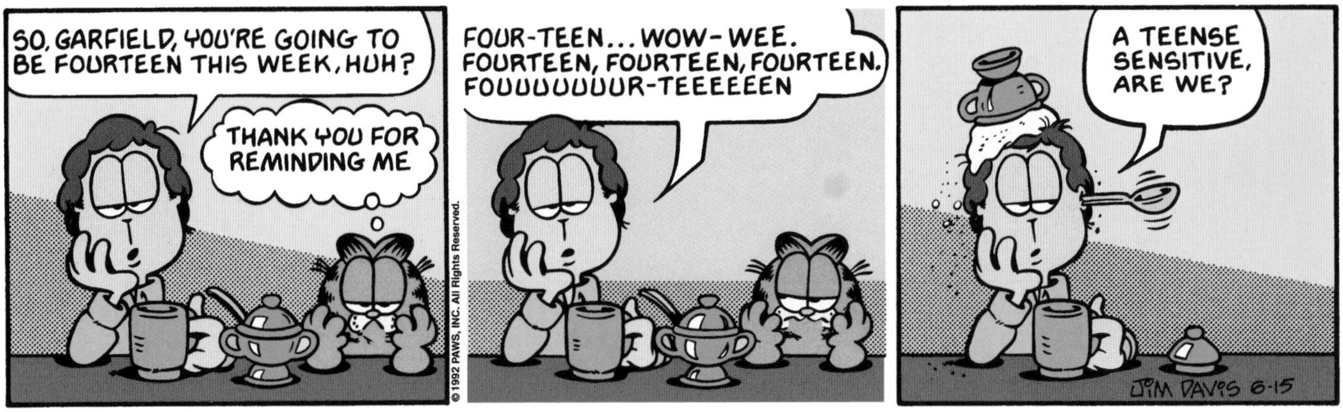
SO, GARFIELD, YOU'RE GOING TO BE FOURTEEN THIS WEEK, HUH?
THANK YOU FOR REMINDING ME
© 1992 PAWS, INC. All Rights Reserved.
FOUR-TEEN... WOW-WEE. FOURTEEN, FOURTEEN, FOURTEEN. FOUUUUUUUR-TEEEEEEN
A TEENSE SENSITIVE, ARE WE?
JIM DAVIS 6-15

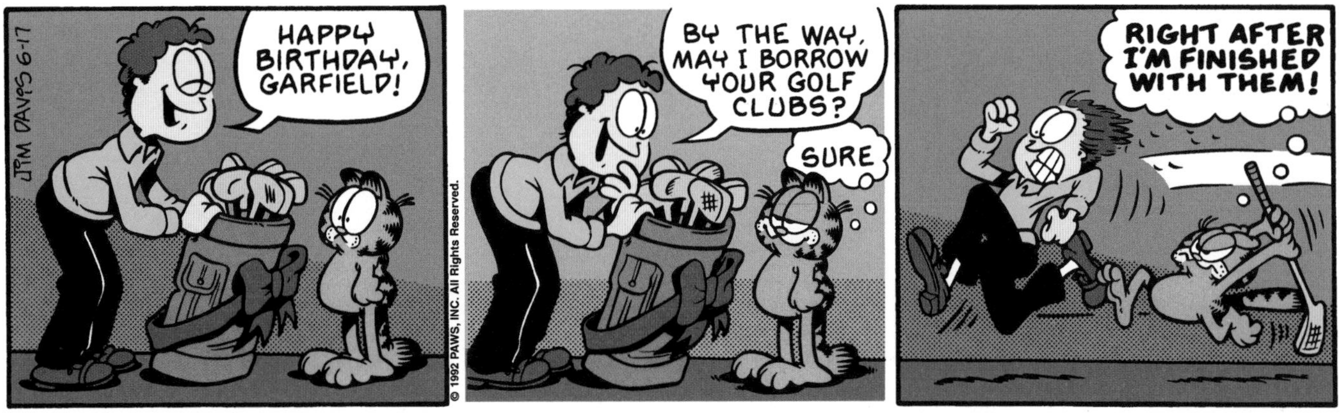
JIM DAVIS 6-17
HAPPY BIRTHDAY, GARFIELD!
© 1992 PAWS, INC. All Rights Reserved.
BY THE WAY, MAY I BORROW YOUR GOLF CLUBS?
SURE
RIGHT AFTER I'M FINISHED WITH THEM!

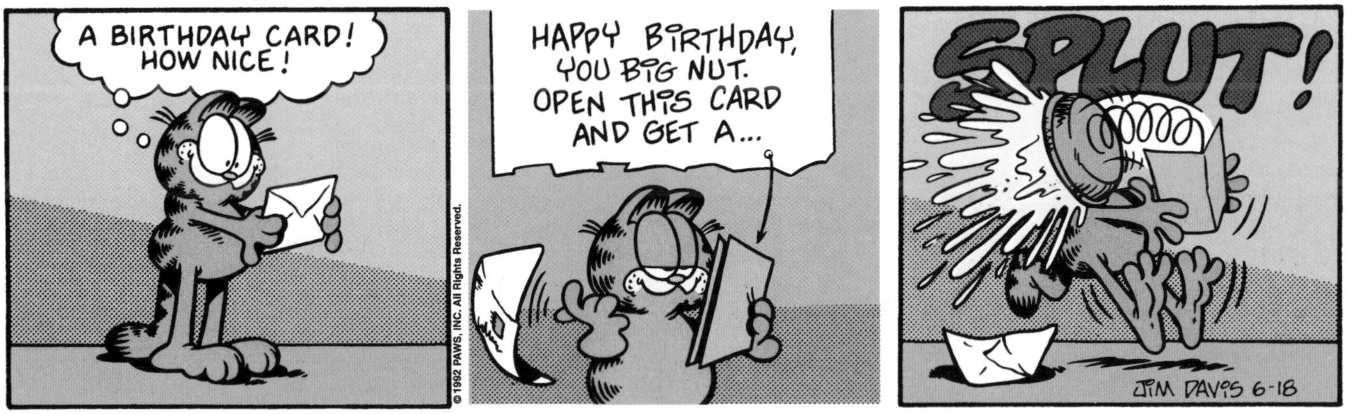
A BIRTHDAY CARD! HOW NICE!
© 1992 PAWS, INC. All Rights Reserved.
HAPPY BIRTHDAY, YOU BIG NUT. OPEN THIS CARD AND GET A...
SPLUT!
JIM DAVIS 6-18

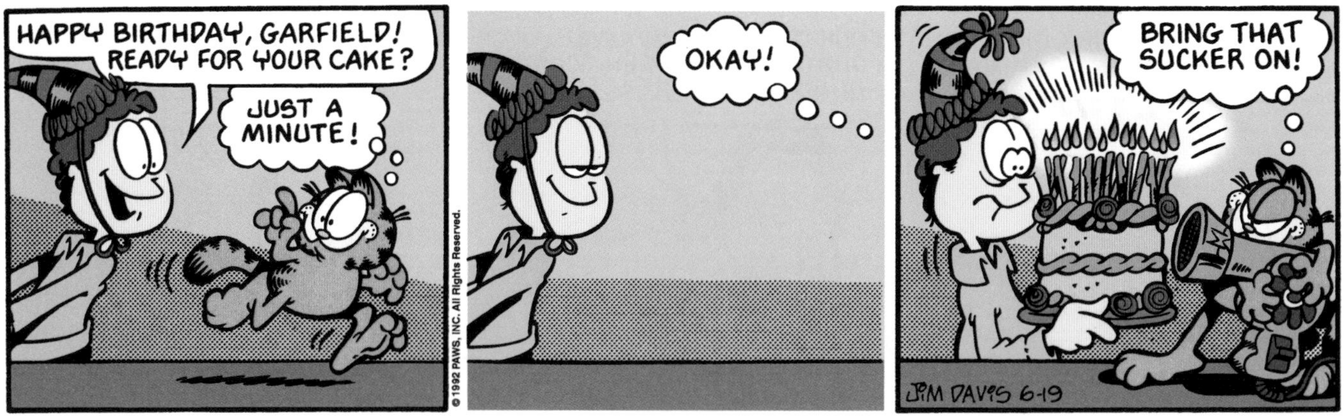
HAPPY BIRTHDAY, GARFIELD! READY FOR YOUR CAKE?
JUST A MINUTE!
OKAY!
BRING THAT SUCKER ON!
© 1992 PAWS, INC. All Rights Reserved.
JIM DAVIS 6-19

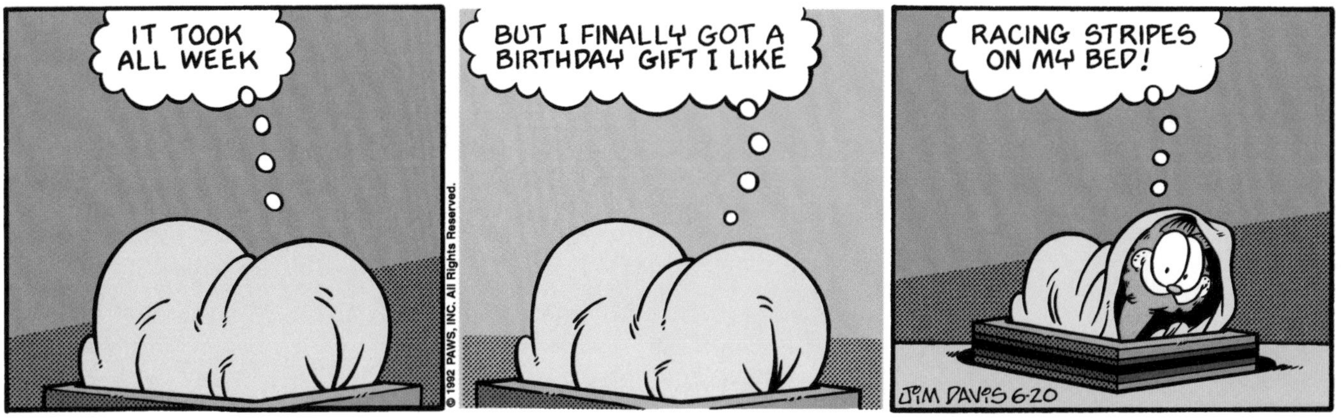
IT TOOK ALL WEEK
BUT I FINALLY GOT A BIRTHDAY GIFT I LIKE
RACING STRIPES ON MY BED!
© 1992 PAWS, INC. All Rights Reserved.
JIM DAVIS 6-20

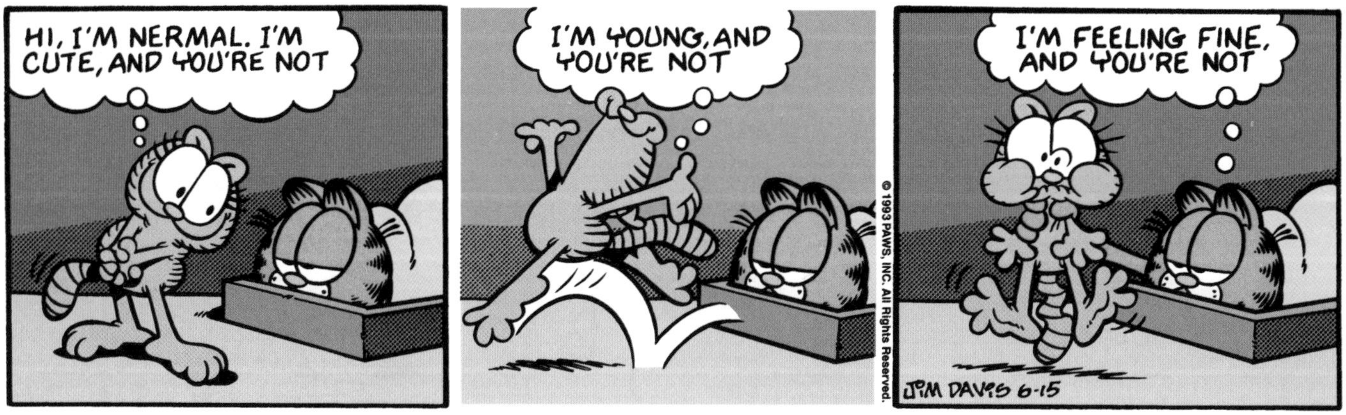
HI, I'M NERMAL. I'M CUTE, AND YOU'RE NOT
I'M YOUNG, AND YOU'RE NOT
I'M FEELING FINE, AND YOU'RE NOT
© 1993 PAWS, INC. All Rights Reserved.
JIM DAVIS 6-15

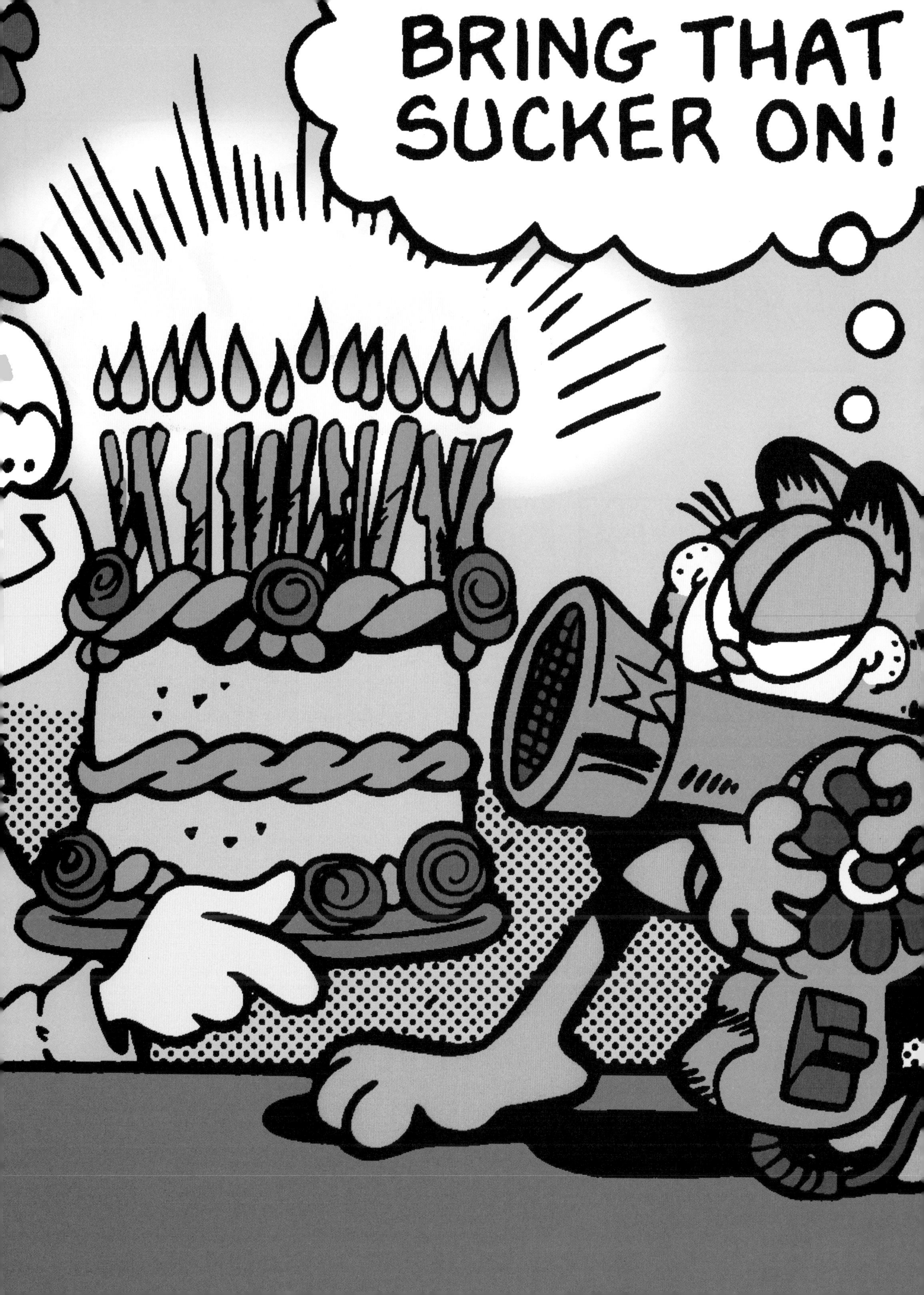
BRING THAT SUCKER ON!

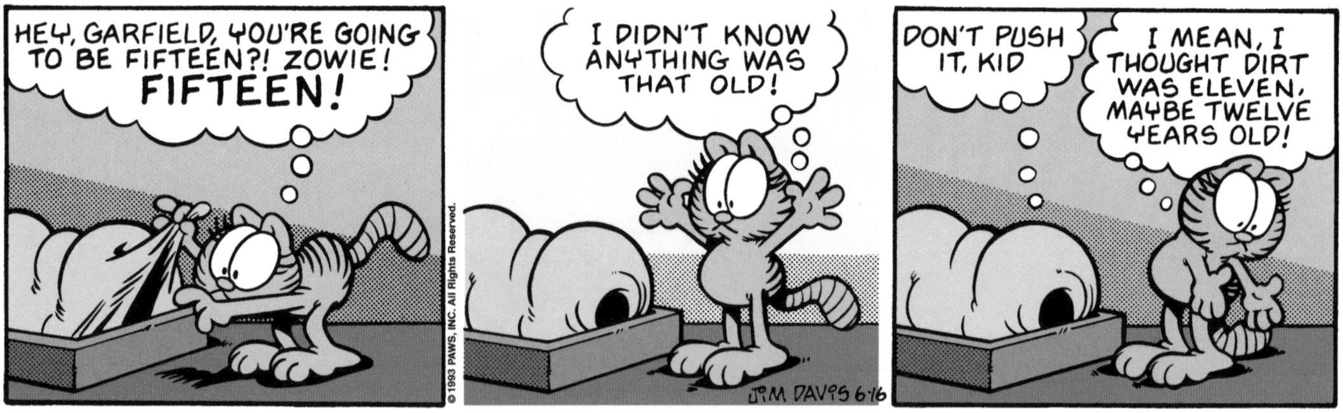
HEY, GARFIELD, YOU'RE GOING TO BE FIFTEEN?! ZOWIE! FIFTEEN!
I DIDN'T KNOW ANYTHING WAS THAT OLD!
DON'T PUSH IT, KID
I MEAN, I THOUGHT DIRT WAS ELEVEN, MAYBE TWELVE YEARS OLD!
© 1993 PAWS, INC. All Rights Reserved.
JIM DAVIS 6-16

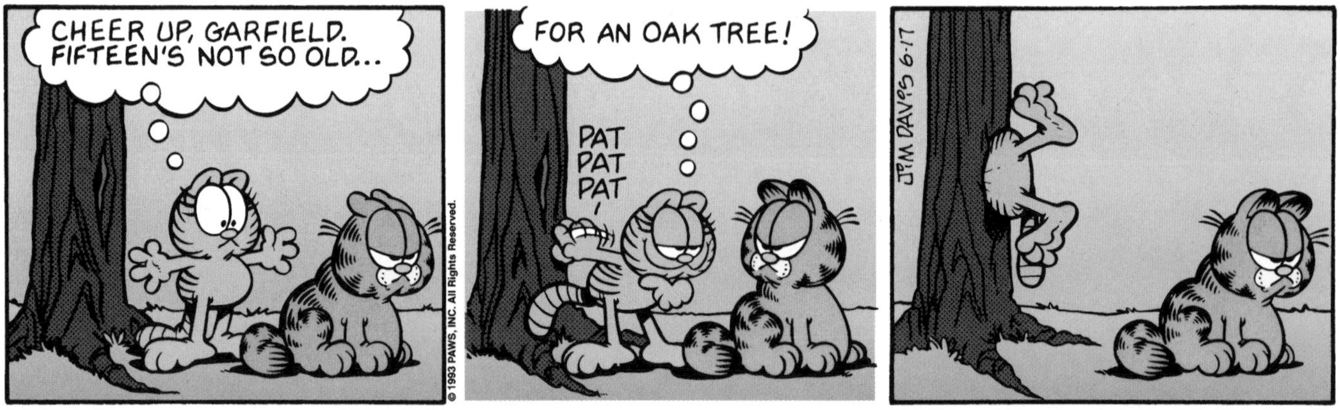
CHEER UP, GARFIELD. FIFTEEN'S NOT SO OLD...
FOR AN OAK TREE!
PAT PAT PAT
© 1993 PAWS, INC. All Rights Reserved.
JIM DAVIS 6-17

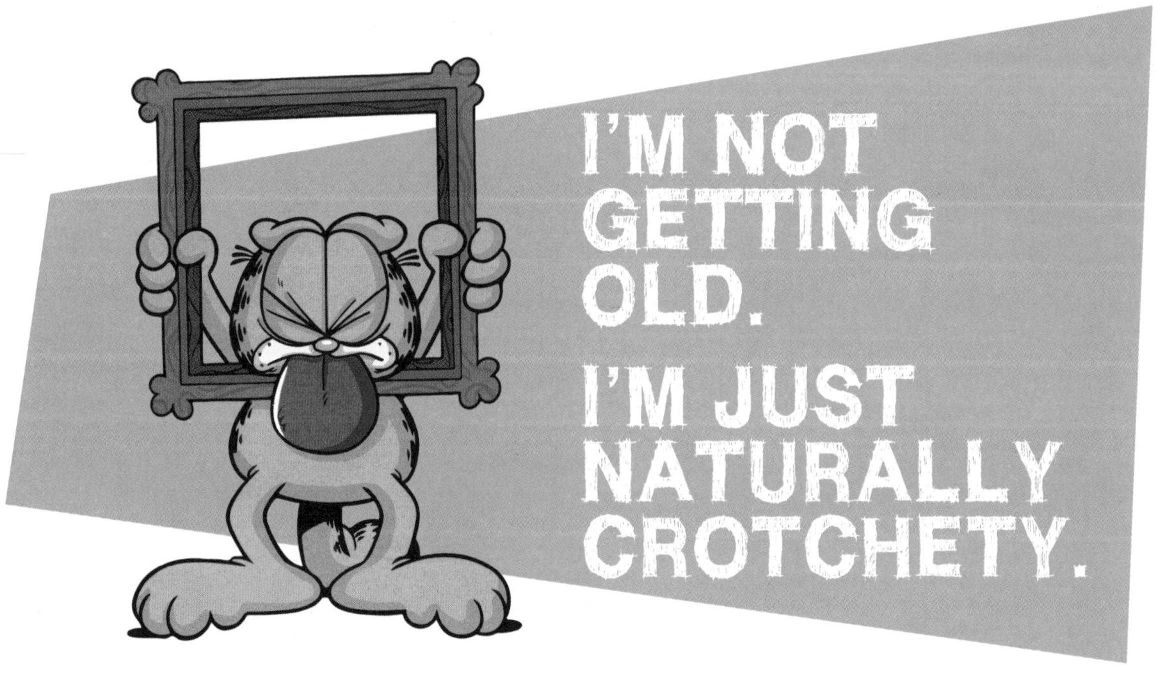
I'M NOT GETTING OLD.
I'M JUST NATURALLY CROTCHETY.

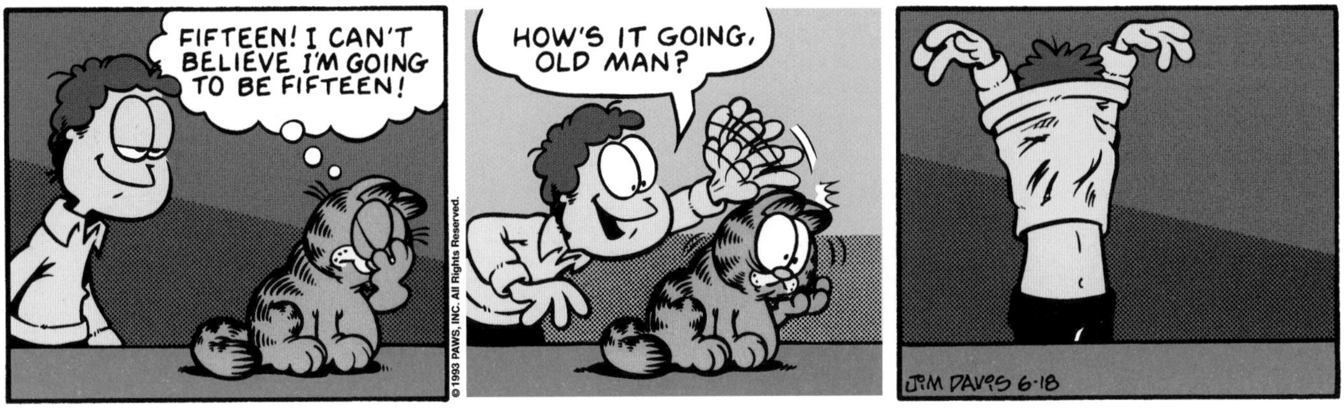
FIFTEEN! I CAN'T BELIEVE I'M GOING TO BE FIFTEEN!
HOW'S IT GOING, OLD MAN?
© 1993 PAWS, INC. All Rights Reserved.
JIM DAVIS 6-18

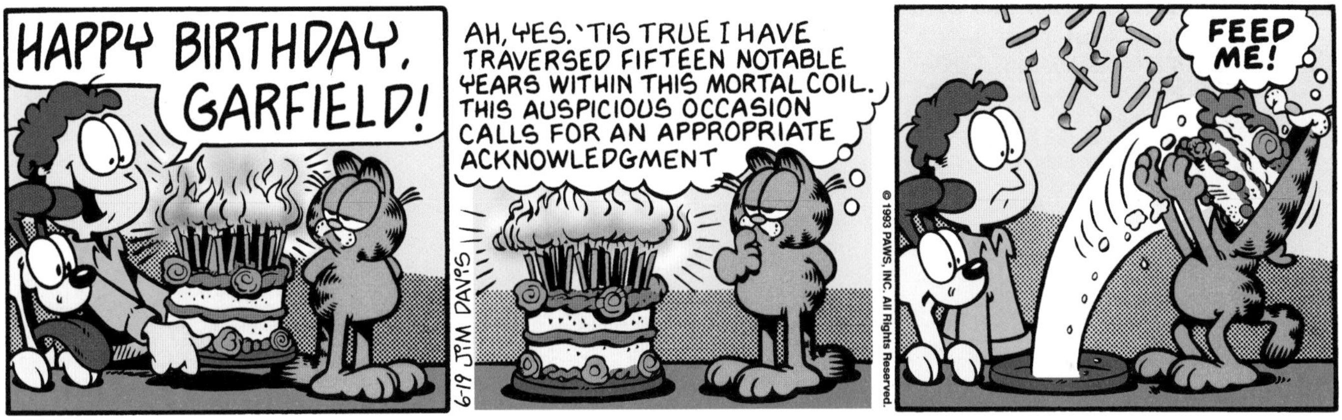
HAPPY BIRTHDAY, GARFIELD!
AH, YES. 'TIS TRUE I HAVE TRAVERSED FIFTEEN NOTABLE YEARS WITHIN THIS MORTAL COIL. THIS AUSPICIOUS OCCASION CALLS FOR AN APPROPRIATE ACKNOWLEDGMENT
6-19 JIM DAVIS
FEED ME!
© 1993 PAWS, INC. All Rights Reserved.

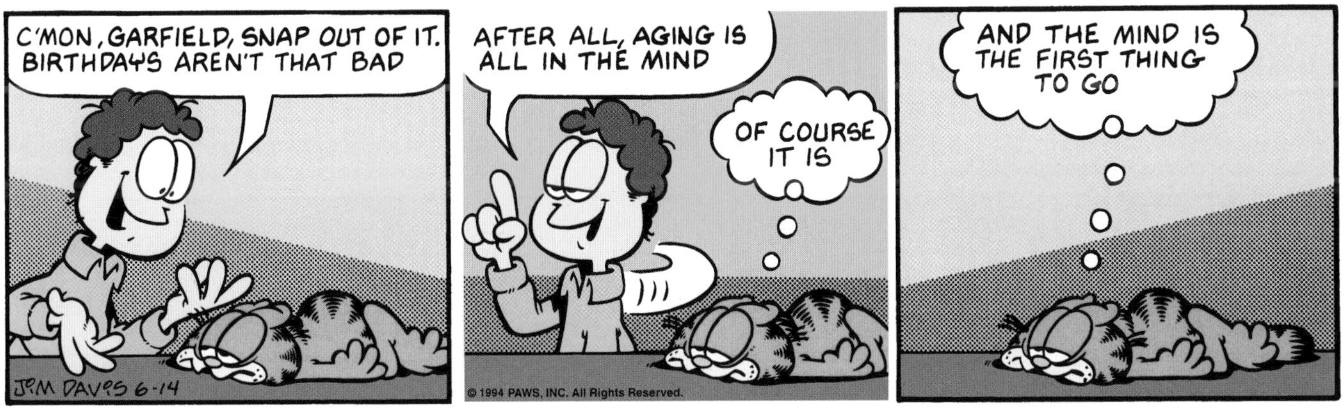
C'MON, GARFIELD, SNAP OUT OF IT. BIRTHDAYS AREN'T THAT BAD
JIM DAVIS 6-14
AFTER ALL, AGING IS ALL IN THE MIND
OF COURSE IT IS
© 1994 PAWS, INC. All Rights Reserved.
AND THE MIND IS THE FIRST THING TO GO

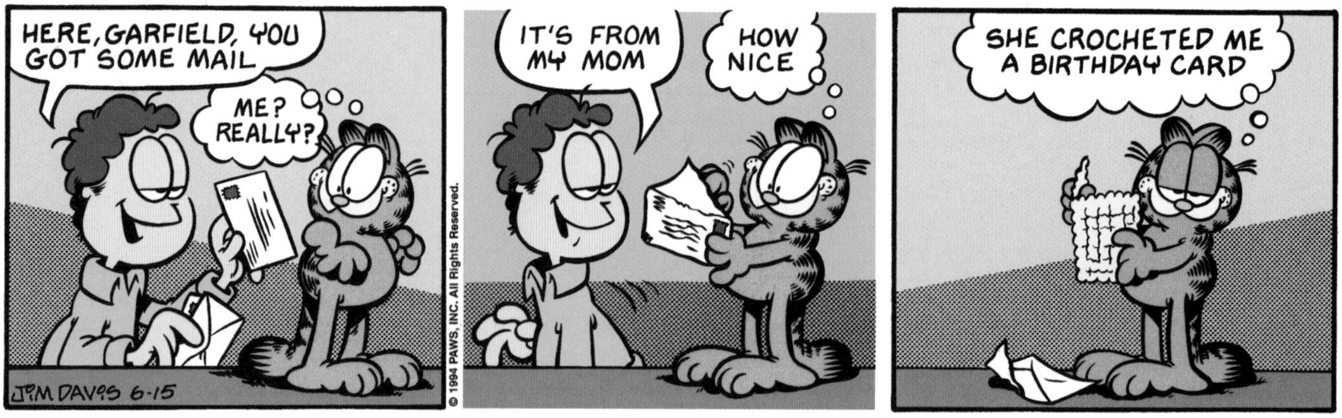
HERE, GARFIELD, YOU GOT SOME MAIL
ME? REALLY?
JIM DAVIS 6-15
© 1994 PAWS, INC. All Rights Reserved.
IT'S FROM MY MOM
HOW NICE
SHE CROCHETED ME A BIRTHDAY CARD

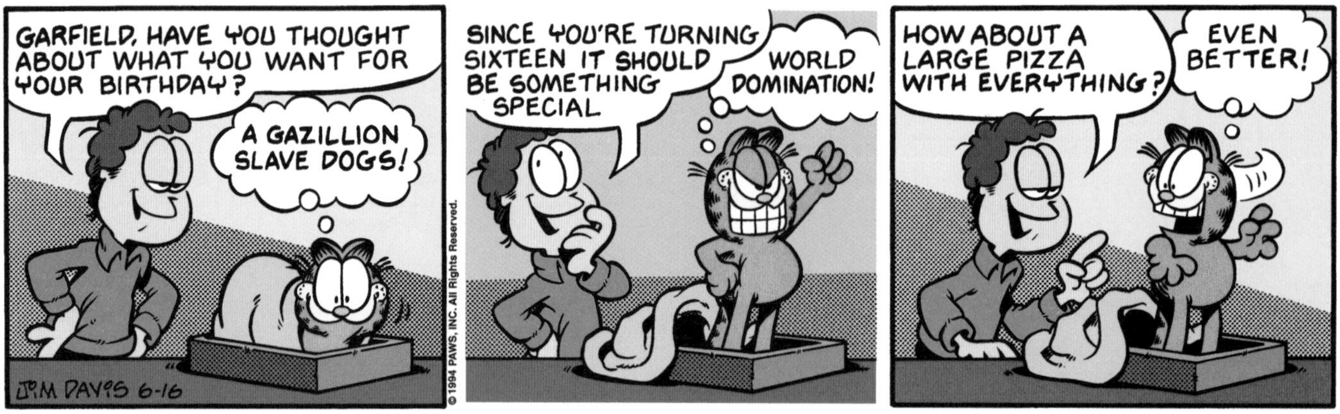
GARFIELD, HAVE YOU THOUGHT ABOUT WHAT YOU WANT FOR YOUR BIRTHDAY?
A GAZILLION SLAVE DOGS!
JIM DAVIS 6-16
© 1994 PAWS, INC. All Rights Reserved.
SINCE YOU'RE TURNING SIXTEEN IT SHOULD BE SOMETHING SPECIAL
WORLD DOMINATION!
HOW ABOUT A LARGE PIZZA WITH EVERYTHING?
EVEN BETTER!

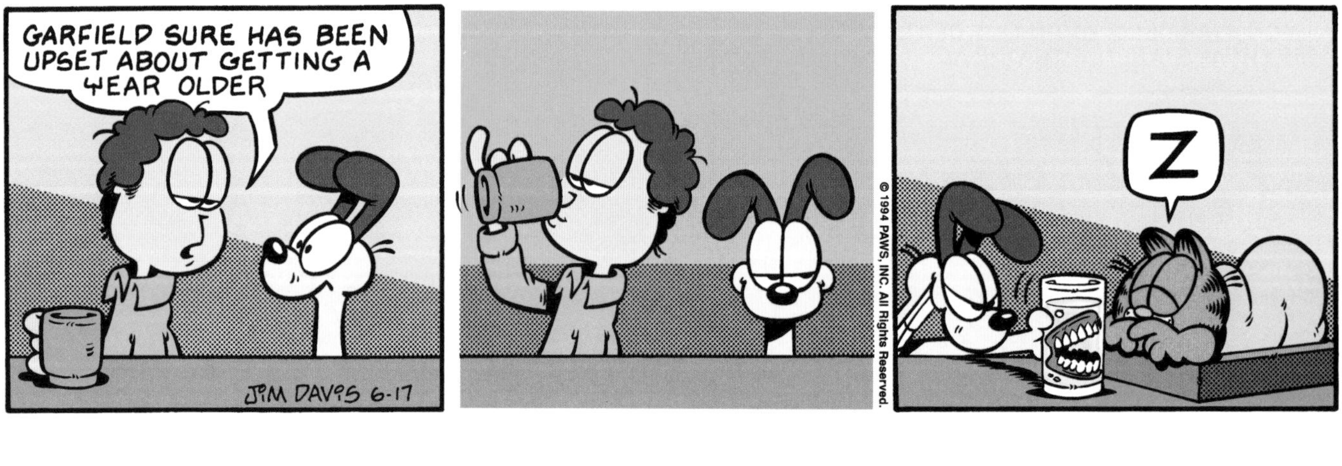
GARFIELD SURE HAS BEEN UPSET ABOUT GETTING A YEAR OLDER
JIM DAVIS 6-17
© 1994 PAWS, INC. All Rights Reserved.
Z

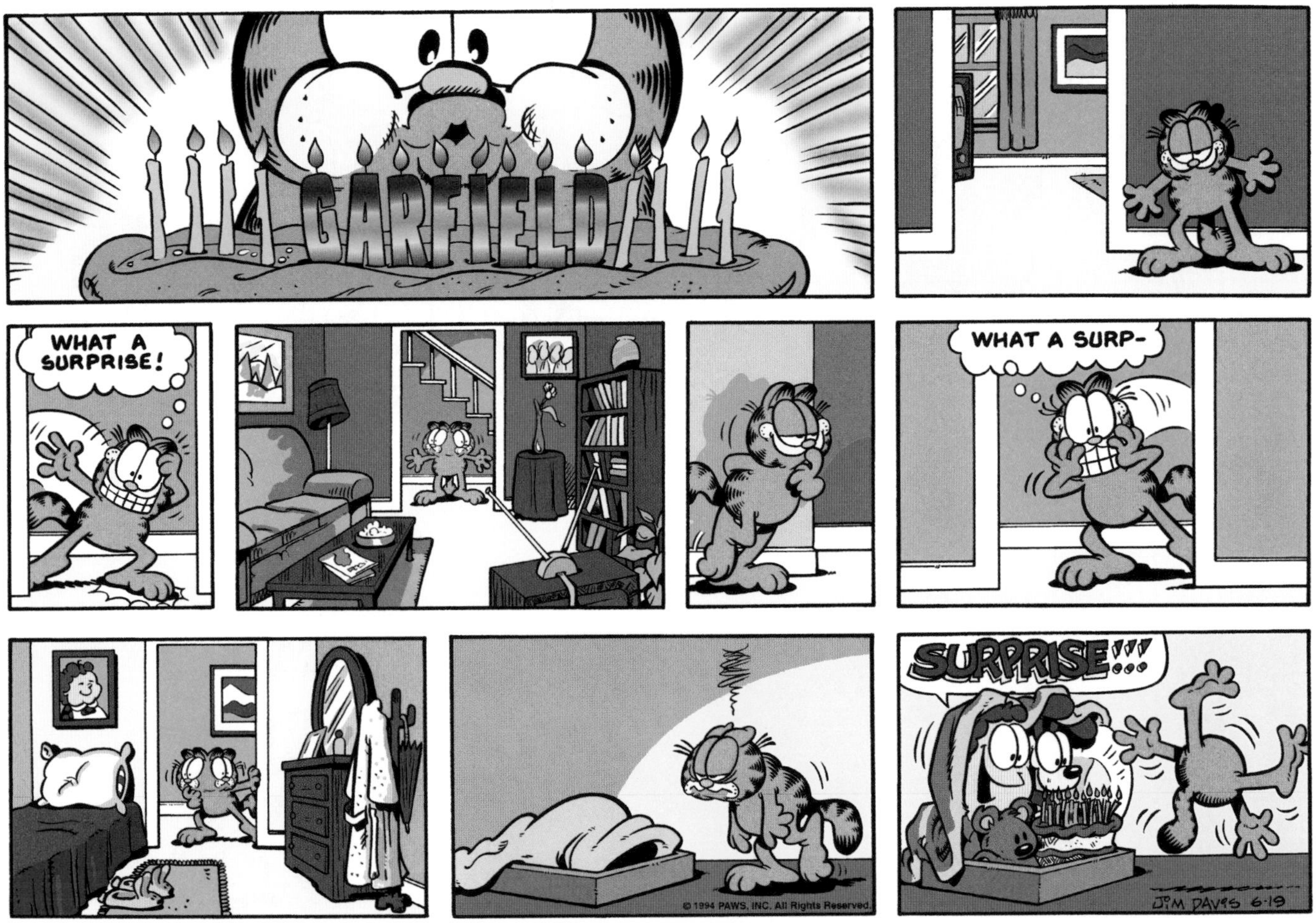
GARFIELD
WHAT A SURPRISE!
WHAT A SURP-
SURPRISE!!!
© 1994 PAWS, INC. All Rights Reserved
JIM DAVIS 6-19

BIRTHDAY TIP #45

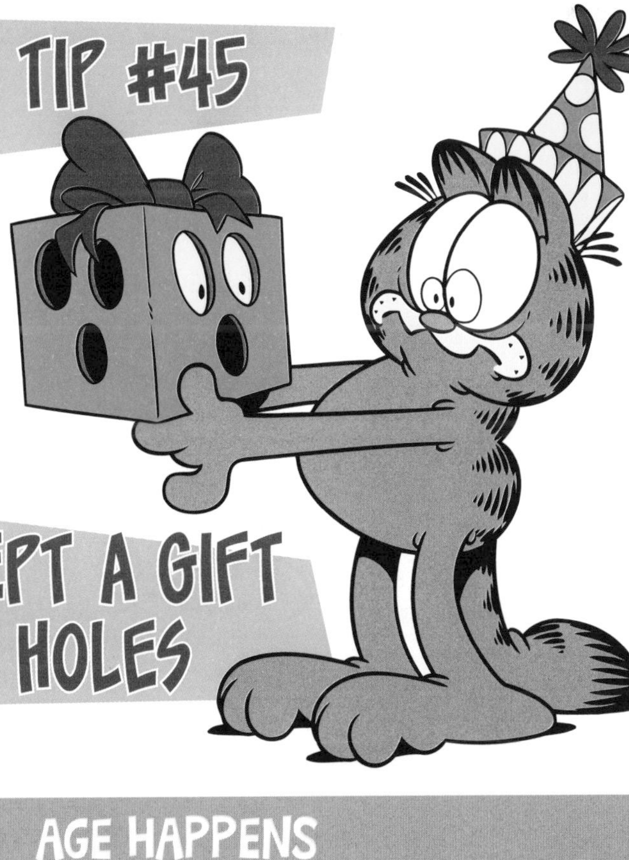

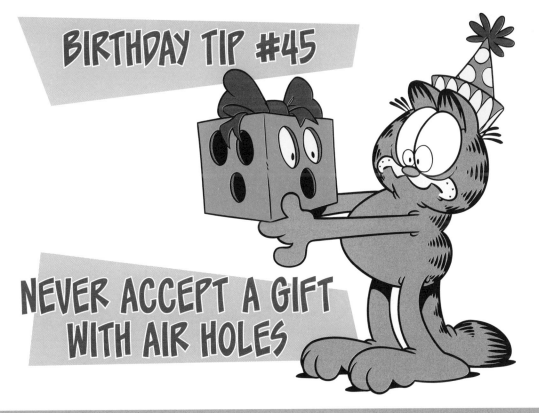

NEVER ACCEPT A GIFT WITH AIR HOLES

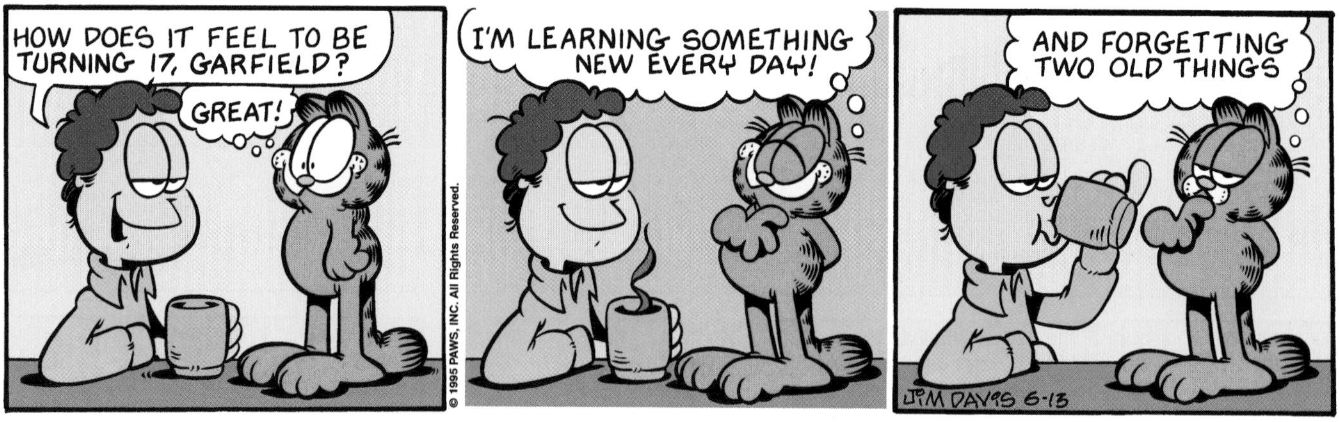
HOW DOES IT FEEL TO BE TURNING 17, GARFIELD?
GREAT!
© 1995 PAWS, INC. All Rights Reserved.
I'M LEARNING SOMETHING NEW EVERY DAY!
AND FORGETTING TWO OLD THINGS
JIM DAVIS 6-13

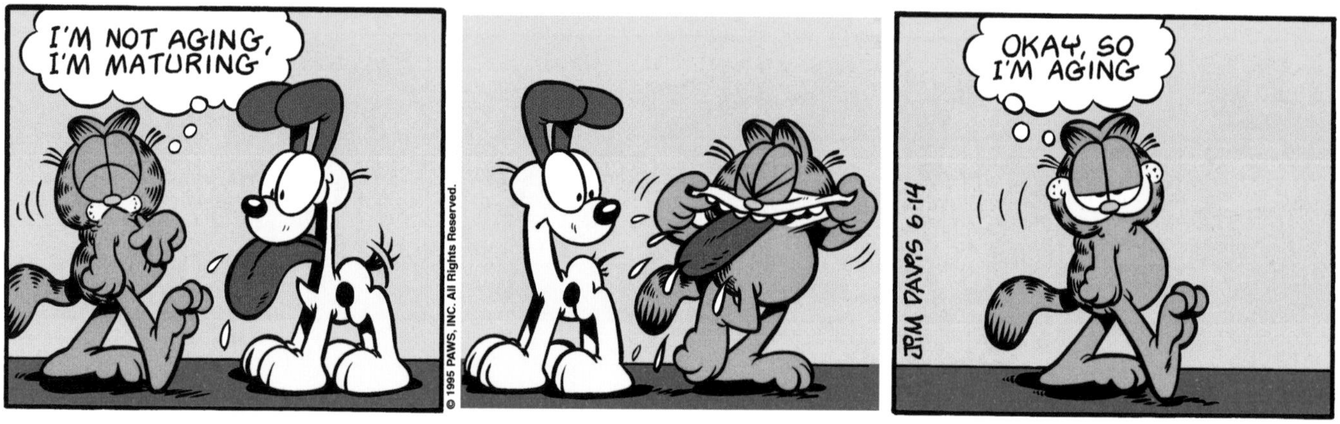
I'M NOT AGING, I'M MATURING
© 1995 PAWS, INC. All Rights Reserved.
OKAY, SO I'M AGING
JIM DAVIS 6-14

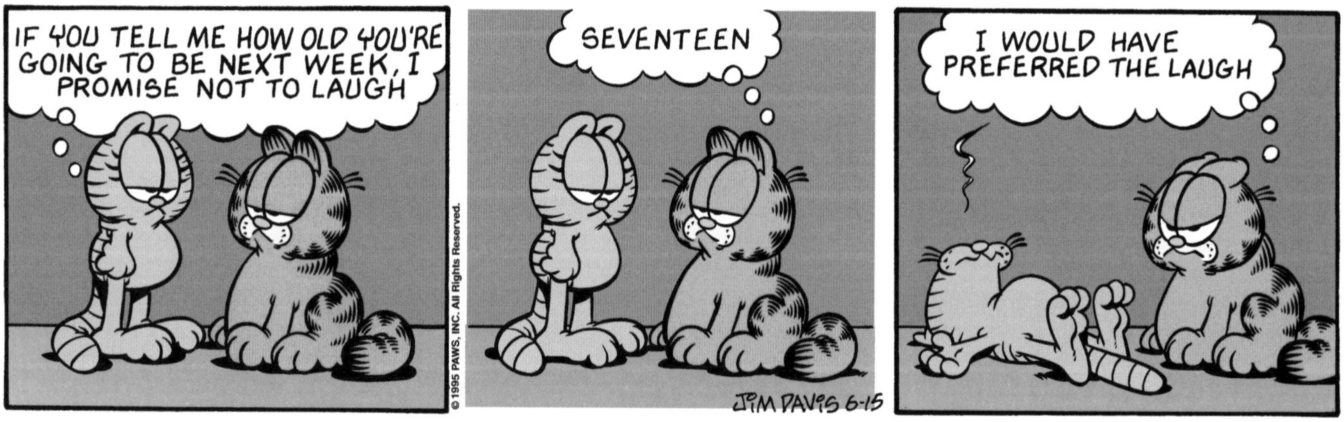
IF YOU TELL ME HOW OLD YOU'RE GOING TO BE NEXT WEEK, I PROMISE NOT TO LAUGH
© 1995 PAWS, INC. All Rights Reserved.
SEVENTEEN
JIM DAVIS 6-15
I WOULD HAVE PREFERRED THE LAUGH

Getting older is great.

I learn something new every day.

AND FORGET TWO OLD THINGS

WHO, ME?
17
GARFIELD
AH CHOO!
HA!
JIM DAVIS 6-18
POO!
© 1995 PAWS, INC. All Rights Reserved.
THANK GOODNESS!

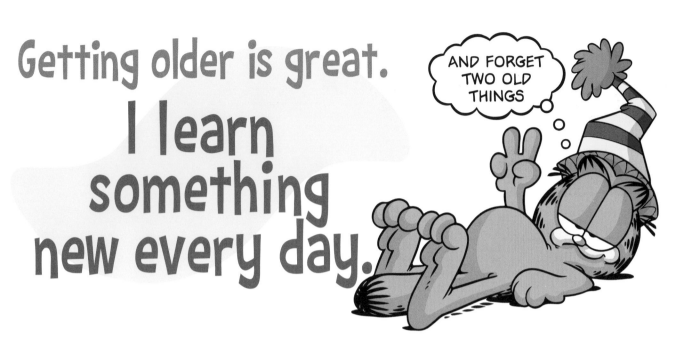

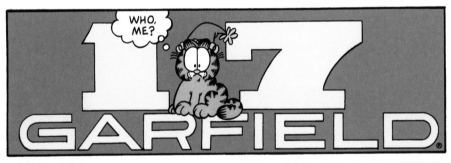

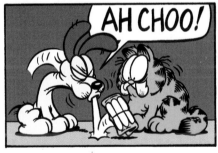

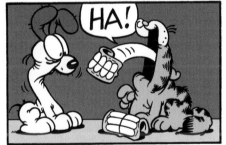

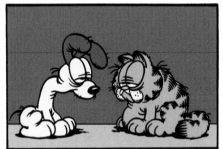

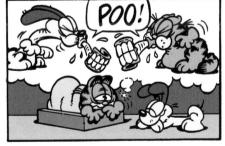

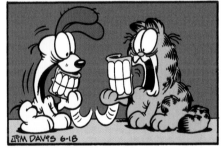

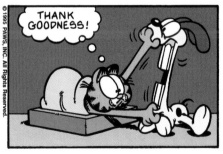

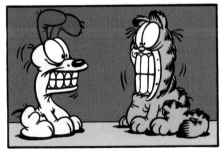

Fat Cat Fan Art

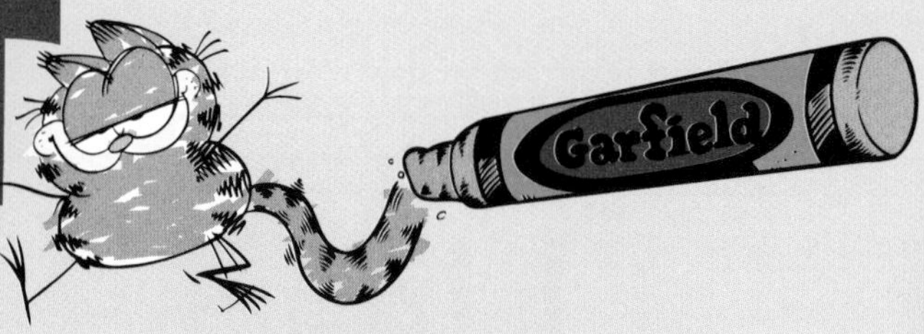
Garfield

Come browse our Garfield gallery of fantastic fan art.

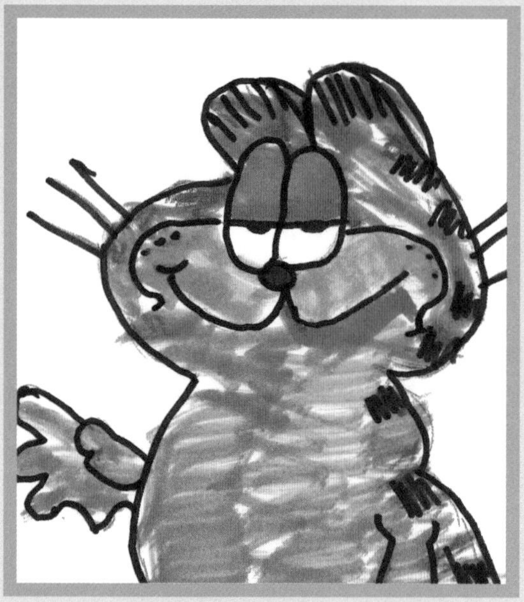

Carly H, age 11
Indiana

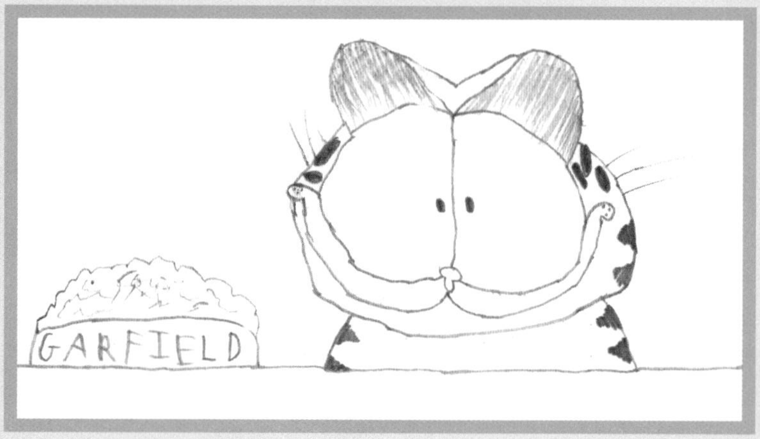
GARFIELD

Stephen P, age 14
Tennessee

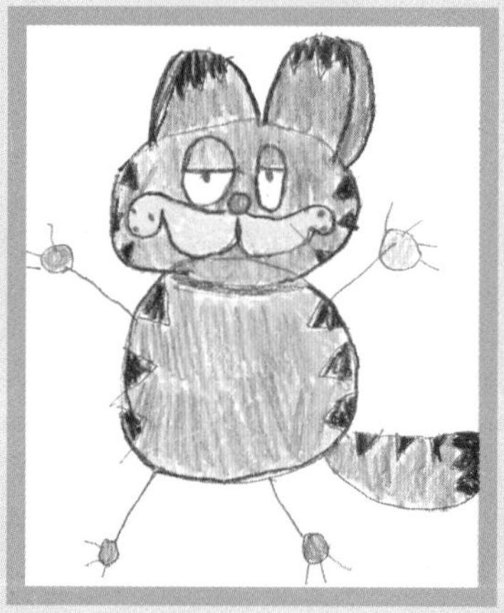

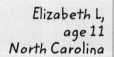

Elizabeth L,
age 11
North Carolina

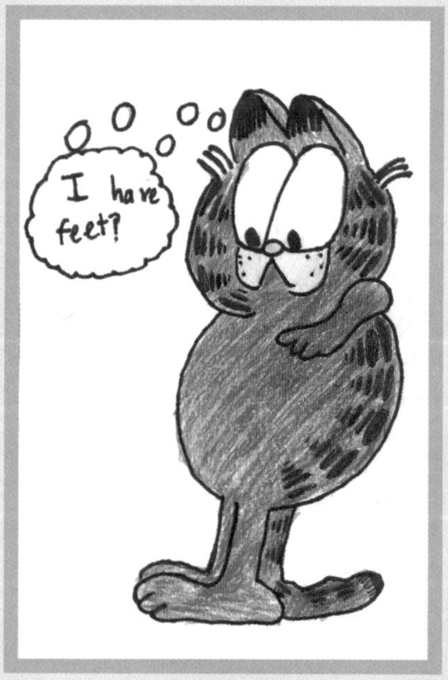
I have feet?

Caroline M, age 10
Utah

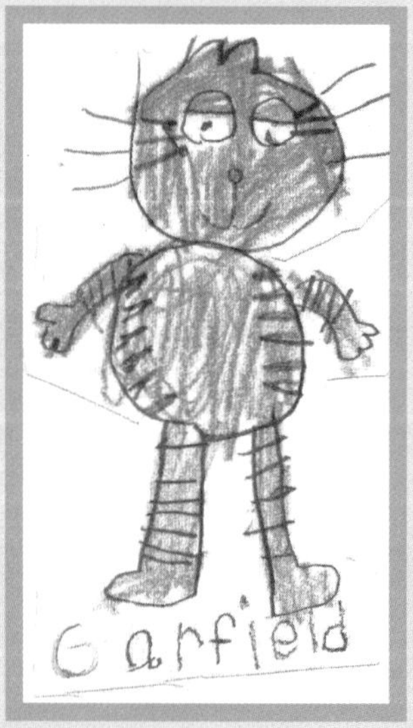
Garfield

Madison R, age 6
Washington

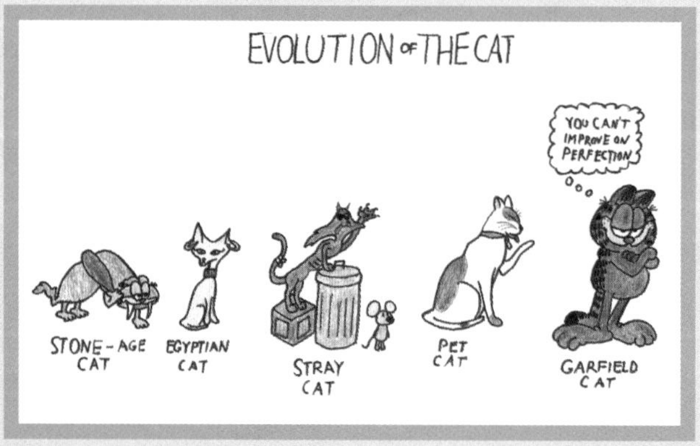
EVOLUTION OF THE CAT
YOU CAN'T IMPROVE ON PERFECTION
STONE-AGE CAT
EGYPTIAN CAT
STRAY CAT
PET CAT
GARFIELD CAT

Jessica R, age 14
Texas

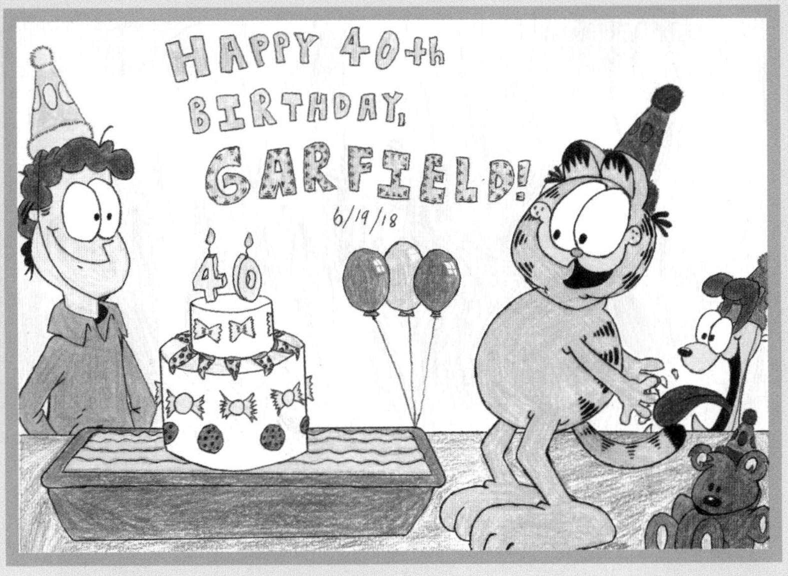
HAPPY 40th
BIRTHDAY,
GARFIELD!
6/19/18

Joseph G, age 12
New Jersey

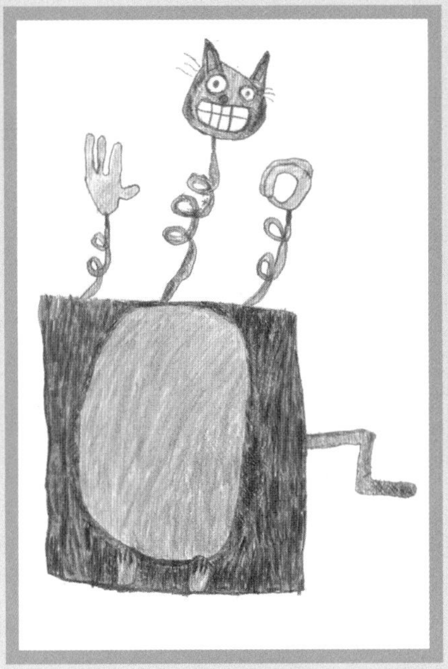

Josh C, age 10
Colorado

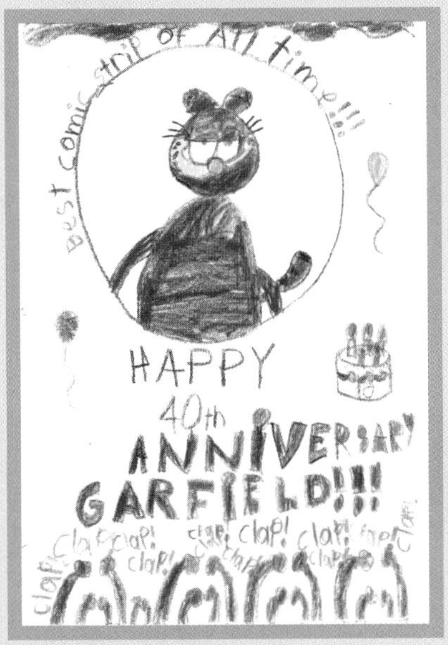
Best comic strip of All time!!!
HAPPY
40th
ANNIVERSARY
GARFIELD!!!

Evan V, age 10
Florida

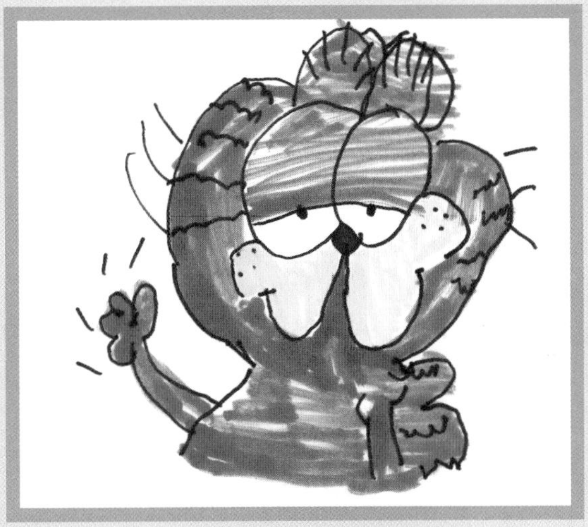

Clayton H, age 6
Indiana

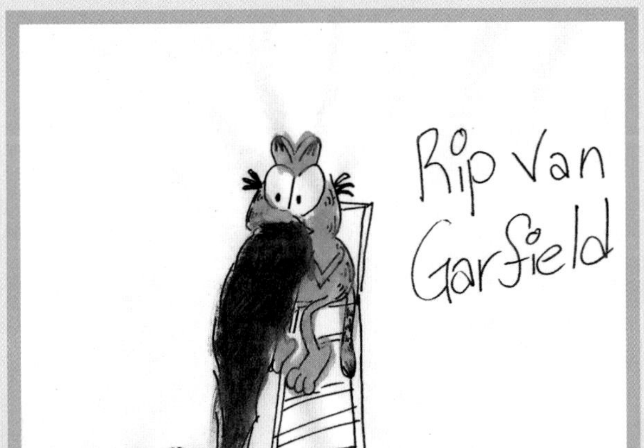
Rip Van
Garfield

Grace A, age 11 (almost 12)
Washington

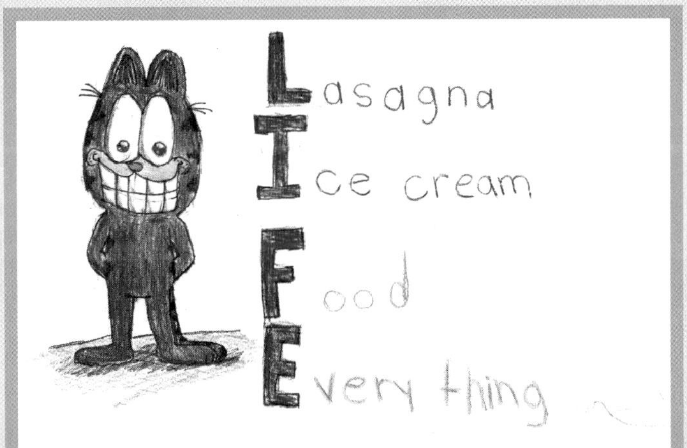
Lasagna
Ice cream
Food
Everything
Is good!

Hannah L, age 10
Texas

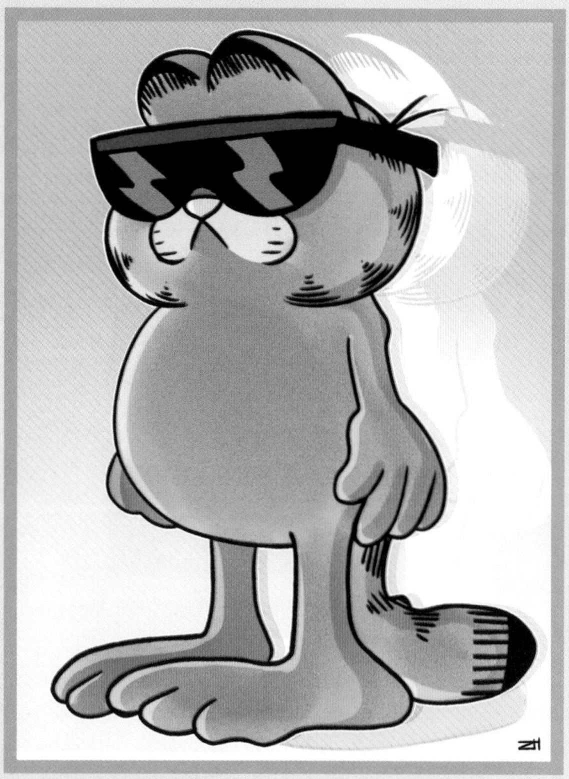

Zackyia H, age 15
Alberta, Canada

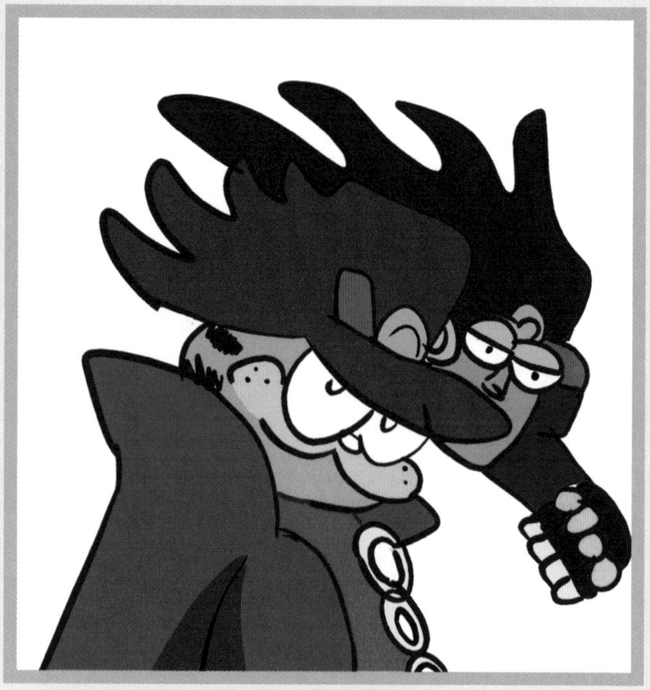

Riley F, age 18
North Carolina

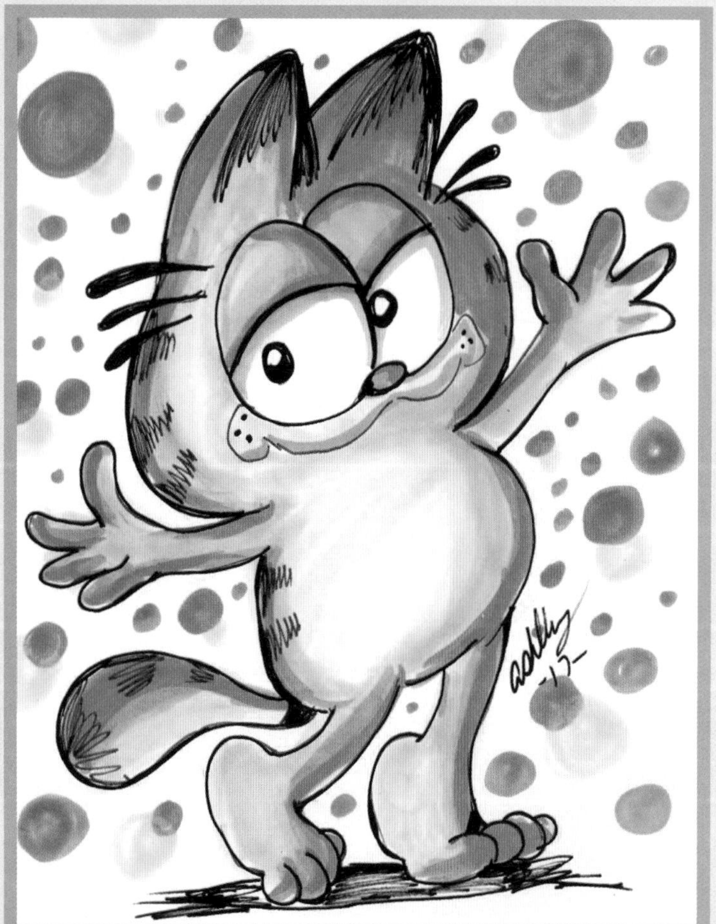

Ashley A, age 31
New York

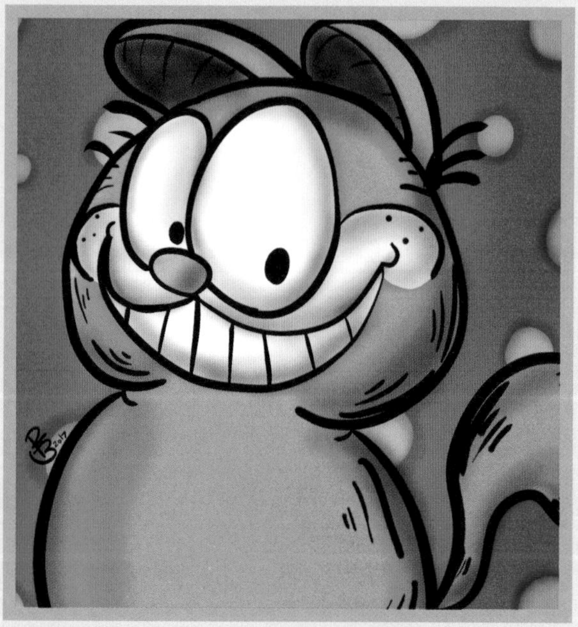

Peter F, age 15
Florida

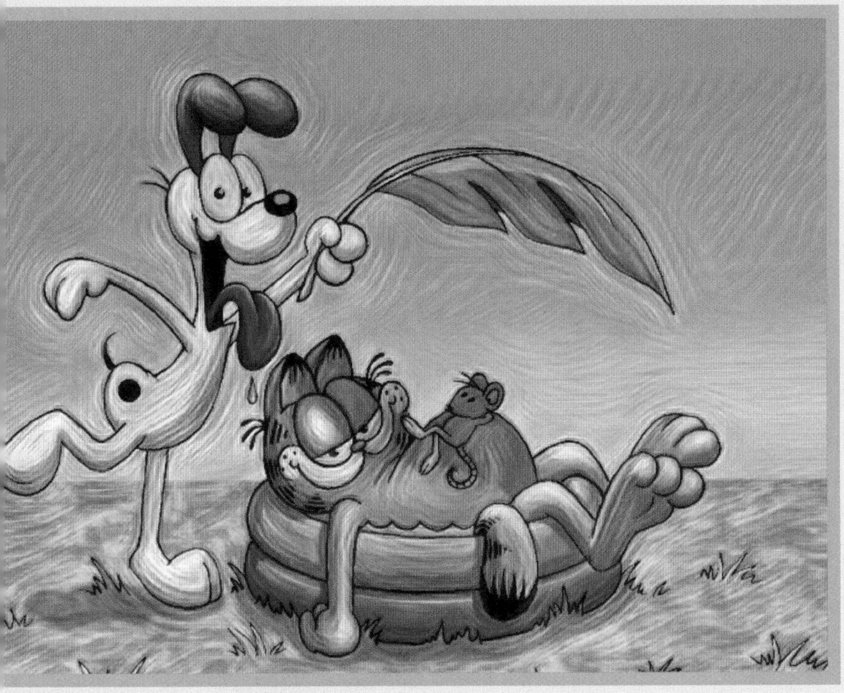

a G, age 36
alifornia

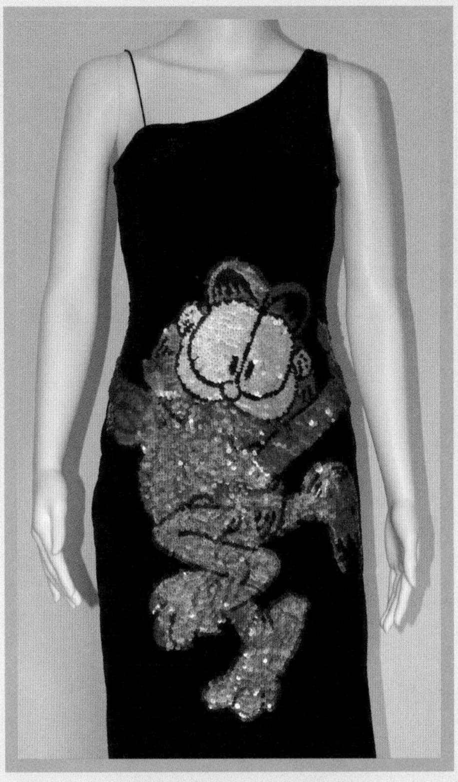

Shannon P, age 41
Utah

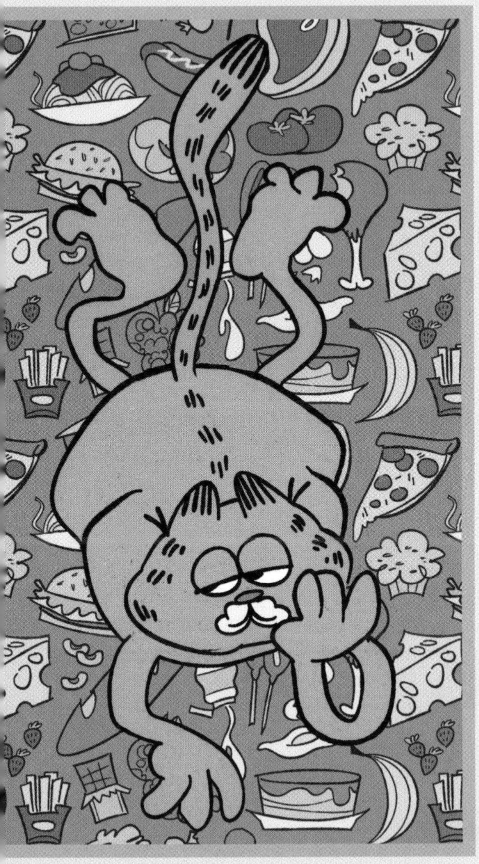

oe M, age 19
exas

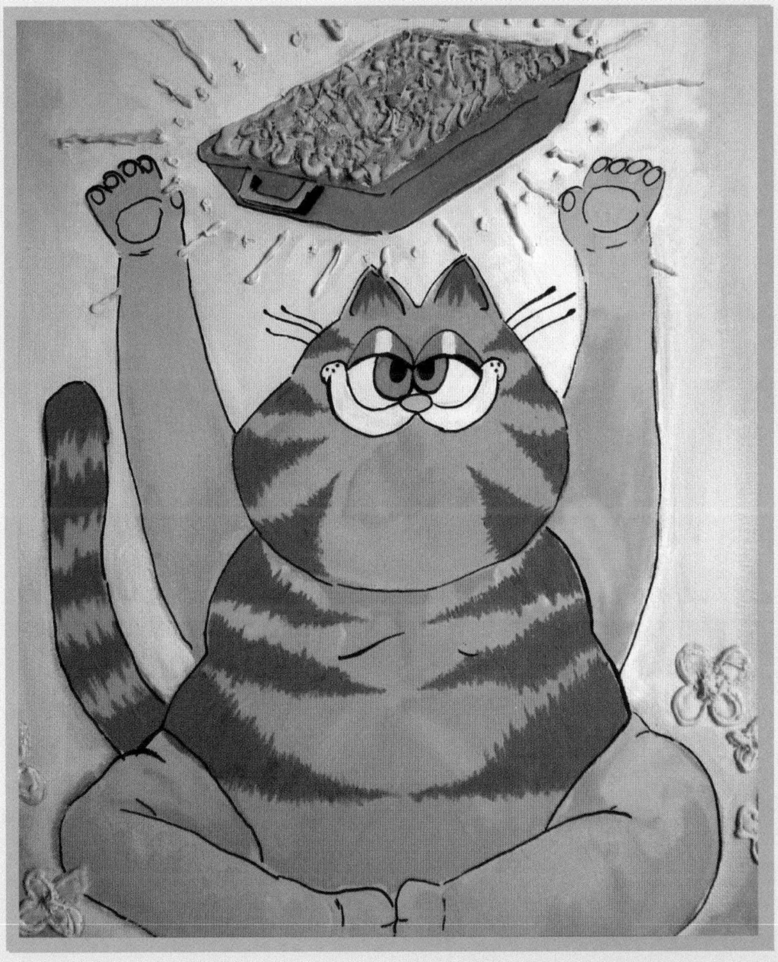

Teller C, age 18
Virginia

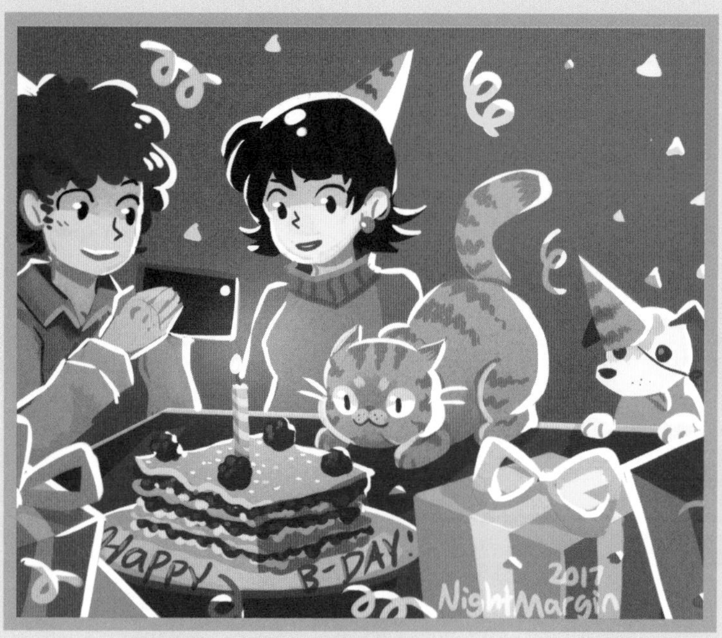
HAPPY B-DAY!
2017
NightMargin

Nightmargin (aka Casey), age 25
Arkansas

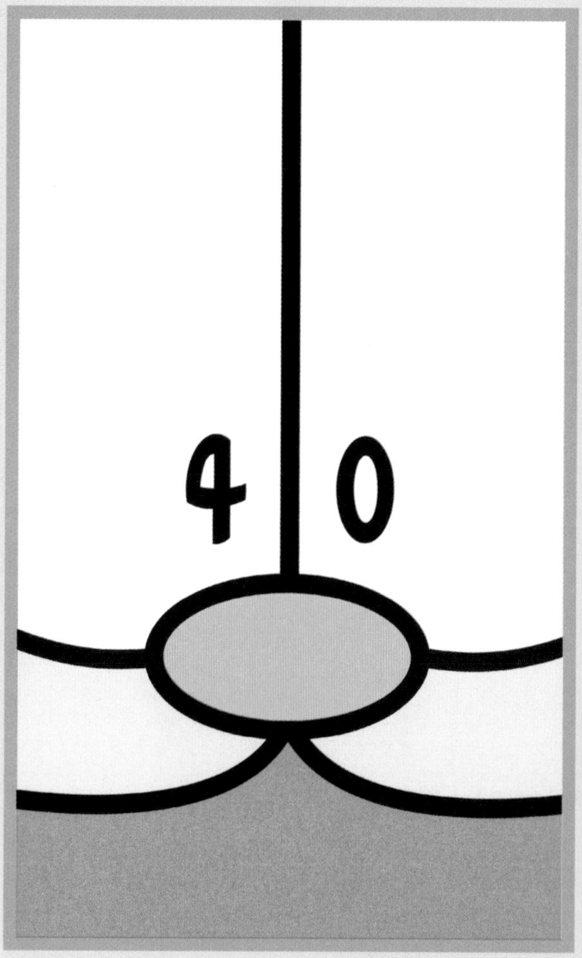
40

Davey P, age 44
Cambridgeshire, U.K.

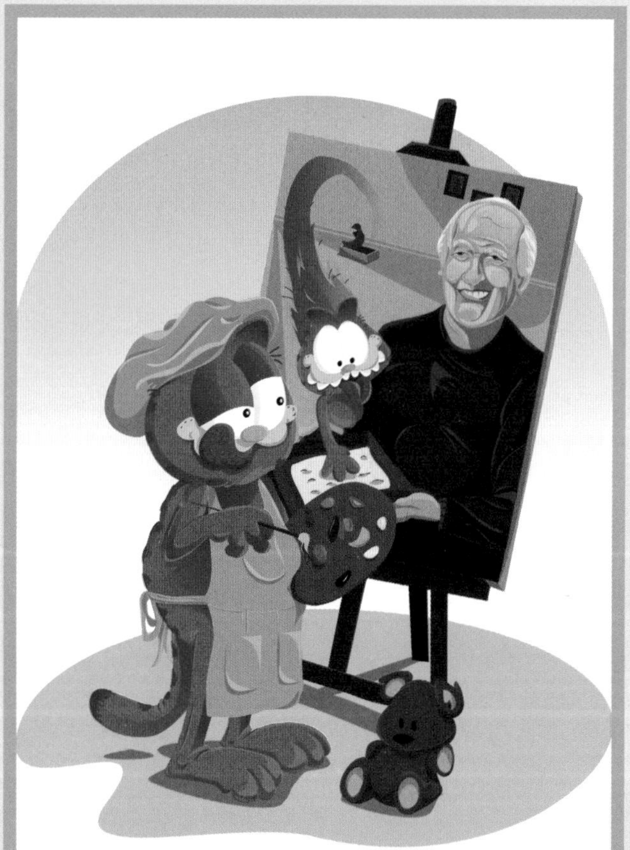

Joshua W, age 36
Indiana

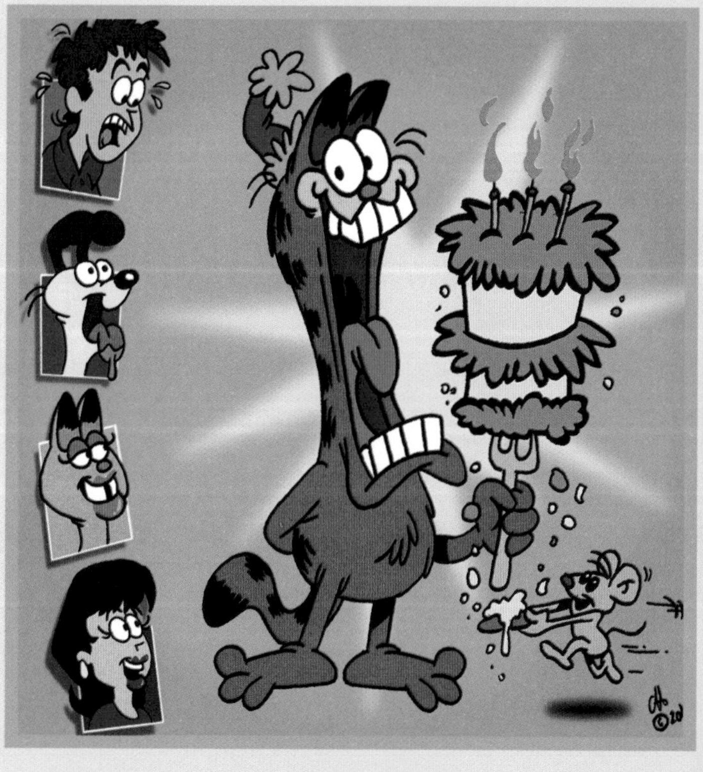

Clint H, age 24
Alberta, Canada

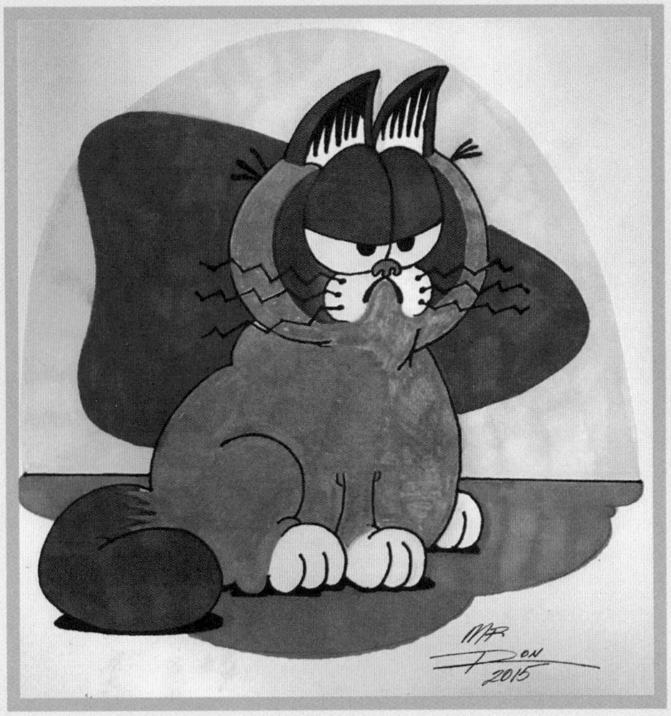

Ron A, age 48
Arkansas

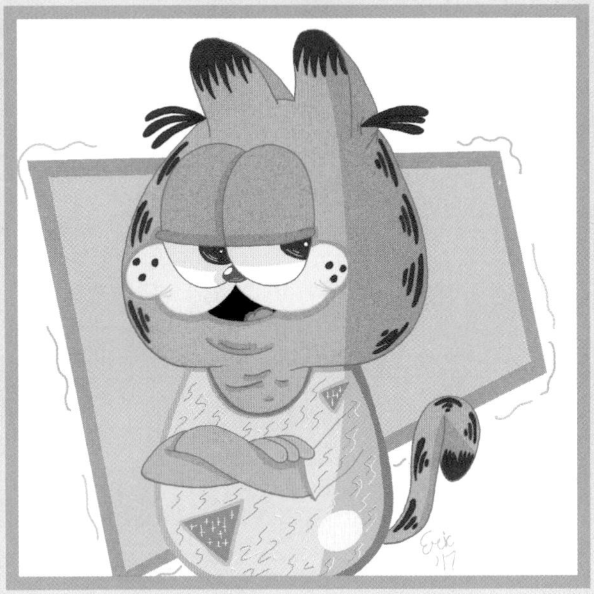

Eric K, age 13
Ontario, Canada

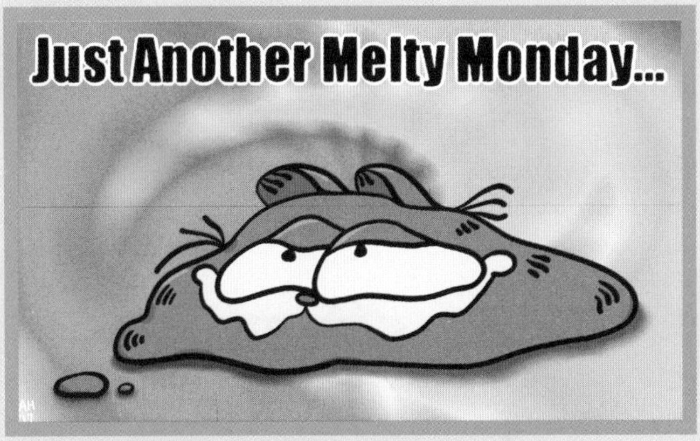
Just Another Melty Monday...

Ari H, age 20
Massachusetts

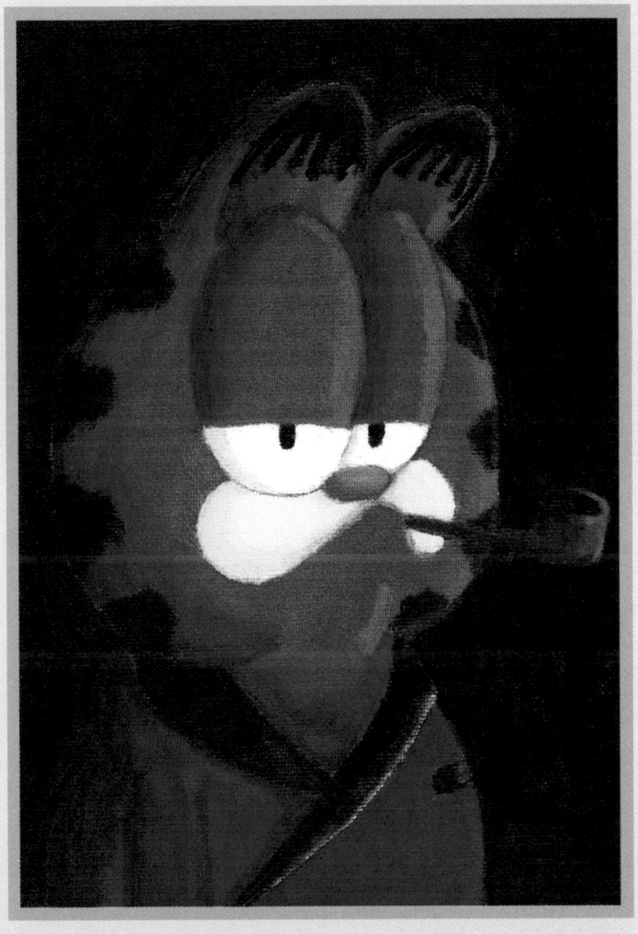

Angelo M, age 23
New York

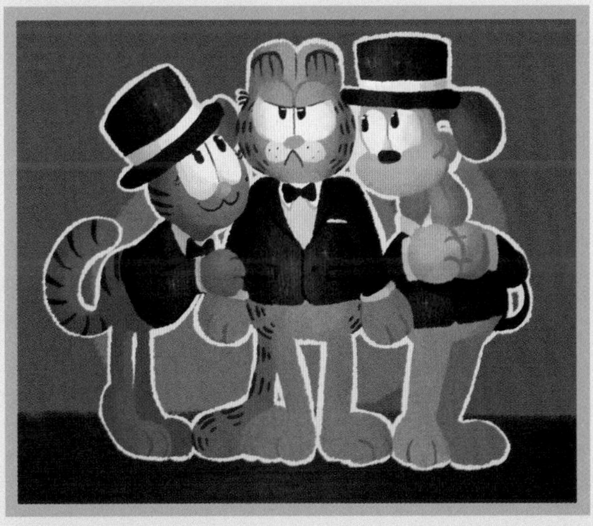

Sarah T, age 16
Iowa

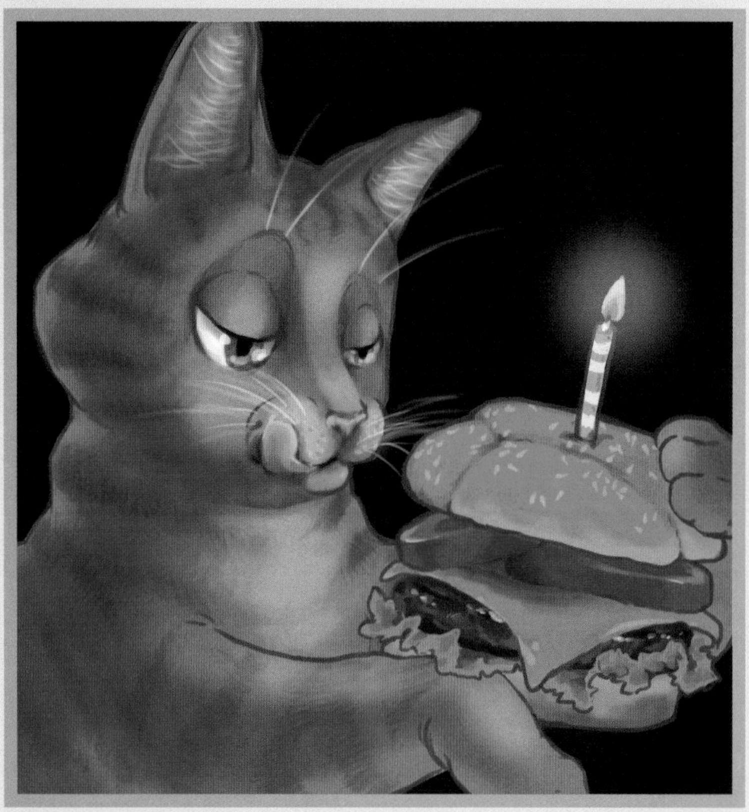

Elaine W, age 18
British Columbia, Canada

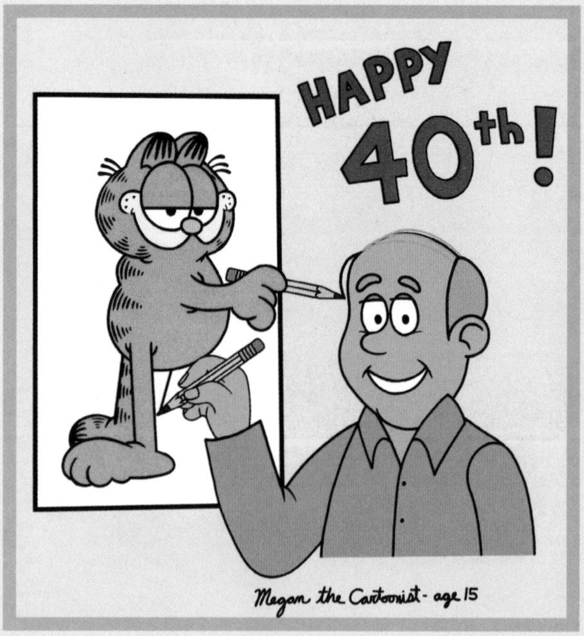
HAPPY
40th!
Megan the Cartoonist - age 15

Megan J, age 15
Ohio

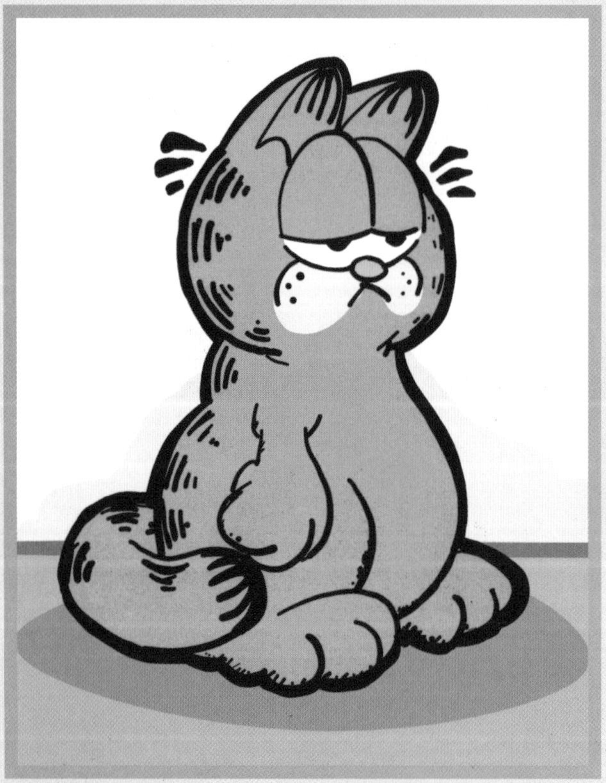

Gary B, age 33
Maryland

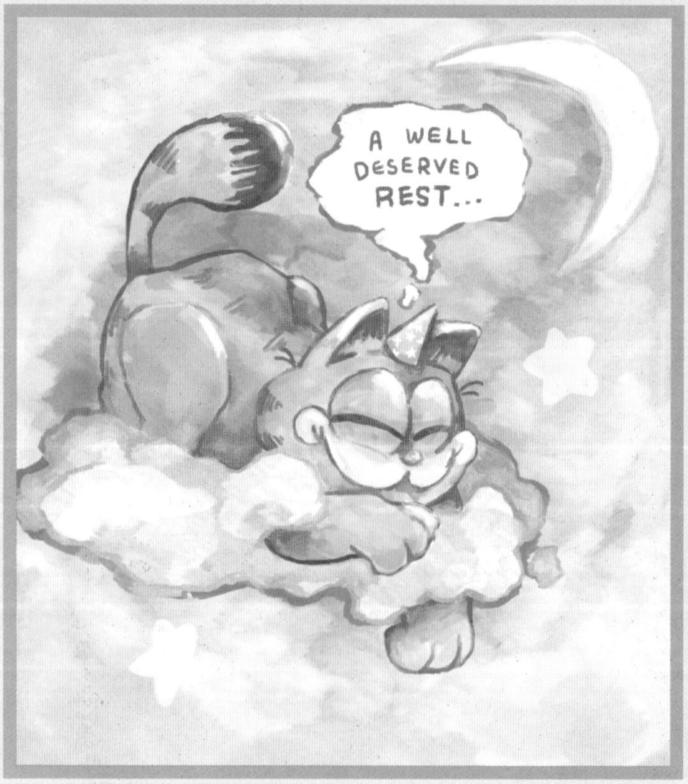
A WELL DESERVED REST...

Emelia L, age 20
California

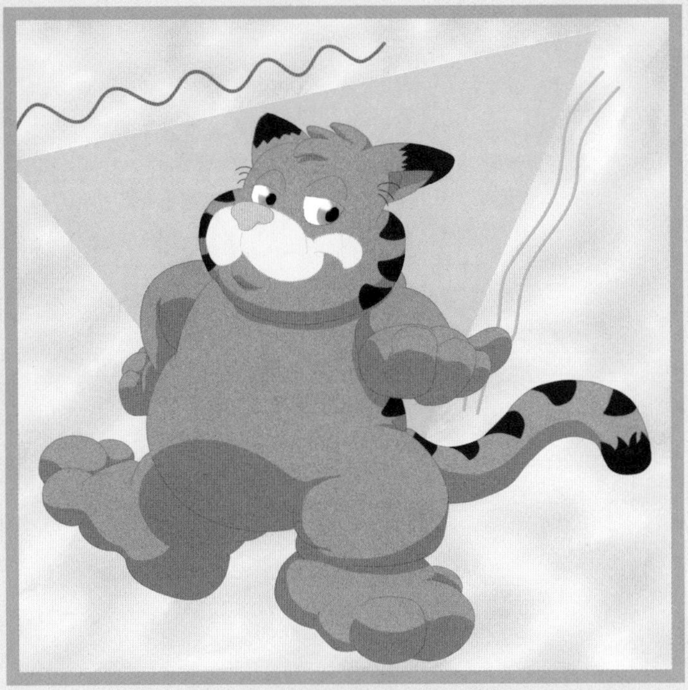

Eric J, age 27
California

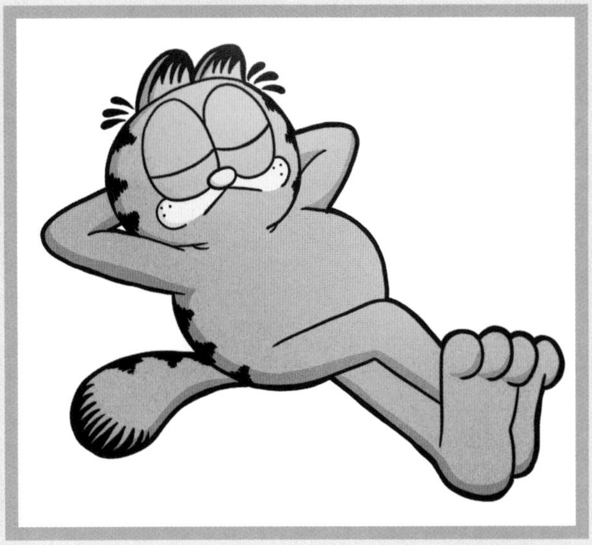

Rosie G, age 17
Colorado

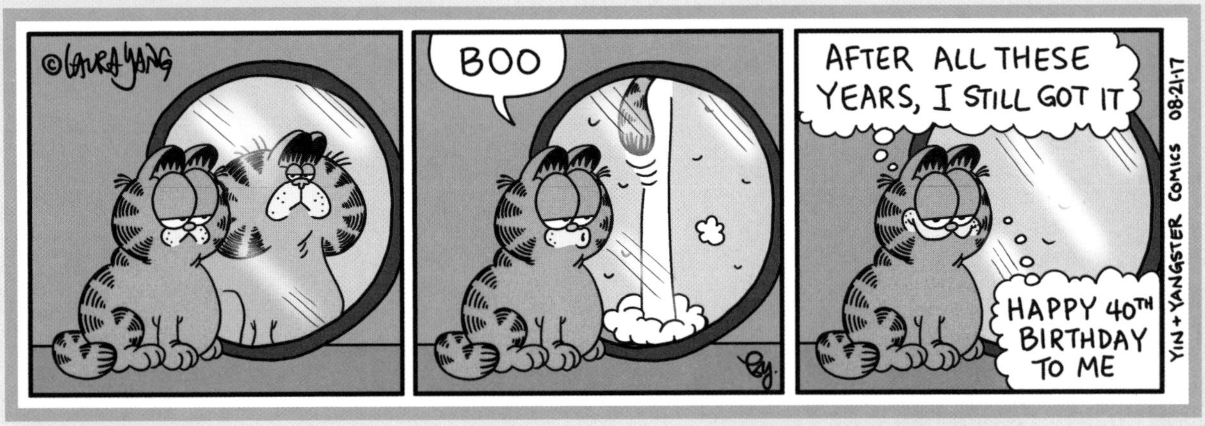
©LAURA YANG
BOO
AFTER ALL THESE YEARS, I STILL GOT IT
HAPPY 40TH BIRTHDAY TO ME
08-21-17
YIN+YANGSTER COMICS

Laura Y, age 27
British Columbia, Canada

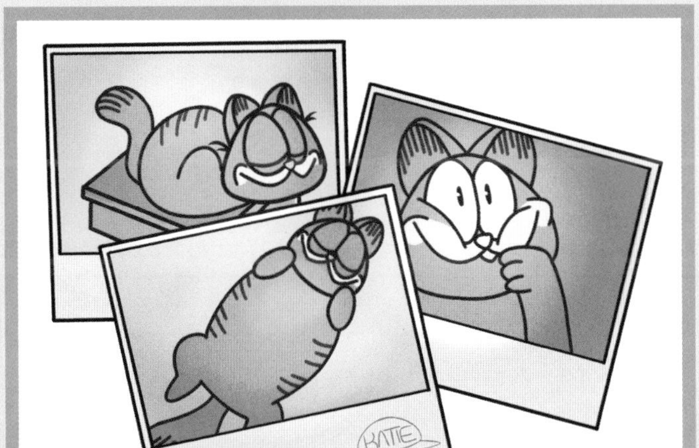
KATIE

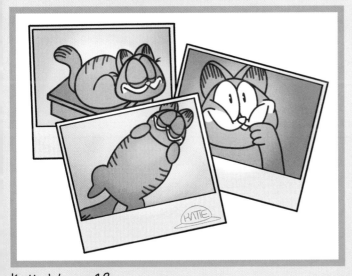

Katie W, age 18
Ohio

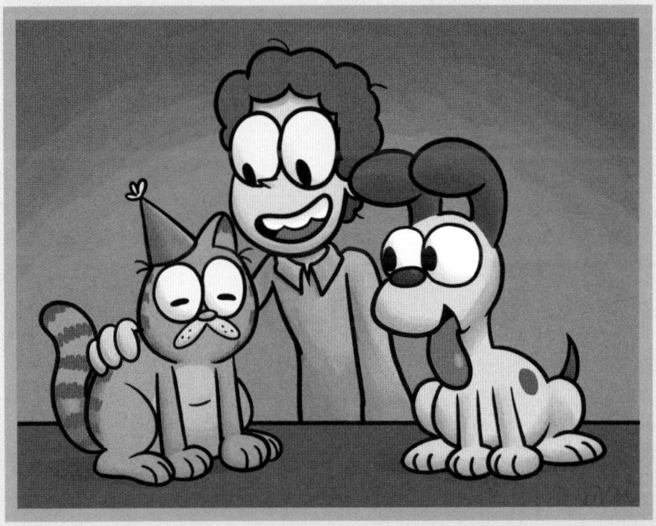

Nigel M, age 17
California

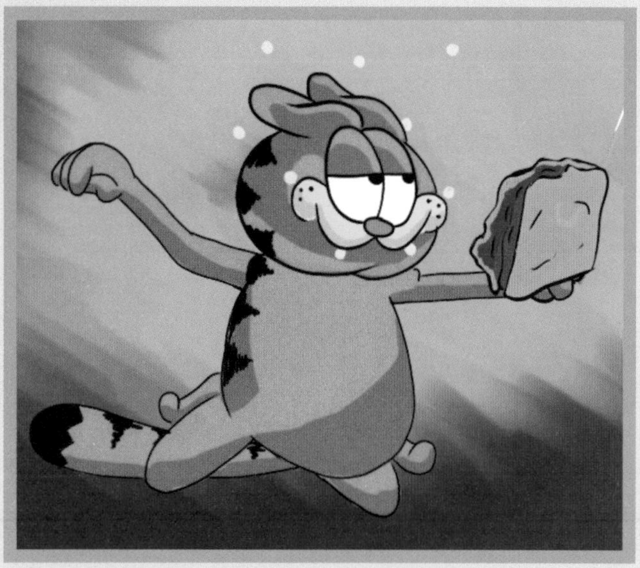

David G, age 21
Missouri

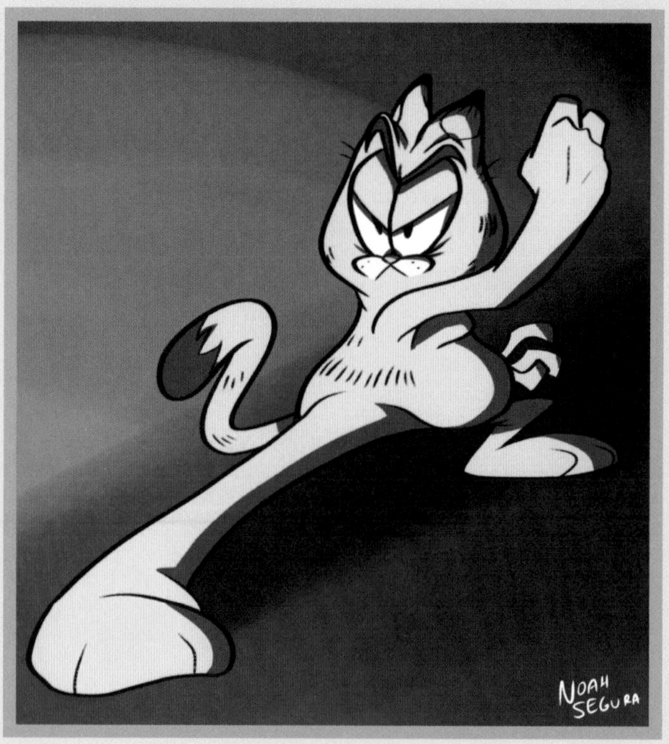
NOAH SEGURA

Noah S, age 18
Colorado

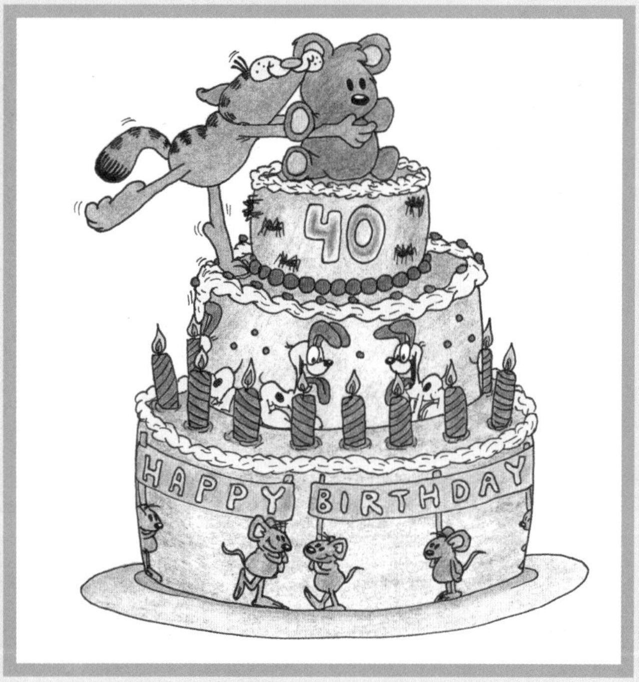
40
HAPPY BIRTHDAY

Bianca S, age 36
Montana

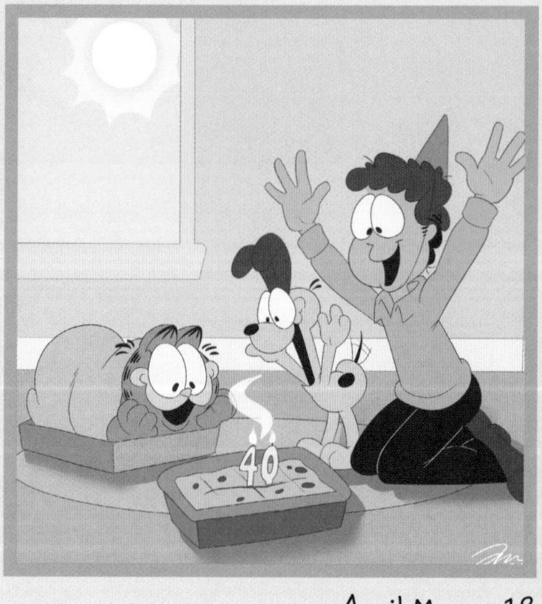
40

April M, age 18
California

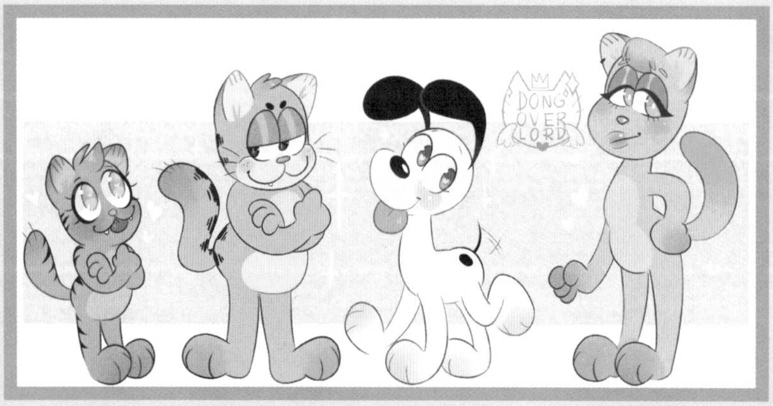
DONG OVER LORD

Nalani R, age 18
Florida

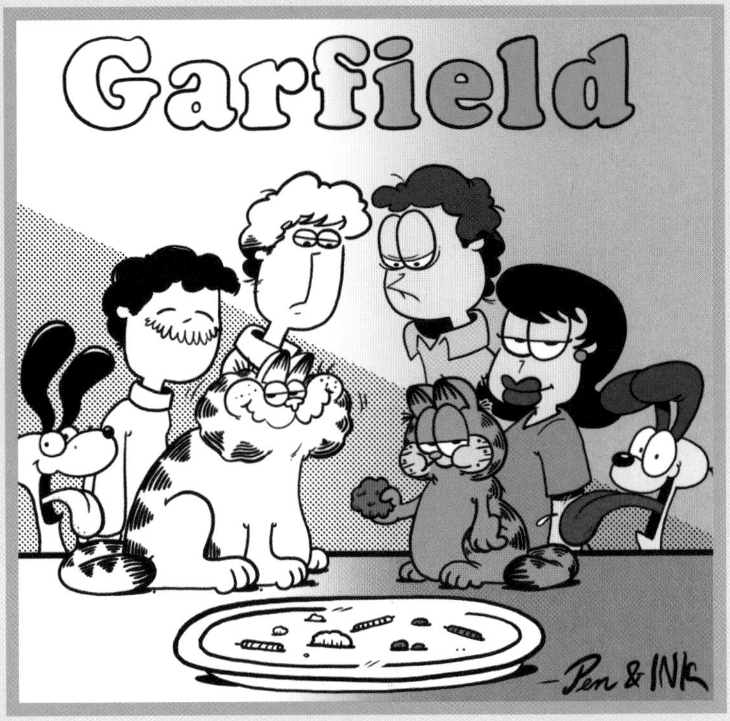
Garfield
Pen & INK

Penny E, age 19
Indiana

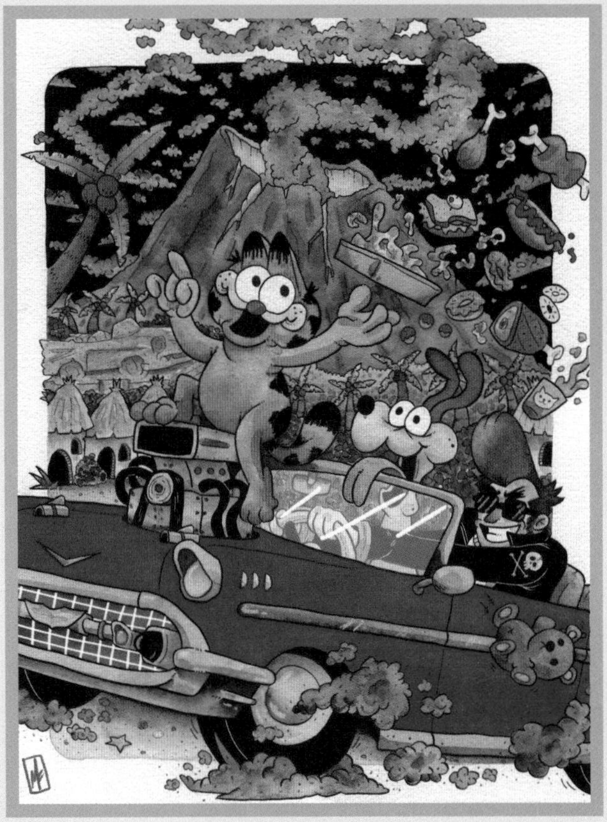

Mark F, age 31
New Jersey

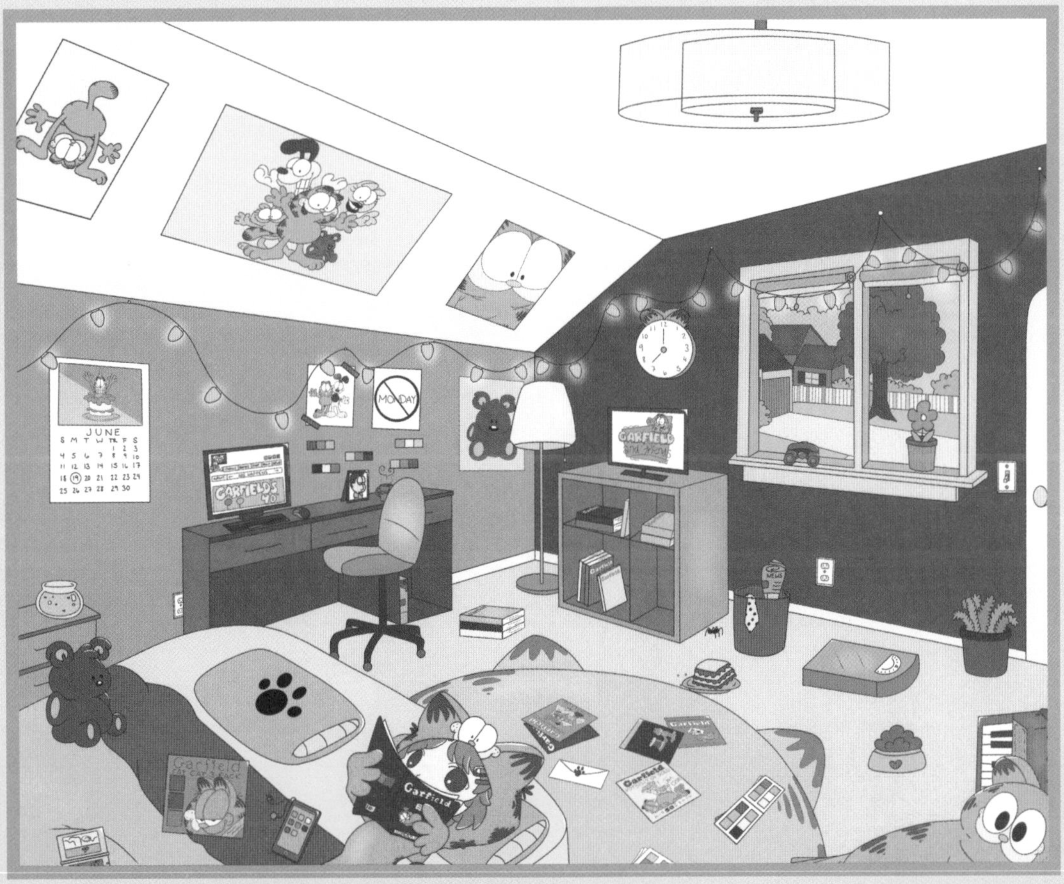
JUNE
MONDAY
Garfield

Krissy L, age 22
Georgia

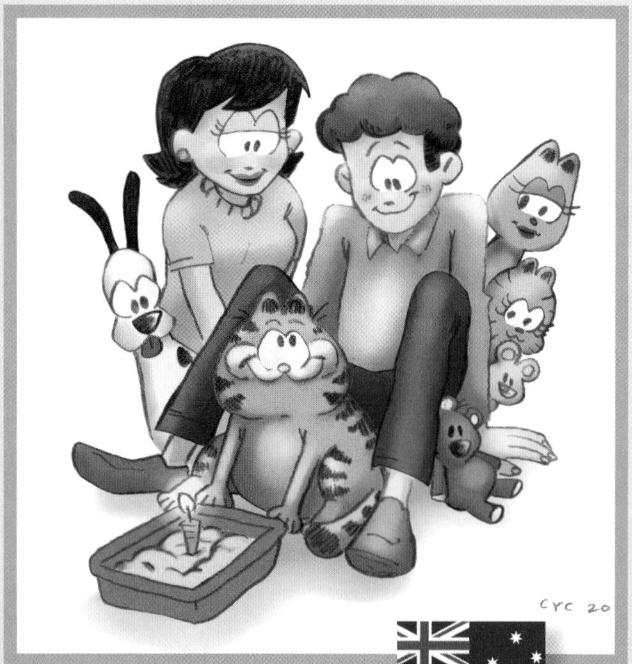
CYC 20

Yee Cheng C, age 19
Victoria, Australia

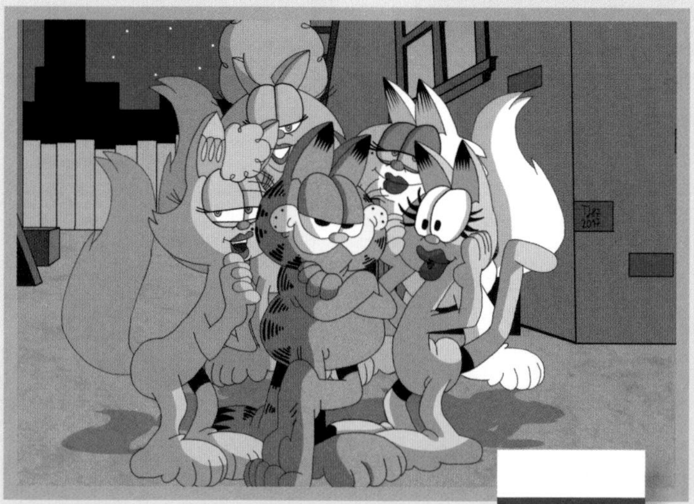

Tomasz D, age 30
Lubin, Poland

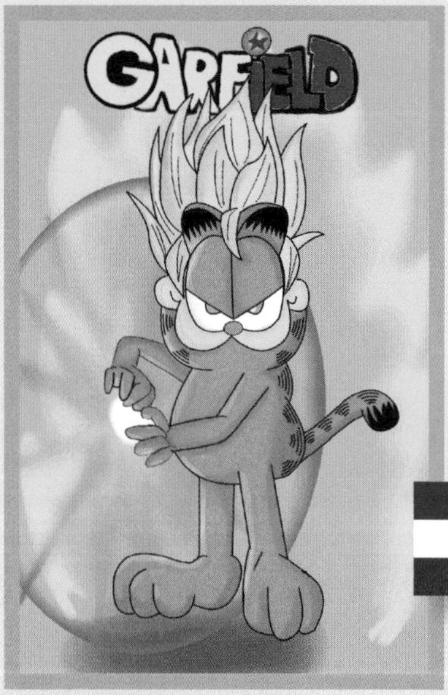
GARFIELD

Michiel G,
age 34
Den Helder,
The Netherlands

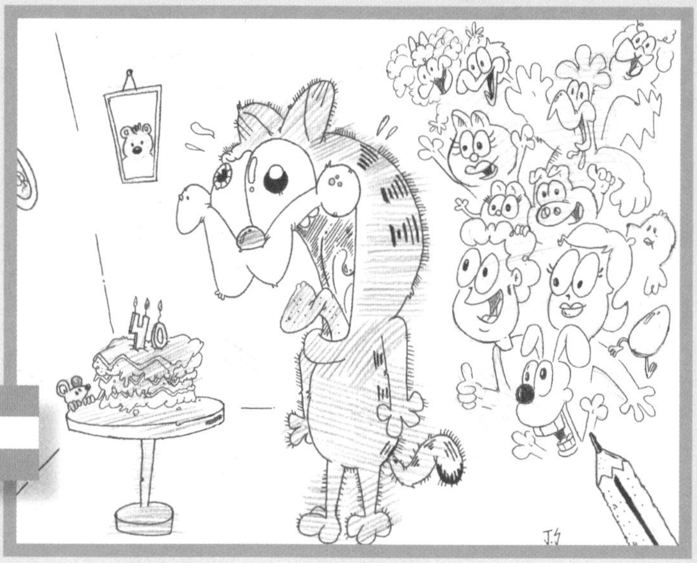
40

Joaquin S, age 17
Buenos Aires, Argentina

Miguel Ángel J, age 21
State of Mexico, Mexico

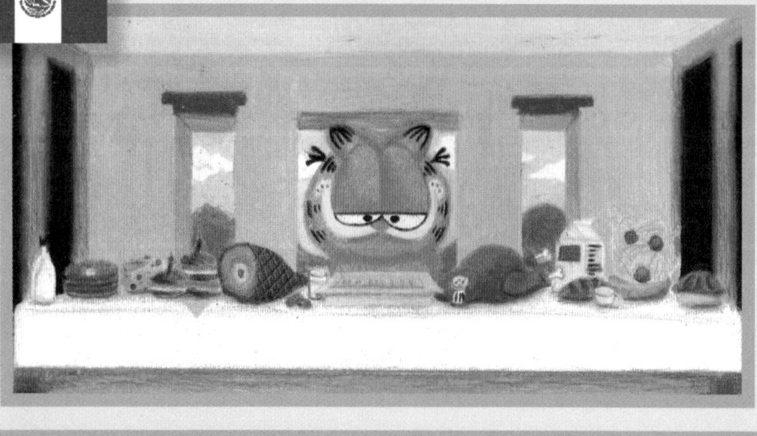

Tara C, age 39
New Brunswick, Canada

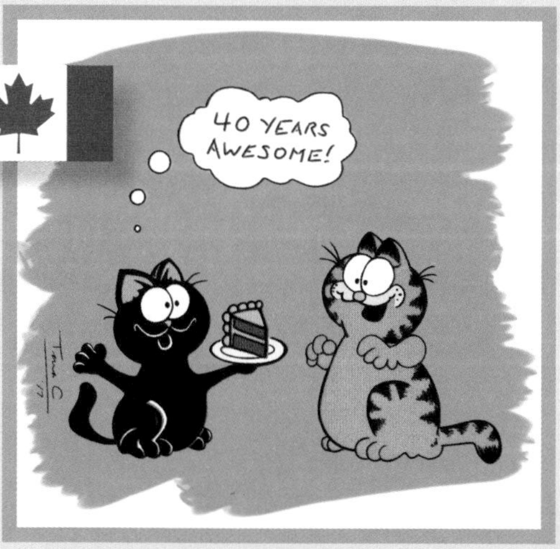
40 YEARS AWESOME!

AGE HAPPENS
Garfield Hits the Big 4-0

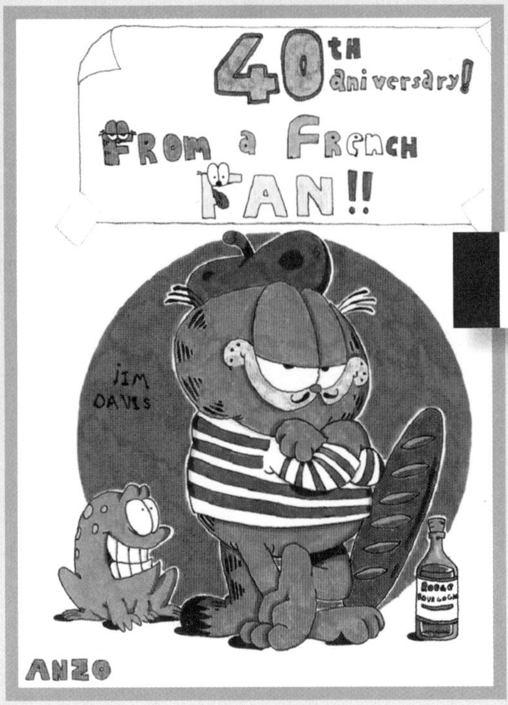
40th anniversary!
From a French
FAN!!
JIM DAVIS
ANZO

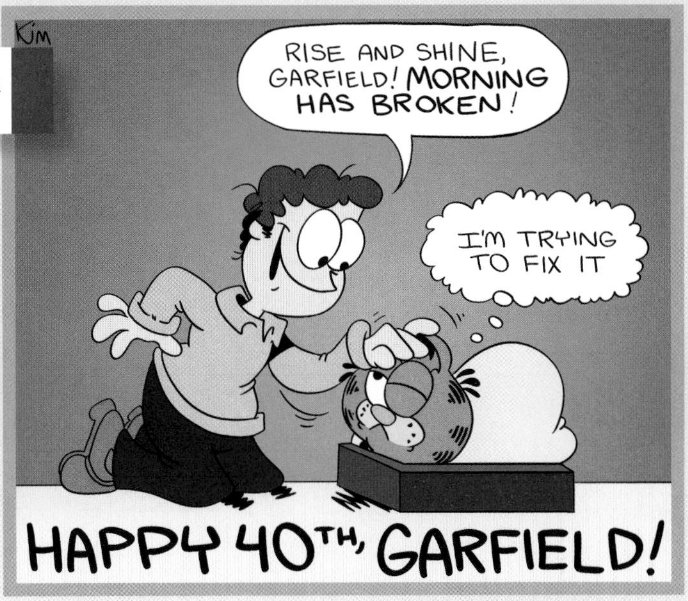
Kim
RISE AND SHINE, GARFIELD! MORNING HAS BROKEN!
I'M TRYING TO FIX IT
HAPPY 40TH, GARFIELD!

Enzo L, age 15
Poitiers, France

Kim B, age 26
Saskatchewan, Canada

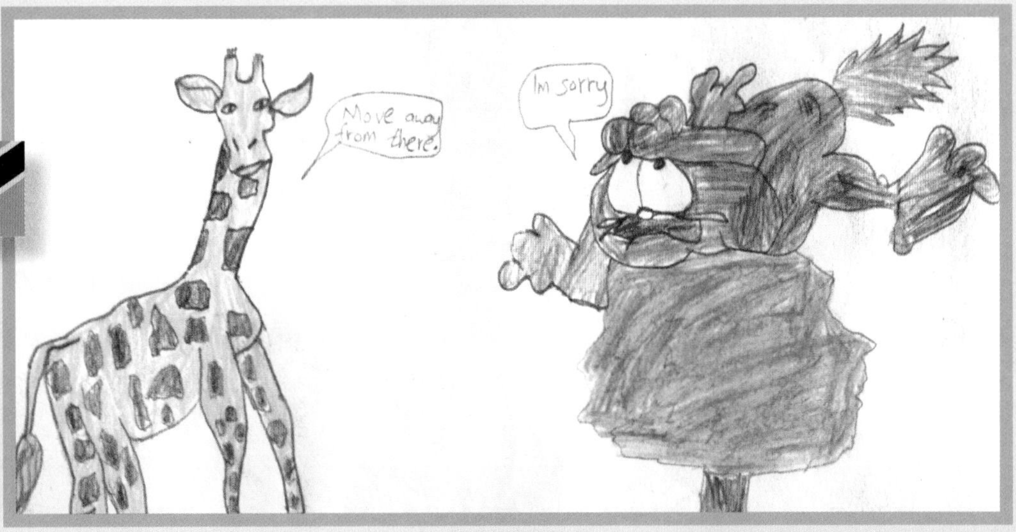
Move away from there.
Im sorry

Claudia R,
age 9
Arusha, Tanzania

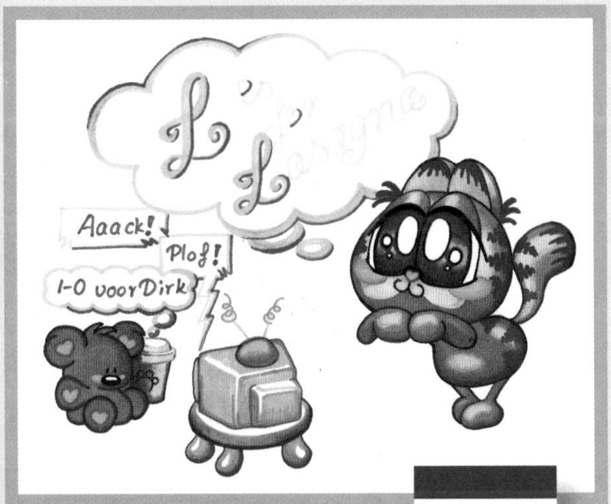
Aaack!
Plof!
1-0 voor Dirk

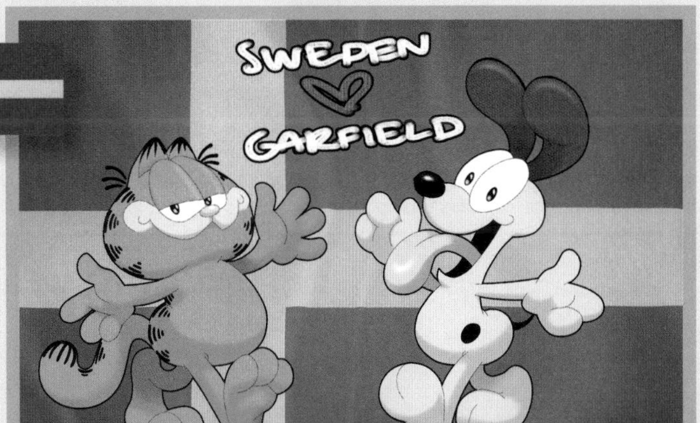
SWEDEN
GARFIELD

Chu-Yun J, age 36
The Netherlands

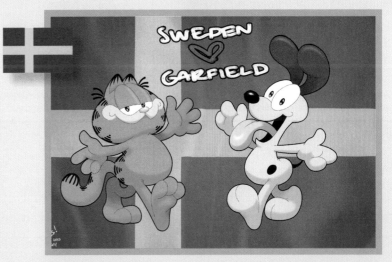

Evelina T, age 25
Brotby, Sweden

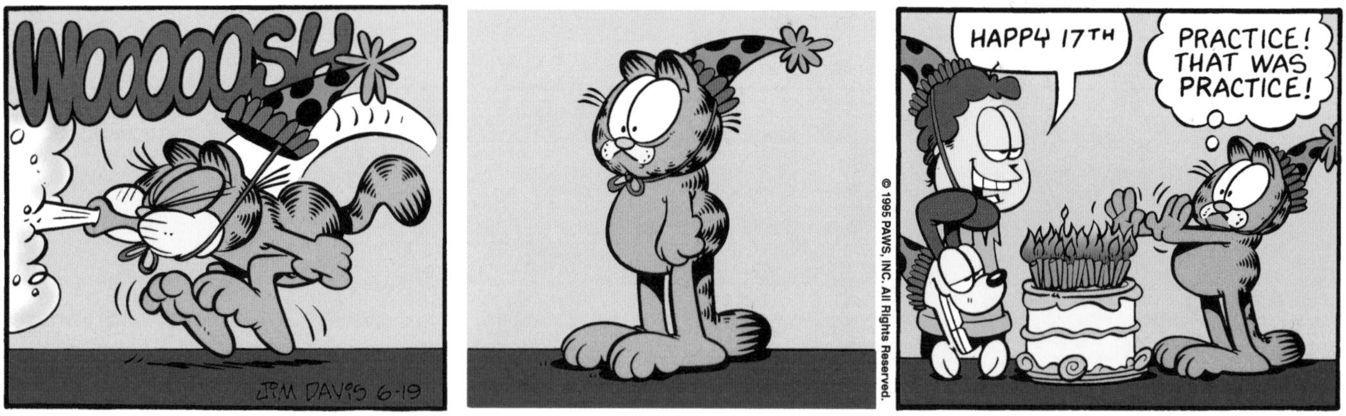

WOOOOOSH
JIM DAVIS 6-19
© 1995 PAWS, INC. All Rights Reserved.
HAPPY 17TH
PRACTICE! THAT WAS PRACTICE!

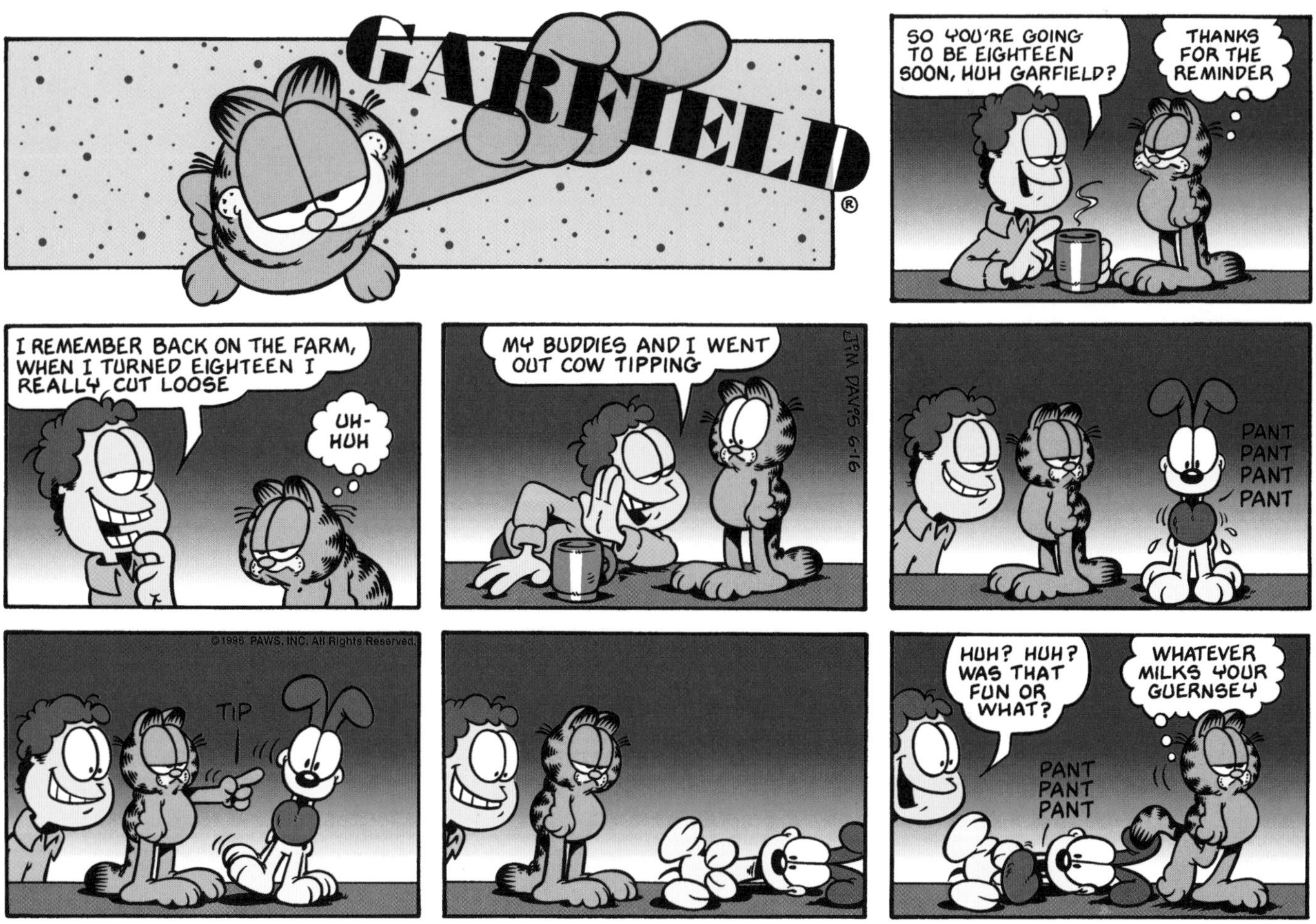

GARFIELD®
SO YOU'RE GOING TO BE EIGHTEEN SOON, HUH GARFIELD?
THANKS FOR THE REMINDER
I REMEMBER BACK ON THE FARM, WHEN I TURNED EIGHTEEN I REALLY CUT LOOSE
UH-HUH
MY BUDDIES AND I WENT OUT COW TIPPING
JIM DAVIS 6-16
PANT PANT PANT PANT
©1996 PAWS, INC. All Rights Reserved.
TIP
HUH? HUH? WAS THAT FUN OR WHAT?
PANT PANT PANT
WHATEVER MILKS YOUR GUERNSEY

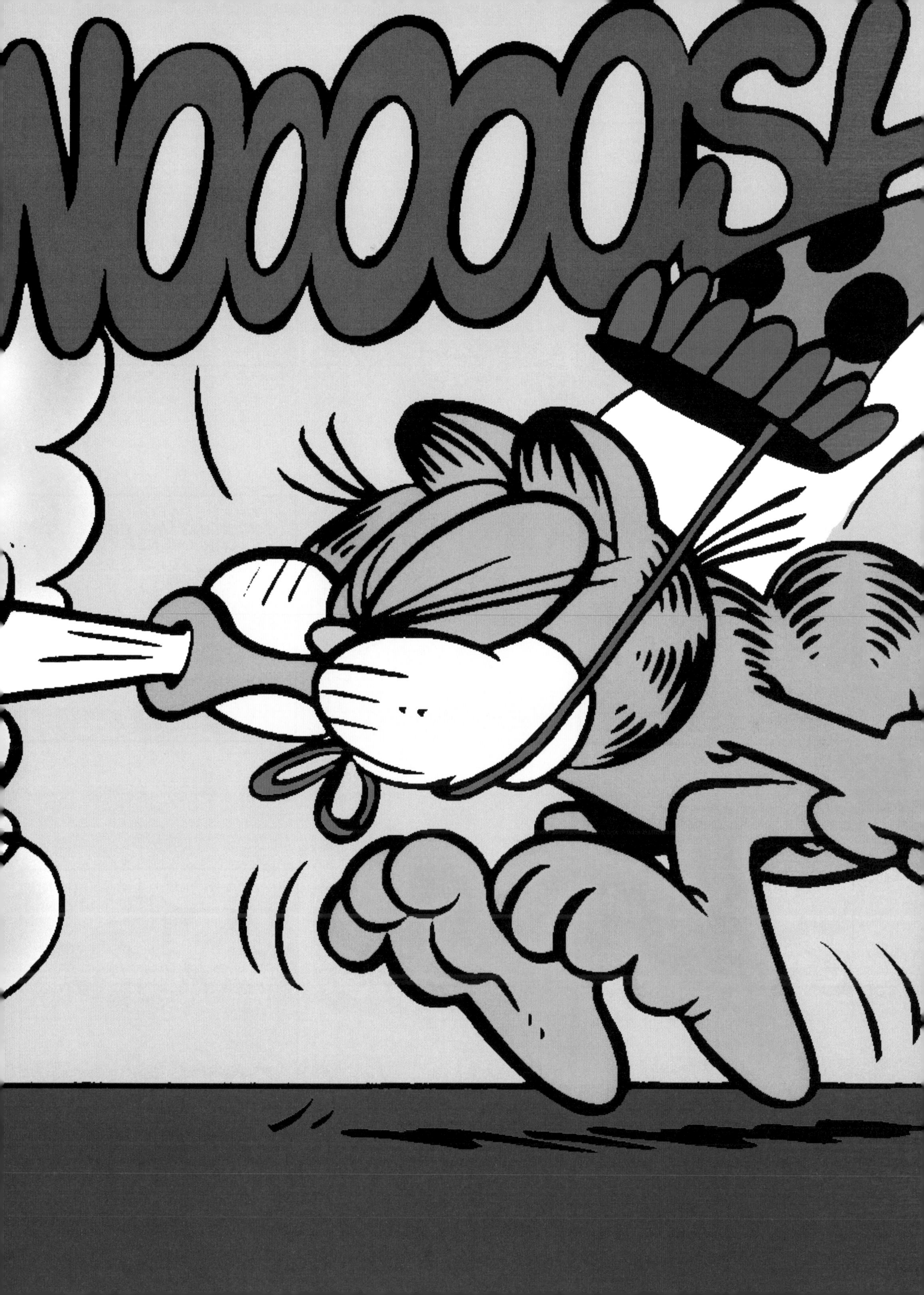

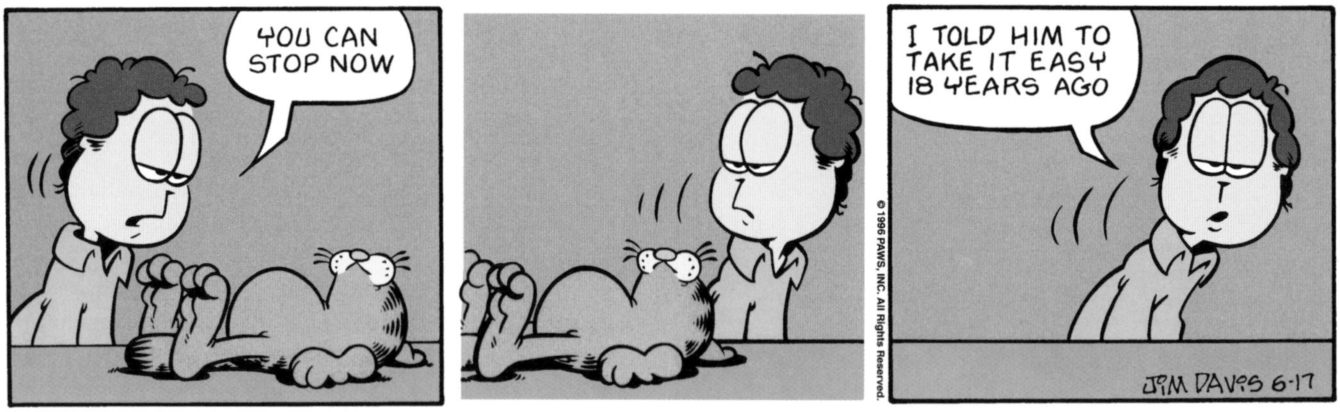
YOU CAN STOP NOW
I TOLD HIM TO TAKE IT EASY 18 YEARS AGO
JIM DAVIS 6-17
© 1996 PAWS, INC. All Rights Reserved.

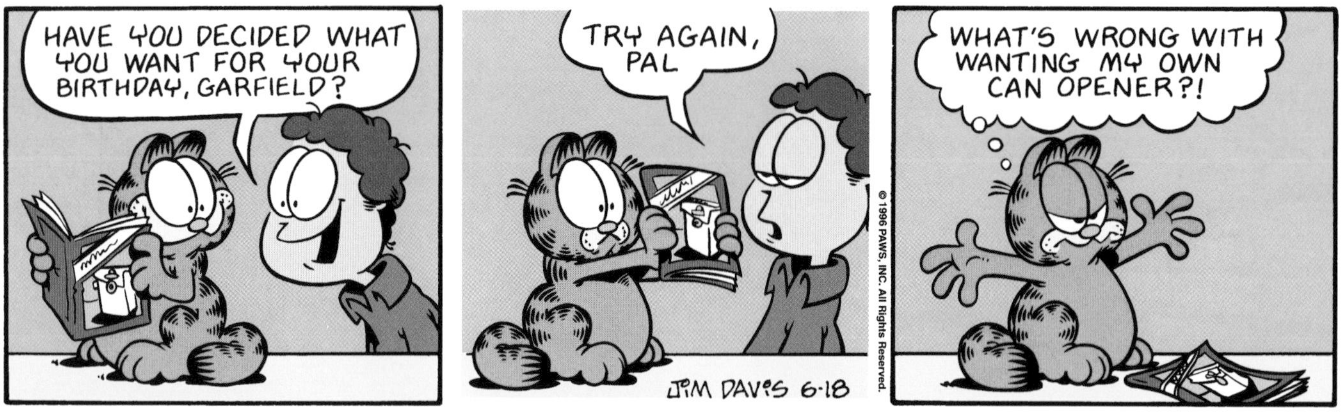
HAVE YOU DECIDED WHAT YOU WANT FOR YOUR BIRTHDAY, GARFIELD?
TRY AGAIN, PAL
WHAT'S WRONG WITH WANTING MY OWN CAN OPENER?!
JIM DAVIS 6-18
© 1996 PAWS, INC. All Rights Reserved.

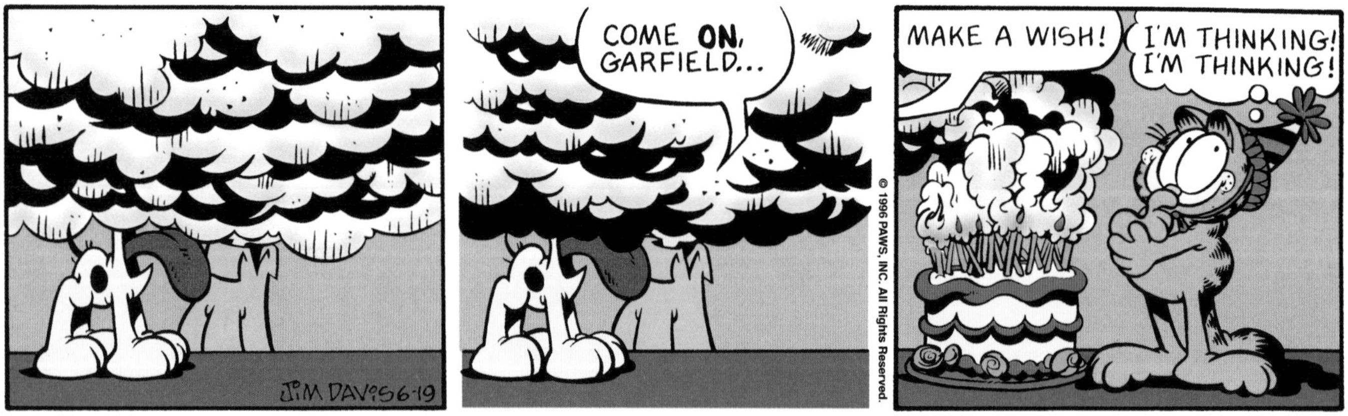
COME **ON**, GARFIELD...
MAKE A WISH!
I'M THINKING! I'M THINKING!
JIM DAVIS 6-19
© 1996 PAWS, INC. All Rights Reserved.

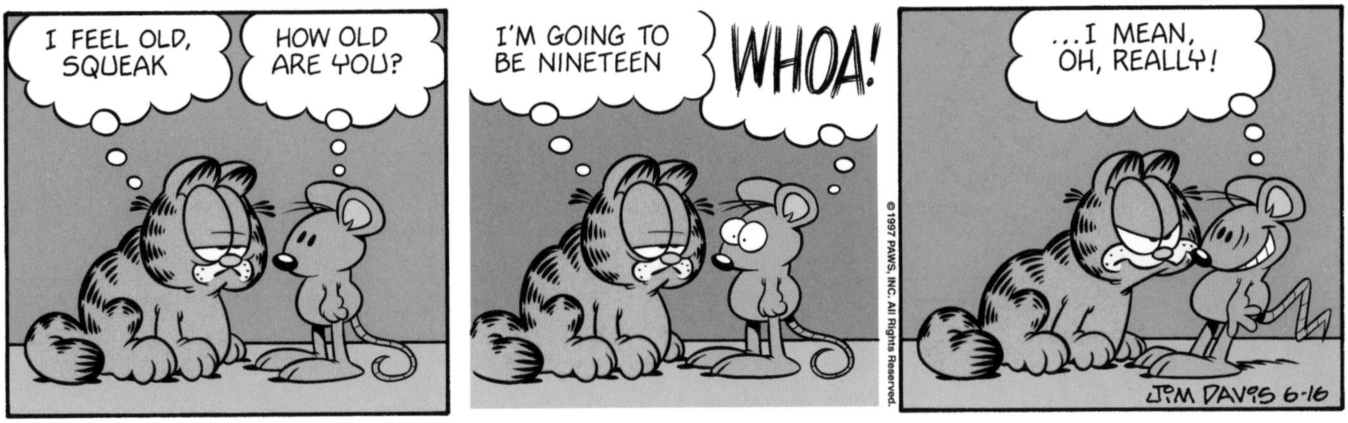
I FEEL OLD, SQUEAK
HOW OLD ARE YOU?
I'M GOING TO BE NINETEEN
WHOA!
...I MEAN, OH, REALLY!
© 1997 PAWS, INC. All Rights Reserved.
JIM DAVIS 6-16

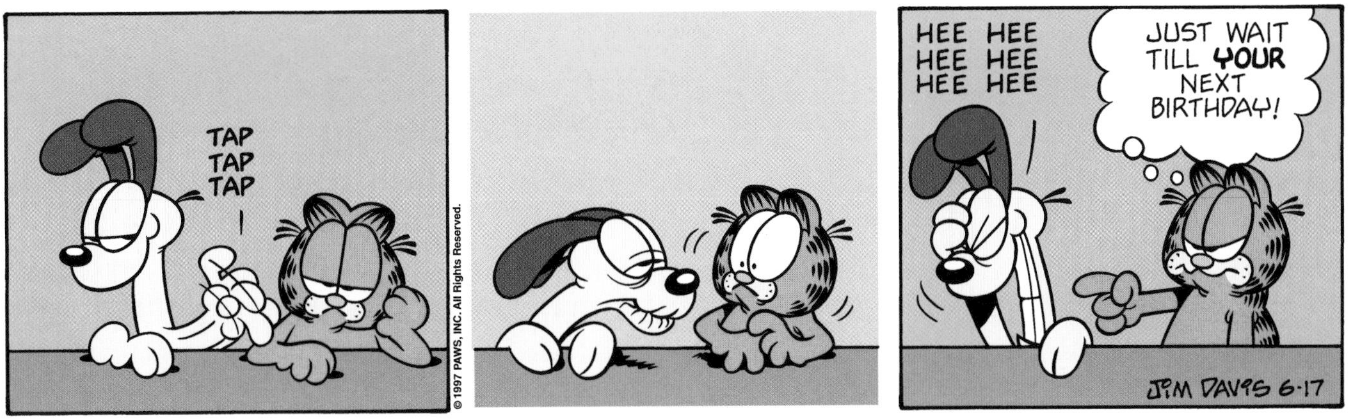
TAP TAP TAP
HEE HEE HEE HEE HEE HEE
JUST WAIT TILL **YOUR** NEXT BIRTHDAY!
© 1997 PAWS, INC. All Rights Reserved.
JIM DAVIS 6-17

You know you're getting old when:
you light your candles with a blowtorch

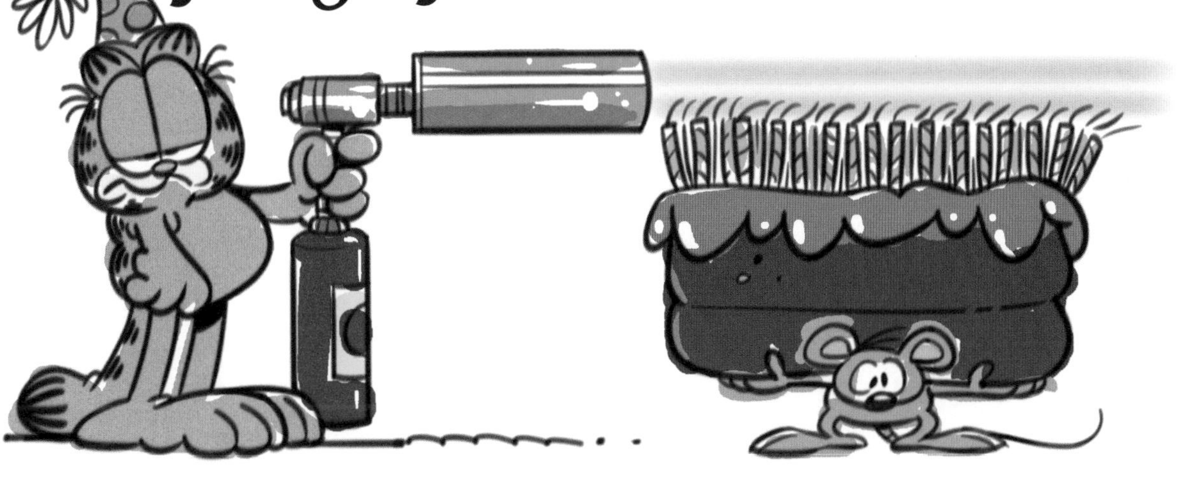

Cat Chat

An Interview with Garfield on His 40th Birthday

In honor of your 40th birthday, I'd like to ask you 40 questions.
Make it 20: I have half the energy and patience I used to have. But, luckily, my voracious appetite is still fully intact.

Can you believe it has been 40 years since you made your debut? How does that make you feel?
Chronologically challenged. That sounds better than old.

So you think of yourself as old?
Actually, I don't. I'm an ageless wonder. And a major hunk!

So what's on your bucket list?
Short-term: a bucket of chicken. Long-term: I'd someday like to go on an African safari. It's one of the few things worth getting off the couch for.

Why a safari?
I'd like to meet some of my distant cat cousins. I think I could improve their live They waste a lot of time and energy hunting; I'd teach them to order pizza.

What are your plans for the immediate future?
A marathon nap...not that I need any beauty sleep.

You're famous for being born to snooze. Was there ever a night you couldn't fall asleep?
Yes, actually. November 8, 1992.

We know you love lasagna. What's your second favorite food?
Everything else (and in large quantites). Except raisins, kale, and tofu.

You don't appear to be slowing down after 40 years. Starting out, did you think you would be in this business for four decades?
In the beginning, I never dreamed of fame and fortune—I just dreamed of a donut the size of a truck tire.

What does 40 mean to you?
Age is like the speed limit...just a big number to ignore.

Do you have any regrets?
Yeah, the time I ate three-day-old sushi. I'll spare you the details...

What keeps you going at your age?
Caffeine and botox.

What do you think of social media?
Like everyone else, I'm hooked on social media. It's a great way to connect with fans...and watch a lot of cat videos.

You teamed up with Grumpy Cat. What was that like?
We both agree it's an honor to work with me.

What is your proudest accomplishment?
Having seven of my books appear simultaneously on the *New York Times* bestseller list was big. But, even better, I once ate my own weight in cheeseballs.

What were the 1980s really like?
I don't know, man. It was all a blur of shoulder pads, mullets, and parachute pants.

How are you celebrating 40 years?
I'm celebrating with gusto: I think I'll order a pizza with 40 different toppings!

What is your most memorable experience of the past 40 years?
With successful movies, Emmy Award–winning TV shows, bestselling books, and having my face stuck on car windows all over the world, it's hard to cite just one memorable experience. (Hey, modesty is overrated.) But it might have been a day—and night—I spent at an all-you-can-eat restaurant in Texas. That was followed by a burp you could hear in Tennessee!

Is there anyone—a celebrity or a cartoon character—that you'd like to do a project with?
I'd love to do something with Leonardo DiCaprio. Leo, call me! I'll get you that second Oscar! As for cartoon characters, Mary Worth seems like a fun old gal!

Last question: Any words of wisdom you'd like to share with your fans?
Yeah, here's some food for thought: Life is uncertain; eat dessert first.

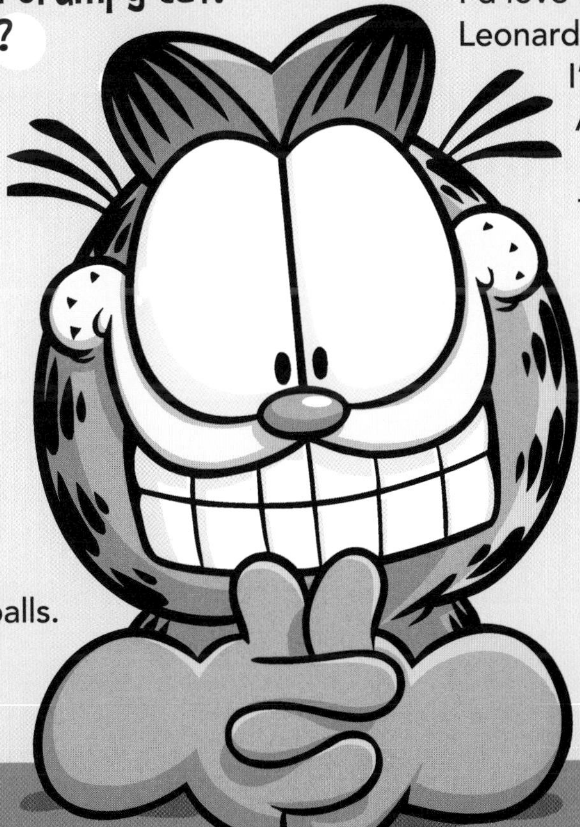

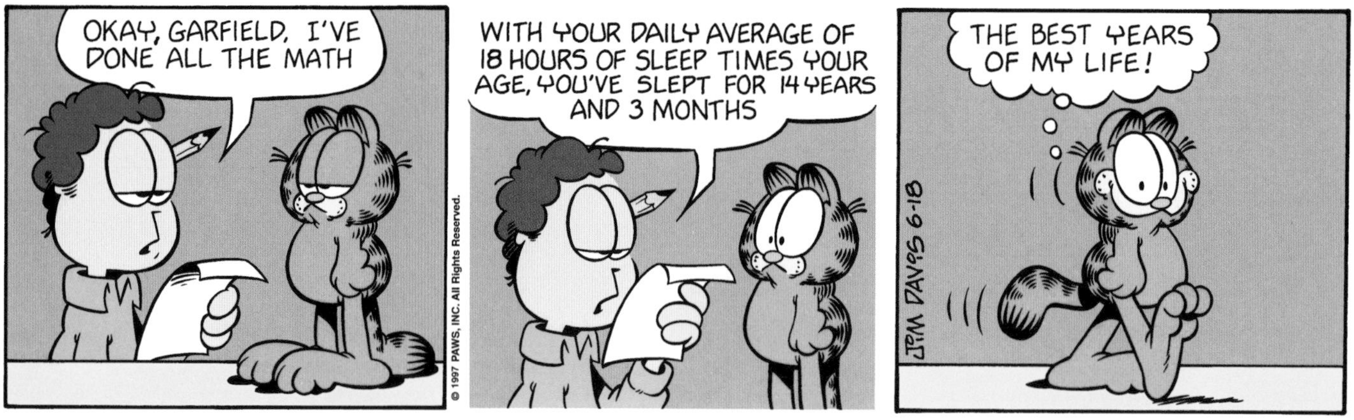
OKAY, GARFIELD, I'VE DONE ALL THE MATH
© 1997 PAWS, INC. All Rights Reserved.
WITH YOUR DAILY AVERAGE OF 18 HOURS OF SLEEP TIMES YOUR AGE, YOU'VE SLEPT FOR 14 YEARS AND 3 MONTHS
THE BEST YEARS OF MY LIFE!

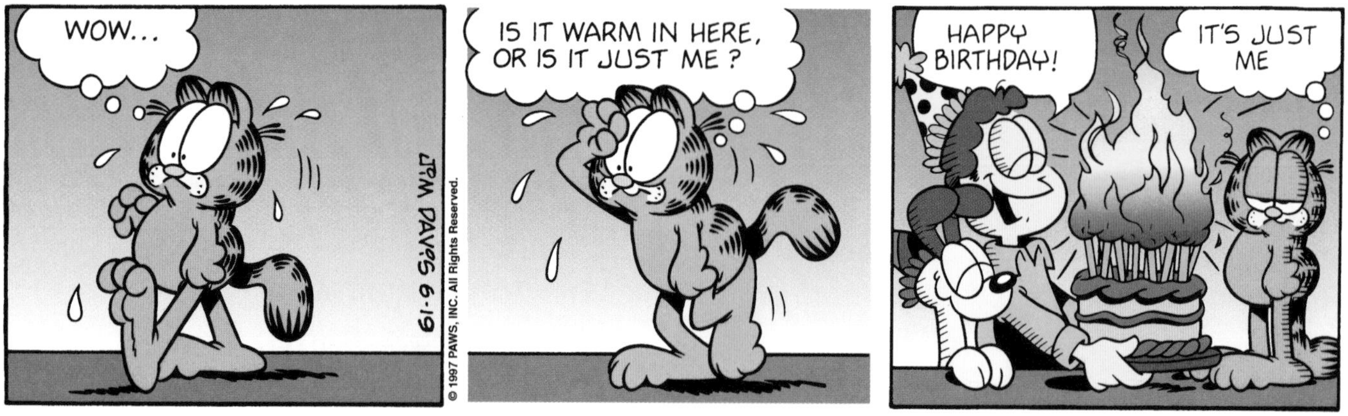
WOW...
© 1997 PAWS, INC. All Rights Reserved.
IS IT WARM IN HERE, OR IS IT JUST ME?
HAPPY BIRTHDAY!
IT'S JUST ME

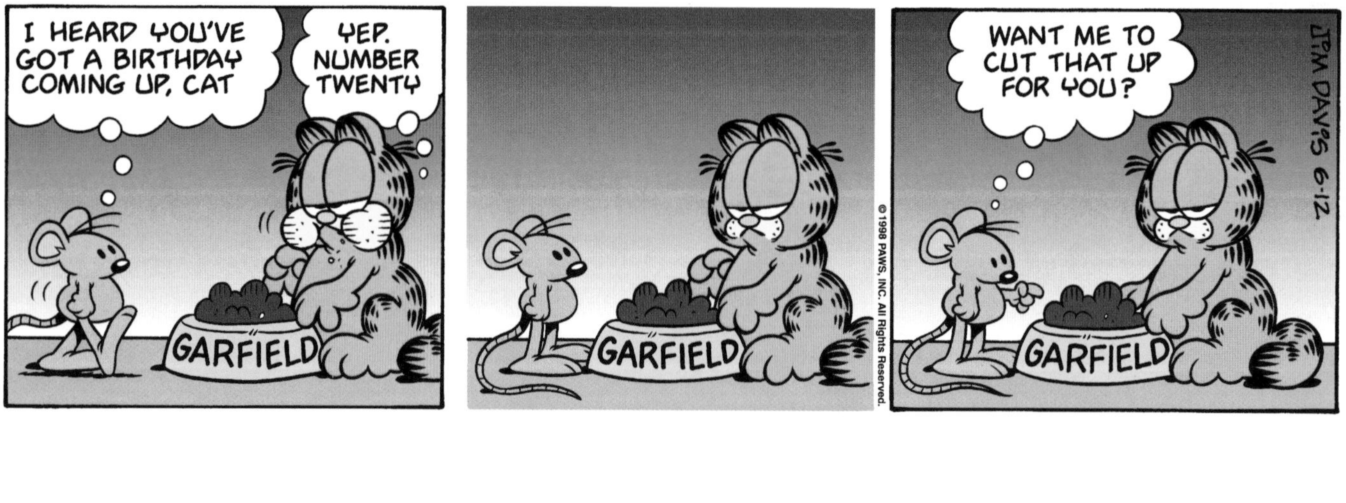
I HEARD YOU'VE GOT A BIRTHDAY COMING UP, CAT
YEP. NUMBER TWENTY
GARFIELD
GARFIELD
© 1998 PAWS, INC. All Rights Reserved.
WANT ME TO CUT THAT UP FOR YOU?
GARFIELD

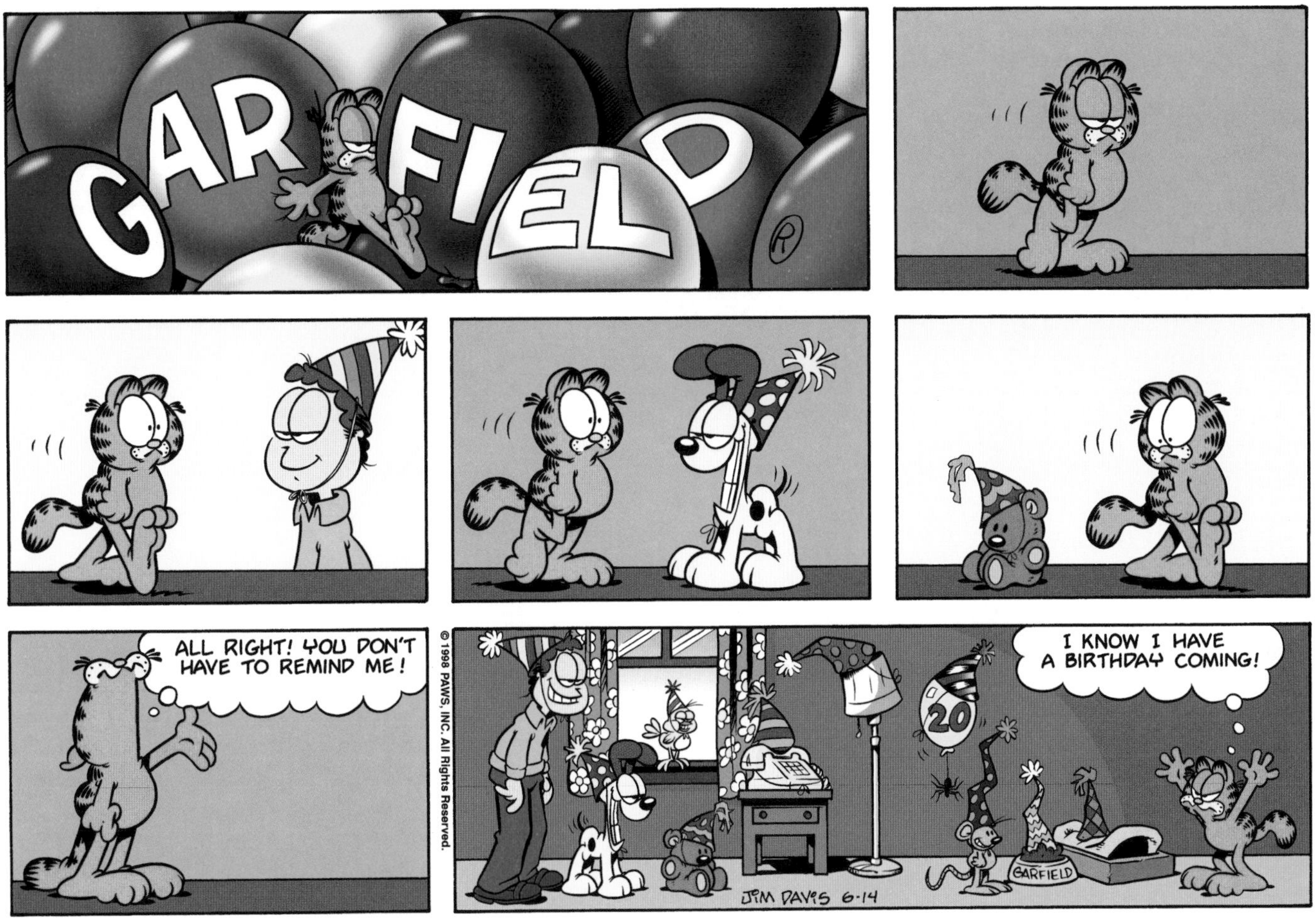
GARFIELD
ALL RIGHT! YOU DON'T HAVE TO REMIND ME!
© 1998 PAWS, INC. All Rights Reserved.
20
I KNOW I HAVE A BIRTHDAY COMING!
GARFIELD
JIM DAVIS 6-14

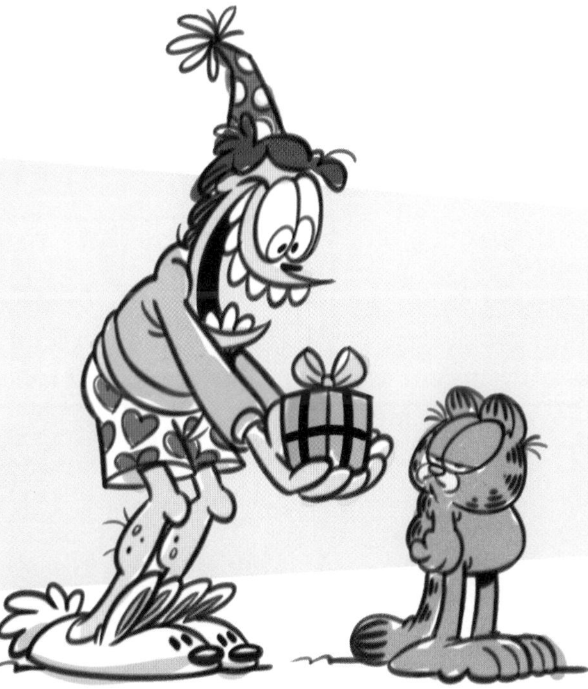

BEWARE OF GEEKS BEARING GIFTS

YOU LOOK DOWN, CAT
MY BIRTHDAY IS COMING UP, SCALE
JIM DAVIS 6-15
© 1998 PAWS, INC. All Rights Reserved.
HOW MANY YEARS?
TWENTY
www.garfield.com
WOW. OLD AND FAT

OH, GREAT...JUST WHO I DON'T NEED TO SEE
WHY?
JIM DAVIS 6-16
© 1998 PAWS, INC. All Rights Reserved.
IF YOU MUST KNOW, I'M HAVING A BIRTHDAY SOON
I THOUGHT IT SMELLED "OLD" IN HERE
www.garfield.com
WHERE'S NERMAL?
OUT GETTING SOME FRESH AIR

WELL, IT'S TIME TO LOOK BACK, AND TAKE STOCK...
JIM DAVIS 6-19
www.garfield.com
TIME TO COUNT MY BLESSINGS...
HAPPY 20TH BIRTHDAY, GARFIELD!
TIME TO START LYING ABOUT MY AGE
© 1998 PAWS, INC. All Rights Reserved.
GARFIELD'S 20 BIRTHDAY

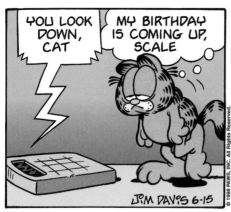

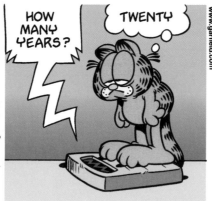

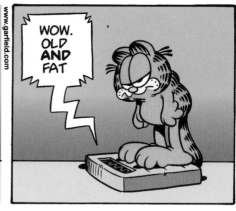

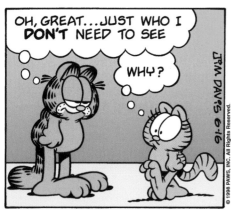

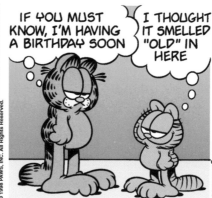

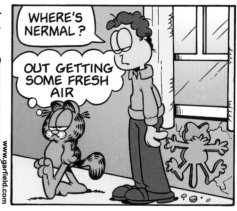

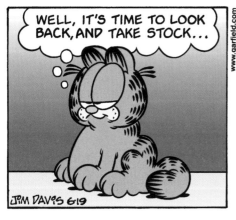

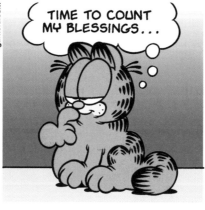

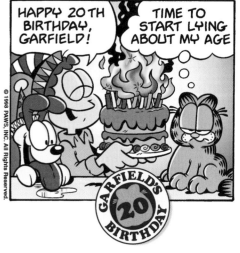

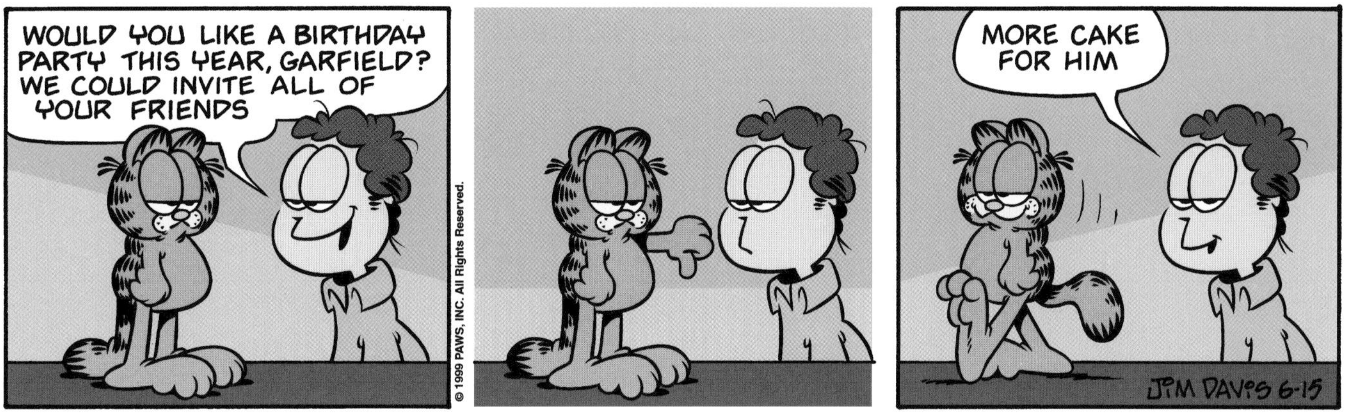
WOULD YOU LIKE A BIRTHDAY PARTY THIS YEAR, GARFIELD? WE COULD INVITE ALL OF YOUR FRIENDS
© 1999 PAWS, INC. All Rights Reserved.
MORE CAKE FOR HIM
JIM DAVIS 6-15

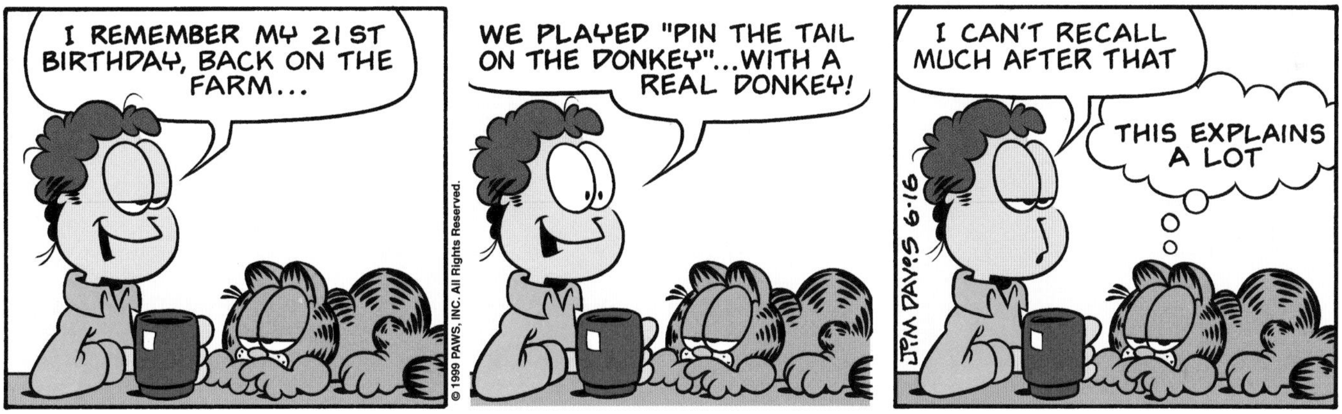
I REMEMBER MY 21ST BIRTHDAY, BACK ON THE FARM...
© 1999 PAWS, INC. All Rights Reserved.
WE PLAYED "PIN THE TAIL ON THE DONKEY"...WITH A REAL DONKEY!
I CAN'T RECALL MUCH AFTER THAT
THIS EXPLAINS A LOT
JIM DAVIS 6-16

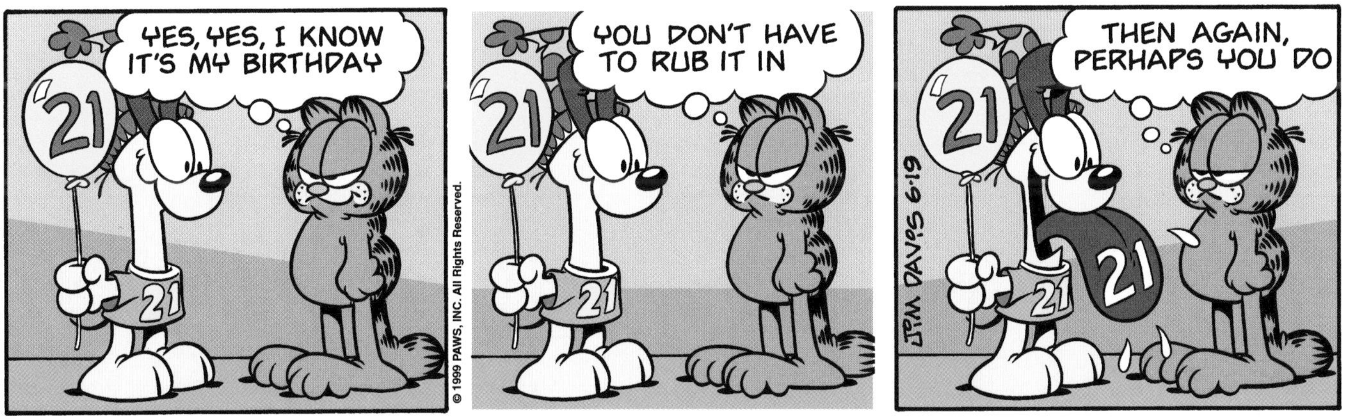
YES, YES, I KNOW IT'S MY BIRTHDAY
21
21
© 1999 PAWS, INC. All Rights Reserved.
YOU DON'T HAVE TO RUB IT IN
THEN AGAIN, PERHAPS YOU DO
21
JIM DAVIS 6-19

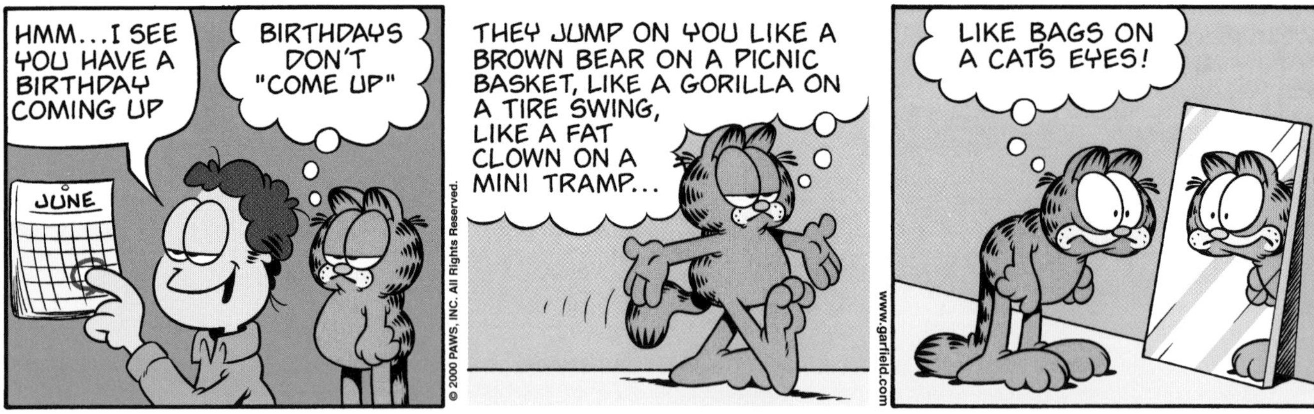
HMM...I SEE YOU HAVE A BIRTHDAY COMING UP
BIRTHDAYS DON'T "COME UP"
JUNE
THEY JUMP ON YOU LIKE A BROWN BEAR ON A PICNIC BASKET, LIKE A GORILLA ON A TIRE SWING, LIKE A FAT CLOWN ON A MINI TRAMP...
LIKE BAGS ON A CAT'S EYES!
JIM DAVIS 6-12
© 2000 PAWS, INC. All Rights Reserved.
www.garfield.com

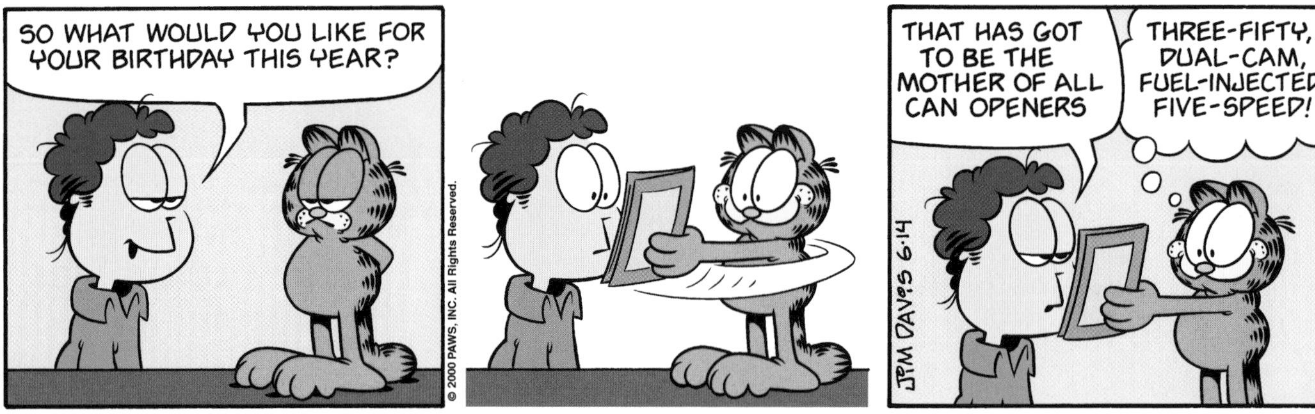
SO WHAT WOULD YOU LIKE FOR YOUR BIRTHDAY THIS YEAR?
THAT HAS GOT TO BE THE MOTHER OF ALL CAN OPENERS
THREE-FIFTY, DUAL-CAM, FUEL-INJECTED FIVE-SPEED!
JIM DAVIS 6-14
© 2000 PAWS, INC. All Rights Reserved.

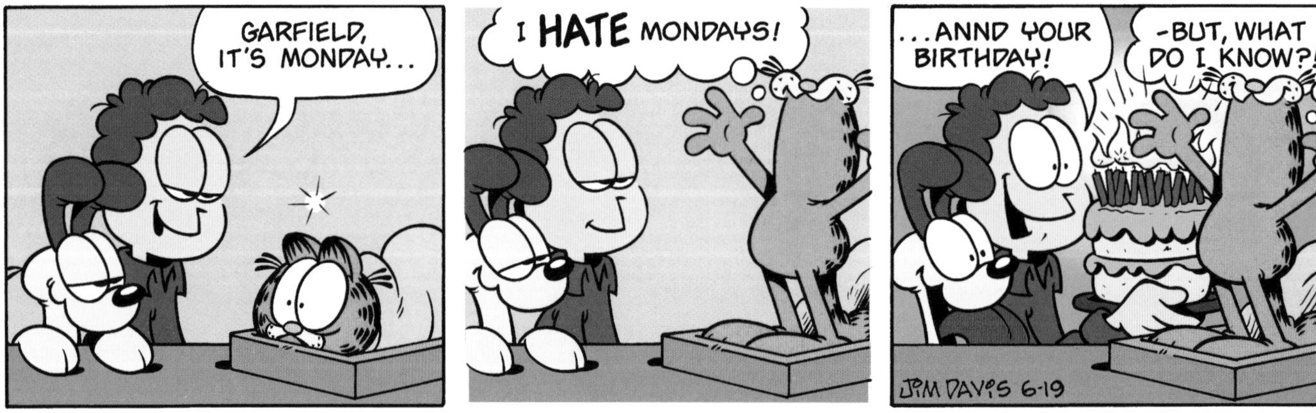
GARFIELD, IT'S MONDAY...
I **HATE** MONDAYS!
...ANND YOUR BIRTHDAY!
-BUT, WHAT DO I KNOW?!
JIM DAVIS 6-19

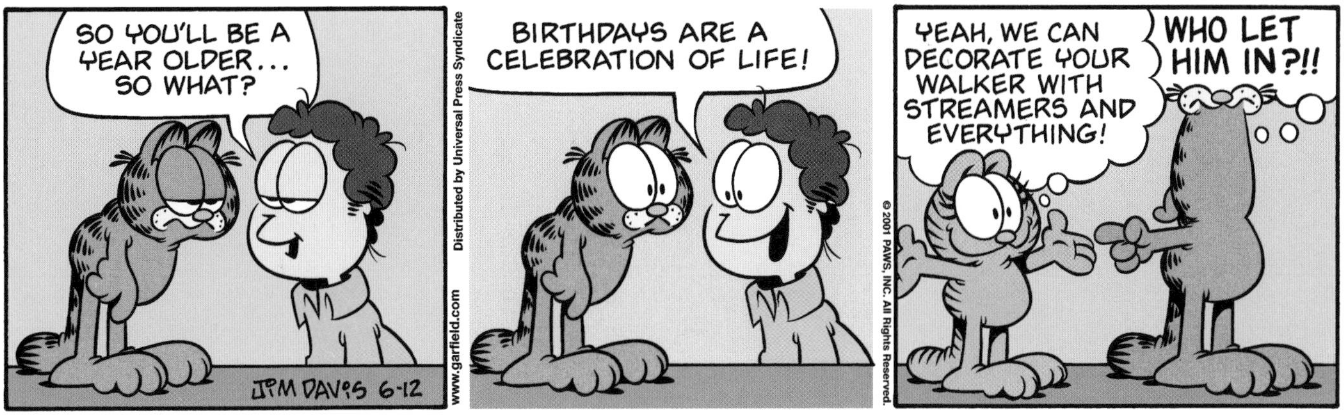
SO YOU'LL BE A YEAR OLDER... SO WHAT?
JIM DAVIS 6-12
www.garfield.com Distributed by Universal Press Syndicate
BIRTHDAYS ARE A CELEBRATION OF LIFE!
© 2001 PAWS, INC. All Rights Reserved.
YEAH, WE CAN DECORATE YOUR WALKER WITH STREAMERS AND EVERYTHING!
WHO LET HIM IN?!!

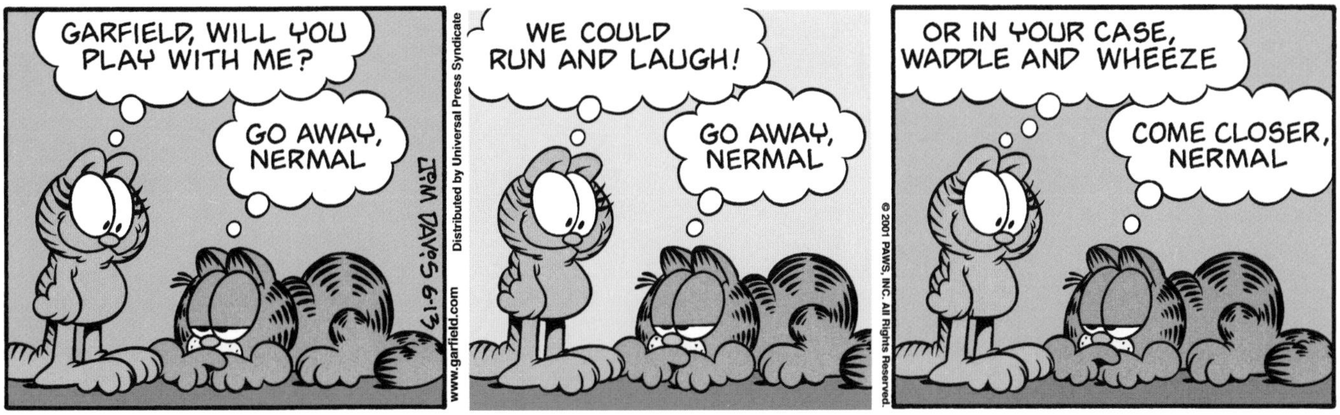
GARFIELD, WILL YOU PLAY WITH ME?
GO AWAY, NERMAL
JIM DAVIS 6-13
www.garfield.com Distributed by Universal Press Syndicate
WE COULD RUN AND LAUGH!
GO AWAY, NERMAL
© 2001 PAWS, INC. All Rights Reserved.
OR IN YOUR CASE, WADDLE AND WHEEZE
COME CLOSER, NERMAL

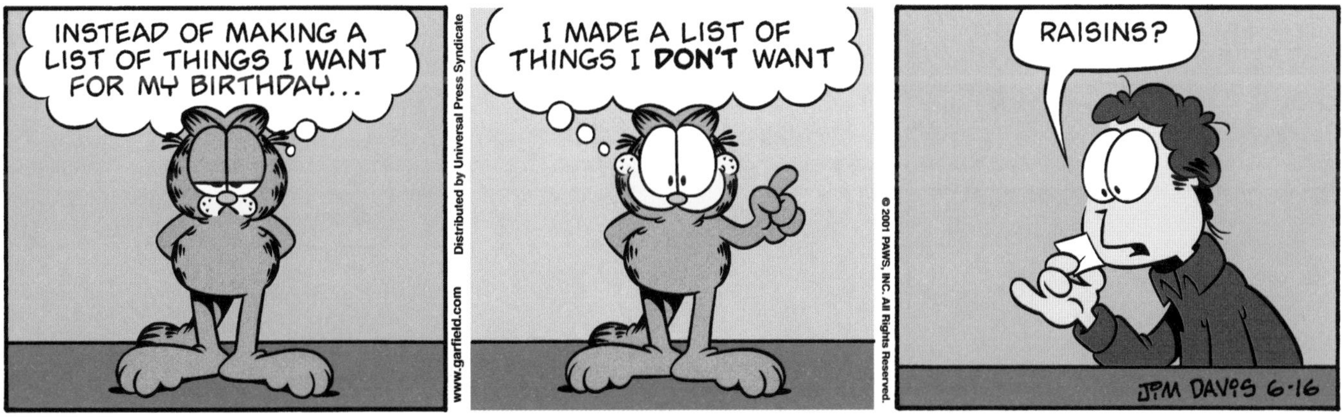
INSTEAD OF MAKING A LIST OF THINGS I WANT FOR MY BIRTHDAY...
www.garfield.com Distributed by Universal Press Syndicate
I MADE A LIST OF THINGS I **DON'T** WANT
© 2001 PAWS, INC. All Rights Reserved.
RAISINS?
JIM DAVIS 6-16

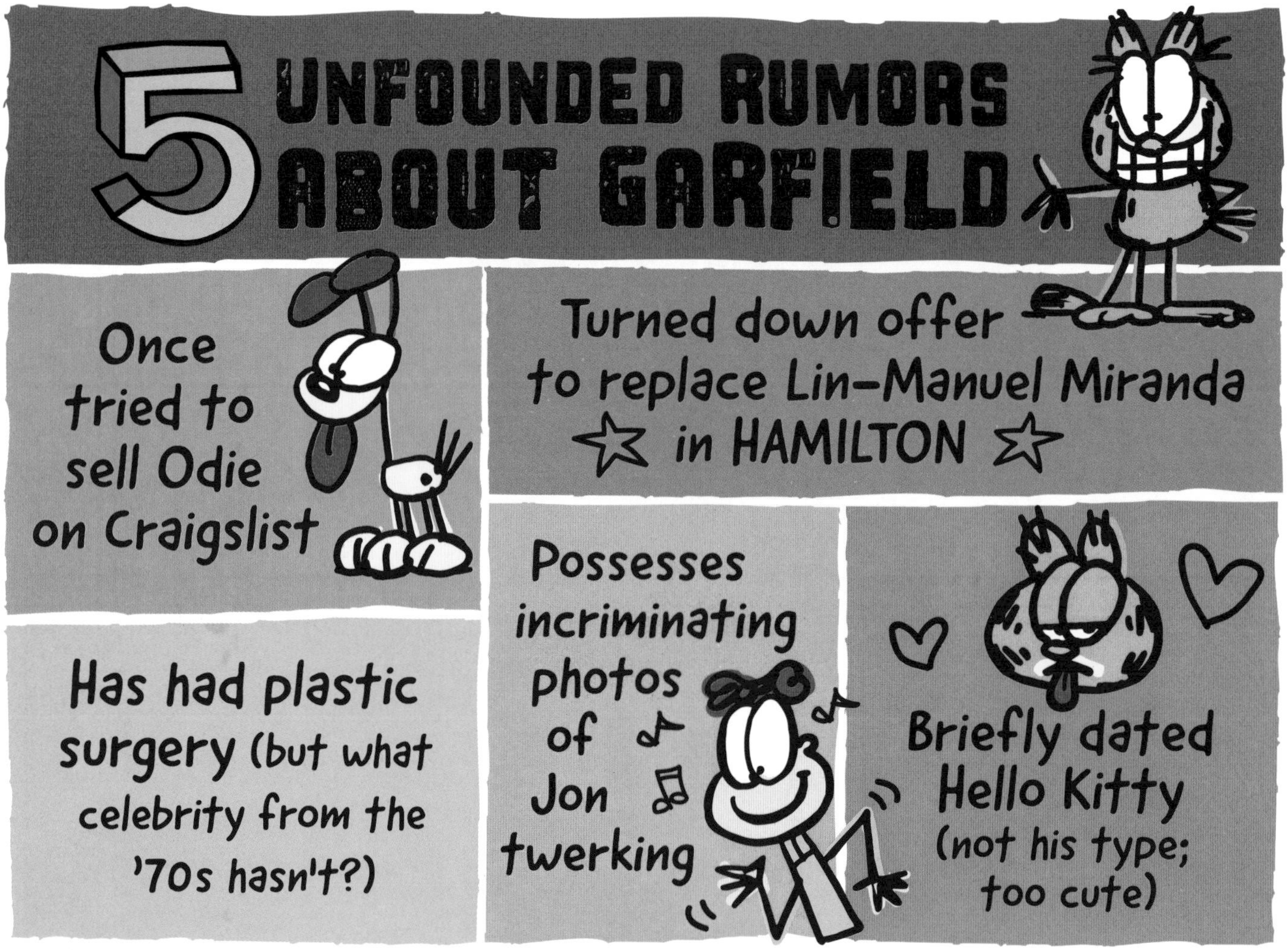
5 UNFOUNDED RUMORS ABOUT GARFIELD
Once tried to sell Odie on Craigslist
Turned down offer to replace Lin-Manuel Miranda in HAMILTON
Has had plastic surgery (but what celebrity from the '70s hasn't?)
Possesses incriminating photos of Jon twerking
Briefly dated Hello Kitty (not his type; too cute)

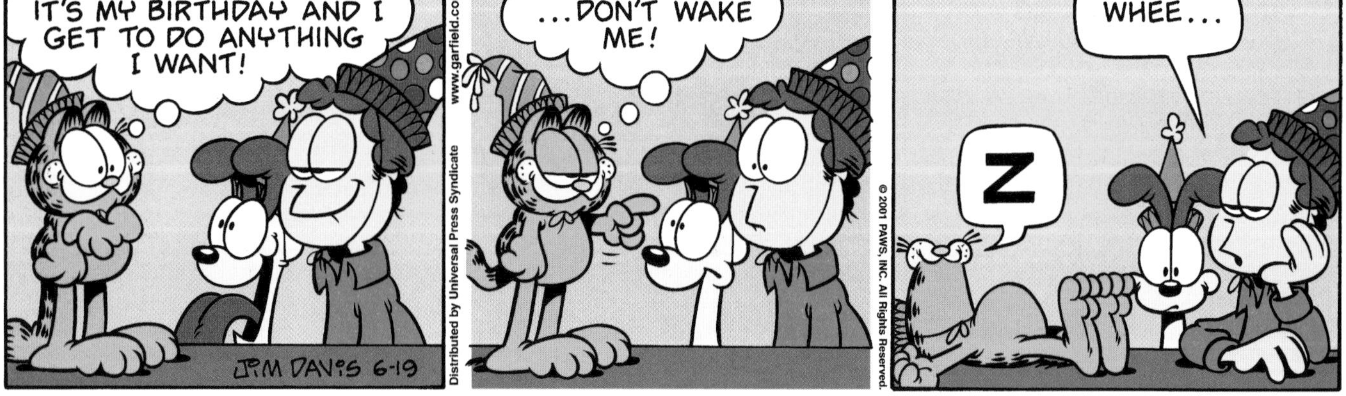
IT'S MY BIRTHDAY AND I GET TO DO ANYTHING I WANT!
JIM DAVIS 6-19
Distributed by Universal Press Syndicate www.garfield.com
...DON'T WAKE ME!
© 2001 PAWS, INC. All Rights Reserved.
WHEE...
Z

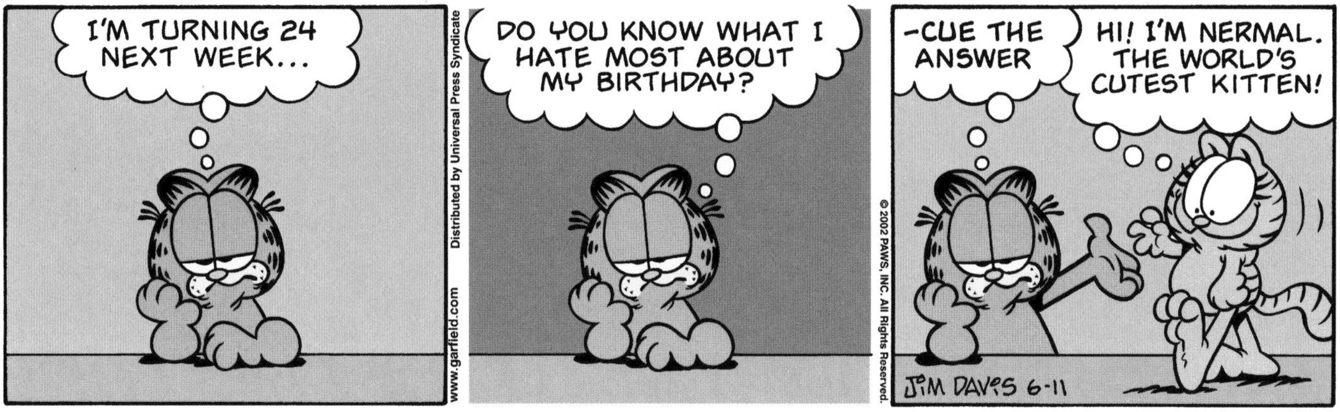
I'M TURNING 24 NEXT WEEK...
www.garfield.com Distributed by Universal Press Syndicate
DO YOU KNOW WHAT I HATE MOST ABOUT MY BIRTHDAY?
© 2002 PAWS, INC. All Rights Reserved.
-CUE THE ANSWER
HI! I'M NERMAL. THE WORLD'S CUTEST KITTEN!
JIM DAVIS 6-11

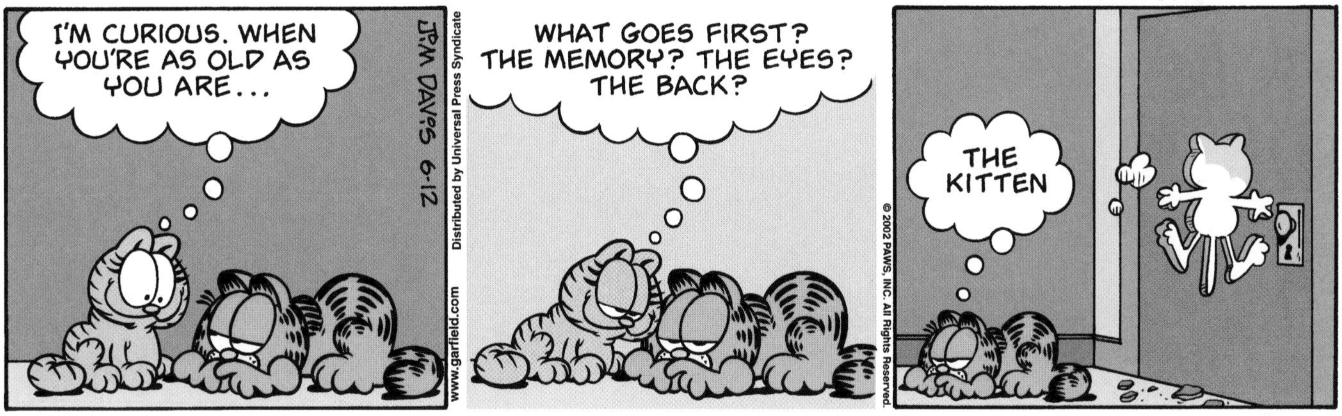
I'M CURIOUS. WHEN YOU'RE AS OLD AS YOU ARE...
JIM DAVIS 6-12
www.garfield.com Distributed by Universal Press Syndicate
WHAT GOES FIRST? THE MEMORY? THE EYES? THE BACK?
© 2002 PAWS, INC. All Rights Reserved.
THE KITTEN

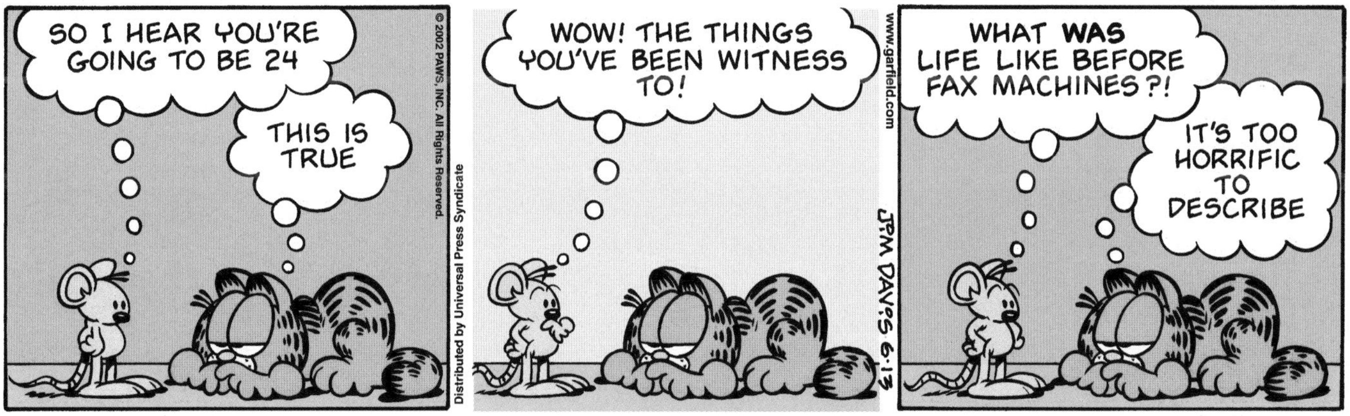
SO I HEAR YOU'RE GOING TO BE 24
THIS IS TRUE
© 2002 PAWS, INC. All Rights Reserved.
Distributed by Universal Press Syndicate
WOW! THE THINGS YOU'VE BEEN WITNESS TO!
www.garfield.com
JIM DAVIS 6-13
WHAT WAS LIFE LIKE BEFORE FAX MACHINES?!
IT'S TOO HORRIFIC TO DESCRIBE

Older, yes.
Wiser, maybe.
Weirder, definitely!

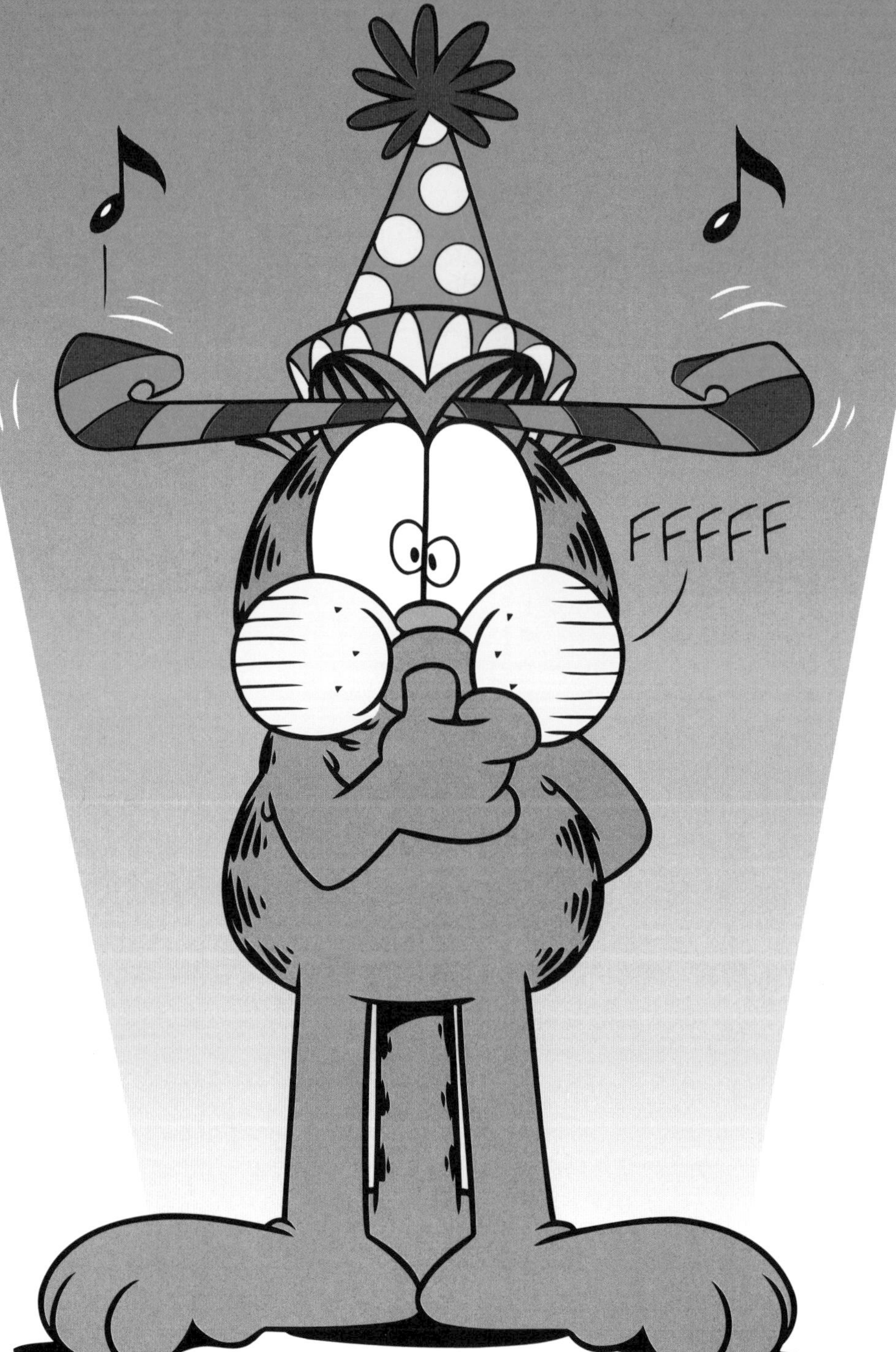
FFFFF

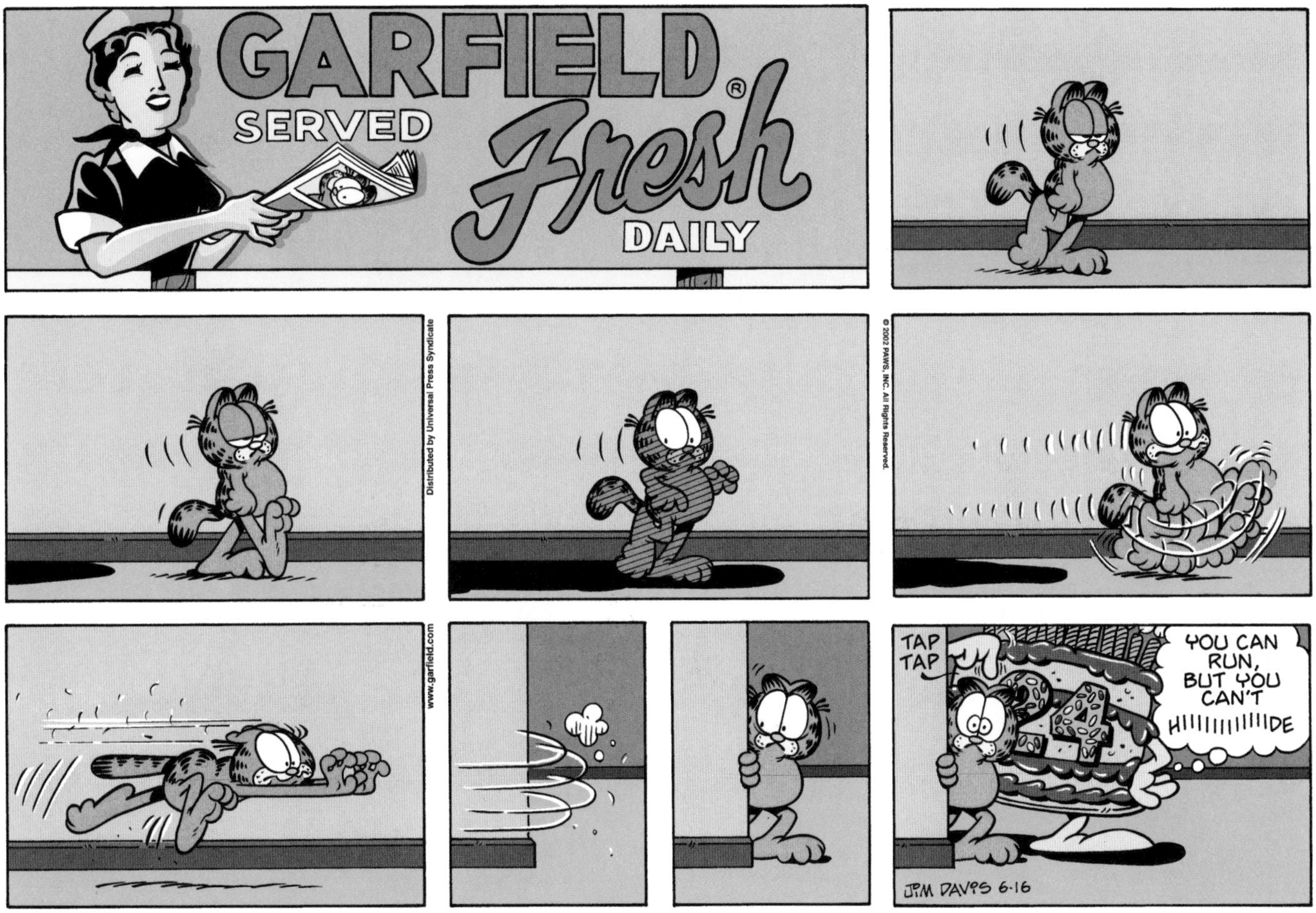
GARFIELD®
SERVED
Fresh
DAILY
Distributed by Universal Press Syndicate
© 2002 PAWS, INC. All Rights Reserved.
www.garfield.com
TAP
TAP
YOU CAN RUN, BUT YOU CAN'T HIIIIIIIIIIDE
JIM DAVIS 6-16

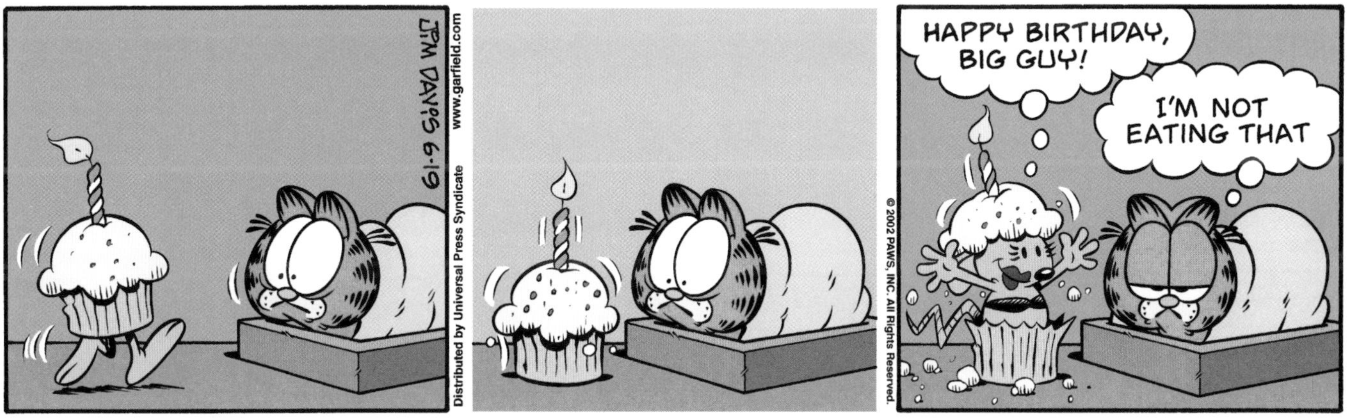
JIM DAVIS 6-19
www.garfield.com
Distributed by Universal Press Syndicate
HAPPY BIRTHDAY, BIG GUY!
I'M NOT EATING THAT
© 2002 PAWS, INC. All Rights Reserved.

OVERHEARD AT A GREAT PARTY

Who am I, and where did I get this chicken?

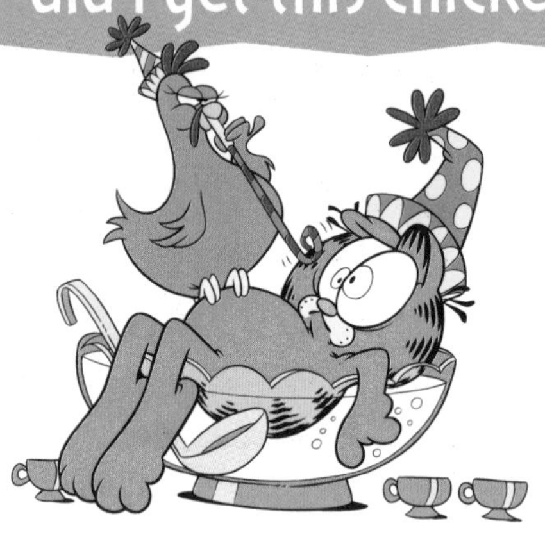

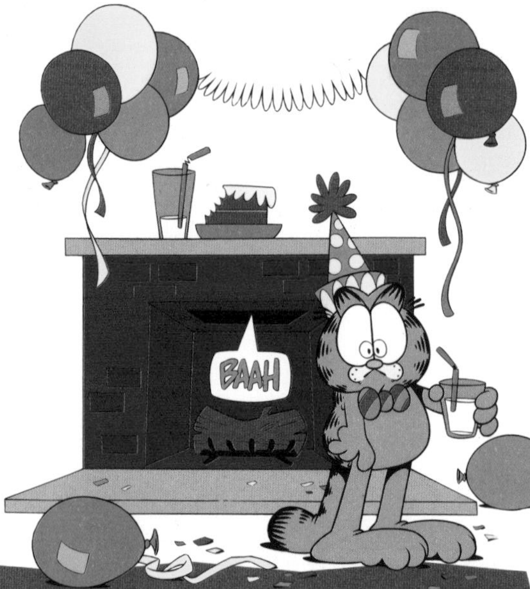
BAAH

HOW DID THAT GOAT GET UP THERE?

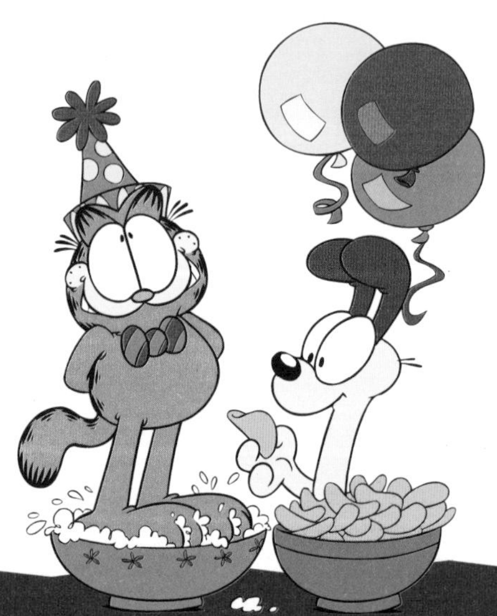

I LOVE THE WAY THIS DIP SQUISHES BETWEEN MY TOES.

Water balloons at twelve o'clock!

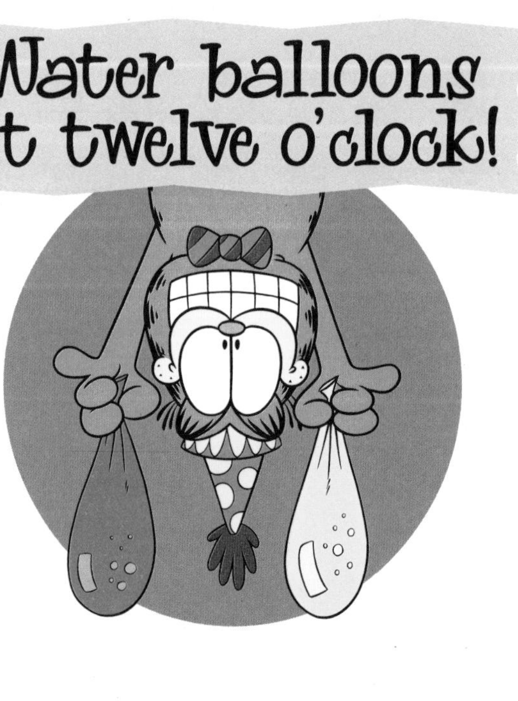

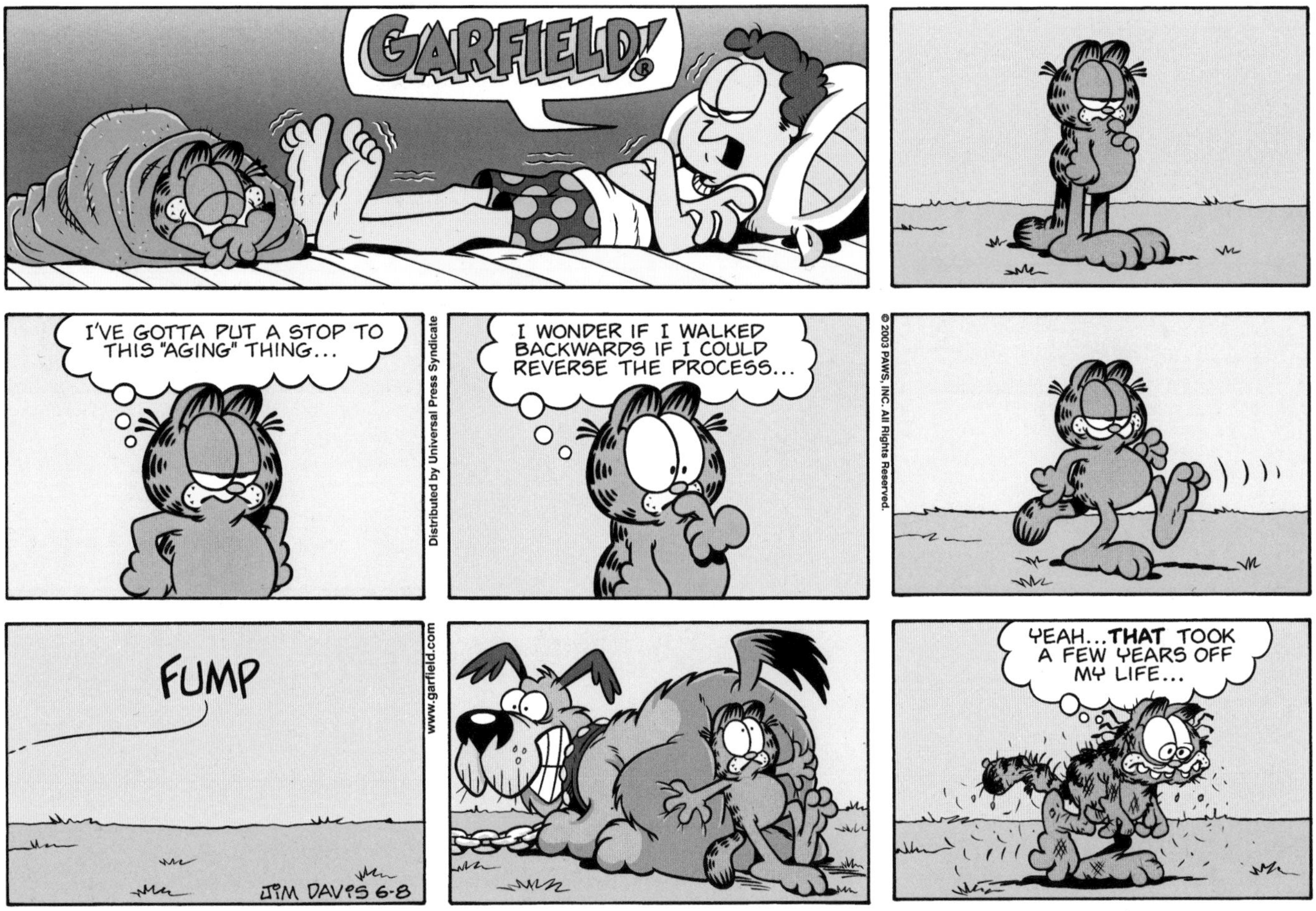
GARFIELD!
I'VE GOTTA PUT A STOP TO THIS "AGING" THING...
Distributed by Universal Press Syndicate
I WONDER IF I WALKED BACKWARDS IF I COULD REVERSE THE PROCESS...
© 2003 PAWS, INC. All Rights Reserved.
FUMP
JIM DAVIS 6-8
www.garfield.com
YEAH...**THAT** TOOK A FEW YEARS OFF MY LIFE...

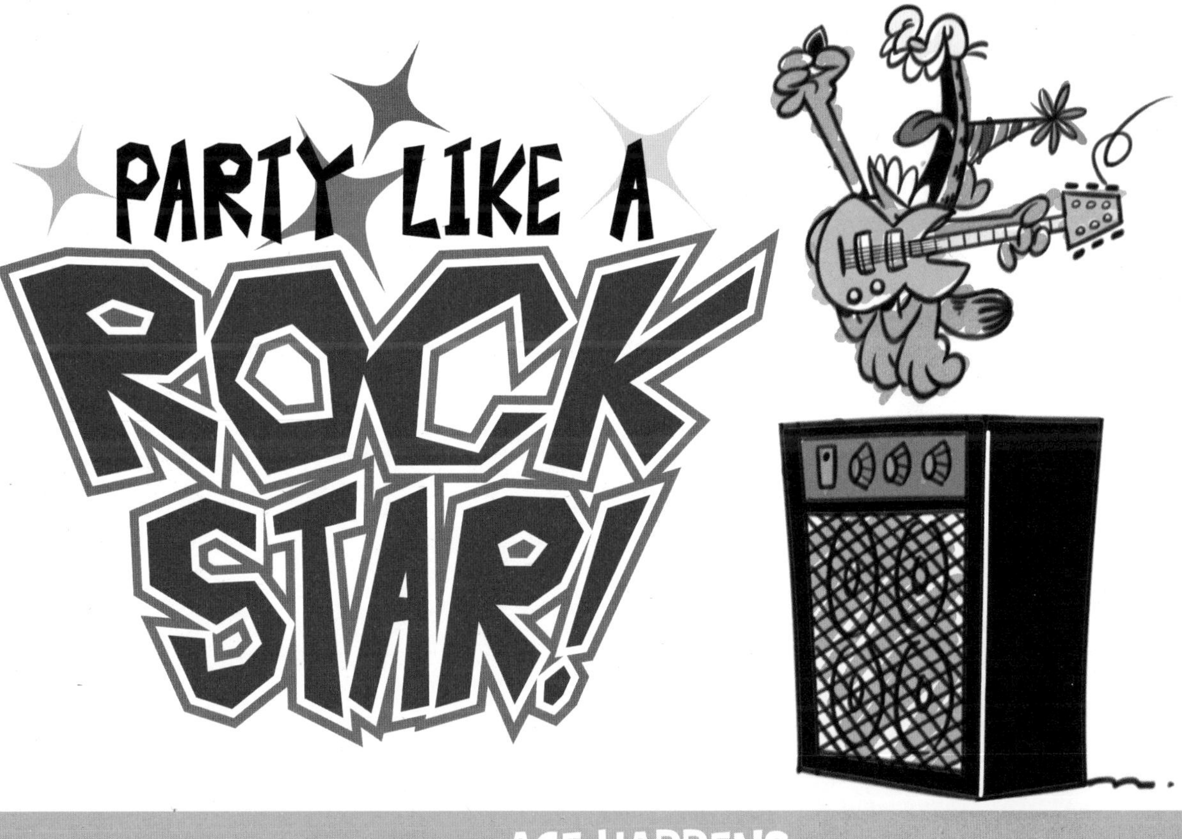
PARTY LIKE A
ROCK
STAR!

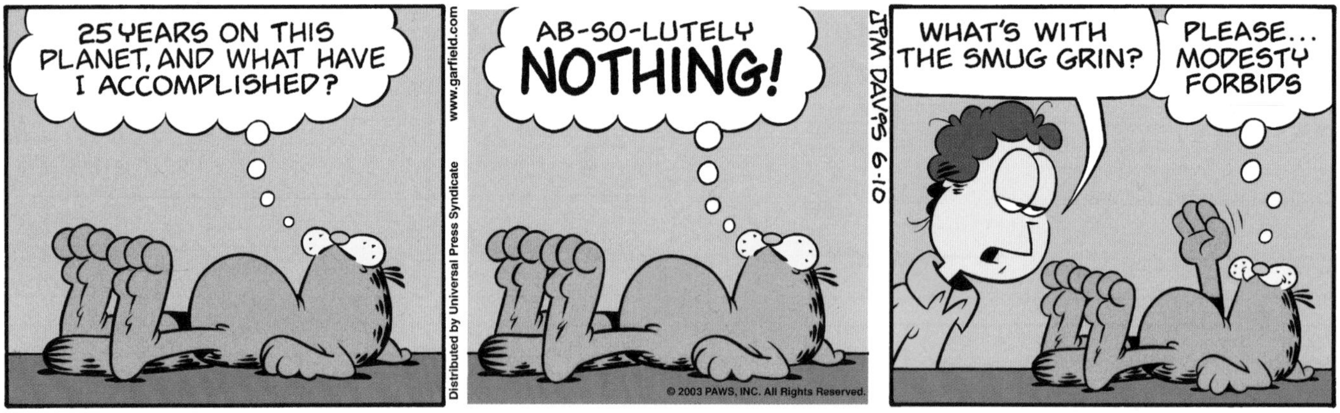
25 YEARS ON THIS PLANET, AND WHAT HAVE I ACCOMPLISHED?
www.garfield.com
Distributed by Universal Press Syndicate
AB-SO-LUTELY NOTHING!
© 2003 PAWS, INC. All Rights Reserved.
JIM DAVIS 6-10
WHAT'S WITH THE SMUG GRIN?
PLEASE... MODESTY FORBIDS

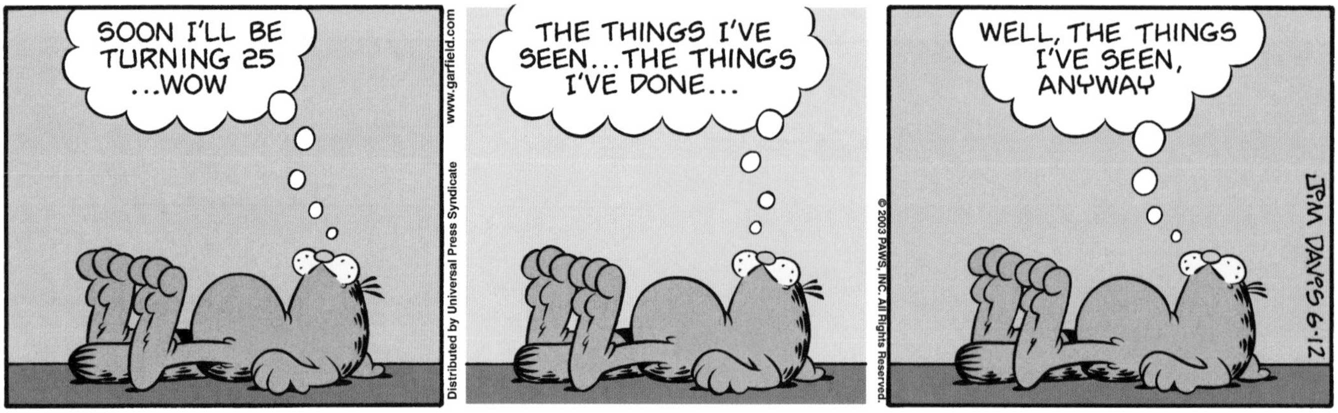
SOON I'LL BE TURNING 25 ...WOW
www.garfield.com
Distributed by Universal Press Syndicate
THE THINGS I'VE SEEN...THE THINGS I'VE DONE...
© 2003 PAWS, INC. All Rights Reserved.
WELL, THE THINGS I'VE SEEN, ANYWAY
JIM DAVIS 6-12

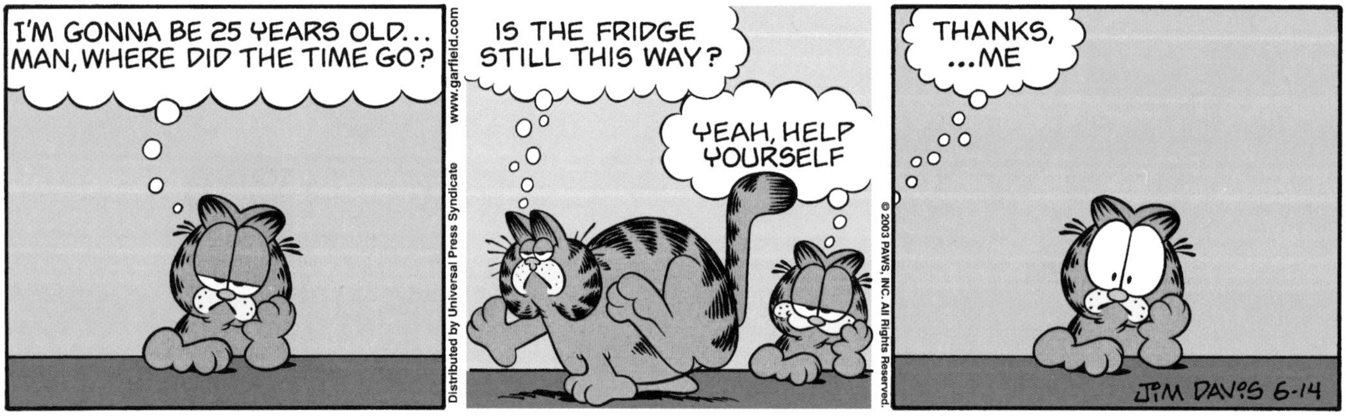
I'M GONNA BE 25 YEARS OLD... MAN, WHERE DID THE TIME GO?
www.garfield.com
Distributed by Universal Press Syndicate
IS THE FRIDGE STILL THIS WAY?
YEAH, HELP YOURSELF
© 2003 PAWS, INC. All Rights Reserved.
THANKS, ...ME
JIM DAVIS 6-14

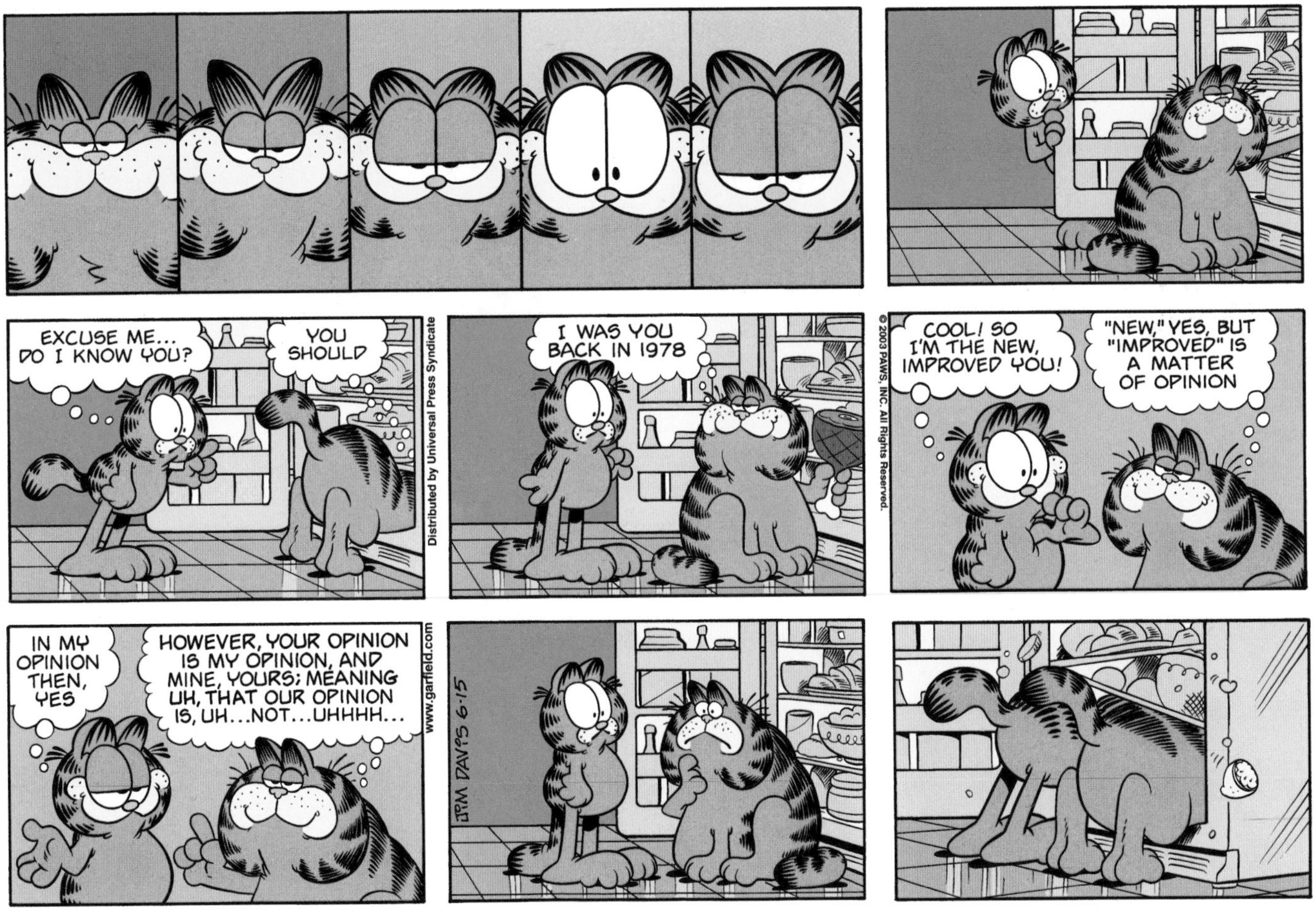
EXCUSE ME... DO I KNOW YOU?
YOU SHOULD
Distributed by Universal Press Syndicate
I WAS YOU BACK IN 1978
© 2003 PAWS, INC. All Rights Reserved.
COOL! SO I'M THE NEW, IMPROVED YOU!
"NEW," YES, BUT "IMPROVED" IS A MATTER OF OPINION
IN MY OPINION THEN, YES
HOWEVER, YOUR OPINION IS MY OPINION, AND MINE, YOURS; MEANING UH, THAT OUR OPINION IS, UH...NOT...UHHHH...
www.garfield.com

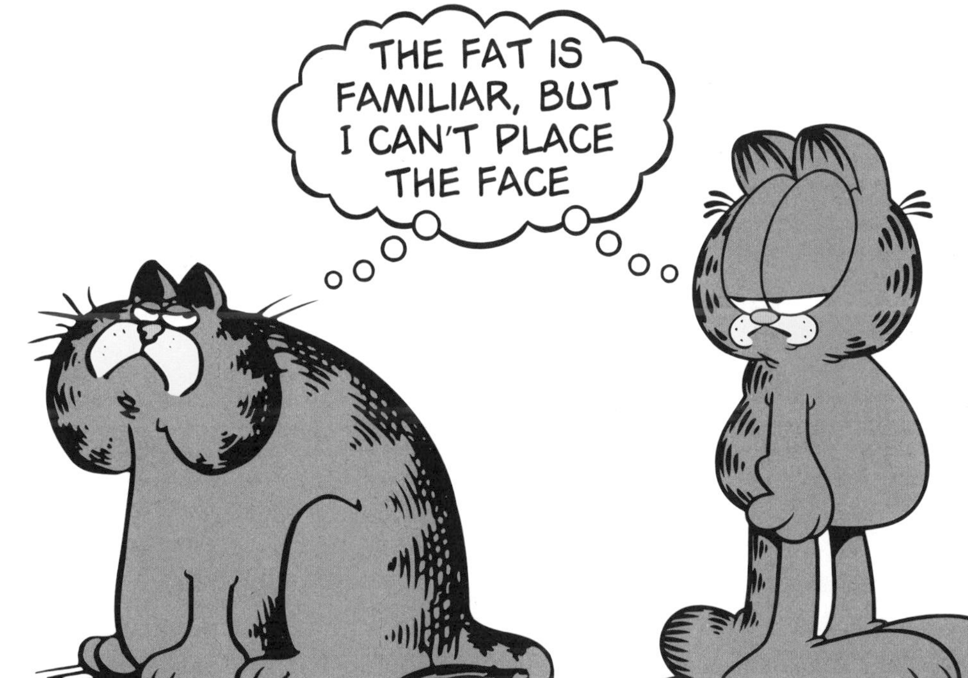
THE FAT IS FAMILIAR, BUT I CAN'T PLACE THE FACE

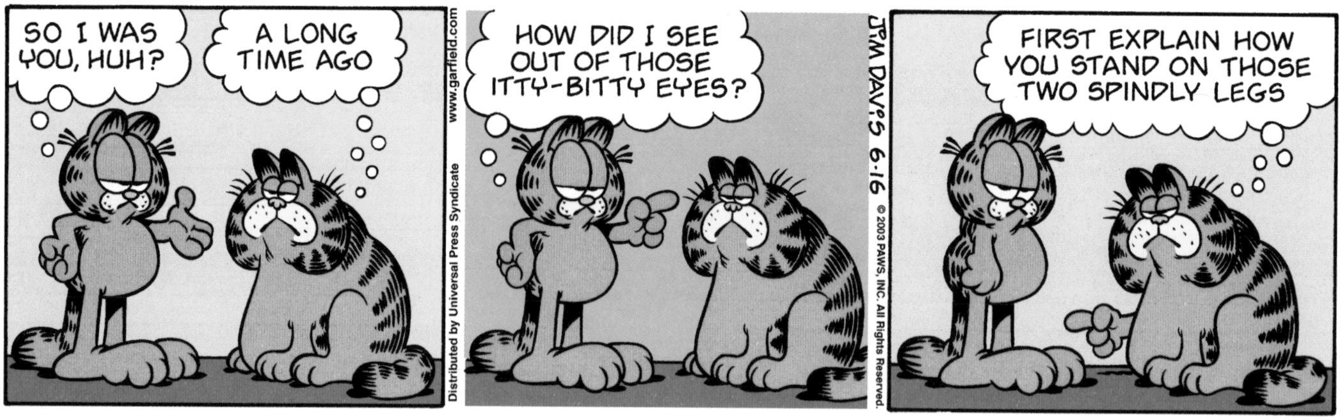
SO I WAS YOU, HUH?
A LONG TIME AGO
HOW DID I SEE OUT OF THOSE ITTY-BITTY EYES?
FIRST EXPLAIN HOW YOU STAND ON THOSE TWO SPINDLY LEGS
www.garfield.com
Distributed by Universal Press Syndicate
JIM DAVIS 6-16
© 2003 PAWS, INC. All Rights Reserved.

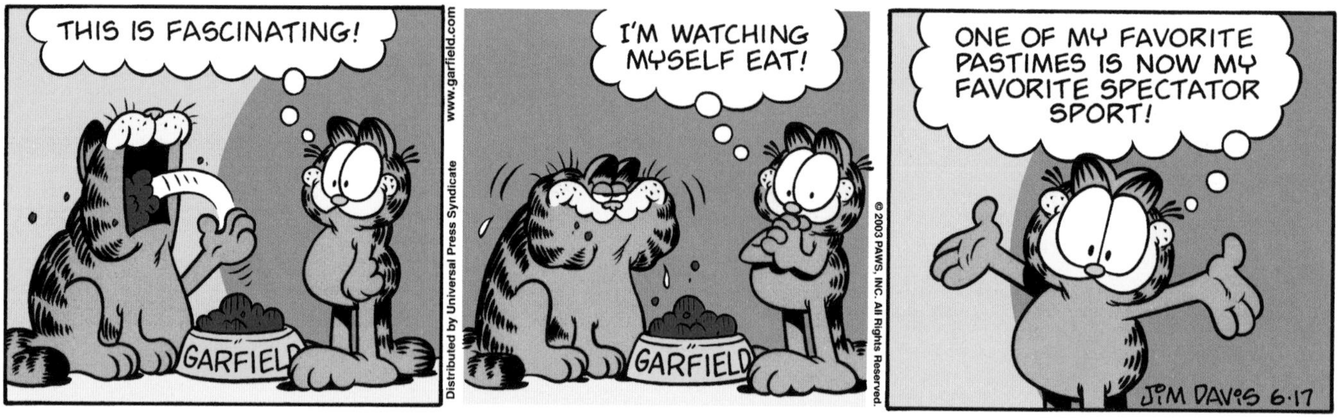
THIS IS FASCINATING!
GARFIELD
I'M WATCHING MYSELF EAT!
GARFIELD
ONE OF MY FAVORITE PASTIMES IS NOW MY FAVORITE SPECTATOR SPORT!
www.garfield.com
Distributed by Universal Press Syndicate
© 2003 PAWS, INC. All Rights Reserved.
JIM DAVIS 6-17

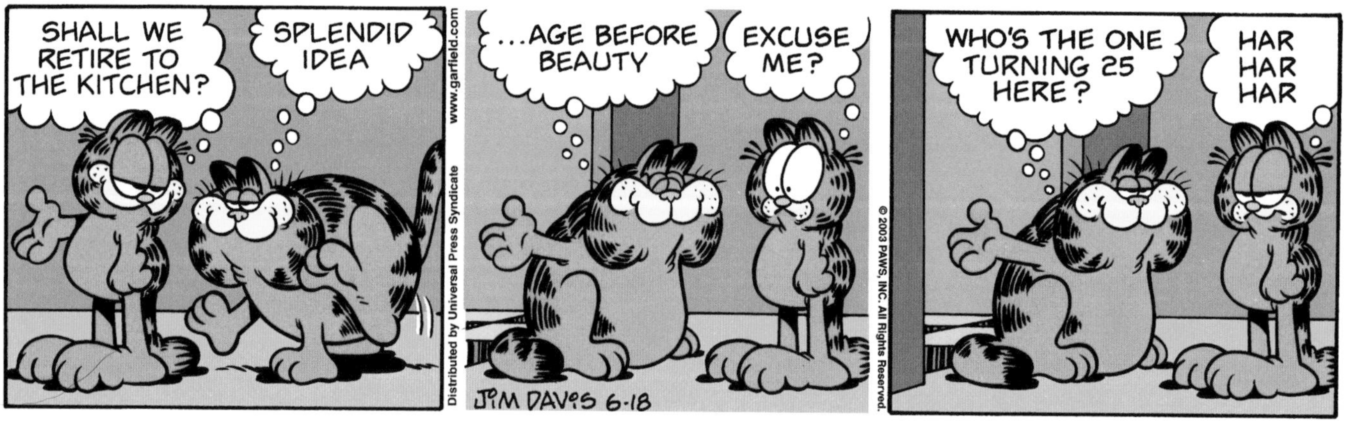
SHALL WE RETIRE TO THE KITCHEN?
SPLENDID IDEA
...AGE BEFORE BEAUTY
EXCUSE ME?
WHO'S THE ONE TURNING 25 HERE?
HAR HAR HAR
www.garfield.com
Distributed by Universal Press Syndicate
JIM DAVIS 6-18
© 2003 PAWS, INC. All Rights Reserved.

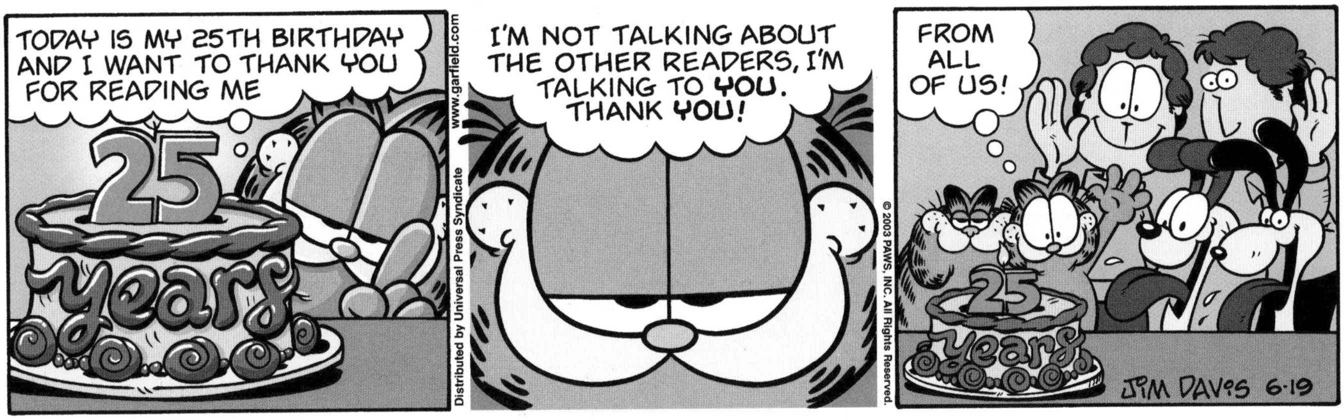
TODAY IS MY 25TH BIRTHDAY AND I WANT TO THANK YOU FOR READING ME
25 years
I'M NOT TALKING ABOUT THE OTHER READERS, I'M TALKING TO YOU. THANK YOU!
FROM ALL OF US!
JIM DAVIS 6·19
www.garfield.com
Distributed by Universal Press Syndicate
© 2003 PAWS, INC. All Rights Reserved.

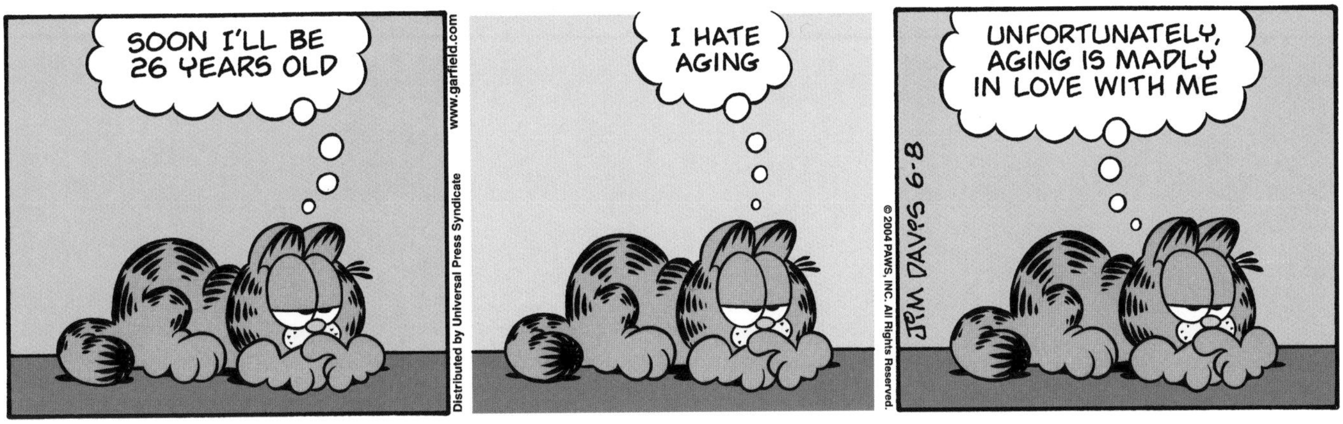
SOON I'LL BE 26 YEARS OLD
I HATE AGING
UNFORTUNATELY, AGING IS MADLY IN LOVE WITH ME
JIM DAVIS 6-8
www.garfield.com
Distributed by Universal Press Syndicate
© 2004 PAWS, INC. All Rights Reserved.

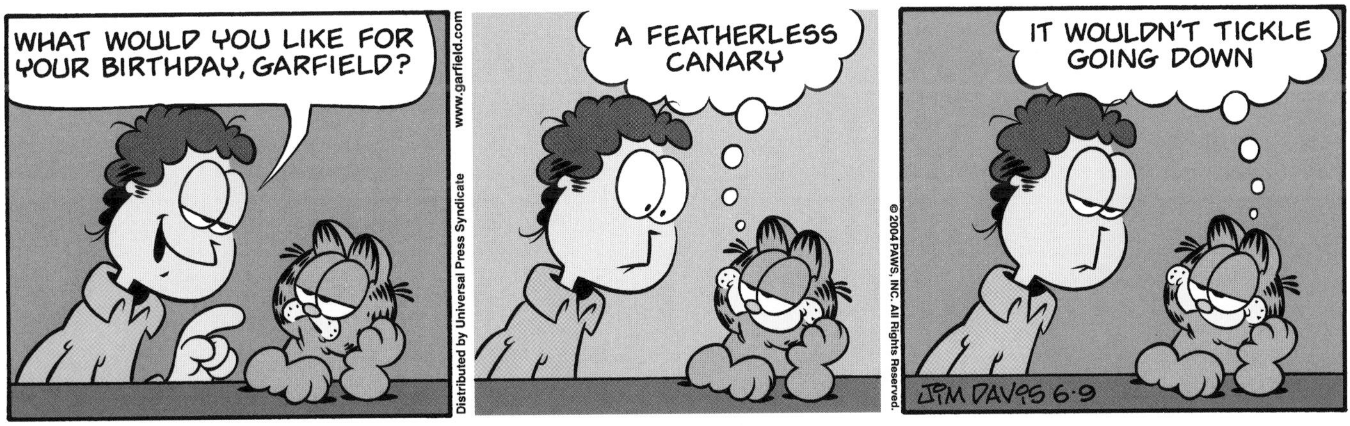
WHAT WOULD YOU LIKE FOR YOUR BIRTHDAY, GARFIELD?
A FEATHERLESS CANARY
IT WOULDN'T TICKLE GOING DOWN
JIM DAVIS 6-9
www.garfield.com
Distributed by Universal Press Syndicate
© 2004 PAWS, INC. All Rights Reserved.

You Know You're Getting Old When...

SOME THINGS DO IMPROVE WITH AGE

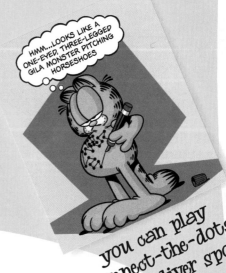

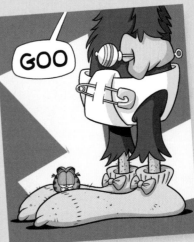

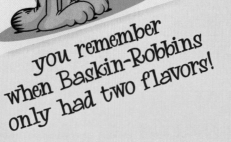

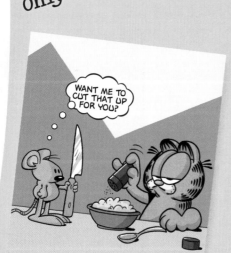

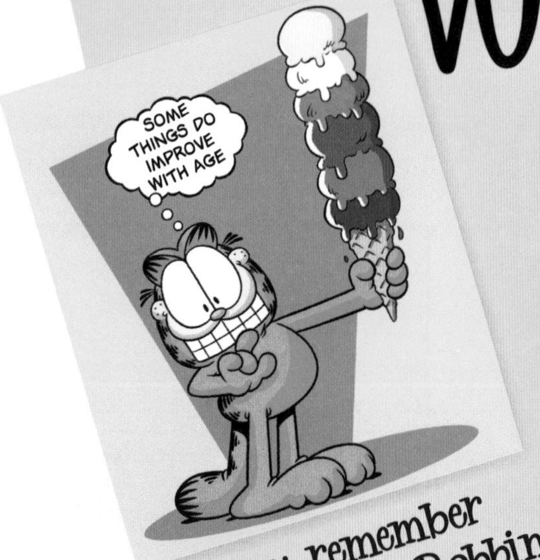

you remember
when Baskin-Robbins
only had two flavors!

GOO

you knew Bigfoot
when he wore booties!

WANT ME TO CUT THAT UP FOR YOU?

you put tenderizer
on your oatmeal!

HMM...LOOKS LIKE A ONE-EYED, THREE-LEGGED GILA MONSTER PITCHING HORSESHOES

you can play
connect-the-dots
on your liver spots!

It's hard to be nostalgic when you can't remember anything.

Gone fishin'

PEOPLE LOVE ME... KNOW WHY?
JIM DAVIS 6·12
www.garfield.com
Distributed by Universal Press Syndicate
BECAUSE I'M CUTE, THAT'S WHY! AND YOU........
© 2004 PAWS, INC. All Rights Reserved.
WELL, YOU'RE DETERIORATING
I WONDER HOW HIGH "CUTE" BOUNCES?

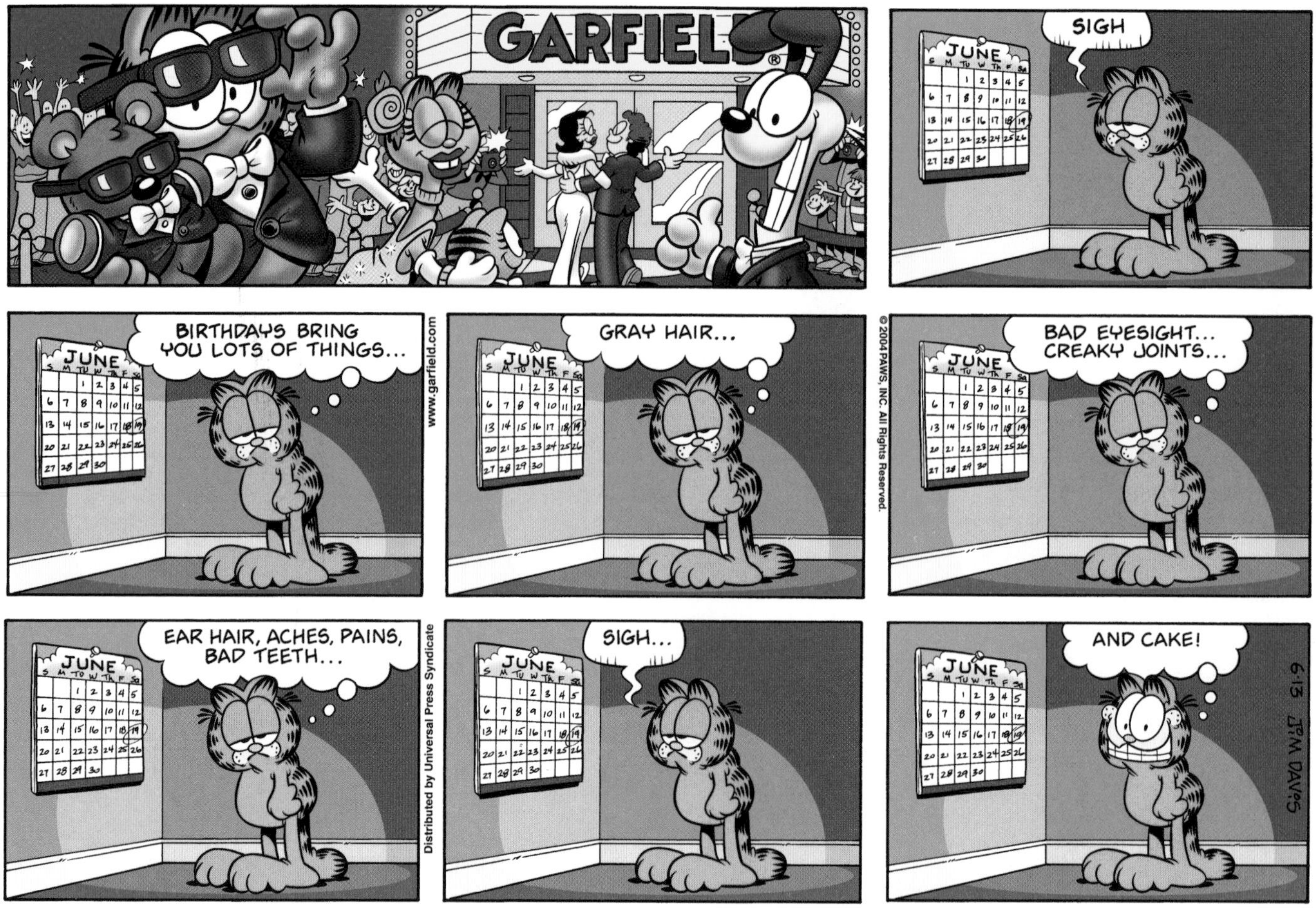
GARFIELD
SIGH
BIRTHDAYS BRING YOU LOTS OF THINGS...
GRAY HAIR...
BAD EYESIGHT... CREAKY JOINTS...
EAR HAIR, ACHES, PAINS, BAD TEETH...
SIGH...
AND CAKE!
JUNE
www.garfield.com
© 2004 PAWS, INC. All Rights Reserved.
Distributed by Universal Press Syndicate
6-13 JIM DAVIS

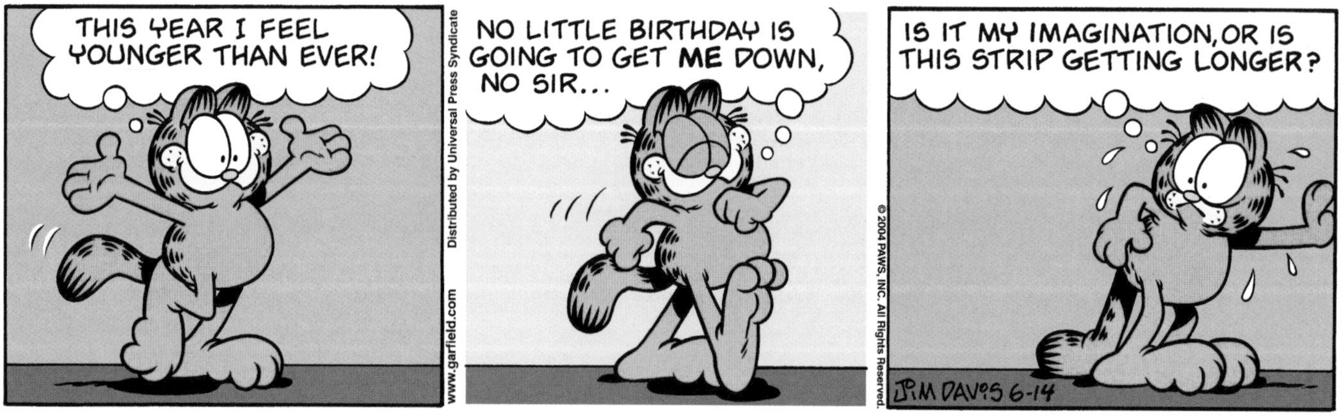
THIS YEAR I FEEL YOUNGER THAN EVER!
NO LITTLE BIRTHDAY IS GOING TO GET ME DOWN, NO SIR...
IS IT MY IMAGINATION, OR IS THIS STRIP GETTING LONGER?
www.garfield.com
Distributed by Universal Press Syndicate
© 2004 PAWS, INC. All Rights Reserved.
JIM DAVIS 6-14

SO WHAT, SO YOU'RE GOING TO BE 26...
-TIME MARCHES ON!
COME BACK!
JIM DAVIS 6-15
www.garfield.com
Distributed by Universal Press Syndicate
© 2004 PAWS, INC. All Rights Reserved.

AGE IS A STATE OF MIND
WITH A HEALTHY DOSE OF DENIAL
JIM DAVIS 6-17
www.garfield.com
Distributed by Universal Press Syndicate
© 2004 PAWS, INC. All Rights Reserved.

AGE IS A STATE OF MIND... WITH A HEALTHY DOSE OF DENIAL.

YOU LIE!
Happy Birthda

Garfield Birthday Trivia

Take a deep breath and try to blow out these burning questions!

1. **Which of these celebrities does NOT share a June 19 birthday with Garfield?**
A.   Zoe Saldana
B.   Carlos Santana
C.   Dirk Nowitzki
D.   Macklemore

2. **What did Jon get Garfield for his second birthday?**
A.   A hideous kitty sweater
B.   An inflatable Odie punching bag
C.   Chewing tobacco
D.   A surprise party

3. **What uninvited guest crashed Garfield's birthday party?**
A.   A tailless donkey
B.   A spider with chutzpah
C.   A warthog with halitosis
D.   A morbidly obese hippo

4. **What did Garfield do when he turned thirteen?**
A.   Got a Guns N' Roses tattoo
B.   Got a kiss from Julia Roberts
C.   Celebrated his bar mitzvah
D.   Found his first gray hair and dyed it

5. **What did Jon's mom send Garfield for his 16th birthday?**
A.   Chicken pot pie—with a live chicken
B.   A crocheted birthday card
C.   A Russian mail-order bride
D.   Pork butt on a stick

6. How did Jon celebrate his 18th birthday?
A. Cow tipping
B. Disco square dancing
C. Making moonshine
D. Watching *The Beverly Hillbillies*

7. What did Garfield want for his 18th birthday?
A. An 18-layer cake
B. A can opener
C. Catnip
D. A fake ID

8. On Jon's 21st birthday, down on the farm, what game did they play?
A. Musical milking stools
B. Cowpie toss
C. Pin the tail on the donkey—with a real donkey
D. Chess

9. What did Garfield want for his 30th birthday?
A. A time machine
B. A trust fund
C. A 30-foot-long cheese coney
D. A glow-in-the-dark litter box

10. On Jon's birthday, what did Garfield give him that wasn't wrapped?
A. A majestic hairball
B. A heartfelt hug
C. A mani-pedi
D. A big proud **BURP!**

11. What did Liz give Jon for his birthday?
A. Rhinestone-studded socks
B. Breath mints
C. A flea dip
D. A kiss

12. What did Garfield think Jon should get Liz for her birthday?
A. Lip reduction surgery
B. A date with Trevor Noah
C. Tuna
D. Cash

Answers:

1. B. 2. D. 3. B. 4. D. 5. B. 6. A. 7. B. 8. C. 9. A. 10. D. 11. D. 12. C.

You're not born lazy...

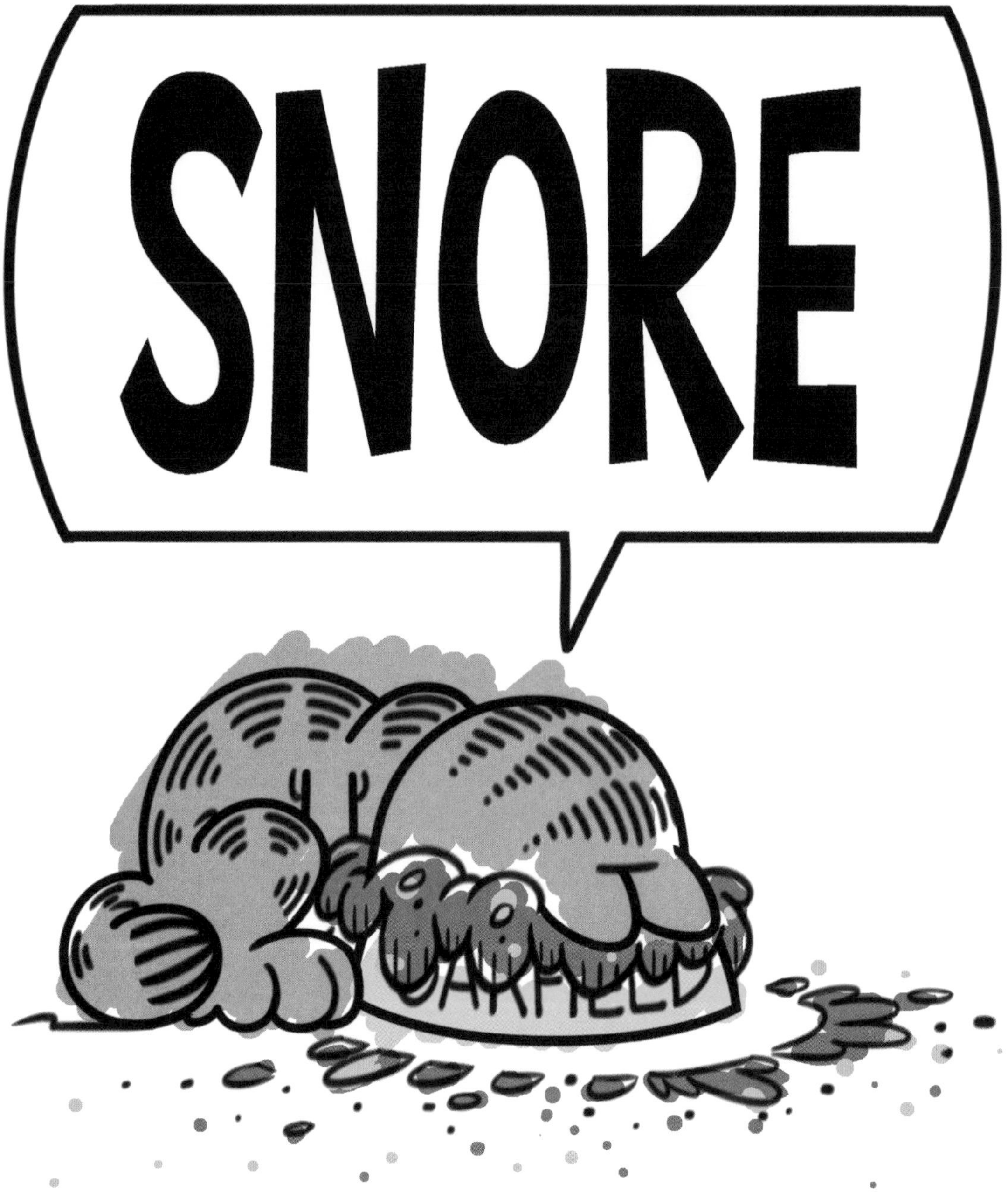
SNORE

it's an acquired skill

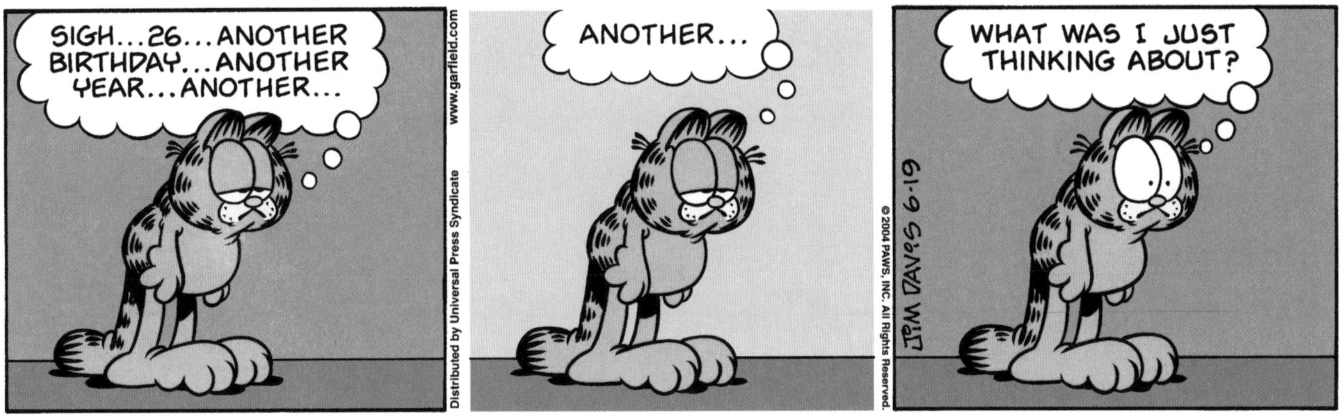
SIGH...26...ANOTHER BIRTHDAY...ANOTHER YEAR...ANOTHER...
ANOTHER...
WHAT WAS I JUST THINKING ABOUT?

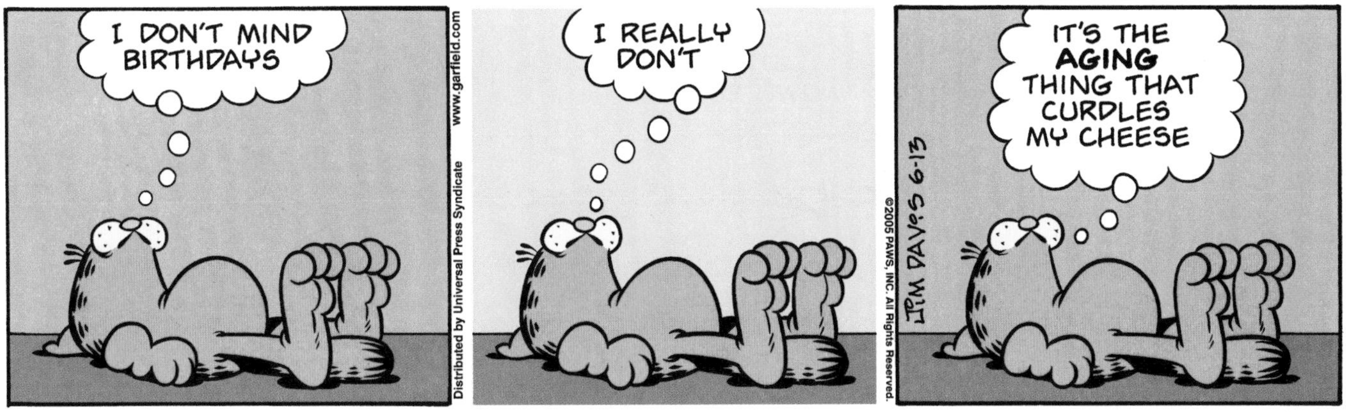
I DON'T MIND BIRTHDAYS
I REALLY DON'T
IT'S THE **AGING** THING THAT CURDLES MY CHEESE

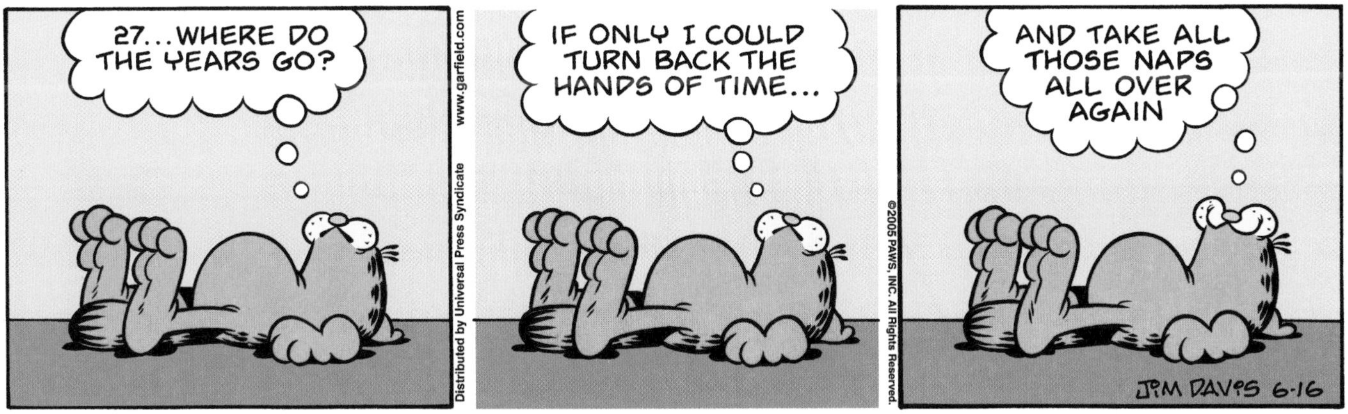
27...WHERE DO THE YEARS GO?
IF ONLY I COULD TURN BACK THE HANDS OF TIME...
AND TAKE ALL THOSE NAPS ALL OVER AGAIN

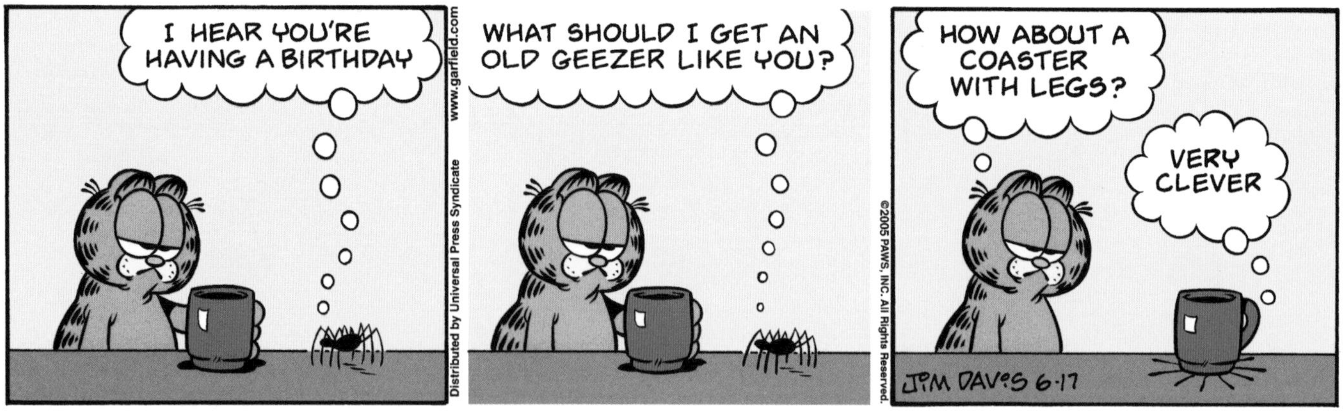
I HEAR YOU'RE HAVING A BIRTHDAY
www.garfield.com
Distributed by Universal Press Syndicate
WHAT SHOULD I GET AN OLD GEEZER LIKE YOU?
©2005 PAWS, INC. All Rights Reserved.
HOW ABOUT A COASTER WITH LEGS?
VERY CLEVER
JIM DAVIS 6-17

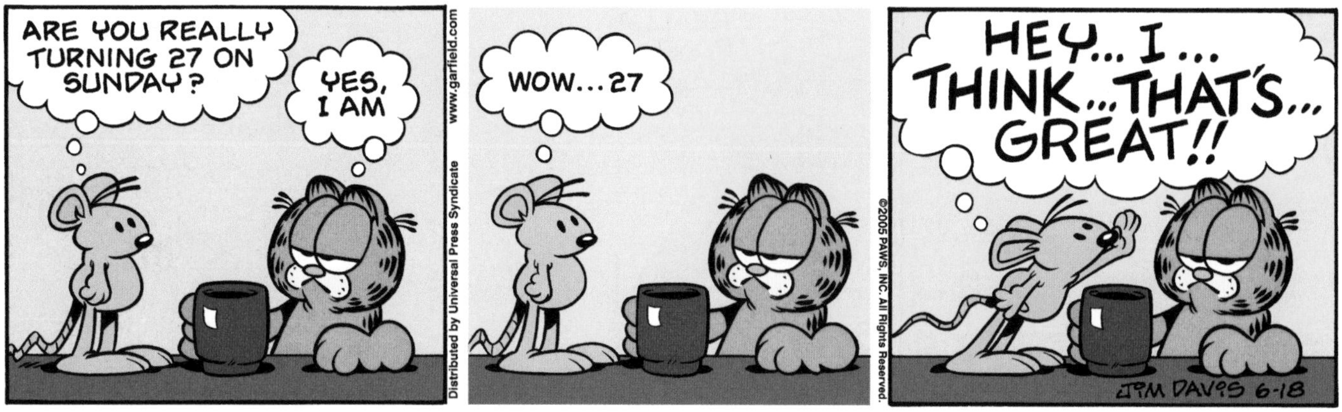
ARE YOU REALLY TURNING 27 ON SUNDAY?
YES, I AM
www.garfield.com
Distributed by Universal Press Syndicate
WOW...27
©2005 PAWS, INC. All Rights Reserved.
HEY... I... THINK...THAT'S... GREAT!!
JIM DAVIS 6-18

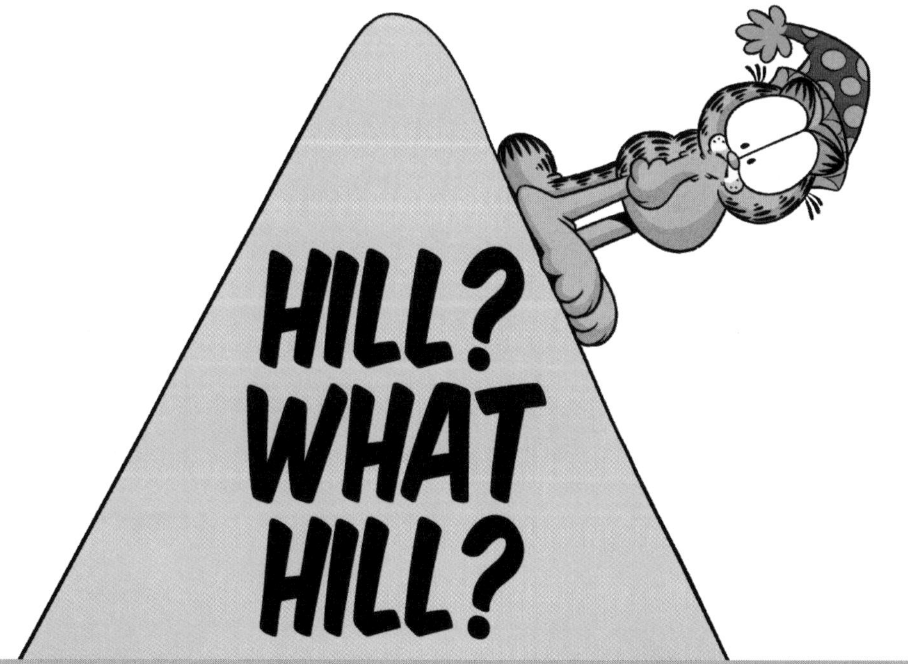
HILL? WHAT HILL?

THE SECRET TO SLOWING DOWN THE AGING PROCESS IS SPEEDING UP THE LYING PROCESS.

I'M 29, AND I HANG MY NOBEL PRIZE FROM THE MIRROR OF MY ROLLS ROYYY... FERRARI! YEAH, FERRARI, THAT'S THE TICKET...

GARFIELD
SIGH...
ANOTHER BIRTHDAY
Distributed by Universal Press Syndicate
THIS ONE'S NUMBER 27...
©2005 PAWS, INC. All Rights Reserved.
AND THAT'S PRETTY OLD FOR A CAT
IF ONLY THERE WERE SOMETHING I COULD DO...
www.garfield.com
YOU'RE WALKING BACKWARDS
IT'S ONLY A THEORY, BUT IT JUST MIGHT WORK
JIM DAVIS 6-19

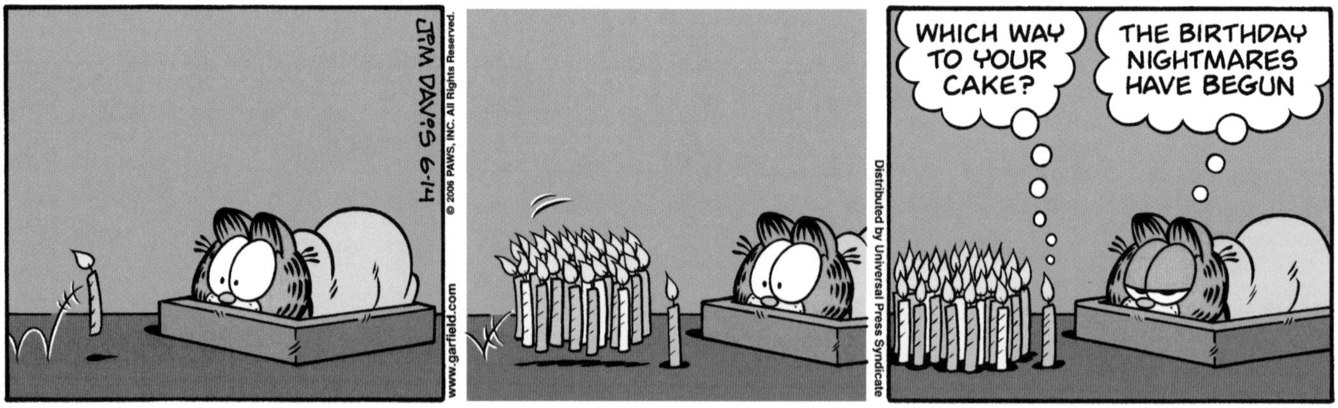
JIM DAVIS 6-14
© 2006 PAWS, INC. All Rights Reserved.
www.garfield.com
Distributed by Universal Press Syndicate
WHICH WAY TO YOUR CAKE?
THE BIRTHDAY NIGHTMARES HAVE BEGUN

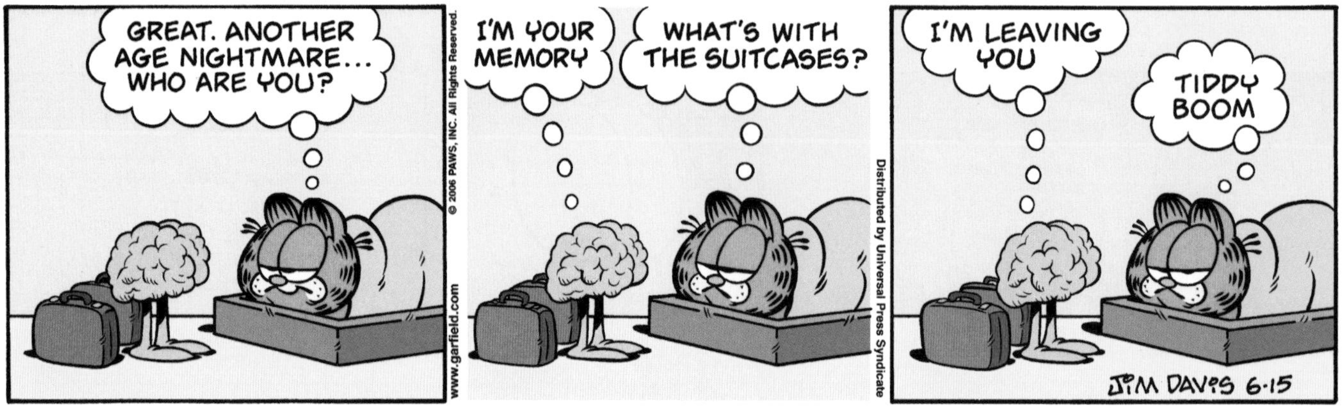
GREAT. ANOTHER AGE NIGHTMARE... WHO ARE YOU?
© 2006 PAWS, INC. All Rights Reserved.
www.garfield.com
I'M YOUR MEMORY
WHAT'S WITH THE SUITCASES?
Distributed by Universal Press Syndicate
I'M LEAVING YOU
TIDDY BOOM
JIM DAVIS 6-15

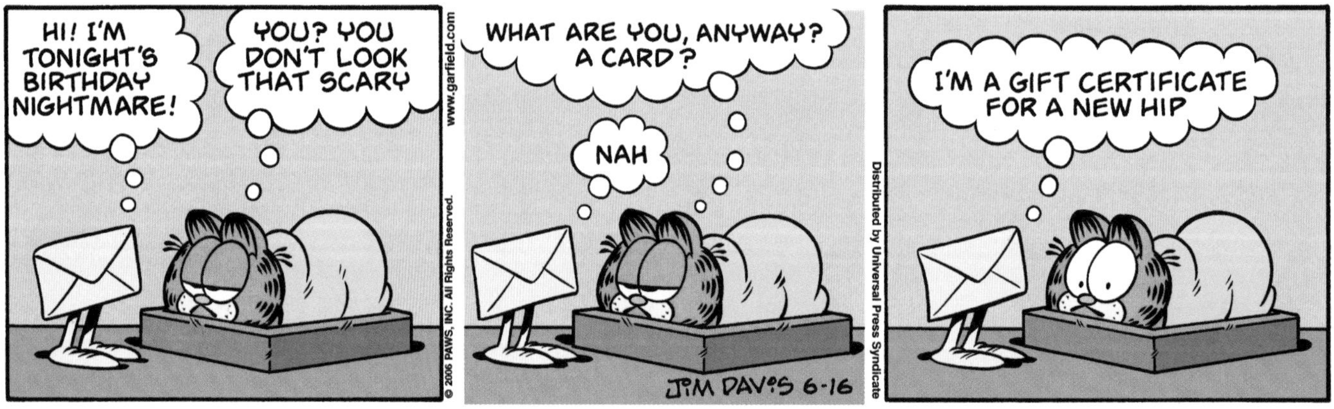
HI! I'M TONIGHT'S BIRTHDAY NIGHTMARE!
YOU? YOU DON'T LOOK THAT SCARY
www.garfield.com
© 2006 PAWS, INC. All Rights Reserved.
WHAT ARE YOU, ANYWAY? A CARD?
NAH
JIM DAVIS 6-16
Distributed by Universal Press Syndicate
I'M A GIFT CERTIFICATE FOR A NEW HIP

JPM DAVIS 6-17
© 2006 PAWS, INC. All Rights Reserved.
www.garfield.com
BETTER WISH FOR MORE SAND THIS YEAR
Distributed by Universal Press Syndicate
HEE HEE HEE
I HATE BIRTHDAY NIGHTMARES

AGE HAPPENS

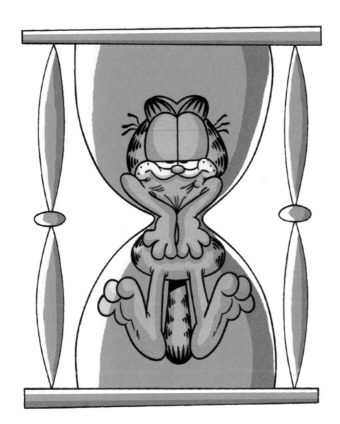

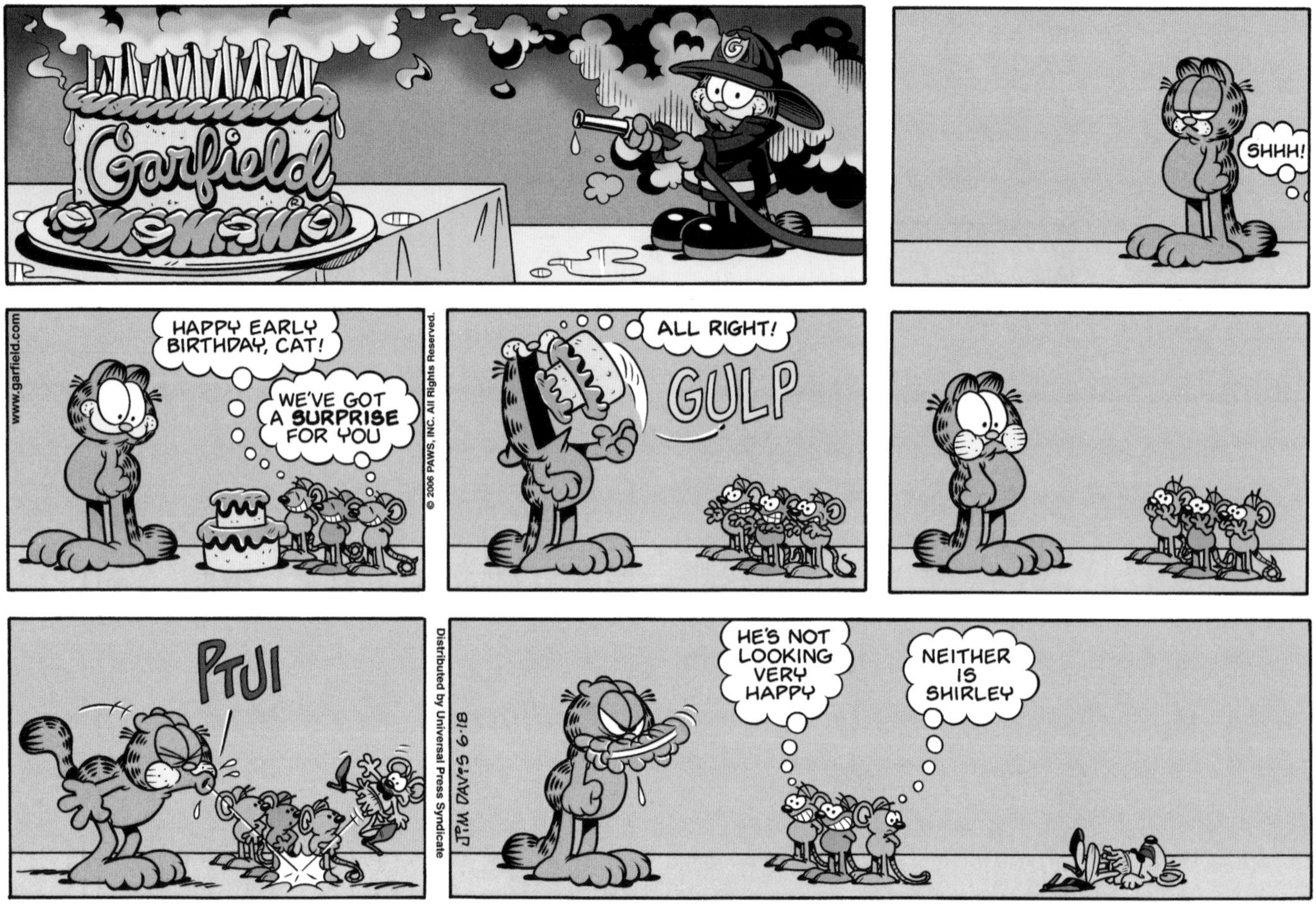
Garfield
SHHH!
www.garfield.com
HAPPY EARLY BIRTHDAY, CAT!
WE'VE GOT A **SURPRISE** FOR YOU
© 2006 PAWS, INC. All Rights Reserved.
ALL RIGHT!
GULP
PTUI
Distributed by Universal Press Syndicate
JIM DAVIS 6-18
HE'S NOT LOOKING VERY HAPPY
NEITHER IS SHIRLEY

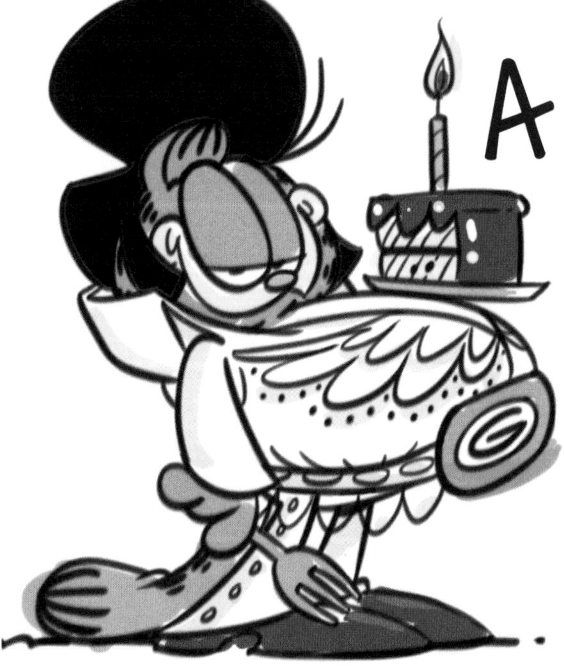

A HUNKA-HUNKA BURNIN' CAKE

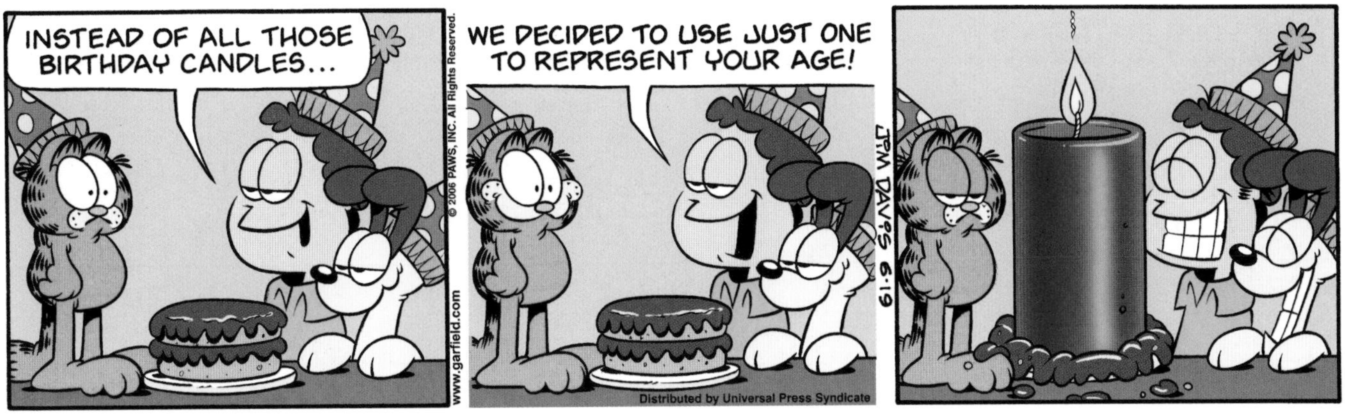
INSTEAD OF ALL THOSE BIRTHDAY CANDLES...
© 2006 PAWS, INC. All Rights Reserved.
www.garfield.com
WE DECIDED TO USE JUST ONE TO REPRESENT YOUR AGE!
Distributed by Universal Press Syndicate
JIM DAVIS 6-19

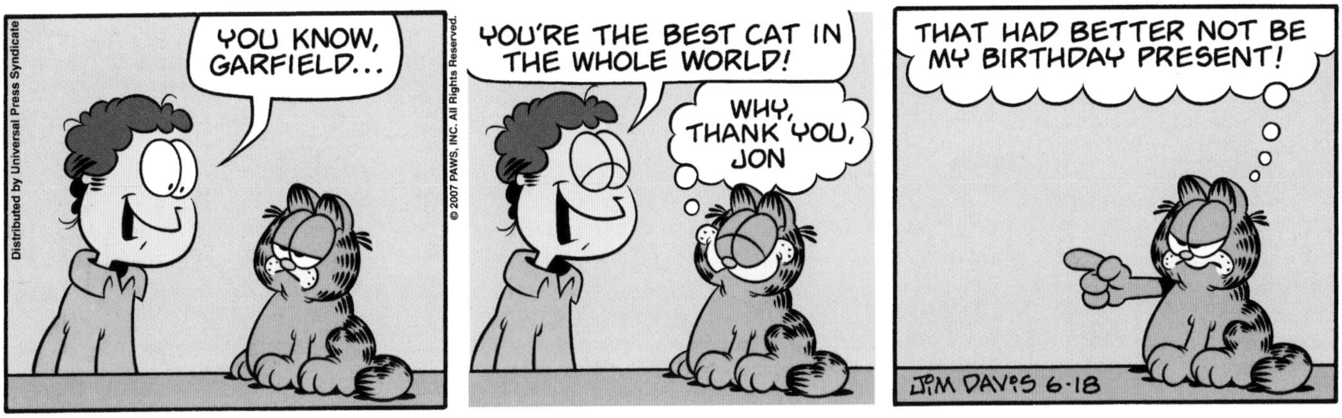
Distributed by Universal Press Syndicate
YOU KNOW, GARFIELD...
© 2007 PAWS, INC. All Rights Reserved.
YOU'RE THE BEST CAT IN THE WHOLE WORLD!
WHY, THANK YOU, JON
THAT HAD BETTER NOT BE MY BIRTHDAY PRESENT!
JIM DAVIS 6-18

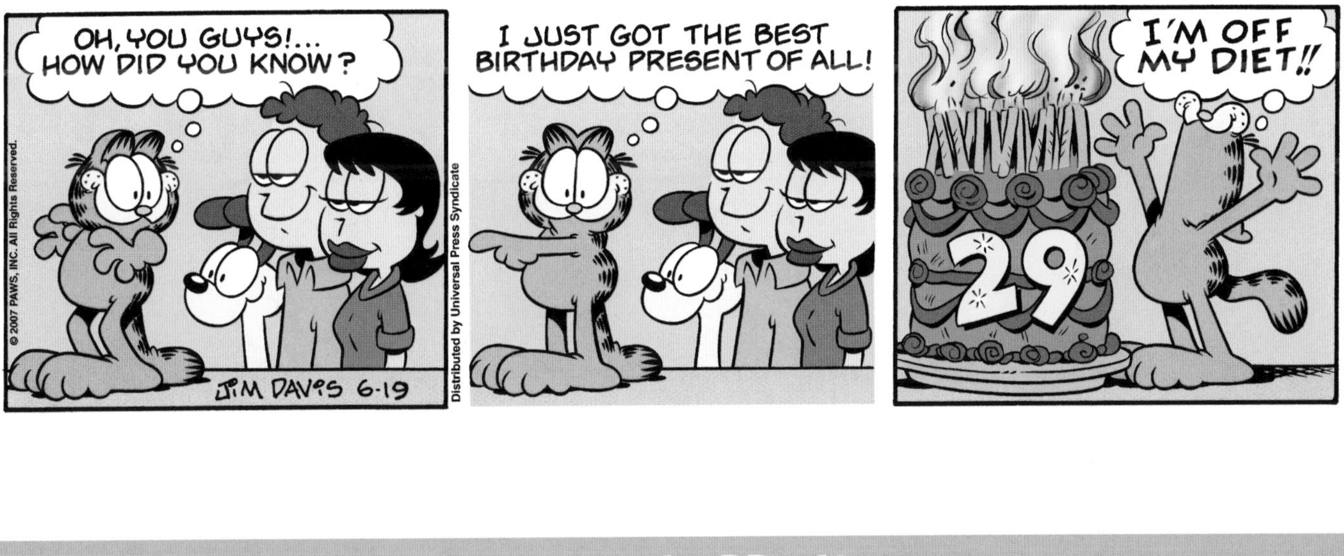
OH, YOU GUYS!... HOW DID YOU KNOW?
© 2007 PAWS, INC. All Rights Reserved.
JIM DAVIS 6-19
Distributed by Universal Press Syndicate
I JUST GOT THE BEST BIRTHDAY PRESENT OF ALL!
29
I'M OFF MY DIET!!

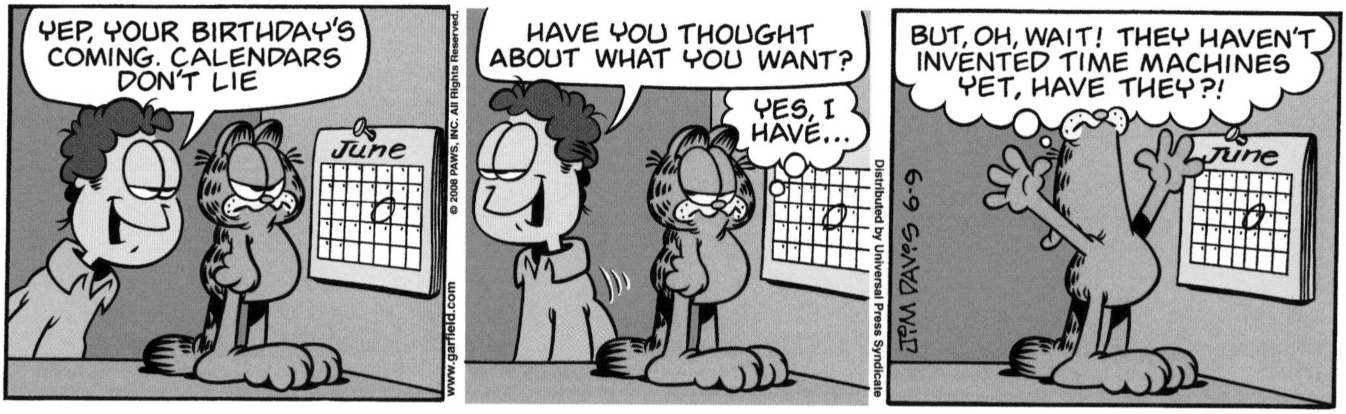
YEP, YOUR BIRTHDAY'S COMING. CALENDARS DON'T LIE
June
© 2008 PAWS, INC. All Rights Reserved.
www.garfield.com
HAVE YOU THOUGHT ABOUT WHAT YOU WANT?
YES, I HAVE...
Distributed by Universal Press Syndicate
JIM DAVIS 6-9
BUT, OH, WAIT! THEY HAVEN'T INVENTED TIME MACHINES YET, HAVE THEY?!
June

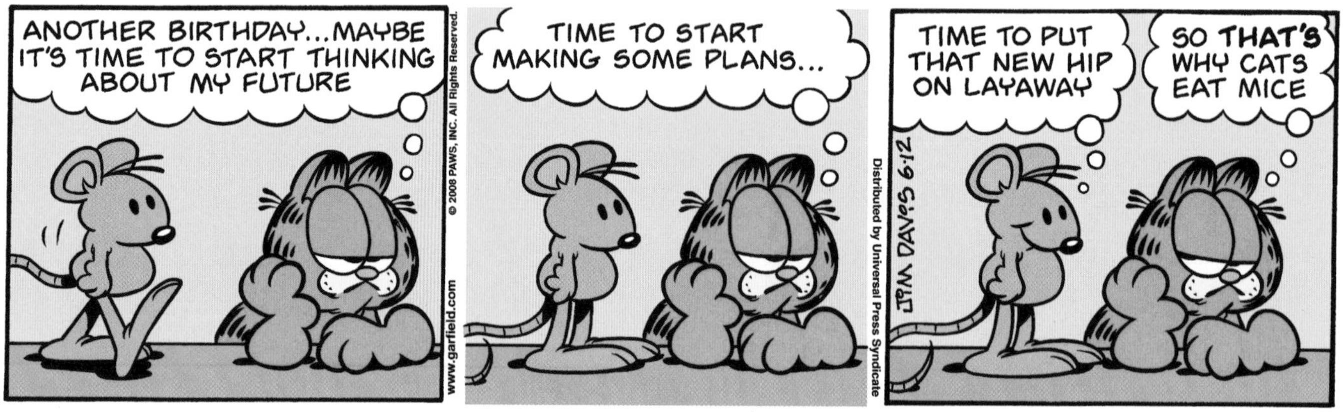
ANOTHER BIRTHDAY...MAYBE IT'S TIME TO START THINKING ABOUT MY FUTURE
© 2008 PAWS, INC. All Rights Reserved.
www.garfield.com
TIME TO START MAKING SOME PLANS...
Distributed by Universal Press Syndicate
JIM DAVIS 6-12
TIME TO PUT THAT NEW HIP ON LAYAWAY
SO THAT'S WHY CATS EAT MICE

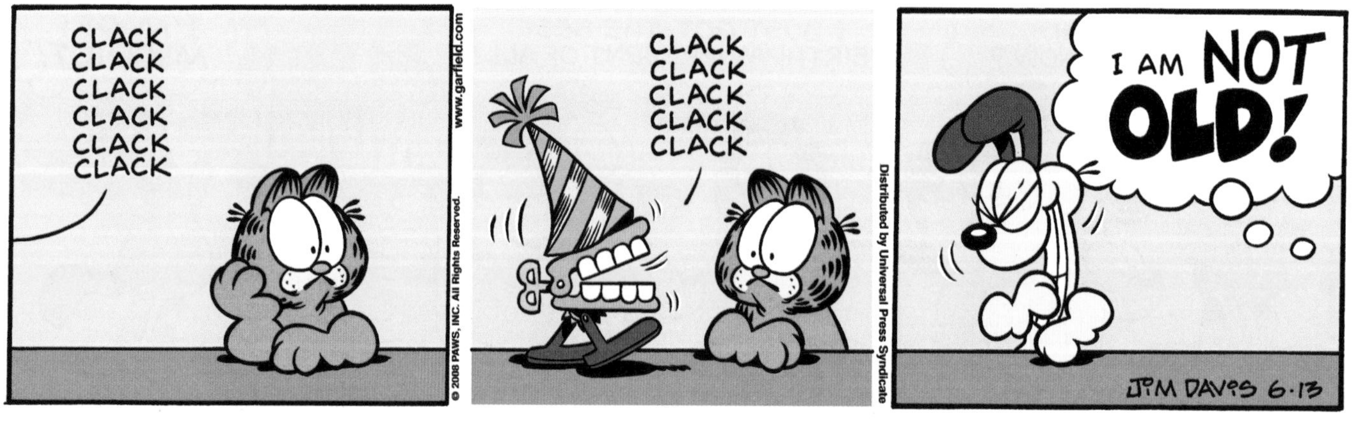
CLACK CLACK CLACK CLACK CLACK CLACK
www.garfield.com
© 2008 PAWS, INC. All Rights Reserved.
CLACK CLACK CLACK CLACK CLACK
Distributed by Universal Press Syndicate
I AM NOT OLD!
JIM DAVIS 6-13

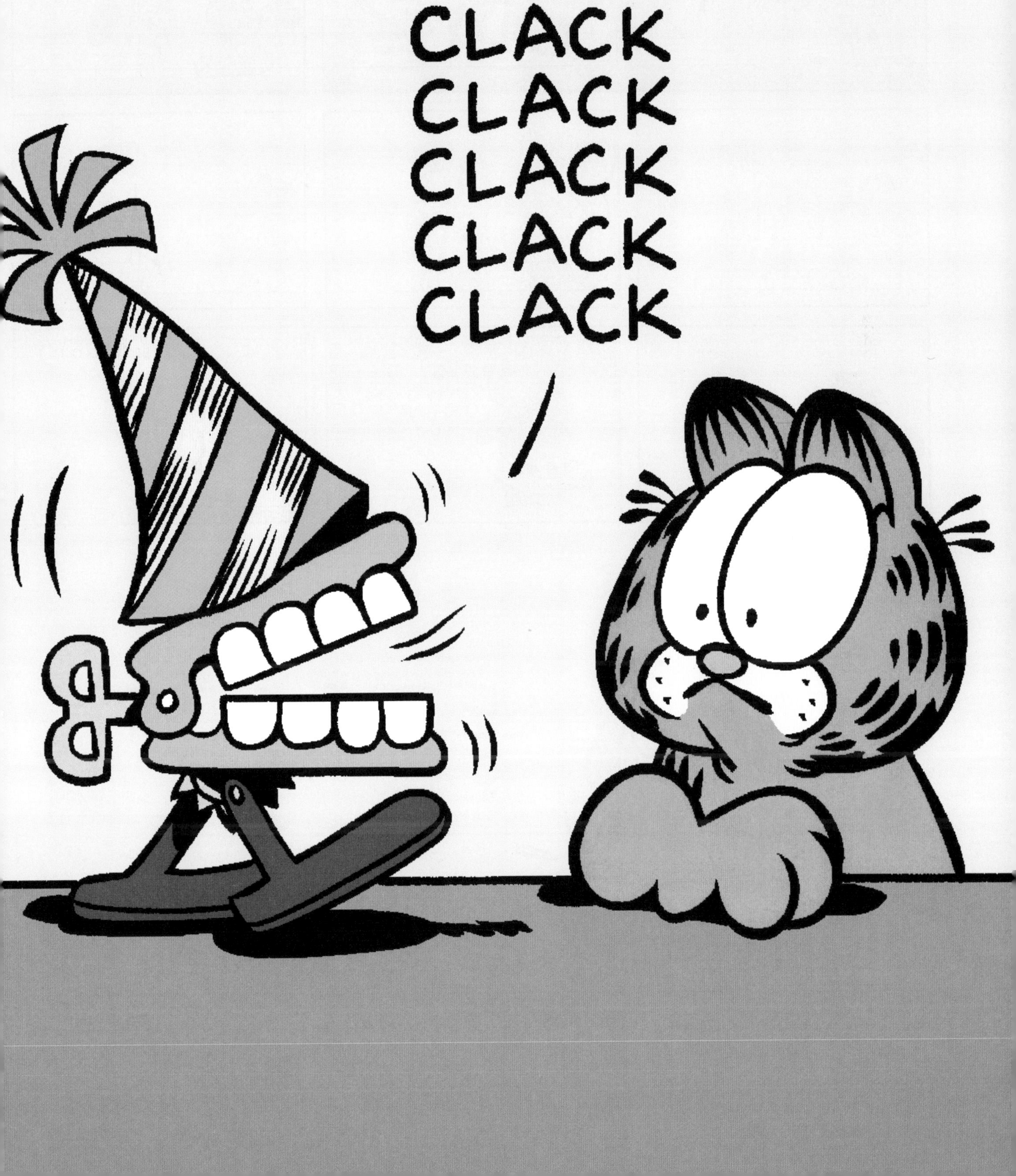
CLACK
CLACK
CLACK
CLACK
CLACK

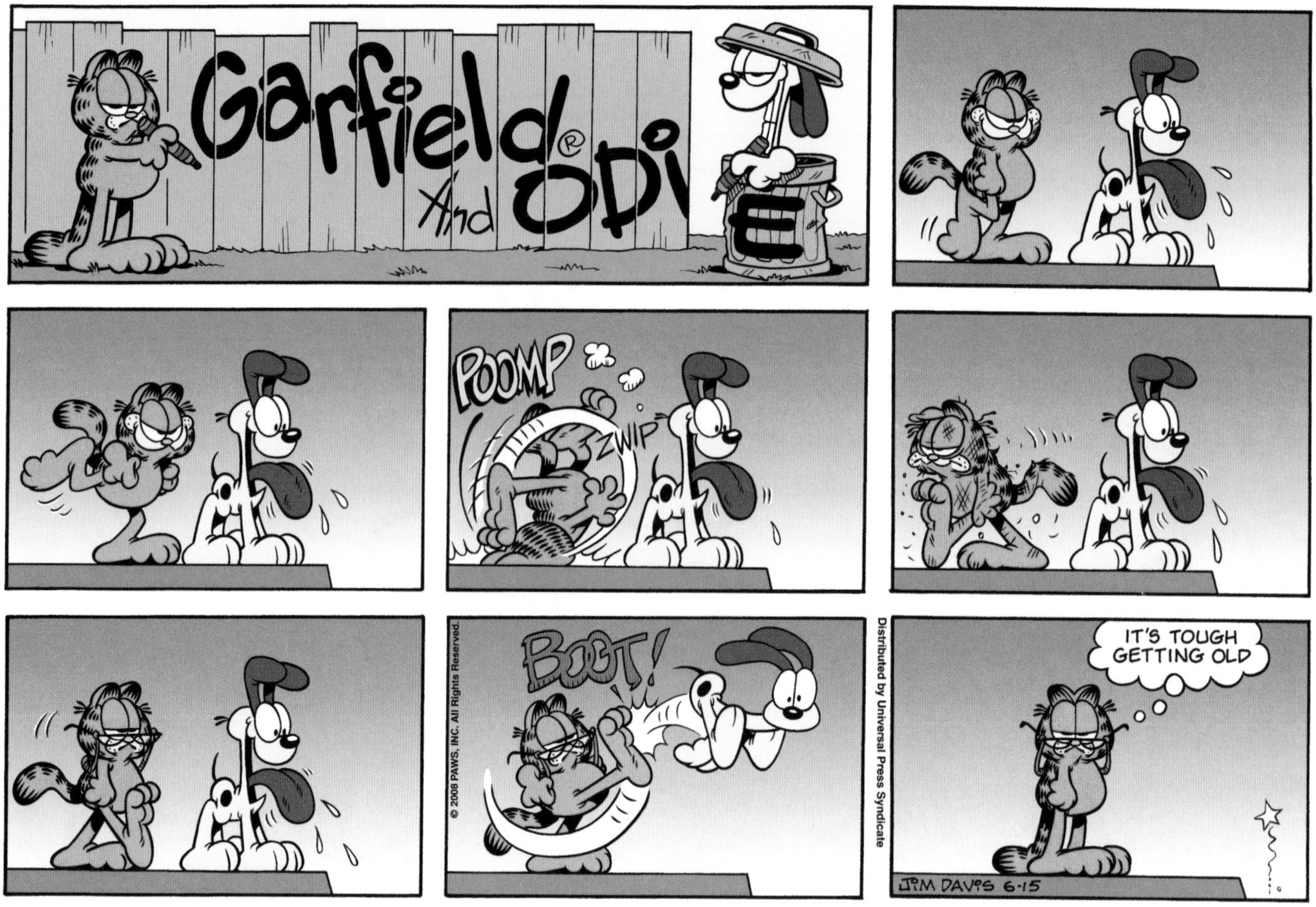

Garfield And ODIE
POOMP
ZWIP
BOOT!
IT'S TOUGH GETTING OLD
© 2008 PAWS, INC. All Rights Reserved.
Distributed by Universal Press Syndicate
JIM DAVIS 6-15

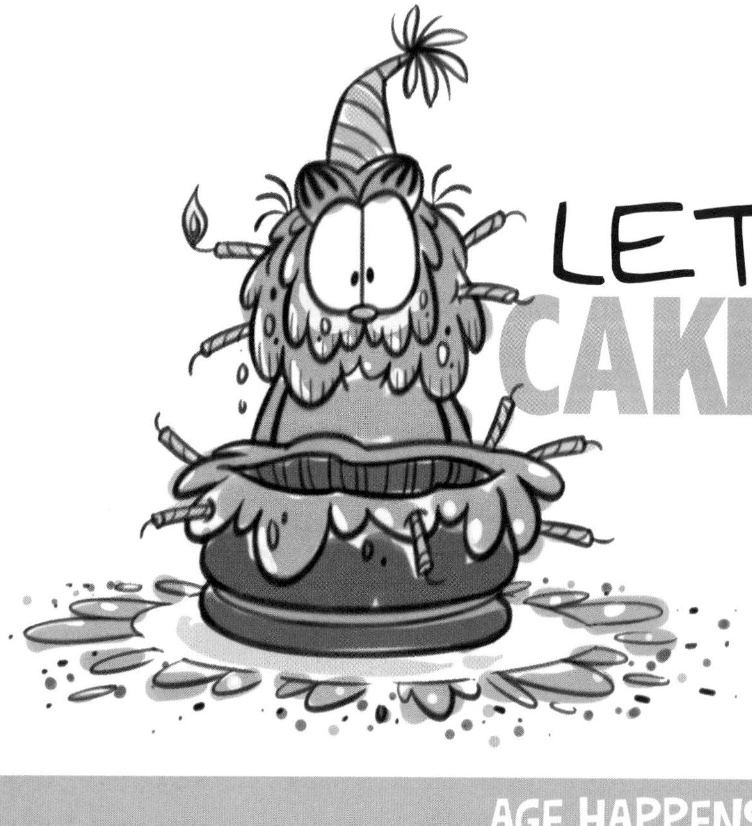

LET'S GET CAKE-FACED!

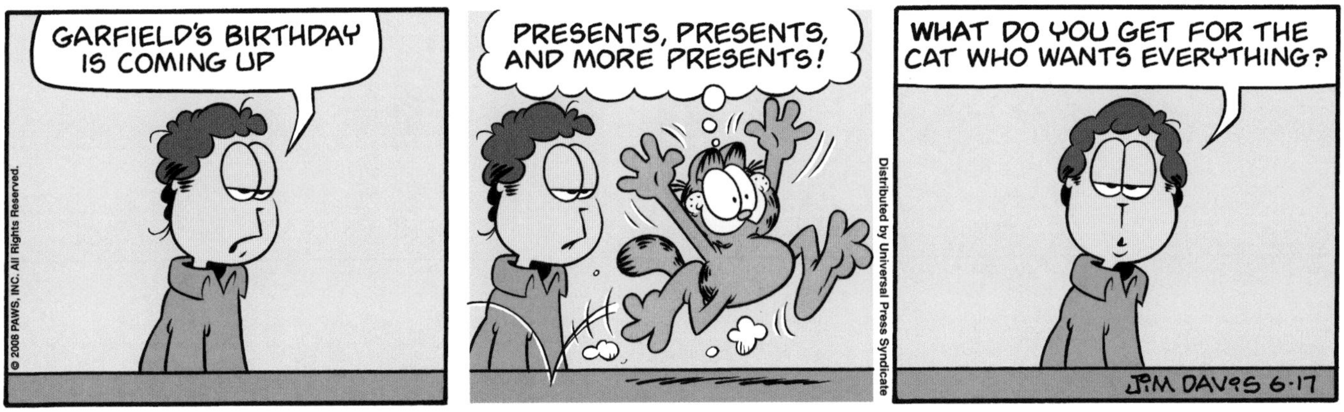
GARFIELD'S BIRTHDAY IS COMING UP
PRESENTS, PRESENTS, AND MORE PRESENTS!
WHAT DO YOU GET FOR THE CAT WHO WANTS EVERYTHING?
JIM DAVIS 6-17
© 2008 PAWS, INC. All Rights Reserved.
Distributed by Universal Press Syndicate

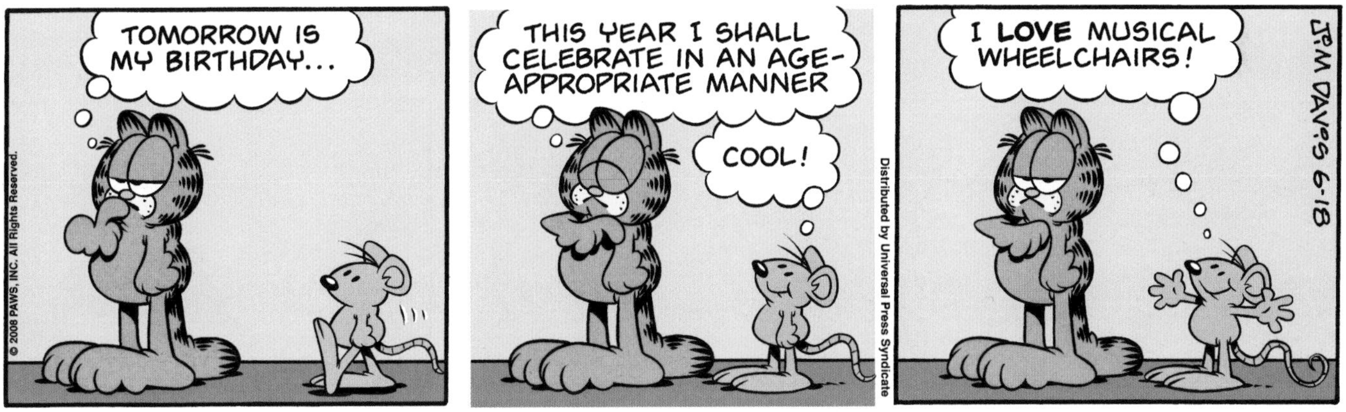
TOMORROW IS MY BIRTHDAY...
THIS YEAR I SHALL CELEBRATE IN AN AGE-APPROPRIATE MANNER
COOL!
I **LOVE** MUSICAL WHEELCHAIRS!
JIM DAVIS 6-18
© 2008 PAWS, INC. All Rights Reserved.
Distributed by Universal Press Syndicate

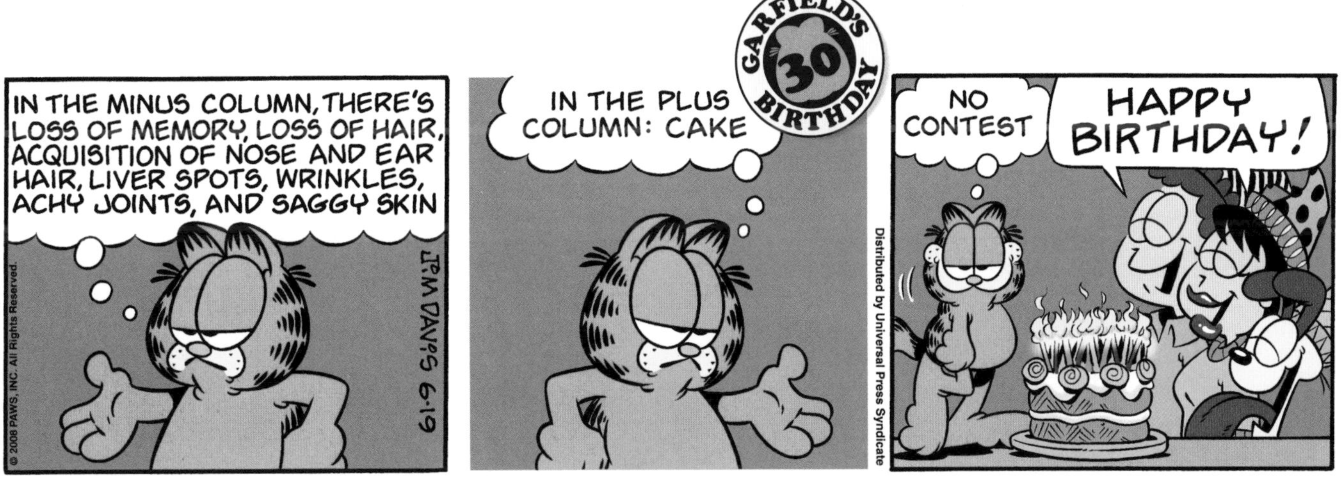
GARFIELD'S 30 BIRTHDAY
IN THE MINUS COLUMN, THERE'S LOSS OF MEMORY, LOSS OF HAIR, ACQUISITION OF NOSE AND EAR HAIR, LIVER SPOTS, WRINKLES, ACHY JOINTS, AND SAGGY SKIN
IN THE PLUS COLUMN: CAKE
NO CONTEST
HAPPY BIRTHDAY!
JIM DAVIS 6-19
© 2008 PAWS, INC. All Rights Reserved.
Distributed by Universal Press Syndicate

AGING... IT'S NOT PRETTY

GARFIELD
HEY, BIRTHDAY BOY!
WHA?...
WE'RE THE THINGS YOU HAVE TO LOOK FORWARD TO!
YEAH! I'M A GREY HAIR!
AND I'M A WRINKLE!
AND DON'T FORGET ME!
WHAT ARE YOU?
I'M A LIVER SPOT!
BUT I CAN'T **SEE** YOU
HI, GUYS! SORRY I'M LATE!
www.garfield.com
Distributed by Universal Press Syndicate
© 2009 PAWS, INC. All Rights Reserved.
JIM DAVIS 6-14

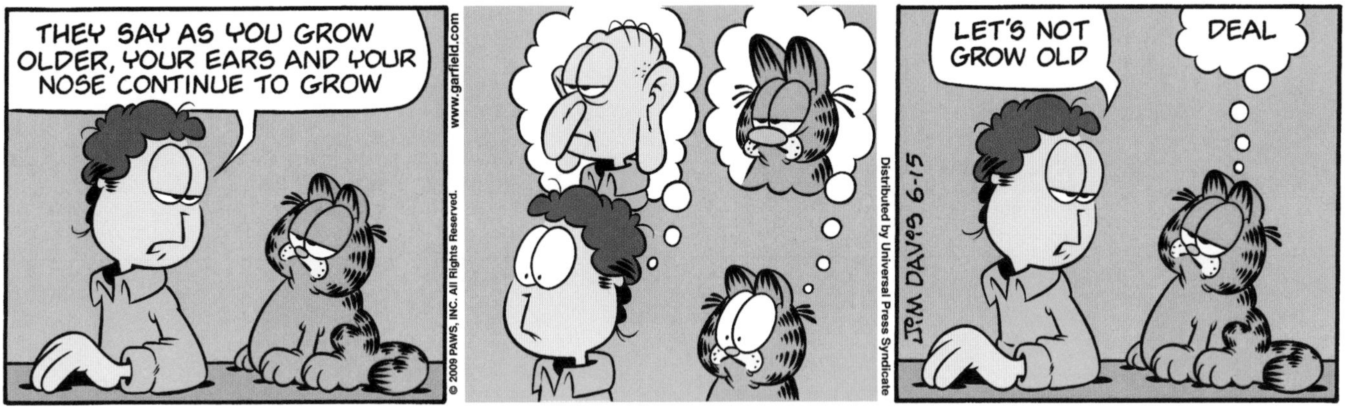
THEY SAY AS YOU GROW OLDER, YOUR EARS AND YOUR NOSE CONTINUE TO GROW
© 2009 PAWS, INC. All Rights Reserved. www.garfield.com
JPM DAVIS 6-15
Distributed by Universal Press Syndicate
LET'S NOT GROW OLD
DEAL

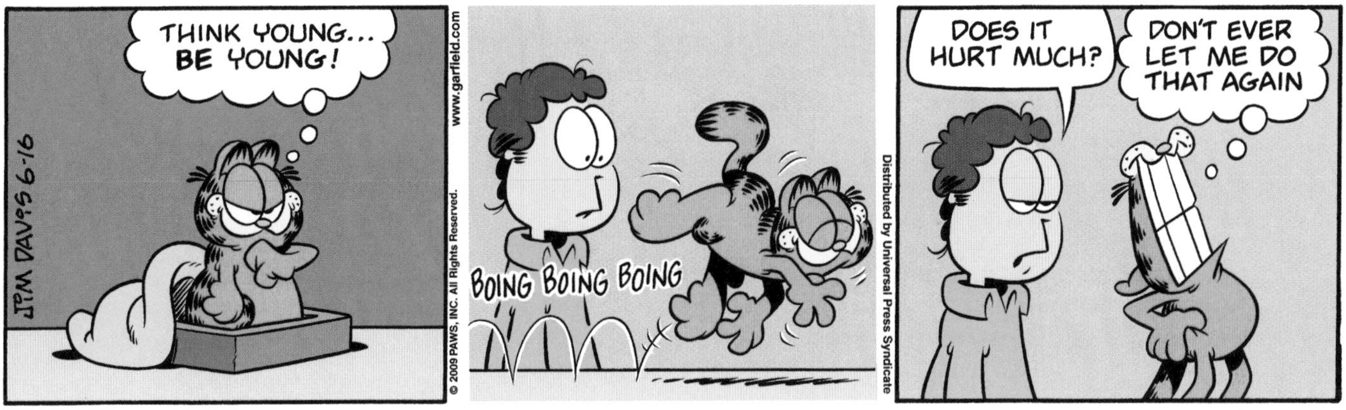
THINK YOUNG... BE YOUNG!
JPM DAVIS 6-16
© 2009 PAWS, INC. All Rights Reserved. www.garfield.com
BOING BOING BOING
Distributed by Universal Press Syndicate
DOES IT HURT MUCH?
DON'T EVER LET ME DO THAT AGAIN

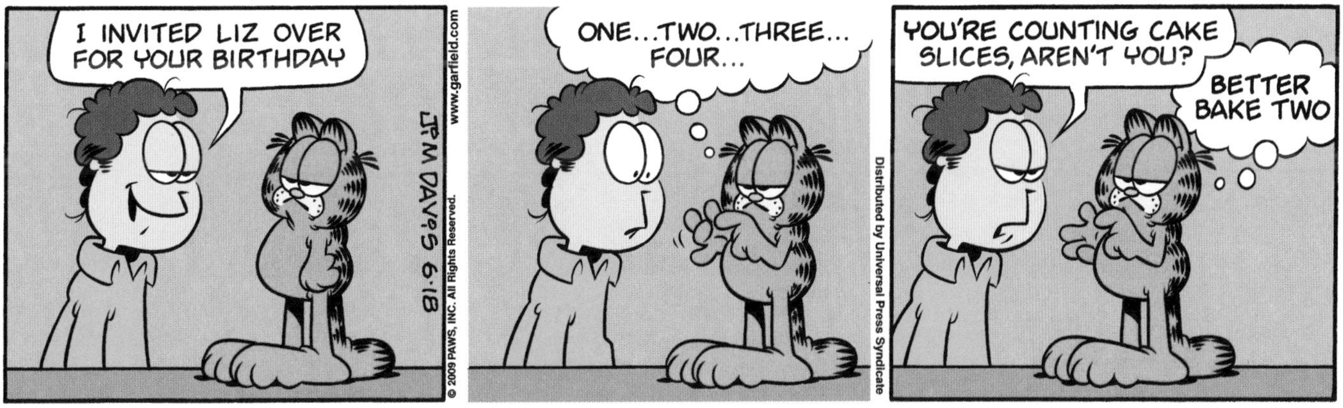
I INVITED LIZ OVER FOR YOUR BIRTHDAY
JPM DAVIS 6-18
© 2009 PAWS, INC. All Rights Reserved. www.garfield.com
ONE...TWO...THREE... FOUR...
Distributed by Universal Press Syndicate
YOU'RE COUNTING CAKE SLICES, AREN'T YOU?
BETTER BAKE TWO

JIM'S TOP 40

His All-Time Favorite Strips from the First Four Decades

1

JUNE 19, 1978

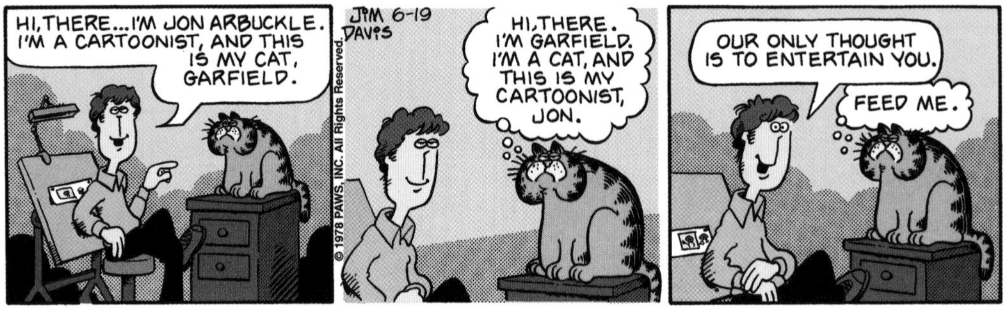
HI, THERE... I'M JON ARBUCKLE. I'M A CARTOONIST, AND THIS IS MY CAT, GARFIELD.
JIM DAVIS 6-19
© 1978 PAWS, INC. All Rights Reserved.
HI, THERE. I'M GARFIELD. I'M A CAT, AND THIS IS MY CARTOONIST, JON.
OUR ONLY THOUGHT IS TO ENTERTAIN YOU.
FEED ME.

"This is my first and my favorite strip. It's one of the very few times that Jon talked about what he does. The strip is a bit prophetic. I still consider myself to be in the entertainment biz."

2

JUNE 21, 1978

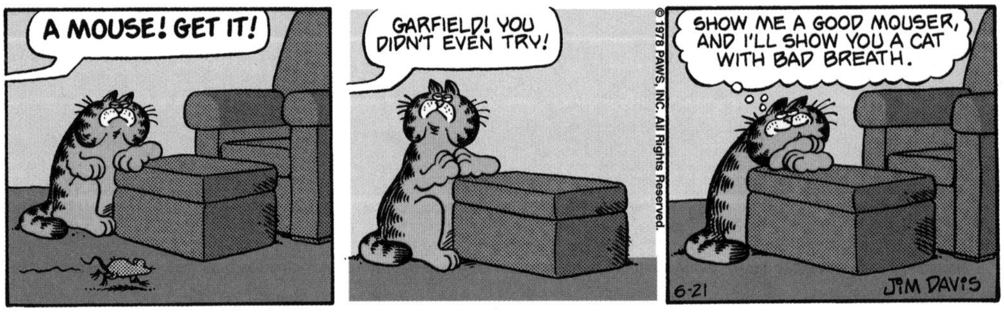
A MOUSE! GET IT!
GARFIELD! YOU DIDN'T EVEN TRY!
© 1978 PAWS, INC. All Rights Reserved.
SHOW ME A GOOD MOUSER, AND I'LL SHOW YOU A CAT WITH BAD BREATH.
6-21
JIM DAVIS

"This was a defining strip for Garfield. He not only set himself apart from stereotypical cats, but he established himself as a human in a cat suit."

FEBRUARY 12, 1982

CLICK!
SHOOP!
FASTER THAN THE SPEED OF DARK
JIM DAVIS 2-12
© 1982 PAWS, INC. All Rights Reserved.

"On very rare occasions, I will use a gag supplied by a trusted source. This trusted source was my dad. I was never able to get him to write another one!"

SEPTEMBER 15, 1985

GARFIELD®
GARFIELD! IT'S TRIPLE-COUPON DAY AT THE SUPERMARKET. WE GOTTA HURRY!
© 1985 PAWS, INC. All Rights Reserved.
HERE IT IS, TRIPLE-COUPON DAY AT THE MARKET. SHOPPERS ARE LINED UP AND EAGERLY AWAITING THE OPENING OF THE STORE
THERE'S THE GREEN FLAG!
AS THE PACK BACKS UP BEHIND THE BUTZ SISTERS, THELDA BALDUCCI DROPS UNDER THE GROOVE AND PASSES INSIDE
BALDUCCI BLOWS A TIRE AND IS T-BONED BY OLD LADY CROWE!
CRASH!
WE GOT THE SALES ITEM FIRST!!!
JIM DAVIS 9-15
DO YOU HAVE A COUPON?
I FORGOT IT
RATS! BLACK FLAGGED ON THE LAST LAP!

"This strip was a deliberate effort to stuff as much art and action into a Sunday page as humanly possible. It was hard work, but great fun! Even Mr. Whipple (remember him?) makes a cameo appearance."

APRIL 27, 1989

JIM DAVIS 4-27
© 1989 PAWS, INC. All Rights Reserved.
"AND NOW... AN EVENING WITH MOZART"
WAR AND PEACE

“This is the only time I’ve shown what Odie is really like off-camera.”

JUNE 9, 1991

GARFIELD
YAAAHHH!!
© 1991 PAWS, INC. All Rights Reserved.
GARFIELD!!!
STOP SCARING THE GOLDFISH!
JIM DAVIS 6-9

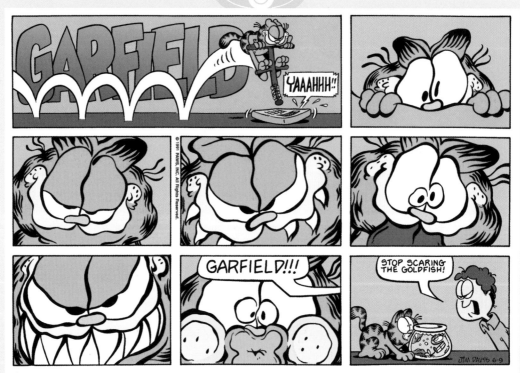

“In the trade, we call this a wallpaper gag with a reveal. I love teasing the reader with seemingly nonsensical action for most of the strip, and then revealing its logic in the last frame. It’s also a great excuse to do silly drawings.”

OCTOBER 7, 1992

THAT'S THE BIGGEST SLINGSHOT I'VE EVER SEEN
JIM DAVIS 10-7
© 1992 PAWS, INC. All Rights Reserved.

"One ingredient of comedy is exaggeration...and it doesn't get much bigger than this."

MARCH 25, 1993

GARFIELD, I HAVE TO ADMIRE YOUR TENACITY
JIM DAVIS 3-25
YOU'VE PULLED SOME DUMB STUNTS
© 1993 PAWS, INC. All Rights Reserved.
BUT THIS IS THE WORST
FEED THE TEETH!

"Some gags don't make a lot of sense...and they don't have to if they're silly enough. This one's very silly."

DECEMBER 18, 1993

WE'RE VISITING JON'S FAMILY FOR CHRISTMAS
IT'S PEACEFUL HERE ON THE FARM
C'MON, GARFIELD! WE'RE GOING TO PLAY "TOUCH THE UDDER"
AND WEIRD
© 1993 PAWS, INC. All Rights Reserved.

"Now and then I can't resist a nostalgic trip back to my childhood on the farm. Oh, the fun Doc Boy and I had...ha, ha, ha...."

DECEMBER 4, 1994

GARFIELD
© 1994 PAWS, INC. All Rights Reserved.
GARFIELD
GARFIELD

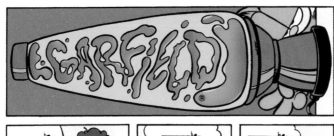

"I read somewhere that the best way to get a pesky tune out of your head was to sing it out loud. Of course, that means that someone else is going to hear it, and pick it up...like a head cold. It's a small world after all."

11

DECEMBER 18, 1994

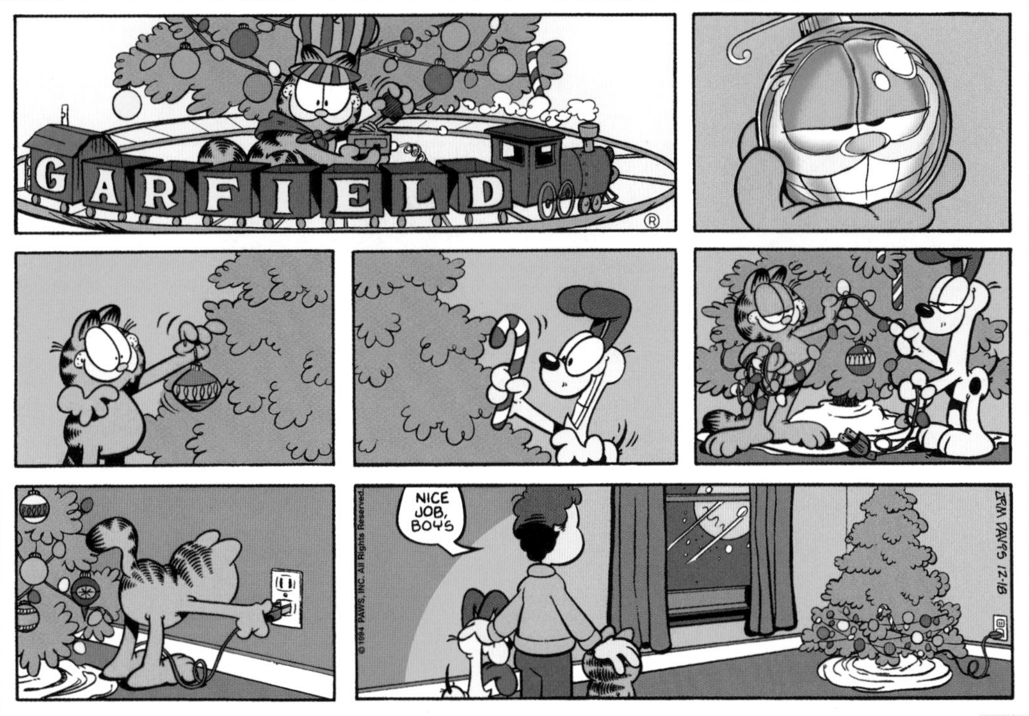
GARFIELD
NICE JOB, BOYS
JIM DAVIS 12-18
© 1994 PAWS, INC. All Rights Reserved.

“When our oldest son was eighteen months old, he wanted to decorate the Christmas tree. He couldn’t reach very high, and all the ornaments were hung together in one spot. It was the most beautiful Christmas tree I’ve even seen.”

12

SEPTEMBER 10, 1995

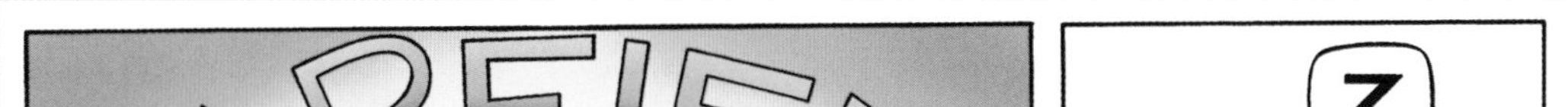
GARFIELD
Z
YAWN
JIM DAVIS 9-10
I HATE MONDAYS. MONDAYS ARE BORING. WOE IS ME...
SCRATCH SCRATCH
© 1995 PAWS, INC. All Rights Reserved.
GET THE PAPER, GARFIELD
SIGH... YES MASTER
IT'S SUNDAY!

“Ever wake up on what you thought was a work/school day and discover that it was a weekend? Remember that feeling of euphoria as you realize it’s going to be a good—nay, great—day? Life is good!”

13

FEBRUARY 11, 1996

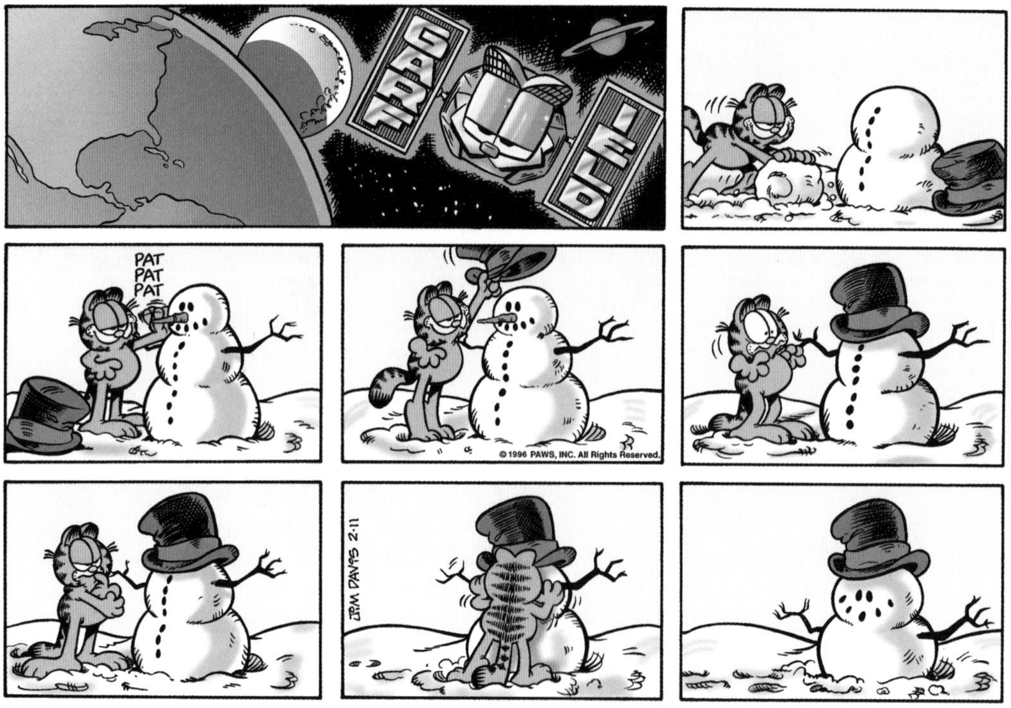
GARFIELD
PAT
PAT
PAT
© 1996 PAWS, INC. All Rights Reserved.
JIM DAVIS 2-11

"The creative process is simply problem solving. How do you get your heroine off the railroad track? How do you get your cartoon cat out of a tree? What do you do if your snowman's hat is too big? This is my nod to the process."

14

NOVEMBER 19, 1997

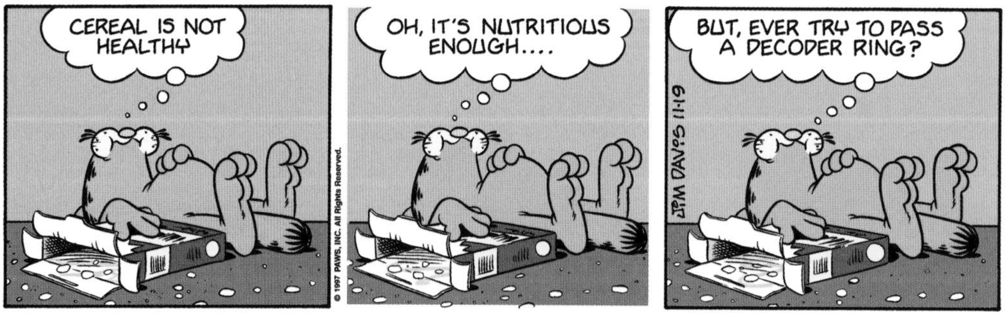
CEREAL IS NOT HEALTHY
© 1997 PAWS, INC. All Rights Reserved.
OH, IT'S NUTRITIOUS ENOUGH....
JIM DAVIS 11-19
BUT, EVER TRY TO PASS A DECODER RING?

"I know, I know. The 'decoder ring' reference really dates me. However, many comics readers are in their forties and up...I hope."

15 APRIL 22, 2001

garfield
SURE IS A BEAUTIFUL SUNSET, DAD
YUP
Distributed by Universal Press Syndicate
© 2001 PAWS, INC. All Rights Reserved.
www.garfield.com
SUNSETS ARE VERY POPULAR ON THE FARM...
JIM DAVIS 4·22
VERY POPULAR

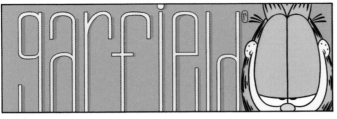

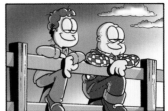

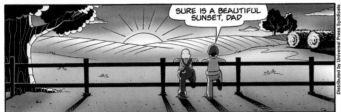

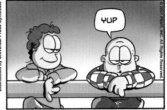

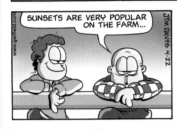

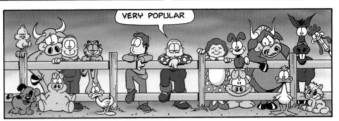

"Growing up on the farm, Dad, Mom, Doc, and I watched a lot of sunsets while leaning on the fence. We didn't talk much, but it was quality time. Orson, Booker, and Roy from the U.S.Acres strip slipped into the last frame."

16 MAY 13, 2001

garfield
www.garfield.com
IF SLEEPING IS AN ART, THEN I'M A MASTERPIECE
JIM DAVIS
5·13

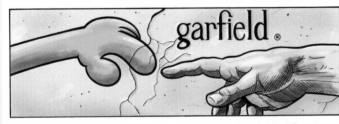

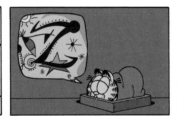

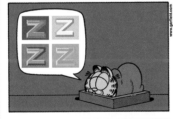

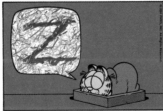

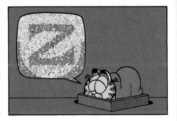

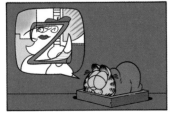

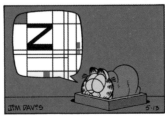

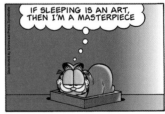

"Technology has finally allowed us to have more fun with the art. Art imitates art in this, my homage to Michelangelo, Miró, Warhol, Pollock, Seurat, Picasso, and Mondrian."

17

AUGUST 16, 2002

SQUEEK
SQUEEK
SQUEEK
SQUEE
I'M ON, AREN'T I ?
Distributed by Universal Press Syndicate
www.garfield.com
© 2002 PAWS, INC. All Rights Reserved.

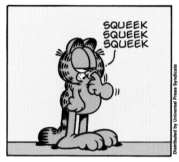

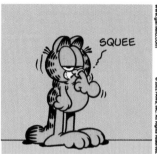

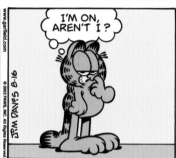

"You can count on one hand the number of times that I've allowed Garfield to step outside of the strip. But I couldn't resist this one."

18

FEBRUARY 26, 2004

HEY, CAT!
THIS IS MY LAWYER, SID. I HAVE A RESTRAINING ORDER AGAINST YOU!
UH, WHY THE SMILE?
I'VE NEVER SQUISHED A LAWYER
www.garfield.com
Distributed by Universal Press Syndicate
© 2004 PAWS, INC. All Rights Reserved.

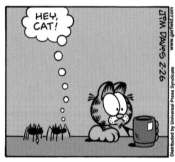

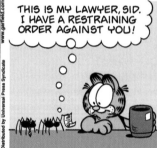

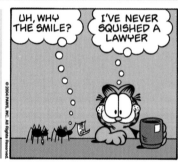

"Luckily, I received no adverse mail from lawyers over this strip. Maybe they don't read the comics...."

19

MAY 28, 2004

NOBODY TELLS ME WHAT TO DO!
www.garfield.com
Distributed by Universal Press Syndicate
HAVE SOMETHING TO EAT
© 2004 PAWS, INC. All Rights Reserved.
JIM DAVIS 5-28
WELL, THIS IS A BIT AWKWARD

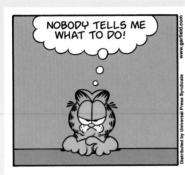

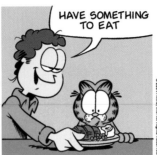

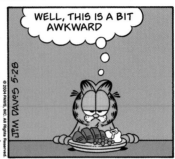

"This is one of the few times that Garfield is at a loss for words. Of course, he's never claimed to be perfect."

20

SEPTEMBER 12, 2004

GARFIELD
BONK!
WHO WANTS A HUG?
www.garfield.com
SOMEBODY?
© 2004 PAWS, INC. All Rights Reserved.
ANYBODY?
NOBODY?
Distributed by Universal Press Syndicate
JIM DAVIS 9-12

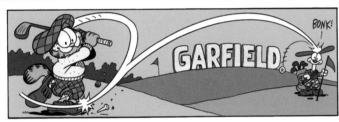

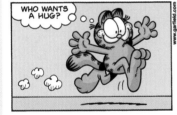

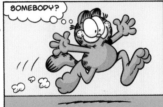

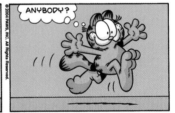

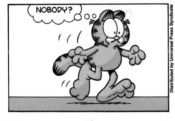

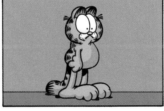

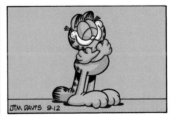

"I don't do political or social commentary in the strip, but sometimes I can't help but share a philosophy. I feel you have to love yourself before you can love others, or, as Garfield says, 'If you don't indulge yourself, nobody will.'"

21

JULY 1, 2005

IN ANSWER TO YOUR MANY LETTERS...
BOOT
www.garfield.com
©2005 PAWS, INC. All Rights Reserved.
YES...
CRASH!
JIM DAVIS 7-1
Distributed by Universal Press Syndicate
ODIE DOES DO ALL HIS OWN STUNTS!

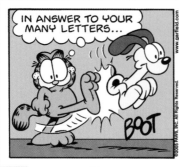

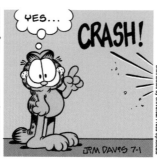

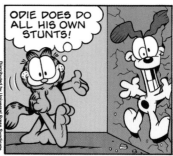

“Fortunately, what may be violence on television is called a sight gag in a comic strip. No dogs were harmed in the performance of this strip.”

22

AUGUST 23, 2005

www.garfield.com
©2005 PAWS, INC. All Rights Reserved.
Distributed by Universal Press Syndicate
SO THAT'S WHY THE CEILING FAN STOPPED
JIM DAVIS 8-23

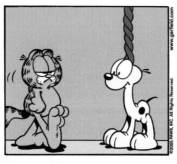

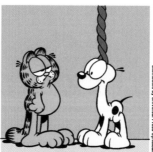

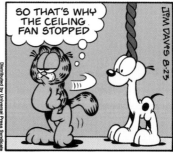

“Sometimes it's what you don't show that makes a gag work. All I do in the last frame is give the reader a hint. Some jokes are funnier if you have to work for them!”

OCTOBER 23, 2005

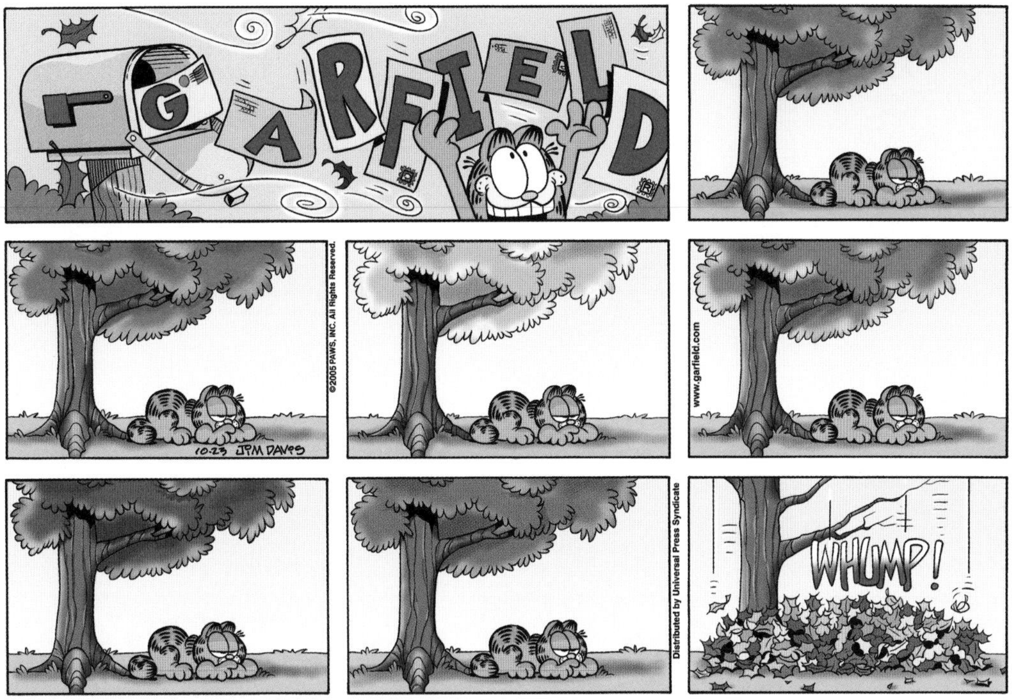
GARFIELD
©2005 PAWS, INC. All Rights Reserved.
10-23 JPM DAVPS
www.garfield.com
Distributed by Universal Press Syndicate
WHUMP!

"Autumn is a wonderful season to feature in a comic strip. It's a colorful and magical time of year. Garfield loves autumn, as do I. There's only one drawback: Autumn is entirely too short."

JANUARY 3, 2006

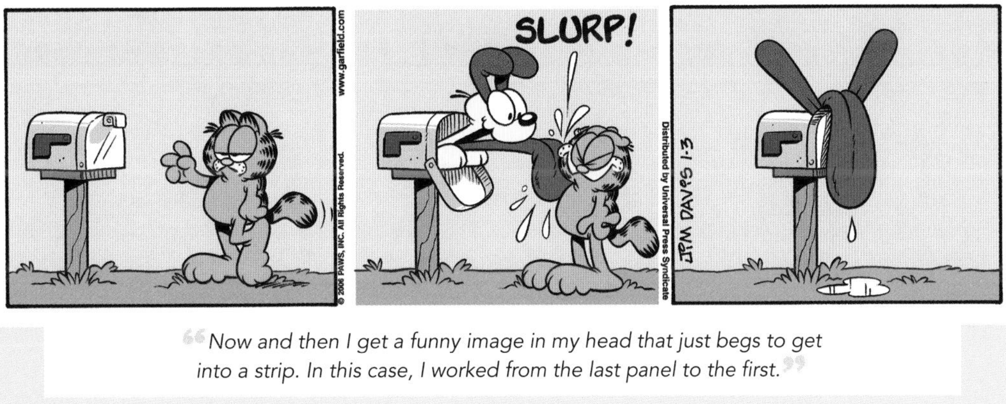
www.garfield.com
© 2006 PAWS, INC. All Rights Reserved.
SLURP!
Distributed by Universal Press Syndicate
JPM DAVPS 1-3

"Now and then I get a funny image in my head that just begs to get into a strip. In this case, I worked from the last panel to the first."

JANUARY 19, 2007

WHAT'S IT ALL MEAN, GARFIELD? WHAT'S LIFE ALL ABOUT?
I'LL SAY TUNA
© 2007 PAWS, INC. All Rights Reserved.
Distributed by Universal Press Syndicate
JIM DAVIS 1-19

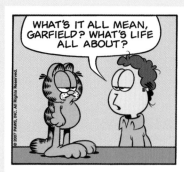

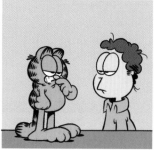

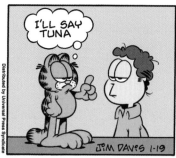

"This is about as deep as Garfield gets. You know what? This may be what life really is about."

FEBRUARY 11, 2007

GARFIELD®
FLOWERS
FLOWERS
Distributed by Universal Press Syndicate
JIM DAVIS 2-11
© 2007 PAWS, INC. All Rights Reserved.

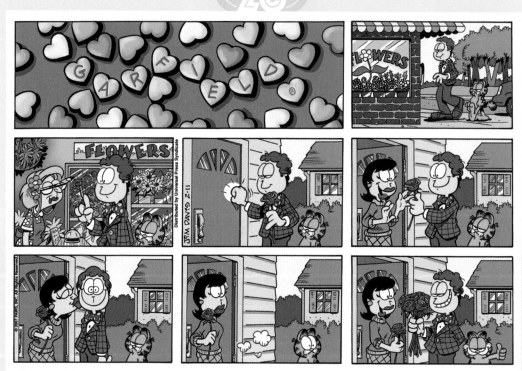

"After Garfield turned twenty-five, we asked our biggest fans if they'd change anything about the strip. The majority said, 'Give Jon a life!' After pursuing Liz for over a quarter of a century, Jon's persistence should count for something...."

MARCH 6, 2007

VEGETARIAN ALIENS FROM OUTER SPACE!
THIS SHOULD BE INTERESTING
TAKE ME TO YOUR BROCCOLI
WITH PLEASURE!
JIM DAVIS 3-6
www.garfield.com
© 2007 PAWS, INC. All Rights Reserved.
Distributed by Universal Press Syndicate

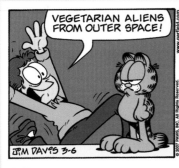

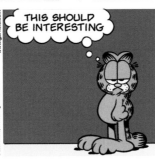

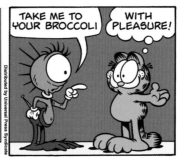

"For some gags to work, the reader has to make a leap of faith. This is about as far as I go."

AUGUST 7, 2007

DOG NEWS
WHOA...
YOU GUYS WILL SNIFF PRETTY MUCH ANYTHING, WON'T YOU?
JIM DAVIS 8-7
www.garfield.com
© 2007 PAWS, INC. All Rights Reserved.
Distributed by Universal Press Syndicate

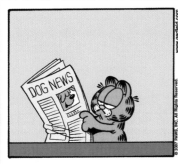

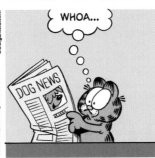

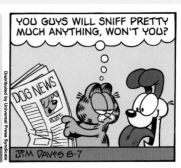

"Part of dog humor is how direct, and, well, earthy they are. You notice that I didn't show a dog actually sniffing anything. I'm too classy for that."

JULY 1, 2007

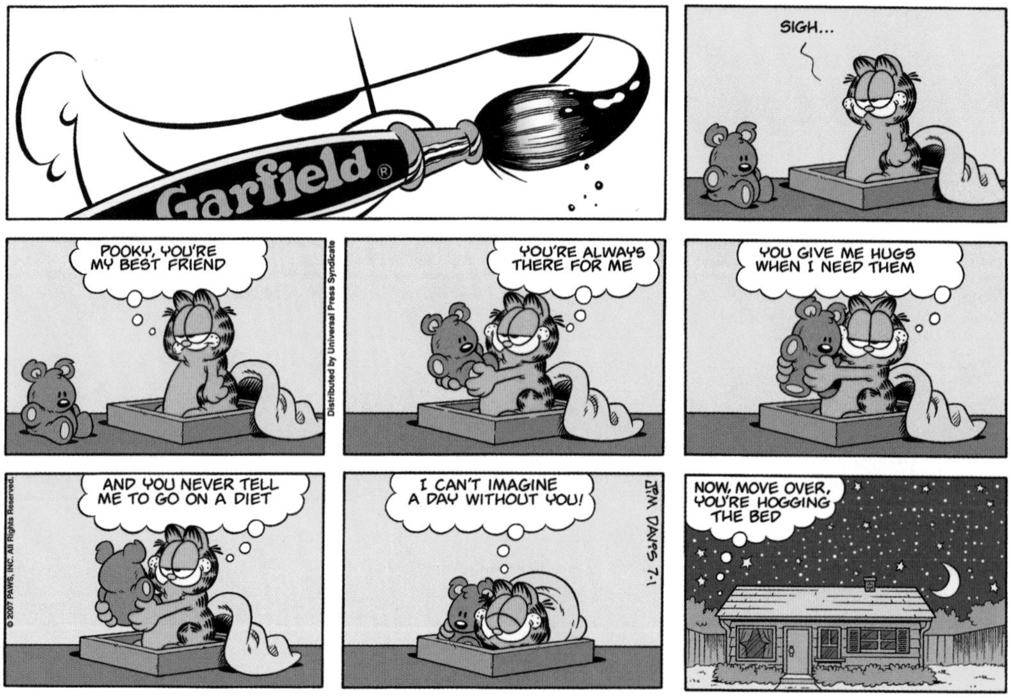
Garfield®
SIGH...
POOKY, YOU'RE MY BEST FRIEND
Distributed by Universal Press Syndicate
YOU'RE ALWAYS THERE FOR ME
YOU GIVE ME HUGS WHEN I NEED THEM
© 2007 PAWS, INC. All Rights Reserved.
AND YOU NEVER TELL ME TO GO ON A DIET
I CAN'T IMAGINE A DAY WITHOUT YOU!
JIM DAVIS 7-1
NOW, MOVE OVER, YOU'RE HOGGING THE BED

"Valette Greene was my first assistant. She was a dear, sweet lady who loved people and pets. She passed away some years back. This strip was written for her. In the last panel, her name is in the stars. I can hear her laughing now."

AUGUST 25, 2007

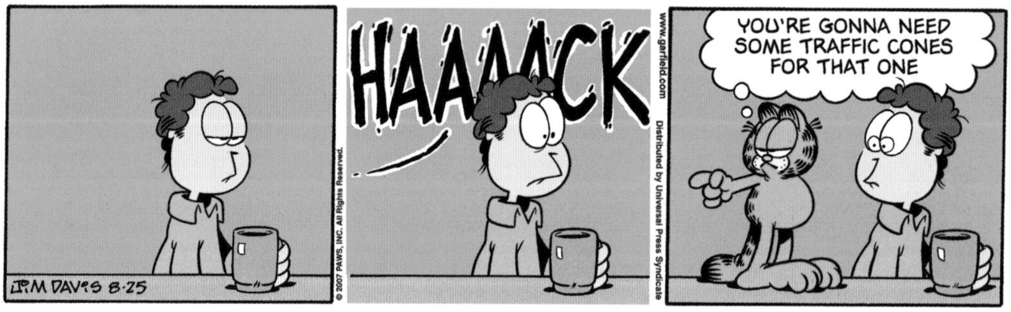
JIM DAVIS 8-25
© 2007 PAWS, INC. All Rights Reserved.
HAAAACK
www.garfield.com
Distributed by Universal Press Syndicate
YOU'RE GONNA NEED SOME TRAFFIC CONES FOR THAT ONE

"This gag is for cat owners. Yes, this graphically exposes the seamy side of owning a cat."

DECEMBER 25, 2009

A NEW STETHOSCOPE! OH, JON!
IT'S ENGRAVED
"FROM MY HEART, TO YOUR EARS. LOVE, JON"
I GOTTA GIVE HIM THIS ONE
www.garfield.com
© 2009 PAWS, INC. All Rights Reserved.
Distributed by Universal Press Syndicate
JIM DAVIS 12-25

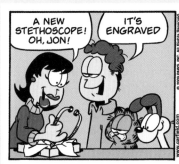

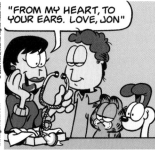

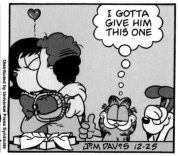

"Even a blind pig finds a truffle now and then."

MAY 5, 2010

CHEER UP, POOKY...
HERE, I HAVE JUST THE THING...
BETTER
www.garfield.com
© 2010 PAWS, INC. All Rights Reserved.
Distributed by Universal Uclick
JIM DAVIS 5-5

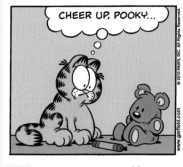

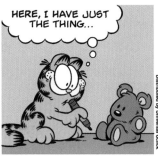

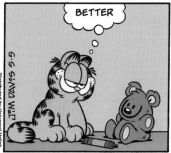

"I ran this on May 5. That's National Cartoonists Day."

33

MAY 1, 2011

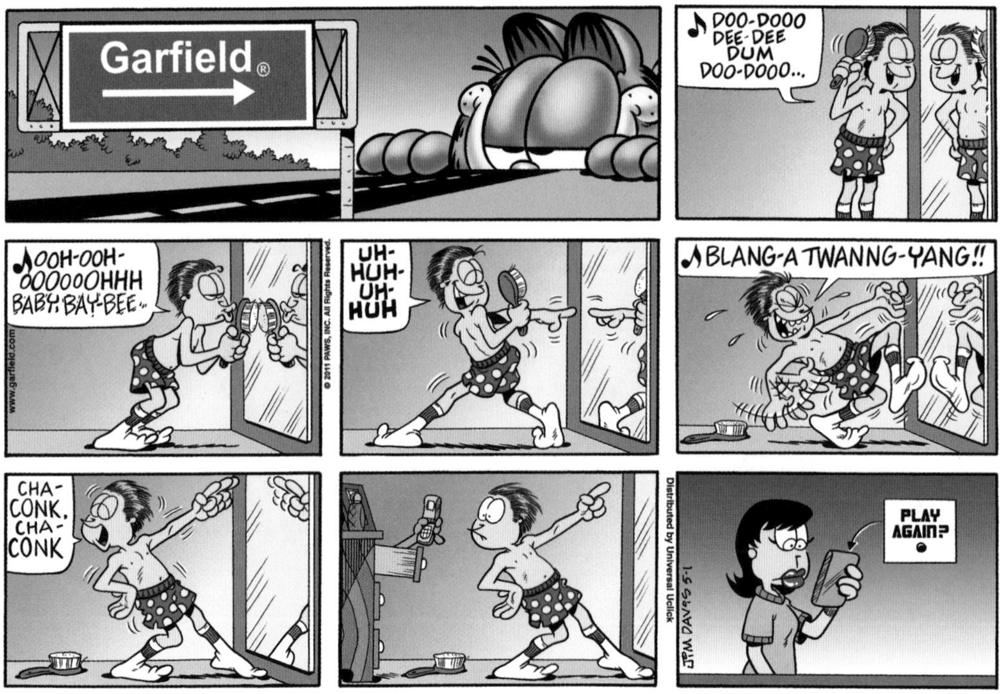

Garfield®
♪DOO-DOOO DEE-DEE DUM DOO-DOOO...
♪OOH-OOH-OOOOOOHHH BABY, BAY-BEE...
www.garfield.com
UH-HUH-UH-HUH
© 2011 PAWS, INC. All Rights Reserved.
♪BLANG-A TWANNG-YANG!!
CHA-CONK, CHA-CONK
Distributed by Universal Uclick
JIM DAVIS 5-1
PLAY AGAIN?

"Garfield has not gone willingly into the digital age (being the analog cat that he is), but there is some humor to be mined there."

34

MAY 5, 2011

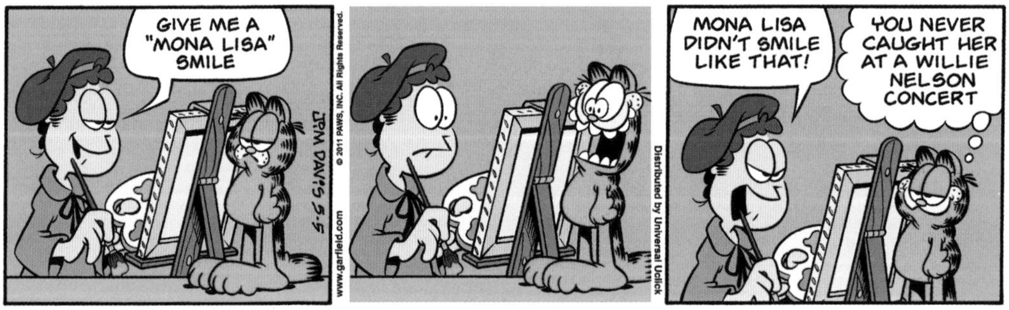

GIVE ME A "MONA LISA" SMILE
JIM DAVIS 5-5
www.garfield.com
© 2011 PAWS, INC. All Rights Reserved.
Distributed by Universal Uclick
MONA LISA DIDN'T SMILE LIKE THAT!
YOU NEVER CAUGHT HER AT A WILLIE NELSON CONCERT

"With very few exceptions, I make sure that each gag works well all around the world. This was one of those exceptions."

JULY 28, 2012

SCRATCH SCRATCH
THAT'S YOUR BIRTHDAY PRESENT. DON'T GET USED TO IT
JIM DAVIS 7-28
Distributed by Universal Uclick
www.facebook.com/garfield
© 2012 PAWS, INC. All Rights Reserved.

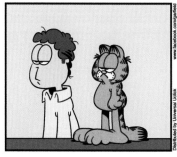

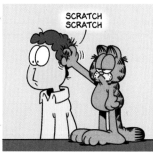

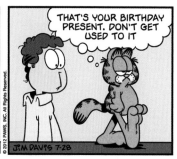

"Here is the sentimental side of Garfield…such as it is. July 28, coincidentally, is also my birthday."

FEBRUARY 19, 2013

YOU LOOK A LITTLE DOWN, GARFIELD
JIM DAVIS 2-19
MAYBE IT'S TIME FOOOOR…
Distributed by Universal Uclick
www.facebook.com/garfield
© 2013 PAWS, INC. All Rights Reserved.
OOO! EEE! OOO! EEE! OOO!
YES, FOLKS, THE HAPPY MONKEY DANCE

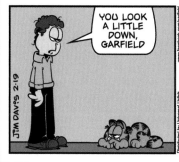

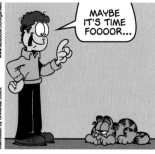

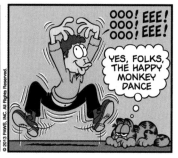

"Don't laugh, but some of my gags are autobiographical… okay, go ahead and laugh."

37

NOVEMBER 2, 2014

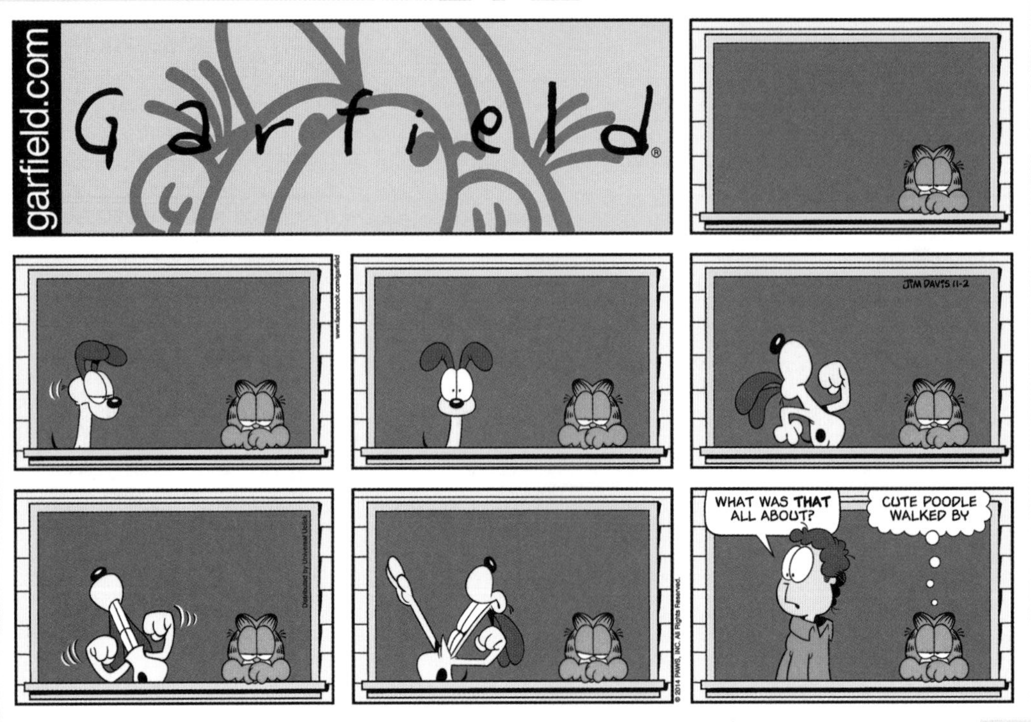
garfield.com
Garfield
WHAT WAS THAT ALL ABOUT?
CUTE POODLE WALKED BY

"A side of Odie that you don't normally see."

38

JANUARY 30, 2015

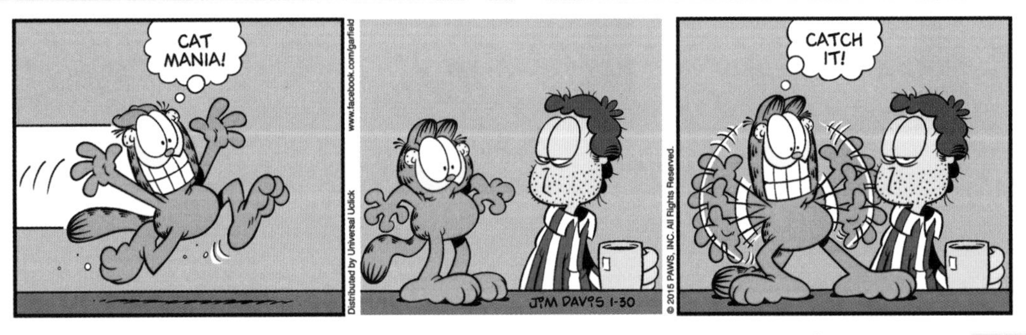
CAT MANIA!
CATCH IT!

"I love the timing of this gag and the fact that it's just, well…silly."

FEBRUARY 14, 2016

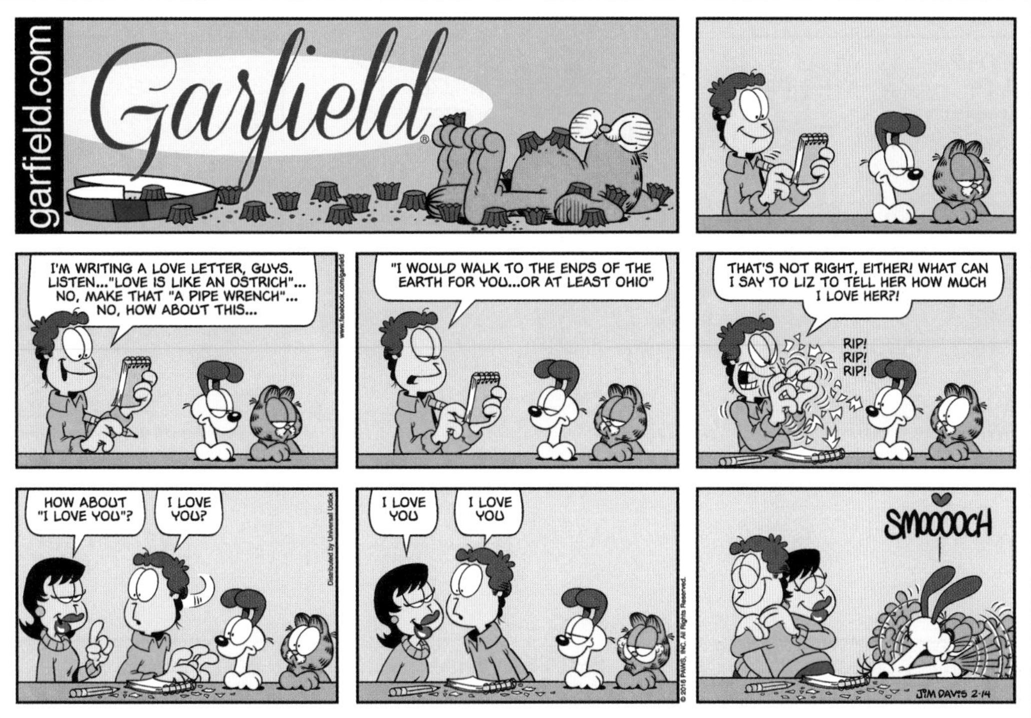
garfield.com
Garfield
I'M WRITING A LOVE LETTER, GUYS. LISTEN..."LOVE IS LIKE AN OSTRICH"... NO, MAKE THAT "A PIPE WRENCH"... NO, HOW ABOUT THIS...
"I WOULD WALK TO THE ENDS OF THE EARTH FOR YOU...OR AT LEAST OHIO"
THAT'S NOT RIGHT, EITHER! WHAT CAN I SAY TO LIZ TO TELL HER HOW MUCH I LOVE HER?!
RIP! RIP! RIP!
HOW ABOUT "I LOVE YOU"?
I LOVE YOU?
I LOVE YOU
I LOVE YOU
SMOOOOCH
JIM DAVIS 2-14

"It only took Jon 38 years to tell Liz that he loved her."

MAY 14, 2017

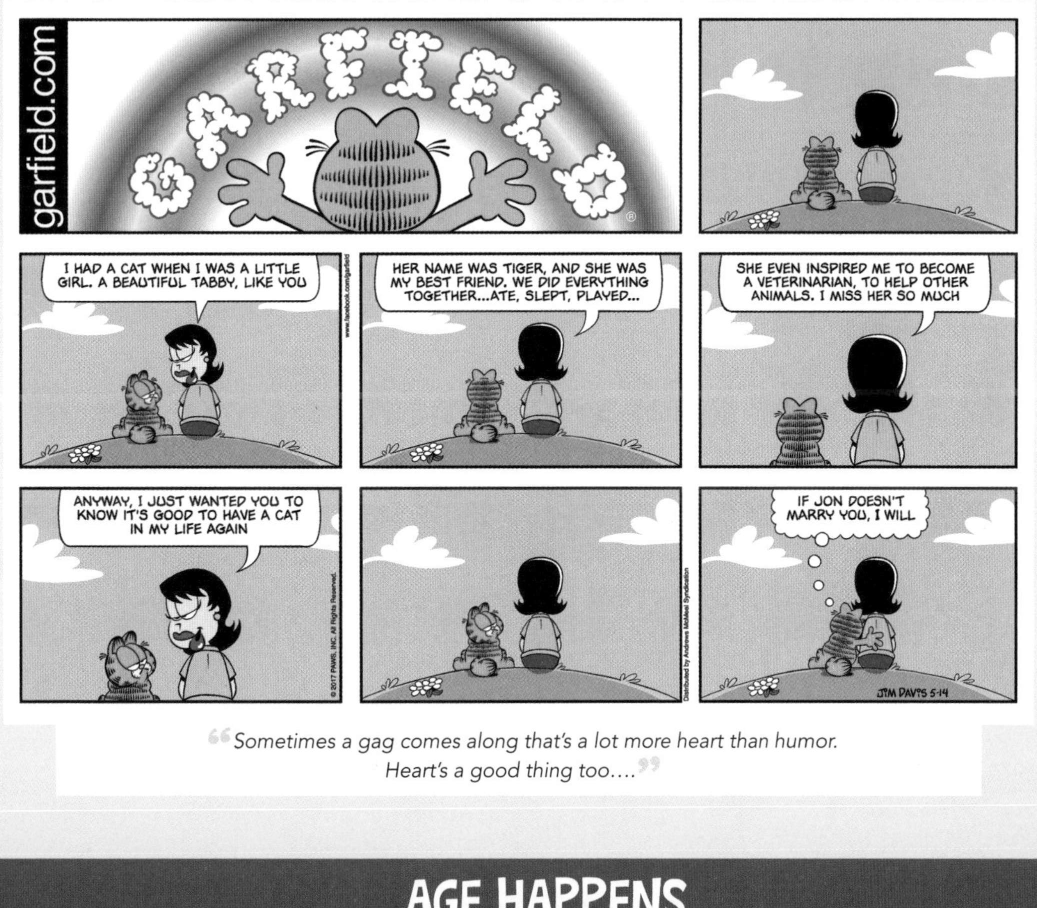
garfield.com
GARFIELD
I HAD A CAT WHEN I WAS A LITTLE GIRL. A BEAUTIFUL TABBY, LIKE YOU
HER NAME WAS TIGER, AND SHE WAS MY BEST FRIEND. WE DID EVERYTHING TOGETHER...ATE, SLEPT, PLAYED...
SHE EVEN INSPIRED ME TO BECOME A VETERINARIAN, TO HELP OTHER ANIMALS. I MISS HER SO MUCH
ANYWAY, I JUST WANTED YOU TO KNOW IT'S GOOD TO HAVE A CAT IN MY LIFE AGAIN
IF JON DOESN'T MARRY YOU, I WILL
JIM DAVIS 5-14

"Sometimes a gag comes along that's a lot more heart than humor. Heart's a good thing too…."

HAPPY BIRTHDAY, GARFIELD!
WHAT'S THIS?
IT'S A LASAGNA-SHAPED CAKE! LIZ MADE IT
COME AWAY WITH ME
© 2009 PAWS, INC. All Rights Reserved.
www.garfield.com
Distributed by Universal Press Syndicate
JPM DAVIS 6-19

SO, WHAT'S IT LIKE TO BE OLD AND FEEBLE?
BETTER THAN BEING YOUNG AND EDIBLE
BUT YOUR WIT IS AS KEEN AS EVER!
KISS-UP
JPM DAVIS 6-20
© 2009 PAWS, INC. All Rights Reserved.
www.garfield.com
Distributed by Universal Press Syndicate

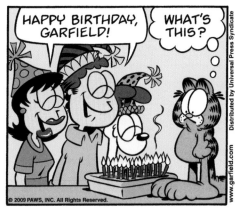

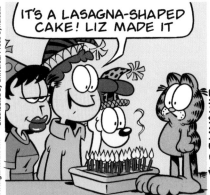

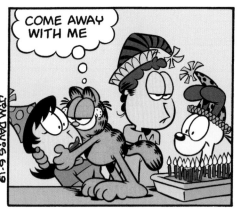

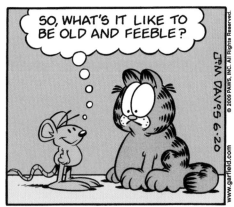

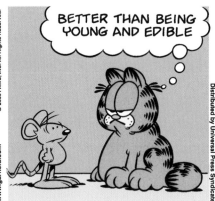

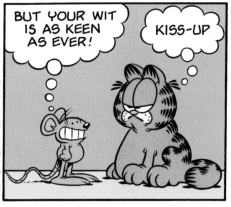

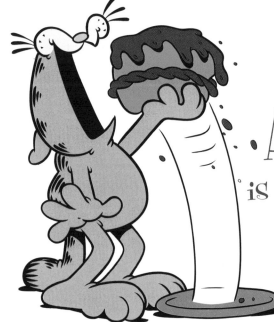

A cake in your mouth is worth two in the fridge.

A fool and his cake are soon parted.

GARFIELD...

WHAT KIND OF BIRTHDAY CAKE WOULD YOU LIKE THIS YEAR, GARFIELD?

GLAD YOU ASKED

I'VE NEVER SEEN A BLUEPRINT FOR A CAKE BEFORE

AND THIS IS THE ELECTRICAL SCHEMATIC

JIM DAVIS 6-13

© 2010 PAWS, INC. All Rights Reserved.

www.garfield.com

Distributed by Universal Uclick

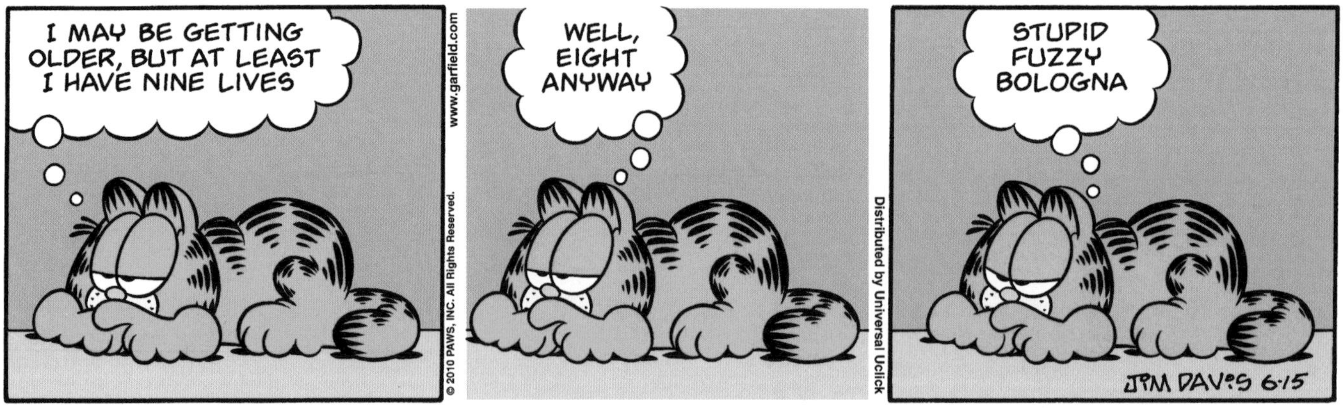
I MAY BE GETTING OLDER, BUT AT LEAST I HAVE NINE LIVES
WELL, EIGHT ANYWAY
STUPID FUZZY BOLOGNA
© 2010 PAWS, INC. All Rights Reserved. www.garfield.com
Distributed by Universal Uclick
JIM DAVIS 6-15

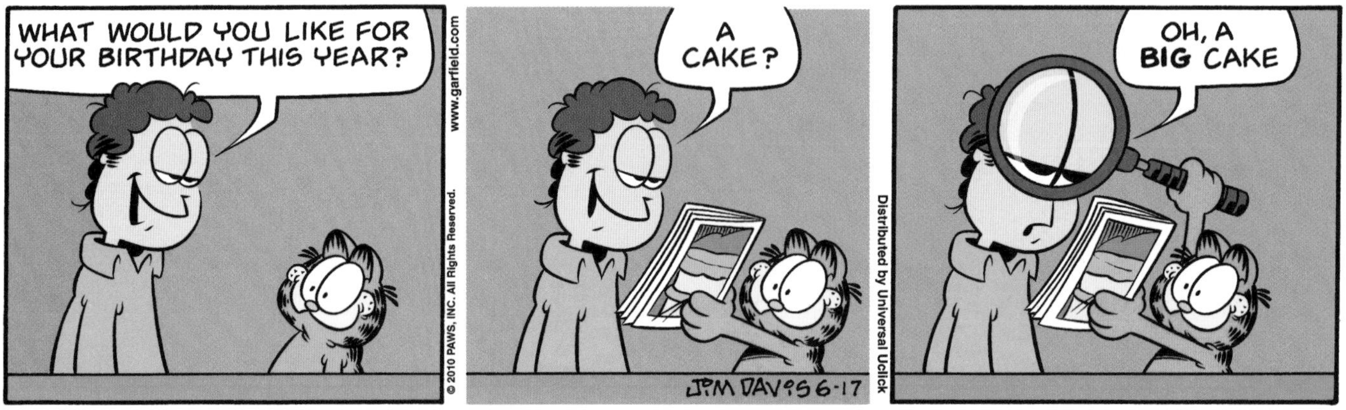
WHAT WOULD YOU LIKE FOR YOUR BIRTHDAY THIS YEAR?
A CAKE?
OH, A BIG CAKE
© 2010 PAWS, INC. All Rights Reserved. www.garfield.com
Distributed by Universal Uclick
JIM DAVIS 6-17

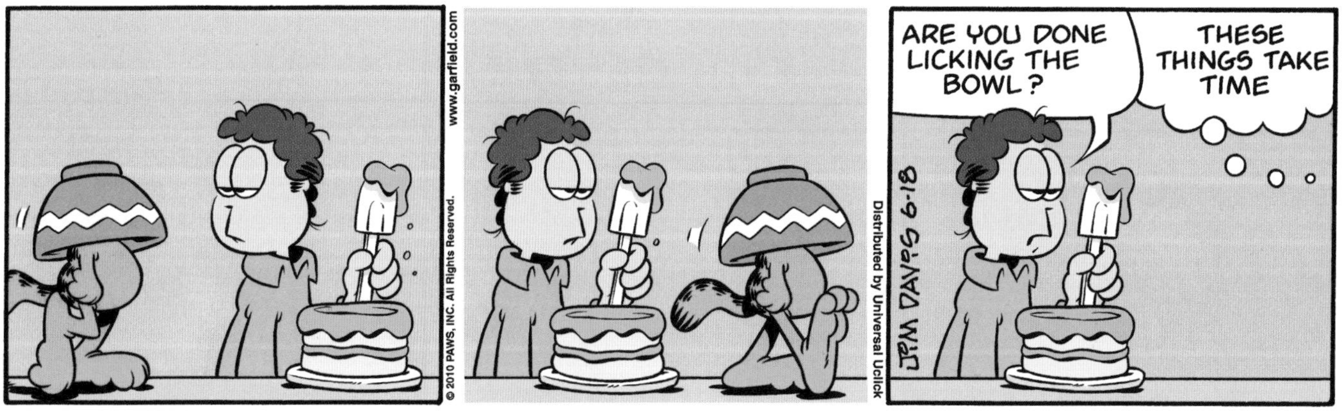
ARE YOU DONE LICKING THE BOWL?
THESE THINGS TAKE TIME
© 2010 PAWS, INC. All Rights Reserved. www.garfield.com
Distributed by Universal Uclick
JIM DAVIS 6-18

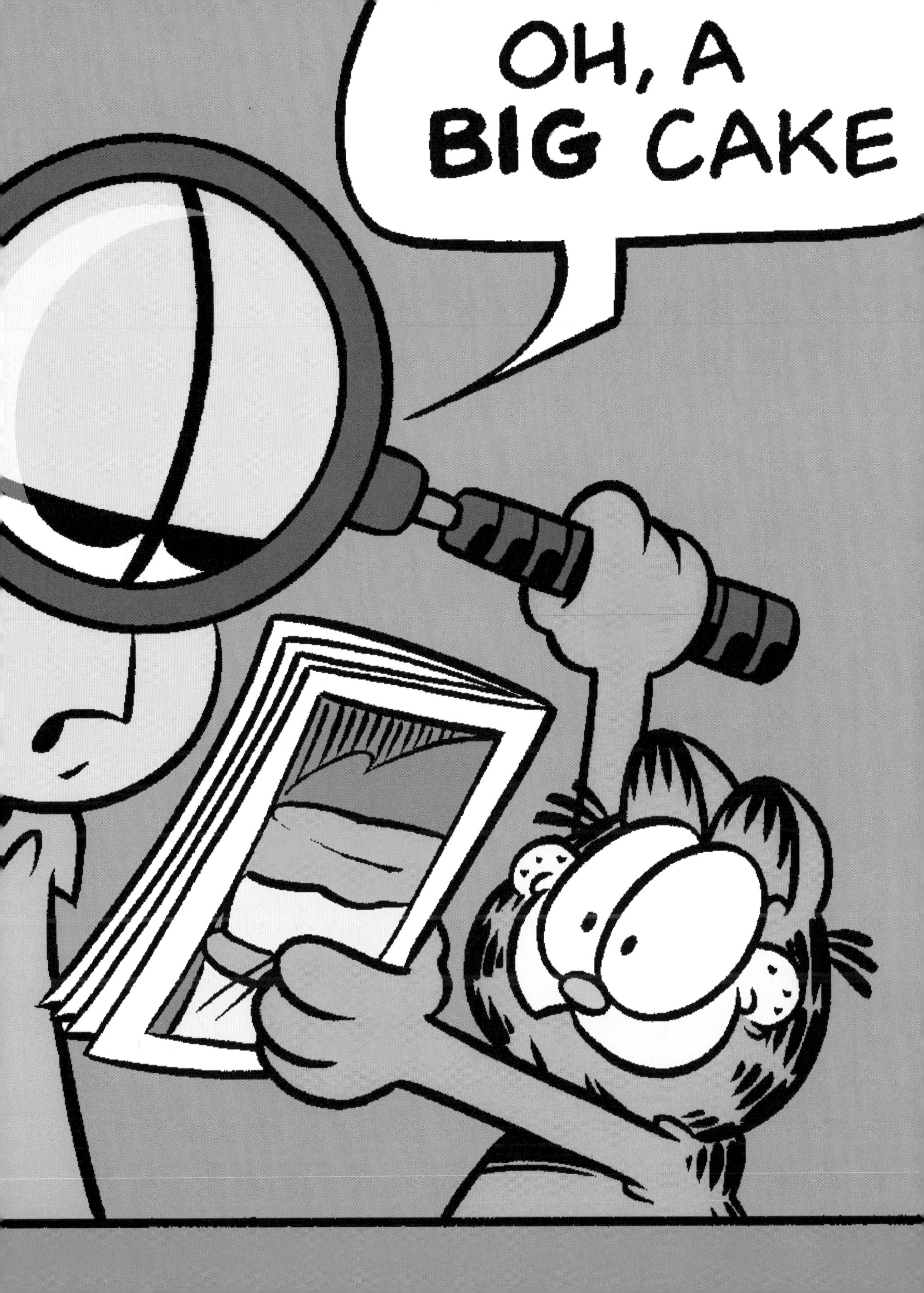
OH, A BIG CAKE

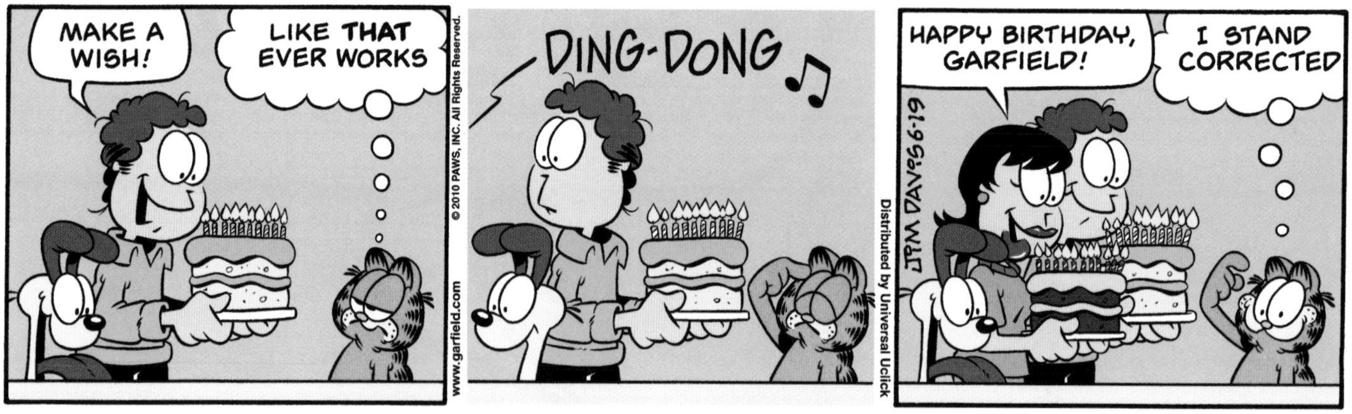
MAKE A WISH!
LIKE THAT EVER WORKS
© 2010 PAWS, INC. All Rights Reserved.
www.garfield.com
DING-DONG
Distributed by Universal Uclick
JIM DAVIS 6-19
HAPPY BIRTHDAY, GARFIELD!
I STAND CORRECTED

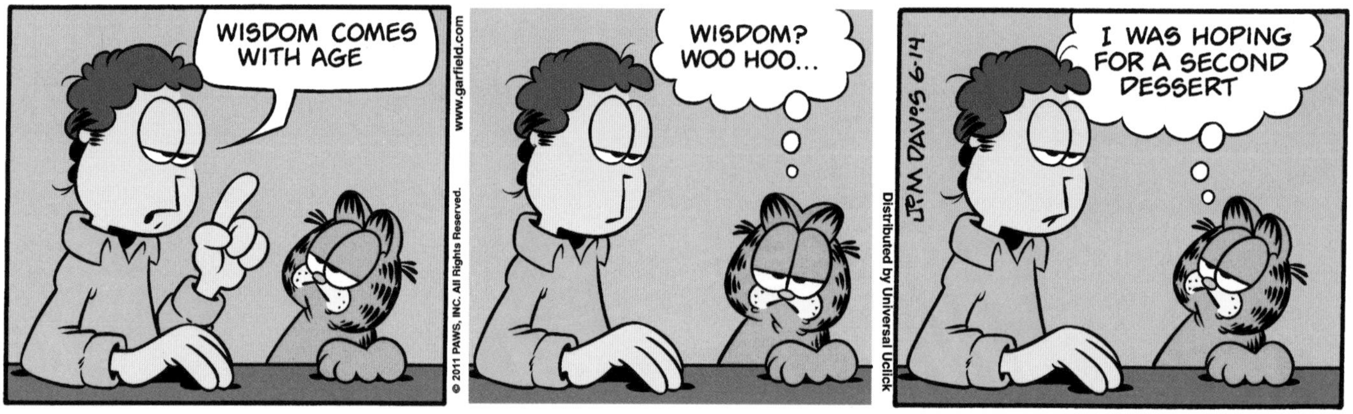
WISDOM COMES WITH AGE
© 2011 PAWS, INC. All Rights Reserved.
www.garfield.com
WISDOM? WOO HOO...
Distributed by Universal Uclick
JIM DAVIS 6-14
I WAS HOPING FOR A SECOND DESSERT

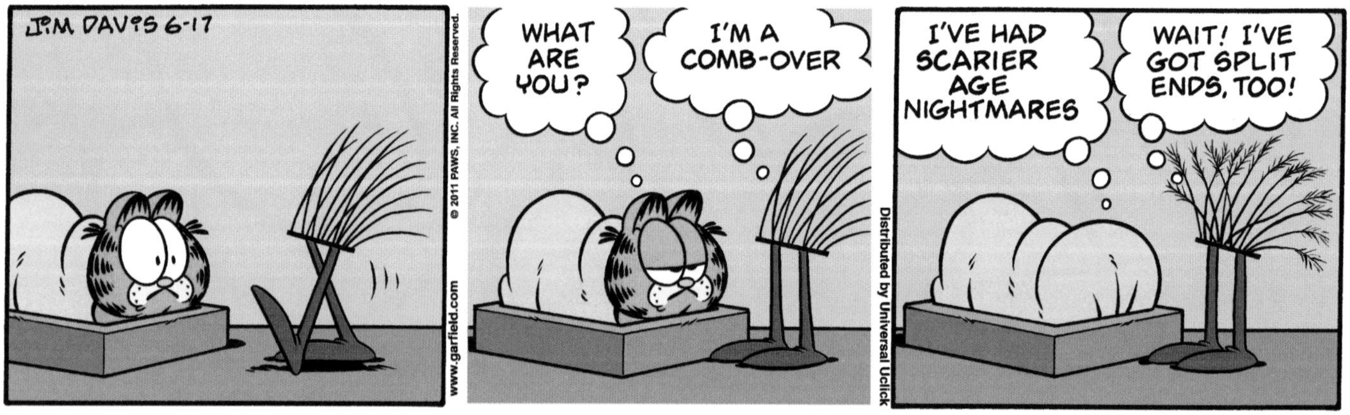
JIM DAVIS 6-17
© 2011 PAWS, INC. All Rights Reserved.
www.garfield.com
WHAT ARE YOU?
I'M A COMB-OVER
Distributed by Universal Uclick
I'VE HAD SCARIER AGE NIGHTMARES
WAIT! I'VE GOT SPLIT ENDS, TOO!

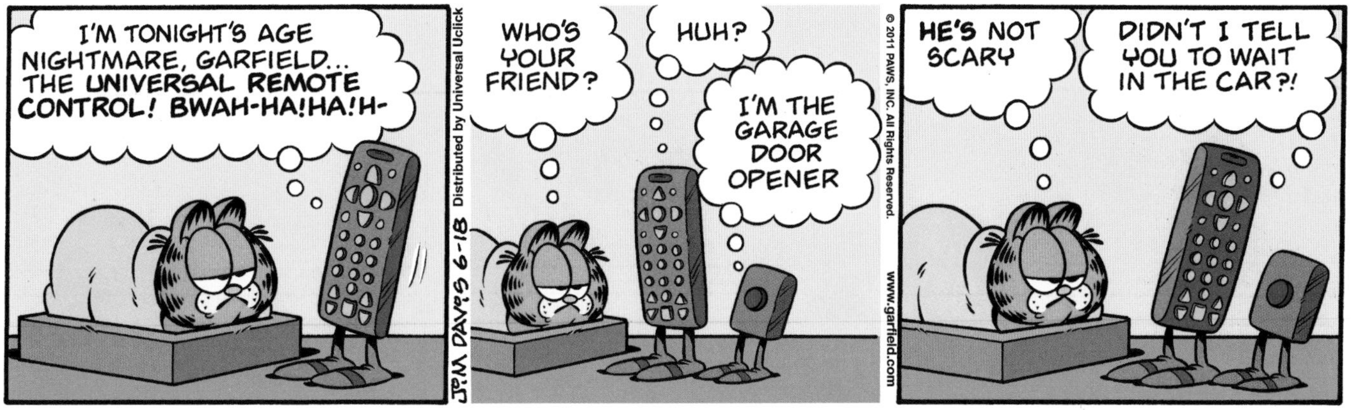

I'M TONIGHT'S AGE NIGHTMARE, GARFIELD... THE UNIVERSAL REMOTE CONTROL! BWAH-HA!HA!H-
JIM DAVIS 6-18
Distributed by Universal Uclick
WHO'S YOUR FRIEND?
HUH?
I'M THE GARAGE DOOR OPENER
© 2011 PAWS, INC. All Rights Reserved.
www.garfield.com
HE'S NOT SCARY
DIDN'T I TELL YOU TO WAIT IN THE CAR?!

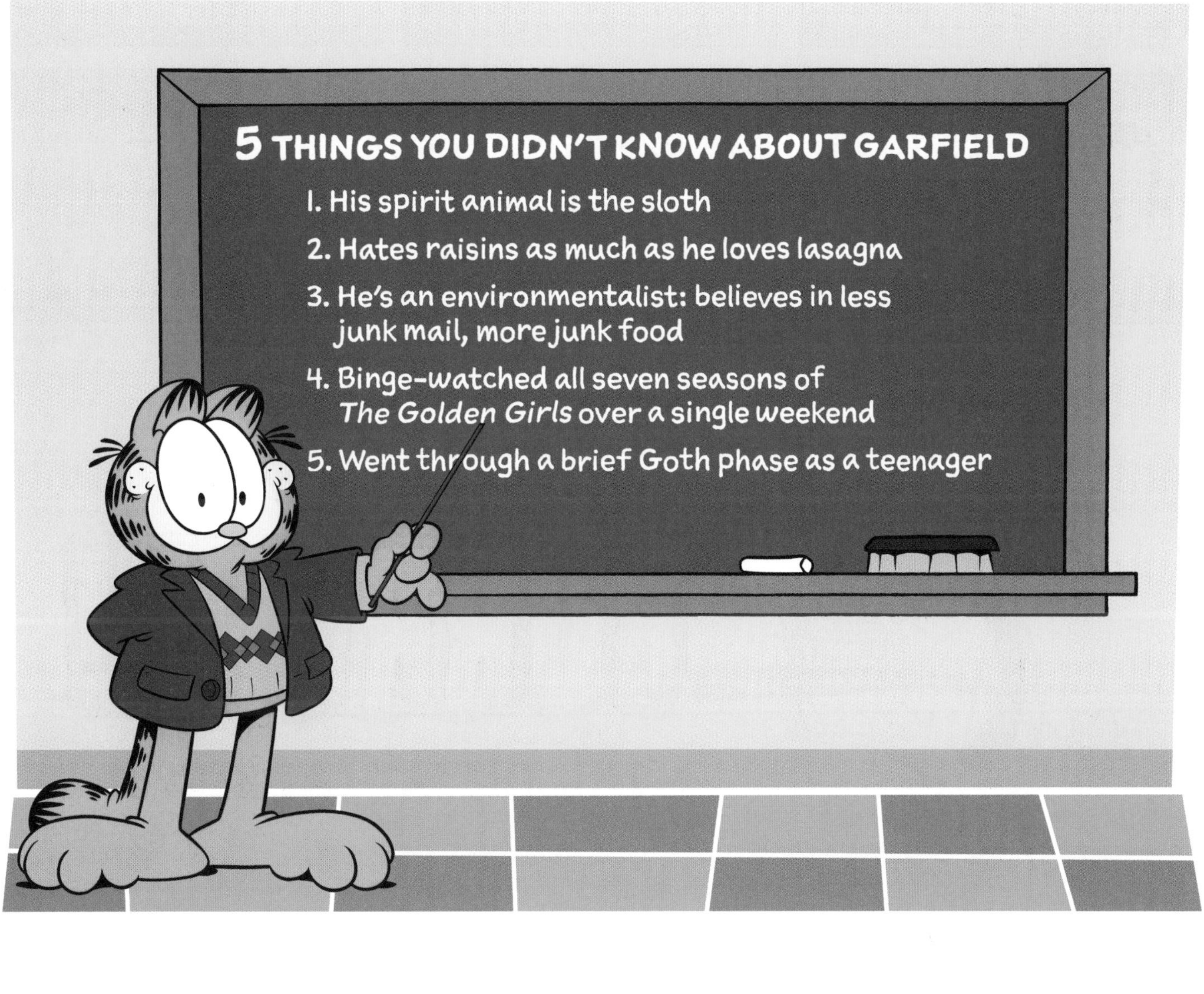

5 THINGS YOU DIDN'T KNOW ABOUT GARFIELD
1. His spirit animal is the sloth
2. Hates raisins as much as he loves lasagna
3. He's an environmentalist: believes in less junk mail, more junk food
4. Binge-watched all seven seasons of The Golden Girls over a single weekend
5. Went through a brief Goth phase as a teenager

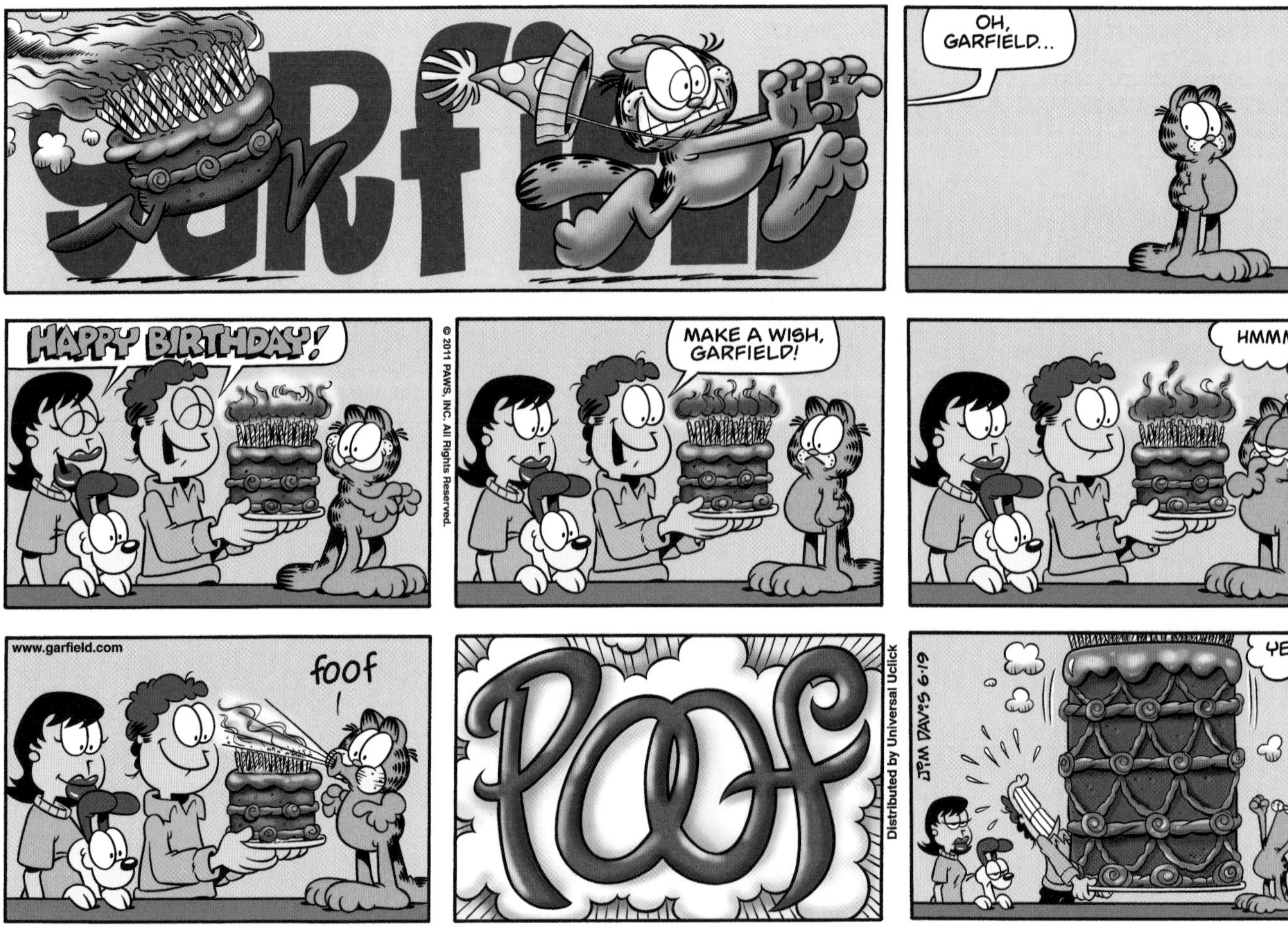
Garfield
OH, GARFIELD...
HAPPY BIRTHDAY!
© 2011 PAWS, INC. All Rights Reserved.
MAKE A WISH, GARFIELD!
HMMM...
www.garfield.com
foof
POOF
Distributed by Universal Uclick
JPM DAVIS 6-19
YES!

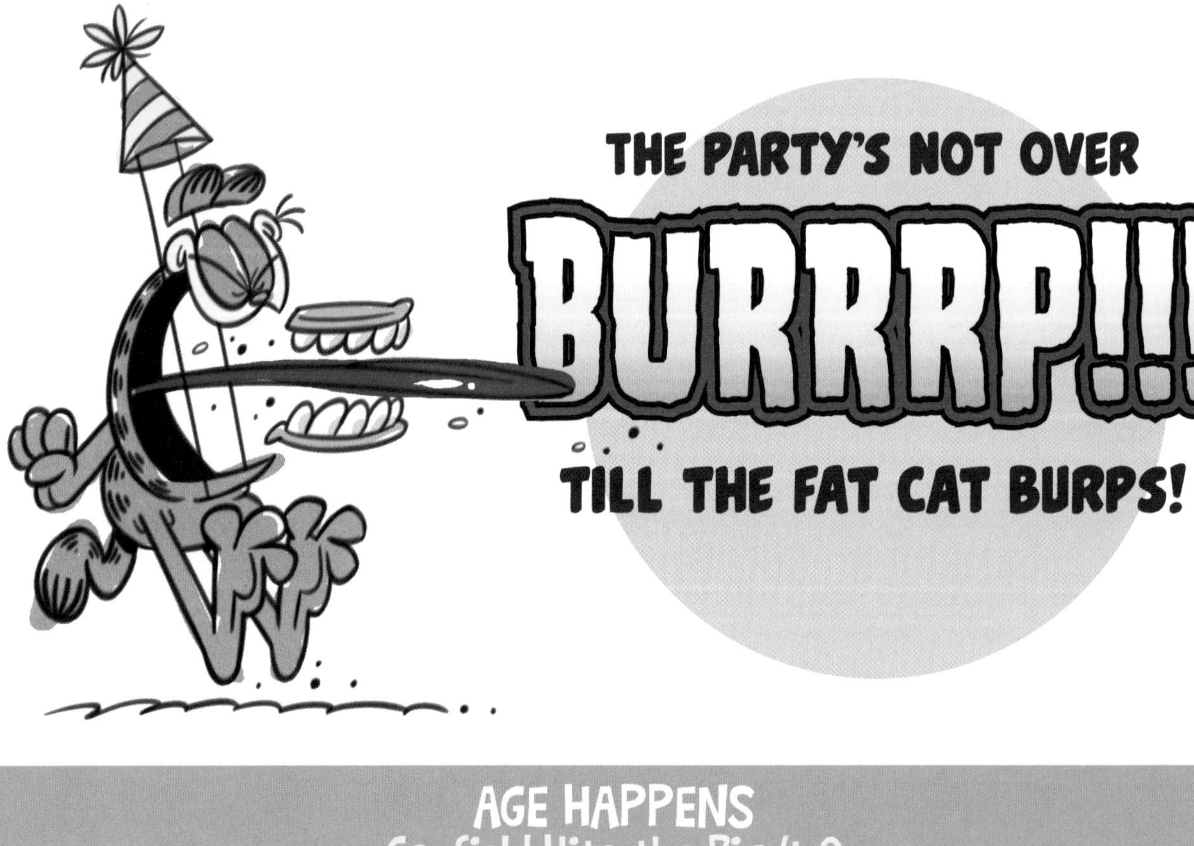
THE PARTY'S NOT OVER
BURRRP!!!
TILL THE FAT CAT BURPS!

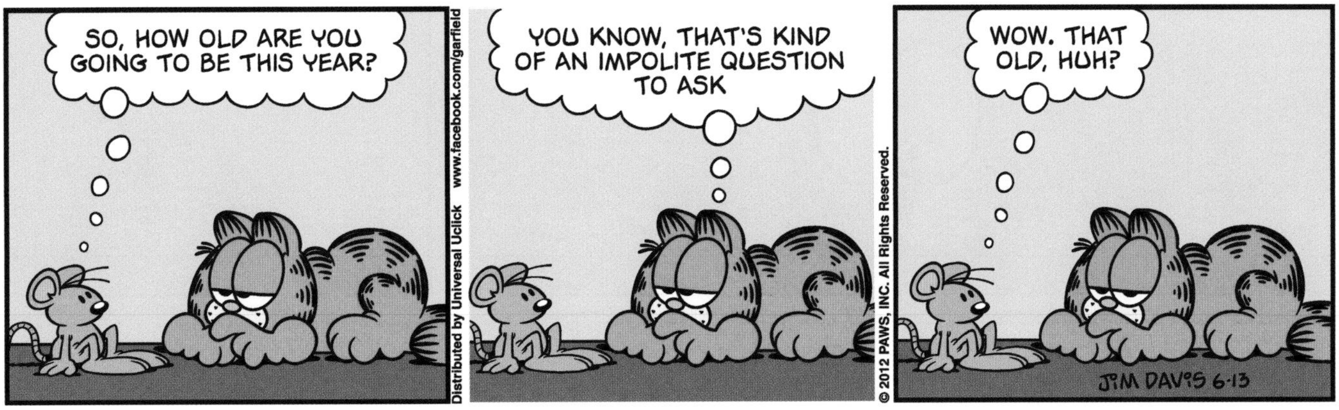
SO, HOW OLD ARE YOU GOING TO BE THIS YEAR?
YOU KNOW, THAT'S KIND OF AN IMPOLITE QUESTION TO ASK
WOW. THAT OLD, HUH?
JIM DAVIS 6-13
Distributed by Universal Uclick www.facebook.com/garfield
© 2012 PAWS, INC. All Rights Reserved.

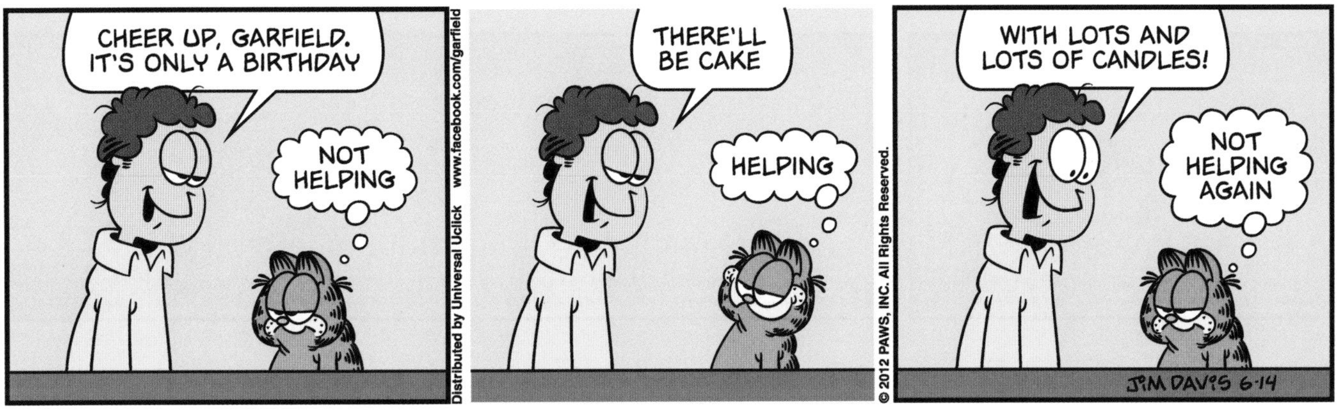
CHEER UP, GARFIELD. IT'S ONLY A BIRTHDAY
NOT HELPING
THERE'LL BE CAKE
HELPING
WITH LOTS AND LOTS OF CANDLES!
NOT HELPING AGAIN
JIM DAVIS 6-14
Distributed by Universal Uclick www.facebook.com/garfield
© 2012 PAWS, INC. All Rights Reserved.

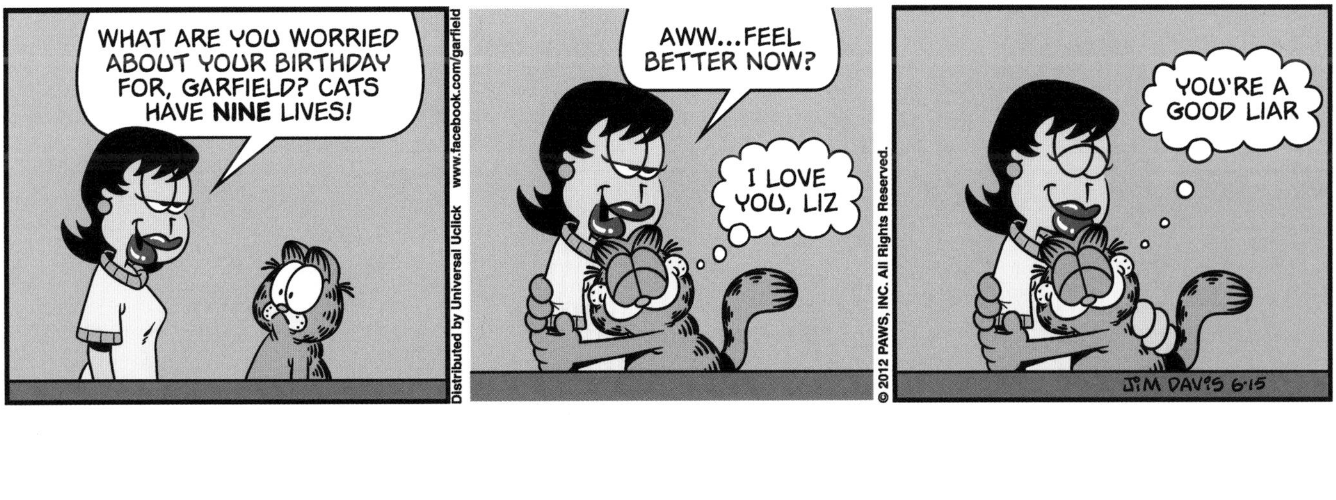
WHAT ARE YOU WORRIED ABOUT YOUR BIRTHDAY FOR, GARFIELD? CATS HAVE **NINE** LIVES!
AWW...FEEL BETTER NOW?
I LOVE YOU, LIZ
YOU'RE A GOOD LIAR
JIM DAVIS 6-15
Distributed by Universal Uclick www.facebook.com/garfield
© 2012 PAWS, INC. All Rights Reserved.

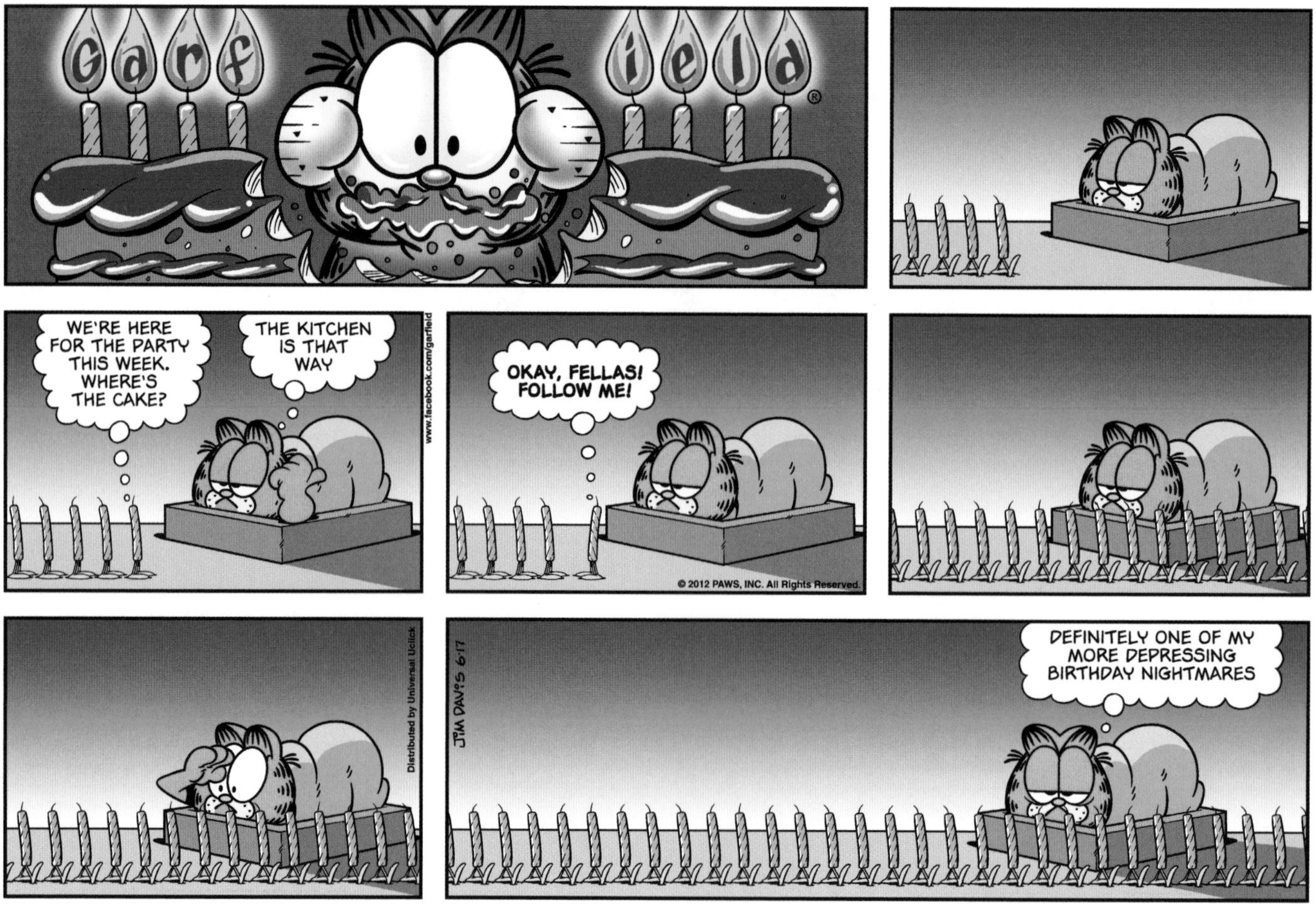
Garfield®
WE'RE HERE FOR THE PARTY THIS WEEK. WHERE'S THE CAKE?
THE KITCHEN IS THAT WAY
www.facebook.com/garfield
OKAY, FELLAS! FOLLOW ME!
© 2012 PAWS, INC. All Rights Reserved.
Distributed by Universal Uclick
JIM DAVIS 6-17
DEFINITELY ONE OF MY MORE DEPRESSING BIRTHDAY NIGHTMARES

SO MANY CANDLES... SO LITTLE LUNG CAPACITY

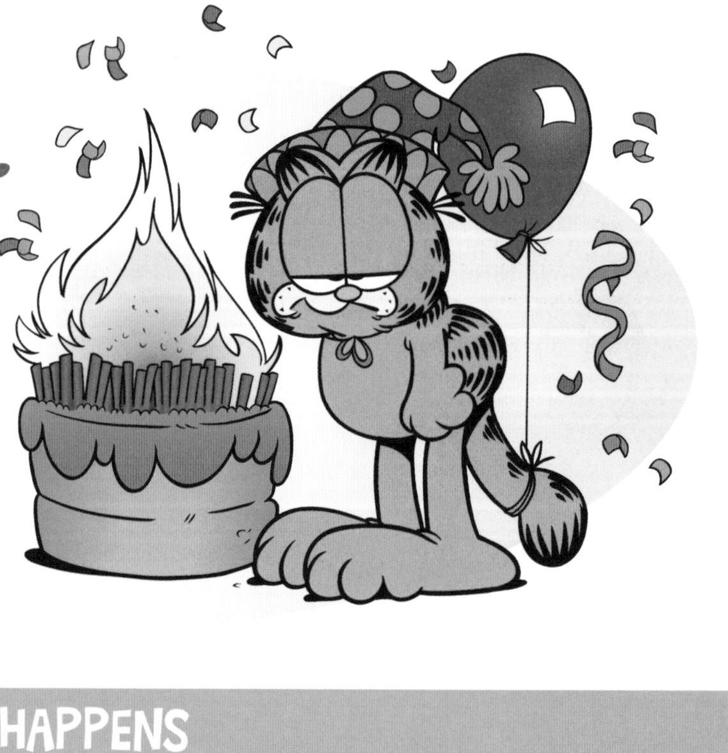

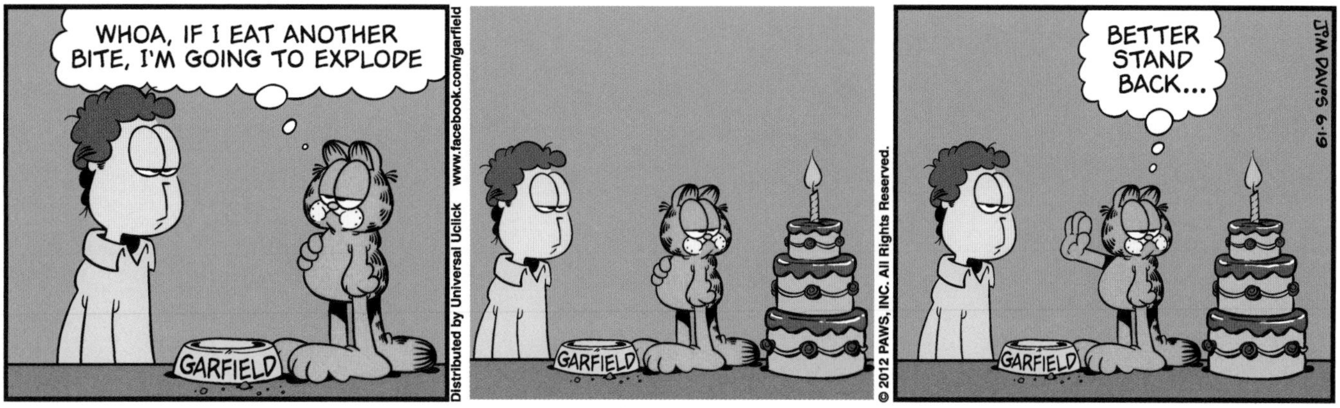
WHOA, IF I EAT ANOTHER BITE, I'M GOING TO EXPLODE
GARFIELD
BETTER STAND BACK...
JIM DAVIS 6-19
Distributed by Universal Uclick www.facebook.com/garfield
© 2012 PAWS, INC. All Rights Reserved.

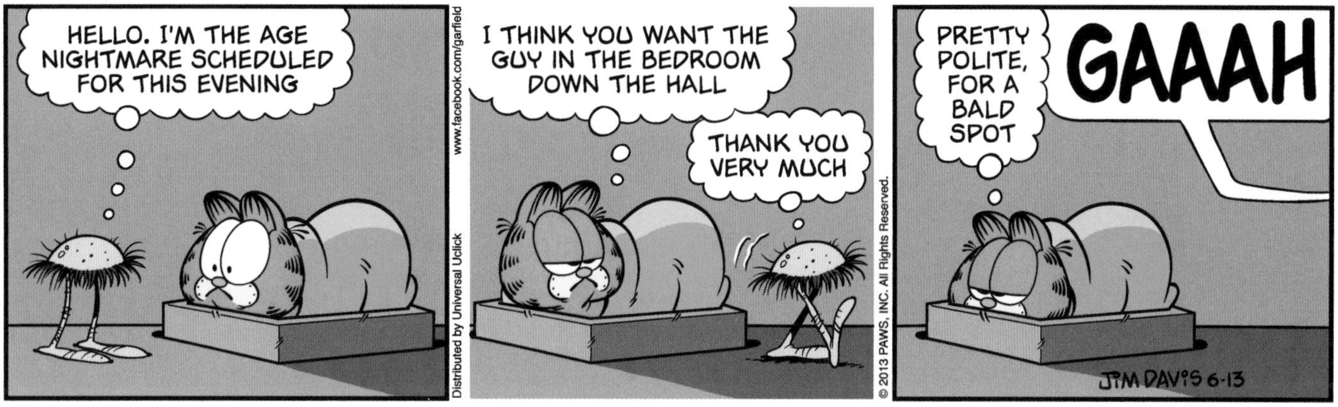
HELLO. I'M THE AGE NIGHTMARE SCHEDULED FOR THIS EVENING
I THINK YOU WANT THE GUY IN THE BEDROOM DOWN THE HALL
THANK YOU VERY MUCH
PRETTY POLITE, FOR A BALD SPOT
GAAAH
JIM DAVIS 6-13
Distributed by Universal Uclick www.facebook.com/garfield
© 2013 PAWS, INC. All Rights Reserved.

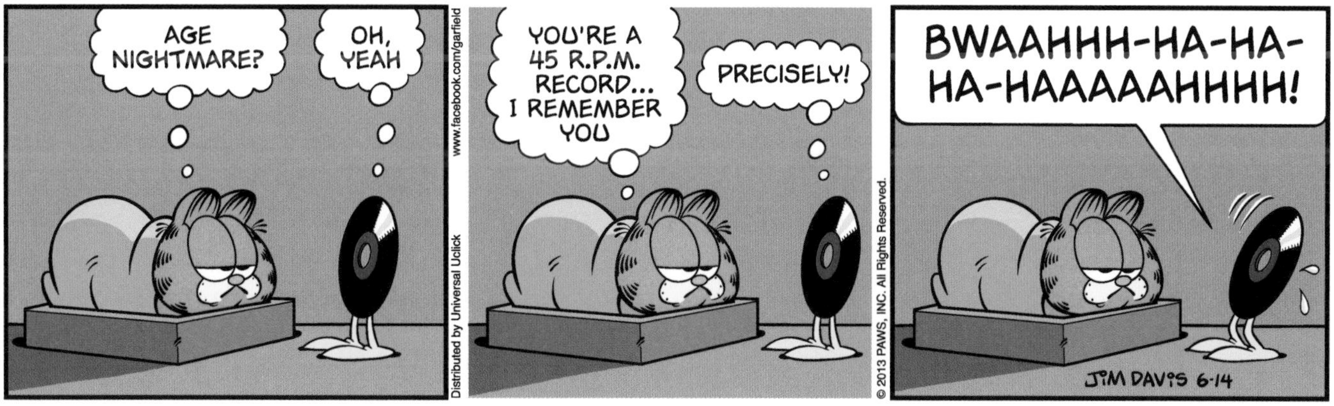
AGE NIGHTMARE?
OH, YEAH
YOU'RE A 45 R.P.M. RECORD... I REMEMBER YOU
PRECISELY!
BWAAHHH-HA-HA-HA-HAAAAAHHHH!
JIM DAVIS 6-14
Distributed by Universal Uclick www.facebook.com/garfield
© 2013 PAWS, INC. All Rights Reserved.

GARFIELD TRIVIA

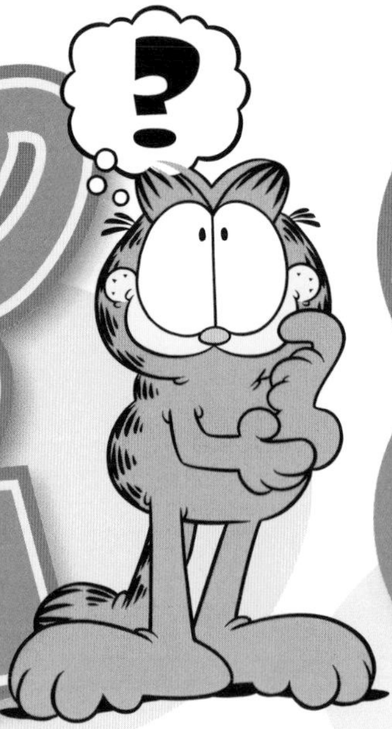
?

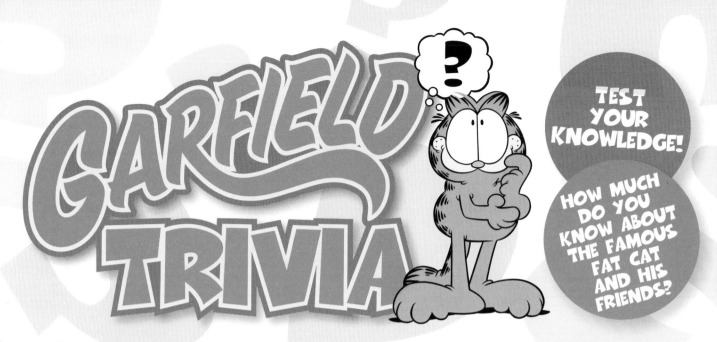

TEST YOUR KNOWLEDGE!

HOW MUCH DO YOU KNOW ABOUT THE FAMOUS FAT CAT AND HIS FRIENDS?

1 In the early years of the strip, who was Jon Arbuckle's roommate?

A. Jack Tripper
B. Lyman
C. Beetle Bailey
D. Binky the Clown

2 Which of the following is NOT an actual Garfield product?

A. Underwear
B. Toilet seat
C. Wart remover
D. Adult diaper

3 What was the name of the "Spider who Saved Christmas"?

A. Hairy Larry
B. Furry Murray
C. Leggy Peggy
D. Bob

4 When Jon saw a mouse in the kitchen, what was it doing?

A. Making a big plate of nachos
B. Pushing a tiny shopping cart
C. Using the free Wi-Fi
D. Finding cheeses

5 What did Greta do when she pet-sat Garfield and Odie on New Year's Eve?

A. Binge-watched the *Twilight Zone* marathon
B. Bent the sofa doing the clean and jerk with it
C. Double-dipped in the guacamole
D. Dressed up as Mary Poppins

6 What did Jon bring Garfield from the pet store?

A.   Live eels
B.   Fake dog ears

C.   A copy of *Weasel Fancier* magazine
D.   A kitty toupee

7 How did Jon take his relationship with Liz to the next level?

A.   Divulged his secret recipe
      for divinity fudge
B.   Shared his Netflix password

C.   Bought matching onesies

D.   Polka-Karaoke Night!

8 Who was Grandma's "Cream of Gladys" soup named after?

A.   Gladys Knight and the Pips
B.   Gladys Kravitz

C.   The chicken who inspired it
D.   Grandma's high school gym teacher

9 Who showed up in Jon's Christmas card photo?

A.   Jon's old girlfriend, Griselda
B.   The Muncie Mall Santa Claus

C.   The pizza guy
D.   Durwood the Plus-Size Elf

10 What did Garfield's neighbor Mrs. Feeny put in her yard?

A.   Booby-trapped tulips
B.   A high-voltage fence

C.   A pool filled with live alligators
D.   An exploding garden gnome

11 What's the name of Garfield's rubber chicken?

A.   McNugget
B.   Rooster Cogburn

C.   Colonel Sanders
D.   Stretch

12 According to Garfield, he isn't overweight; he's_____.

A.   Calorie-infused
B.   A bit blimpy

C.   Large and luscious
D.   Undertall

ANSWERS:

1.B, 2.D, 3.A, 4.B, 5.B, 6.B, 7.D, 8.C, 9.C, 10.B, 11.D, 12.D

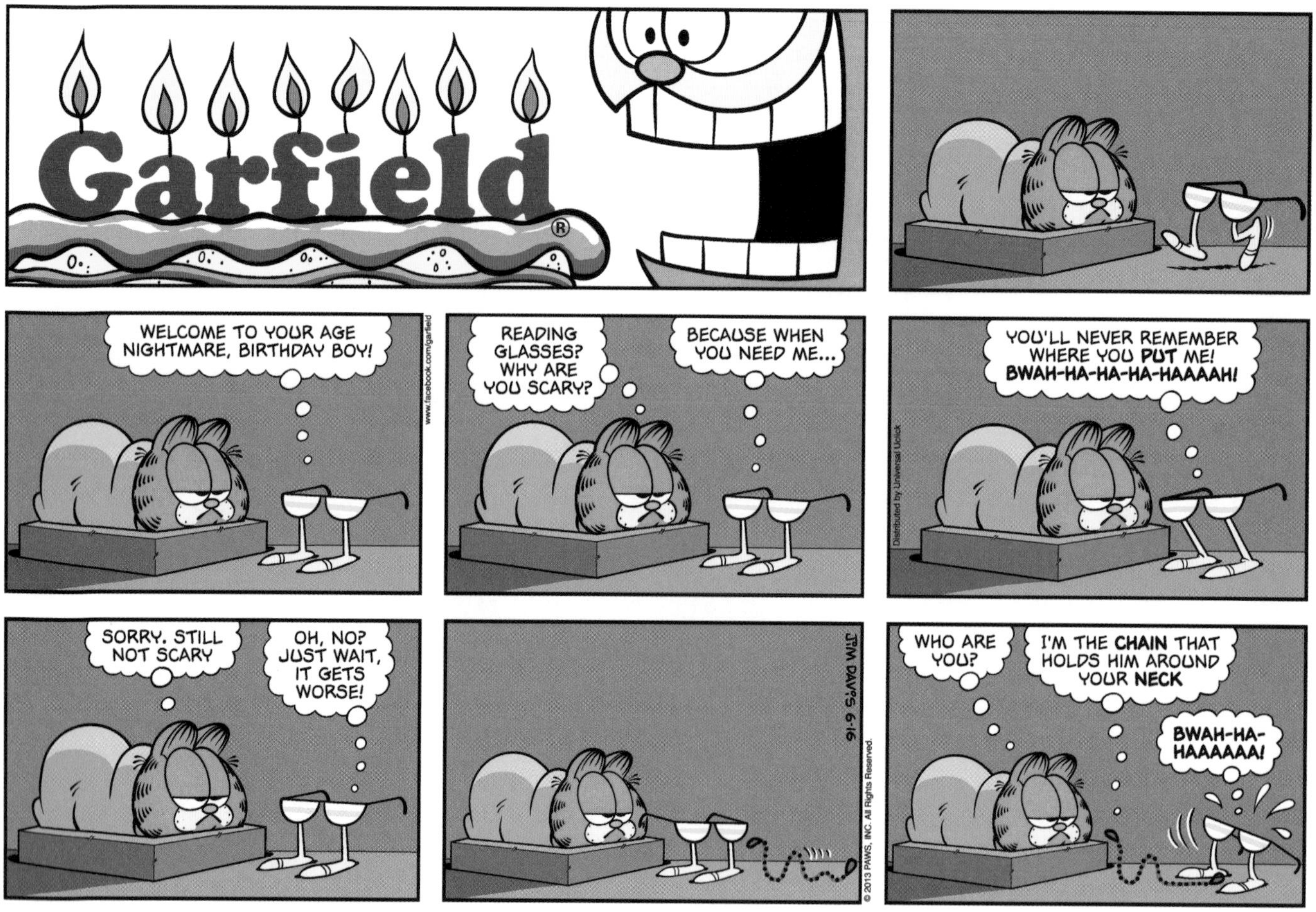
Garfield®
WELCOME TO YOUR AGE NIGHTMARE, BIRTHDAY BOY!
www.facebook.com/garfield
READING GLASSES? WHY ARE YOU SCARY?
BECAUSE WHEN YOU NEED ME...
YOU'LL NEVER REMEMBER WHERE YOU PUT ME! BWAH-HA-HA-HA-HAAAAH!
Distributed by Universal Uclick
SORRY. STILL NOT SCARY
OH, NO? JUST WAIT, IT GETS WORSE!
JIM DAVIS 6-16
© 2013 PAWS, INC. All Rights Reserved.
WHO ARE YOU?
I'M THE CHAIN THAT HOLDS HIM AROUND YOUR NECK
BWAH-HA-HAAAAAA!

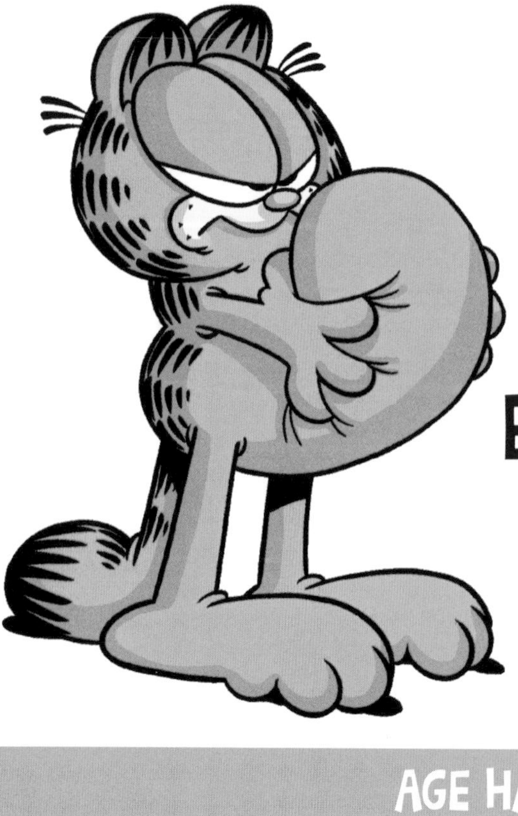

A BIRTHDAY IS LIKE A BELLY BUTTON. EVERYBODY HAS ONE. BUT WHO NEEDS IT ANYMORE?

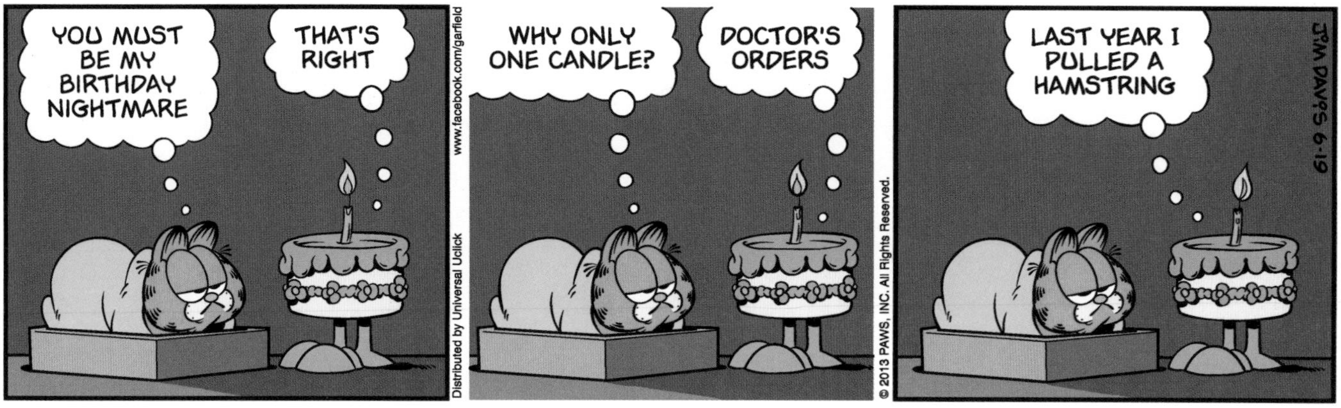
YOU MUST BE MY BIRTHDAY NIGHTMARE
THAT'S RIGHT
WHY ONLY ONE CANDLE?
DOCTOR'S ORDERS
LAST YEAR I PULLED A HAMSTRING
JIM DAVIS 6-19
www.facebook.com/garfield
Distributed by Universal Uclick
© 2013 PAWS, INC. All Rights Reserved.

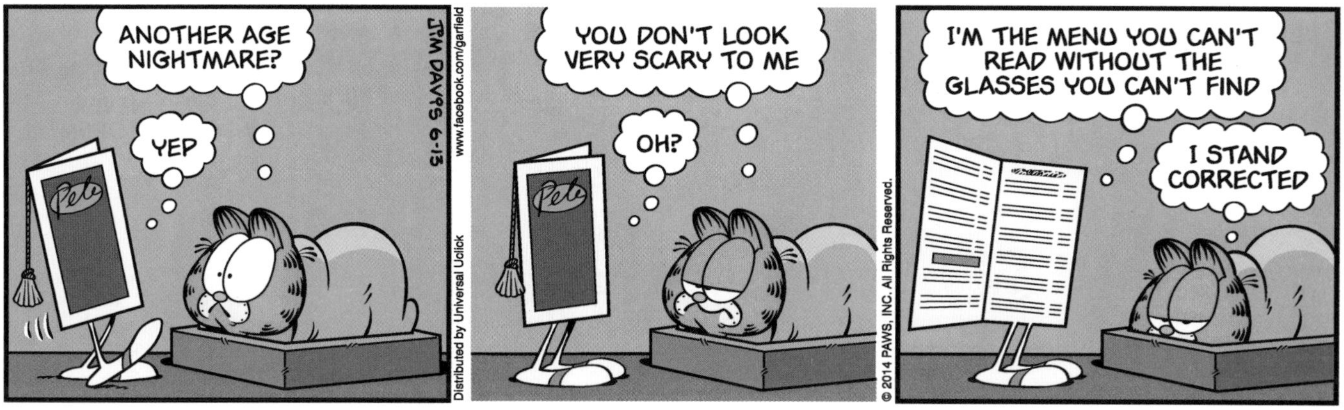
ANOTHER AGE NIGHTMARE?
YEP
YOU DON'T LOOK VERY SCARY TO ME
OH?
I'M THE MENU YOU CAN'T READ WITHOUT THE GLASSES YOU CAN'T FIND
I STAND CORRECTED
JIM DAVIS 6-13
www.facebook.com/garfield
Distributed by Universal Uclick
© 2014 PAWS, INC. All Rights Reserved.

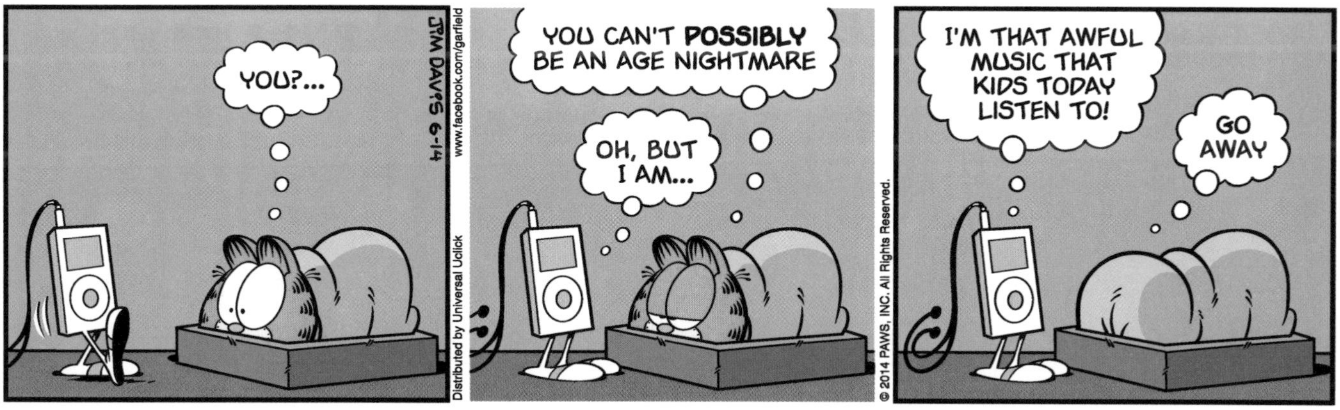
YOU?...
YOU CAN'T **POSSIBLY** BE AN AGE NIGHTMARE
OH, BUT I AM...
I'M THAT AWFUL MUSIC THAT KIDS TODAY LISTEN TO!
GO AWAY
JIM DAVIS 6-14
www.facebook.com/garfield
Distributed by Universal Uclick
© 2014 PAWS, INC. All Rights Reserved.

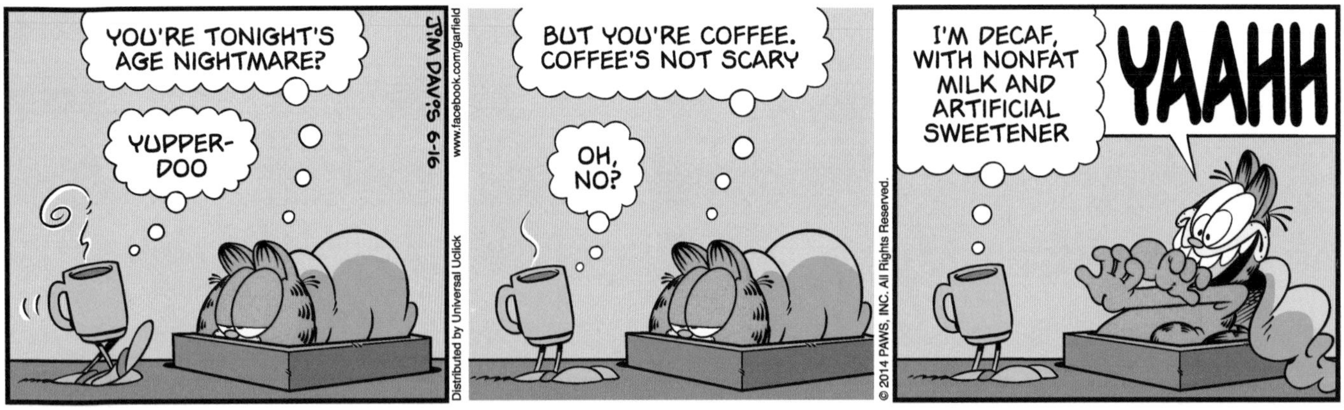
YOU'RE TONIGHT'S AGE NIGHTMARE?
YUPPER-DOO
JIM DAVIS 6-16
www.facebook.com/garfield
Distributed by Universal Uclick
BUT YOU'RE COFFEE. COFFEE'S NOT SCARY
OH, NO?
© 2014 PAWS, INC. All Rights Reserved.
I'M DECAF, WITH NONFAT MILK AND ARTIFICIAL SWEETENER
YAAHH

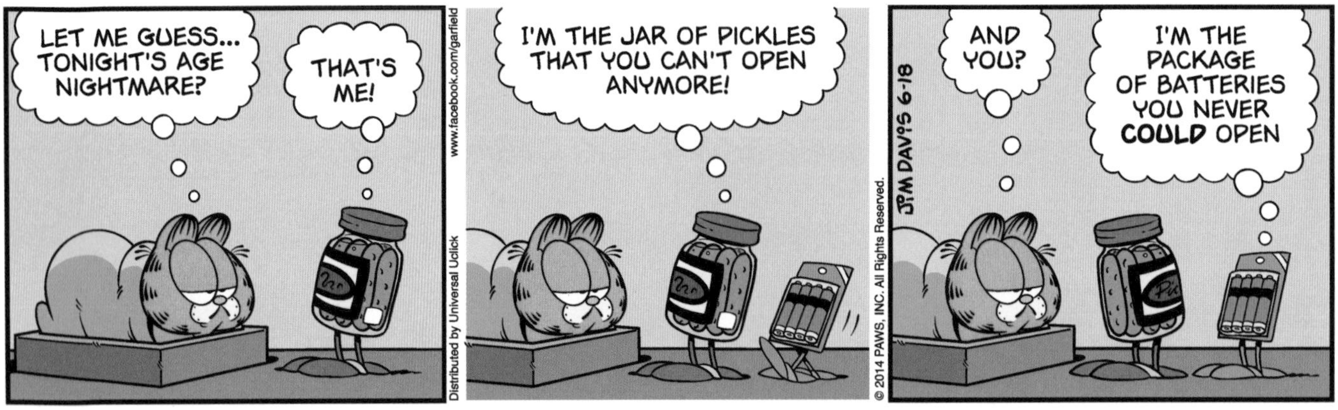
LET ME GUESS... TONIGHT'S AGE NIGHTMARE?
THAT'S ME!
www.facebook.com/garfield
Distributed by Universal Uclick
I'M THE JAR OF PICKLES THAT YOU CAN'T OPEN ANYMORE!
© 2014 PAWS, INC. All Rights Reserved.
JIM DAVIS 6-18
AND YOU?
I'M THE PACKAGE OF BATTERIES YOU NEVER COULD OPEN

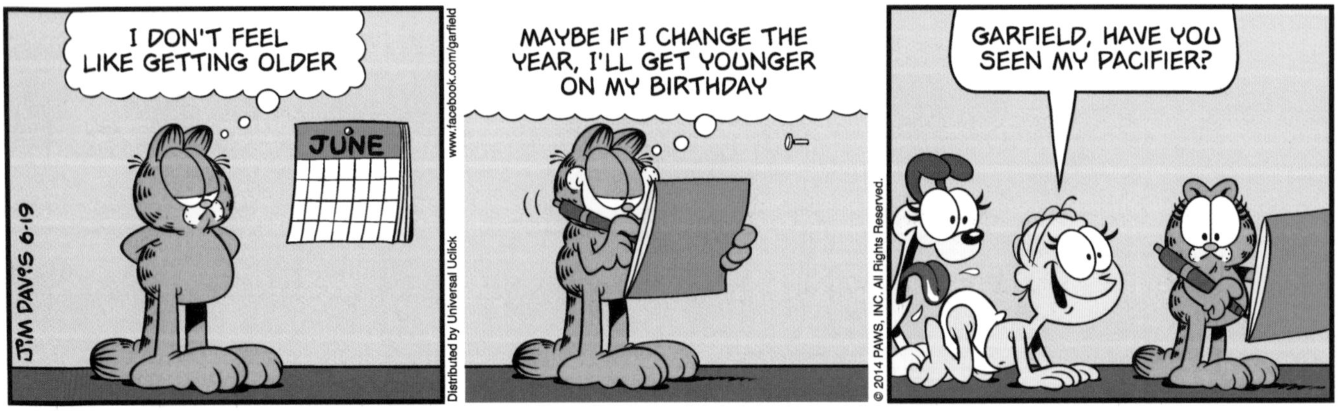
I DON'T FEEL LIKE GETTING OLDER
JUNE
JIM DAVIS 6-19
www.facebook.com/garfield
Distributed by Universal Uclick
MAYBE IF I CHANGE THE YEAR, I'LL GET YOUNGER ON MY BIRTHDAY
© 2014 PAWS, INC. All Rights Reserved.
GARFIELD, HAVE YOU SEEN MY PACIFIER?

I'M TOO OLD TO GROW UP

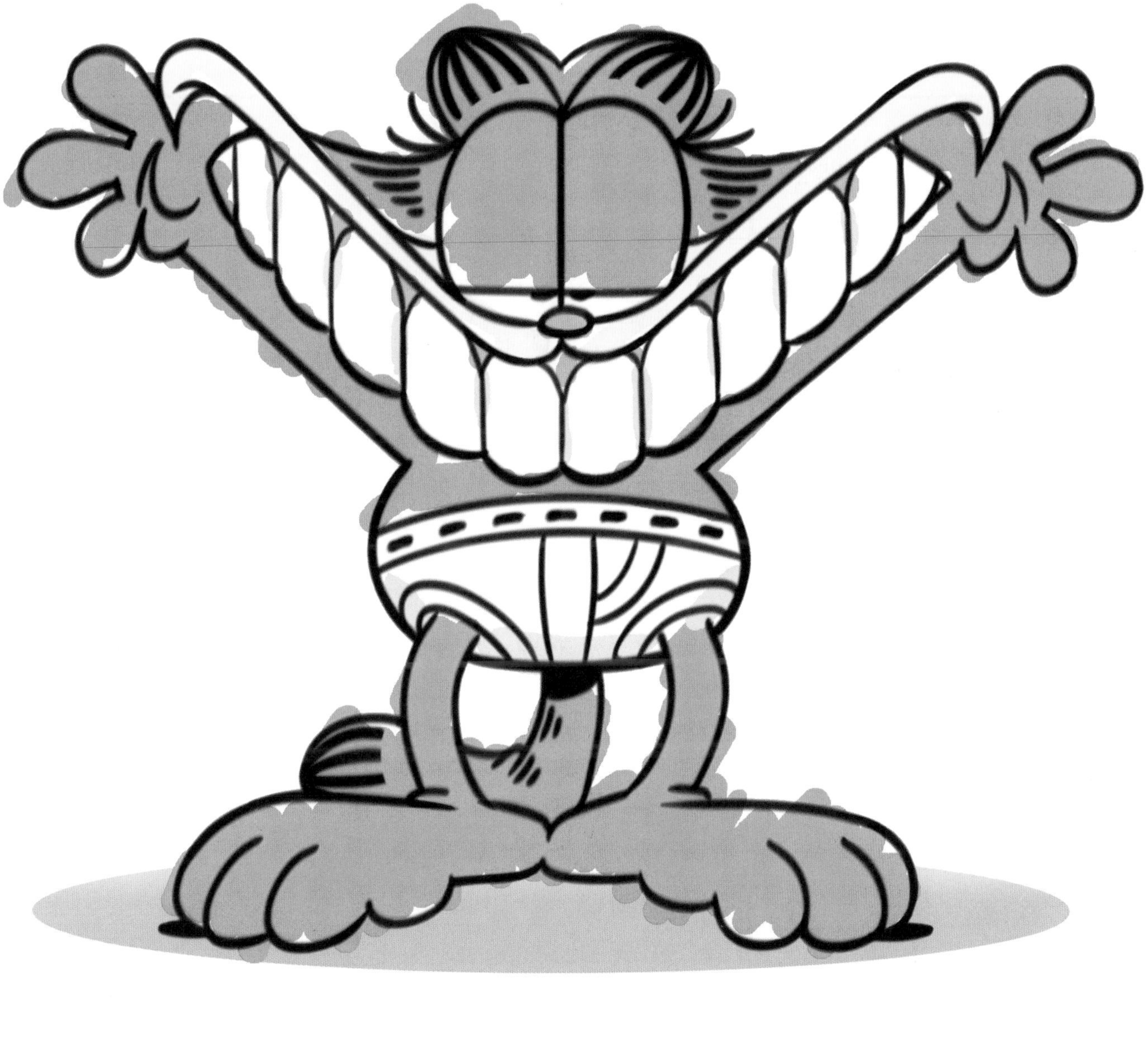

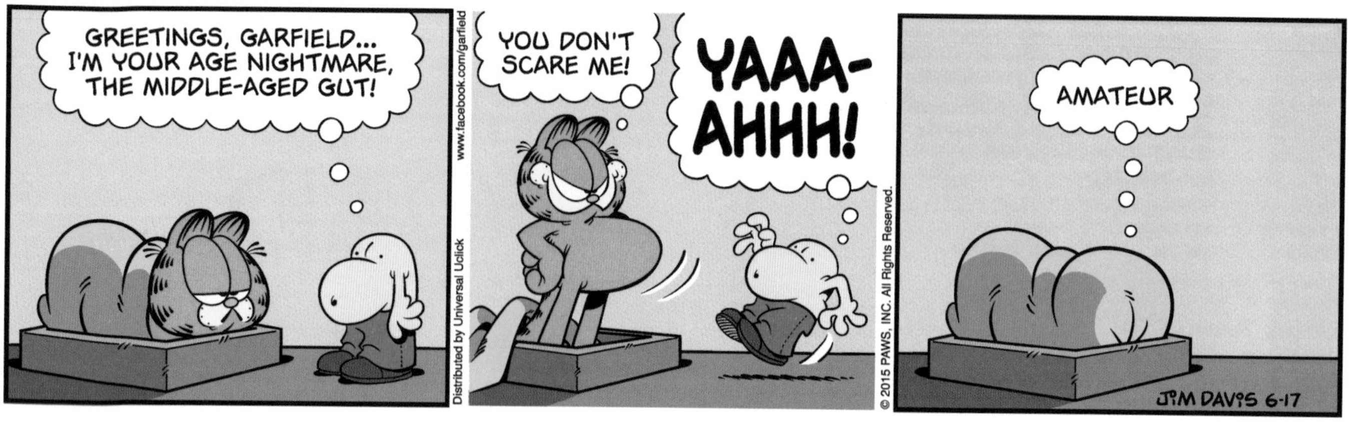
GREETINGS, GARFIELD... I'M YOUR AGE NIGHTMARE, THE MIDDLE-AGED GUT!
YOU DON'T SCARE ME!
YAAA-AHHH!
AMATEUR
JIM DAVIS 6-17
© 2015 PAWS, INC. All Rights Reserved.
Distributed by Universal Uclick www.facebook.com/garfield

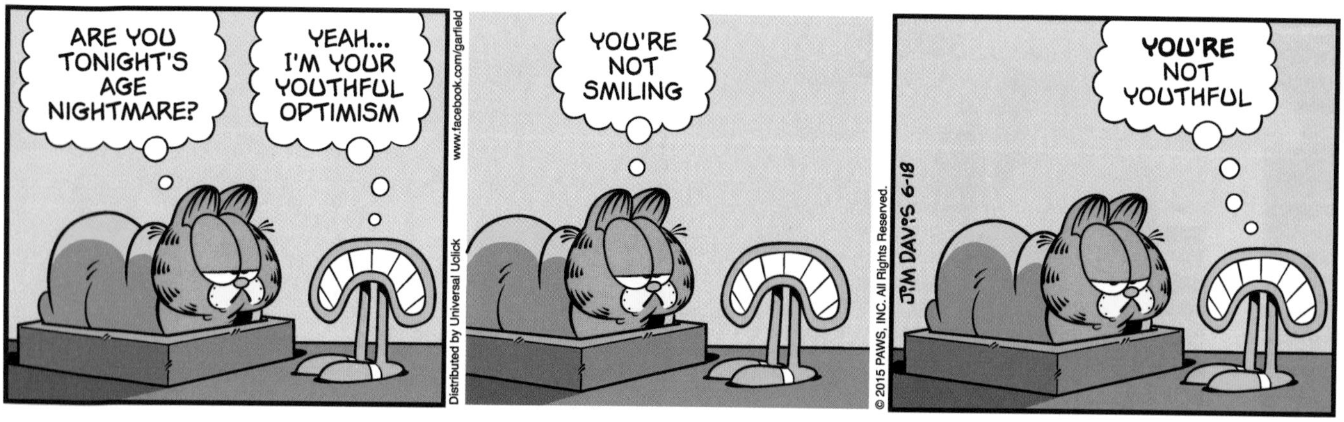
ARE YOU TONIGHT'S AGE NIGHTMARE?
YEAH... I'M YOUR YOUTHFUL OPTIMISM
YOU'RE NOT SMILING
YOU'RE NOT YOUTHFUL
JIM DAVIS 6-18
© 2015 PAWS, INC. All Rights Reserved.
Distributed by Universal Uclick www.facebook.com/garfield

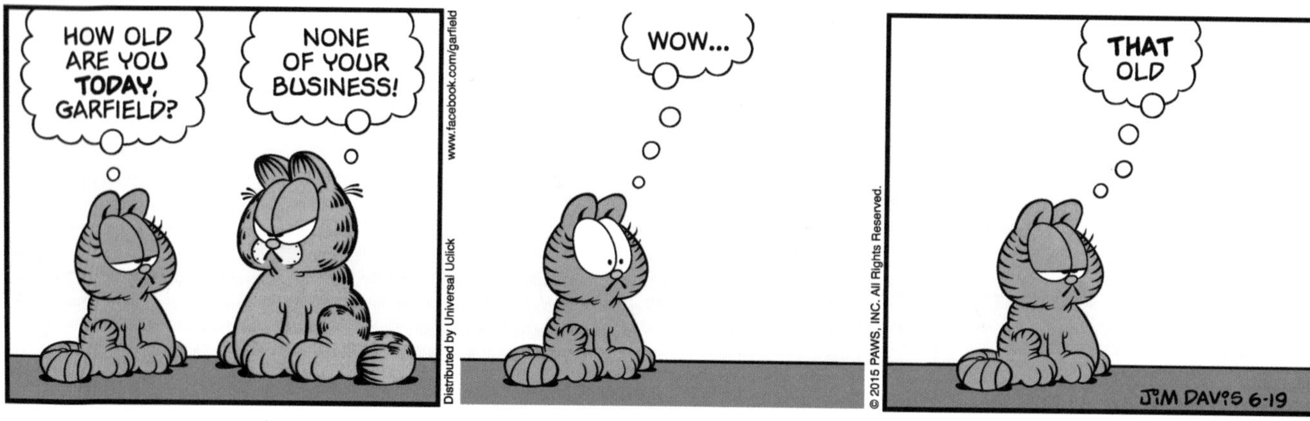
HOW OLD ARE YOU TODAY, GARFIELD?
NONE OF YOUR BUSINESS!
WOW...
THAT OLD
JIM DAVIS 6-19
© 2015 PAWS, INC. All Rights Reserved.
Distributed by Universal Uclick www.facebook.com/garfield

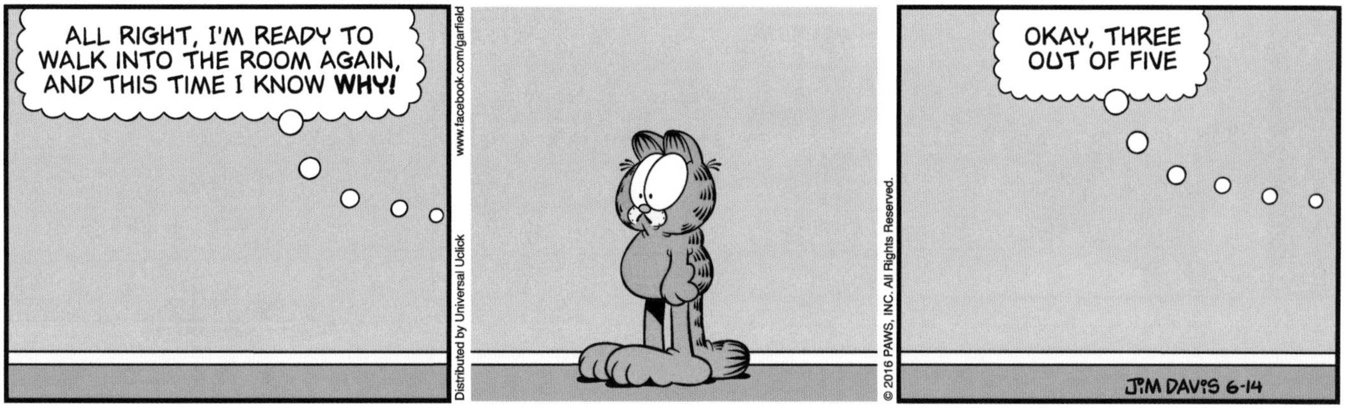
ALL RIGHT, I'M READY TO WALK INTO THE ROOM AGAIN, AND THIS TIME I KNOW WHY!
Distributed by Universal Uclick www.facebook.com/garfield
© 2016 PAWS, INC. All Rights Reserved.
OKAY, THREE OUT OF FIVE
JIM DAVIS 6-14

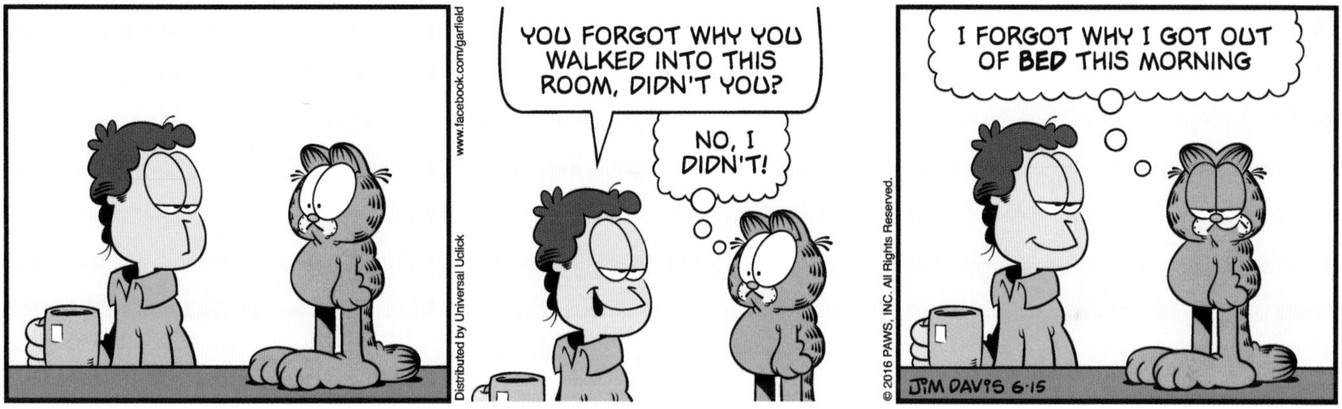
Distributed by Universal Uclick www.facebook.com/garfield
YOU FORGOT WHY YOU WALKED INTO THIS ROOM, DIDN'T YOU?
NO, I DIDN'T!
© 2016 PAWS, INC. All Rights Reserved.
I FORGOT WHY I GOT OUT OF BED THIS MORNING
JIM DAVIS 6-15

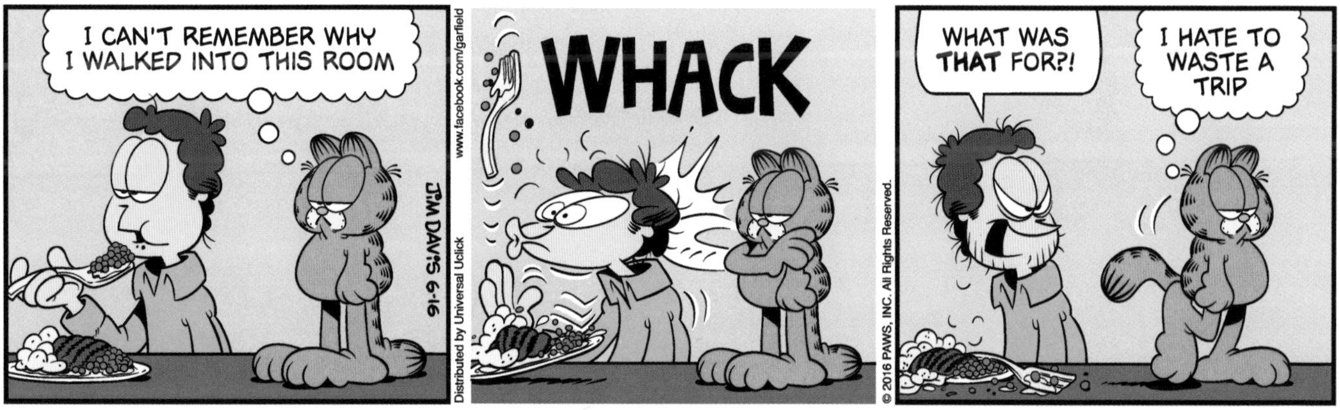
I CAN'T REMEMBER WHY I WALKED INTO THIS ROOM
JIM DAVIS 6-16
Distributed by Universal Uclick www.facebook.com/garfield
WHACK
© 2016 PAWS, INC. All Rights Reserved.
WHAT WAS THAT FOR?!
I HATE TO WASTE A TRIP

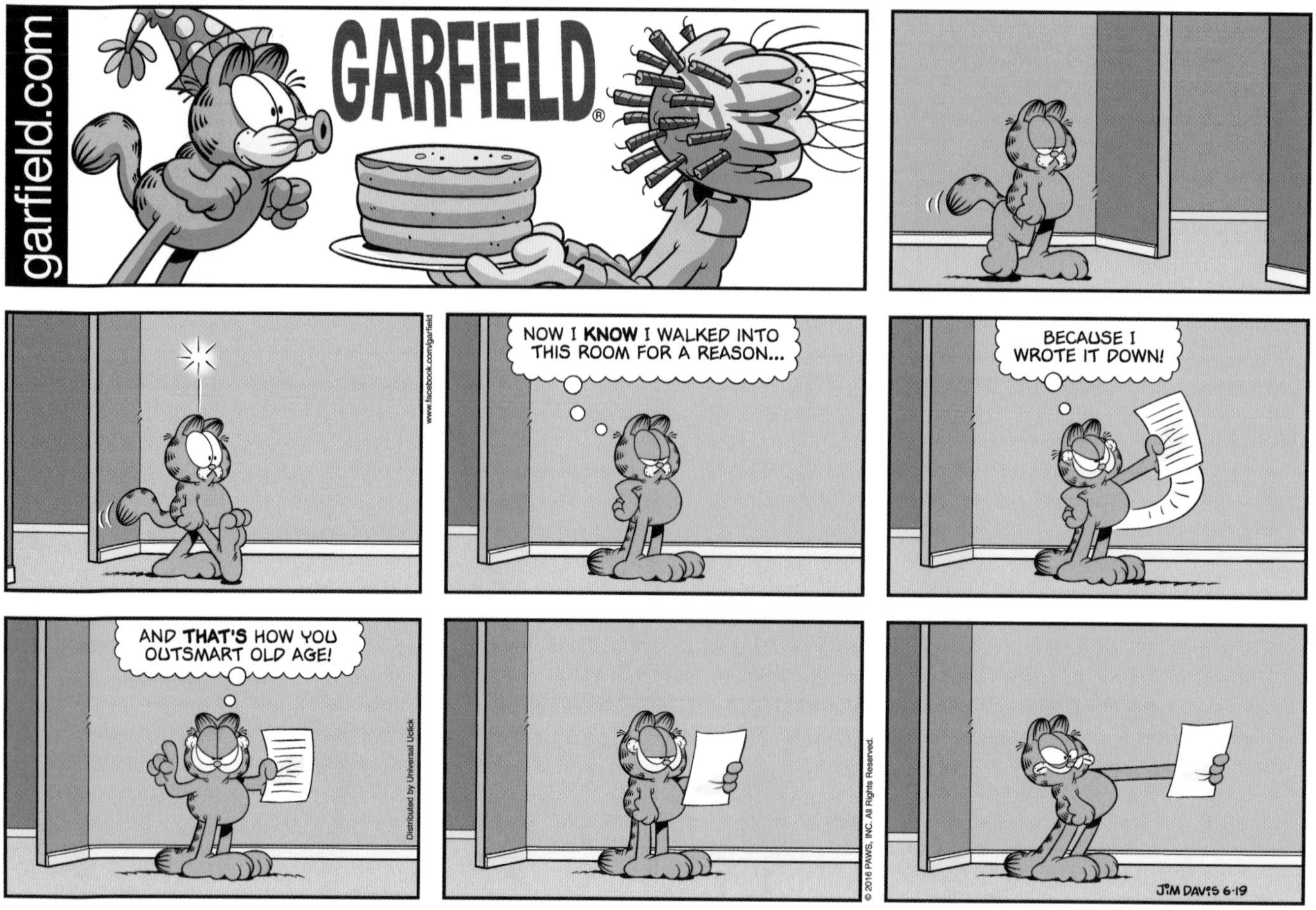
garfield.com
GARFIELD
www.facebook.com/garfield
NOW I KNOW I WALKED INTO THIS ROOM FOR A REASON...
BECAUSE I WROTE IT DOWN!
AND THAT'S HOW YOU OUTSMART OLD AGE!
Distributed by Universal Uclick
© 2016 PAWS, INC. All Rights Reserved.
JIM DAVIS 6-19

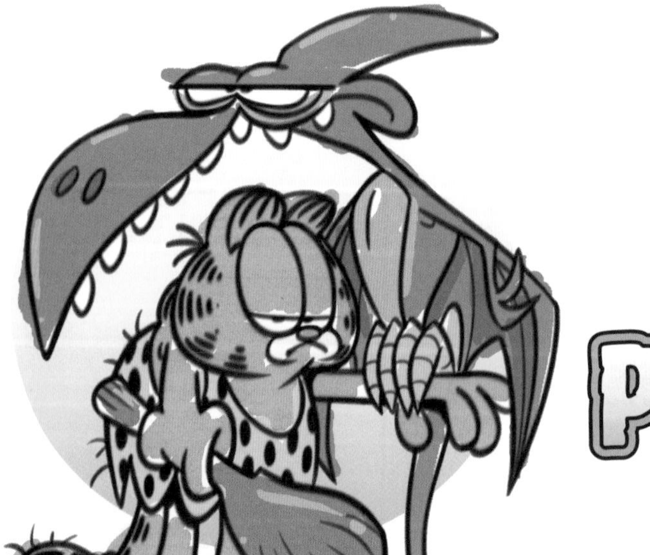

YOU KNOW YOU'RE OLD WHEN:

YOUR PET BIRD WAS A PTERODACTYL

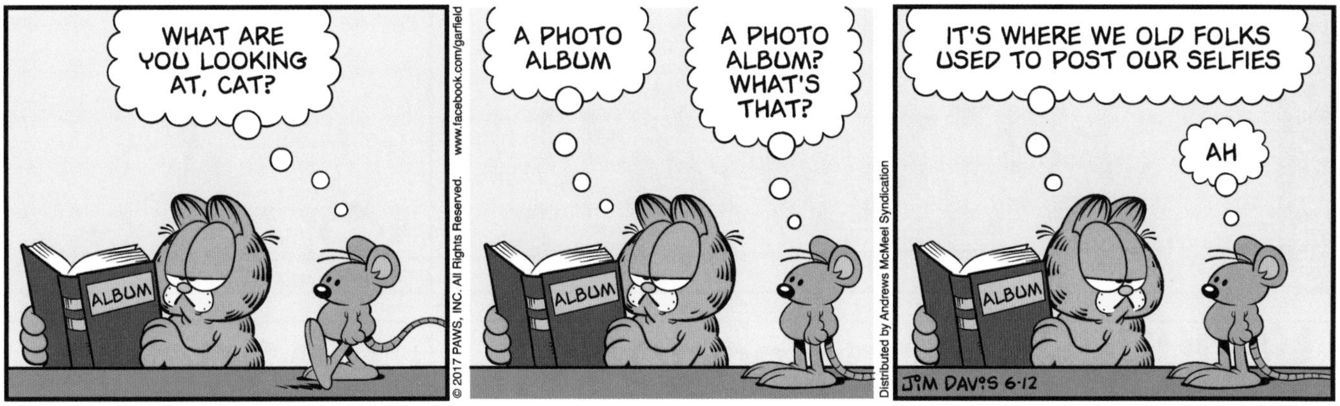
WHAT ARE YOU LOOKING AT, CAT?
ALBUM
A PHOTO ALBUM
A PHOTO ALBUM? WHAT'S THAT?
IT'S WHERE WE OLD FOLKS USED TO POST OUR SELFIES
AH
JIM DAVIS 6-12
© 2017 PAWS, INC. All Rights Reserved. www.facebook.com/garfield
Distributed by Andrews McMeel Syndication

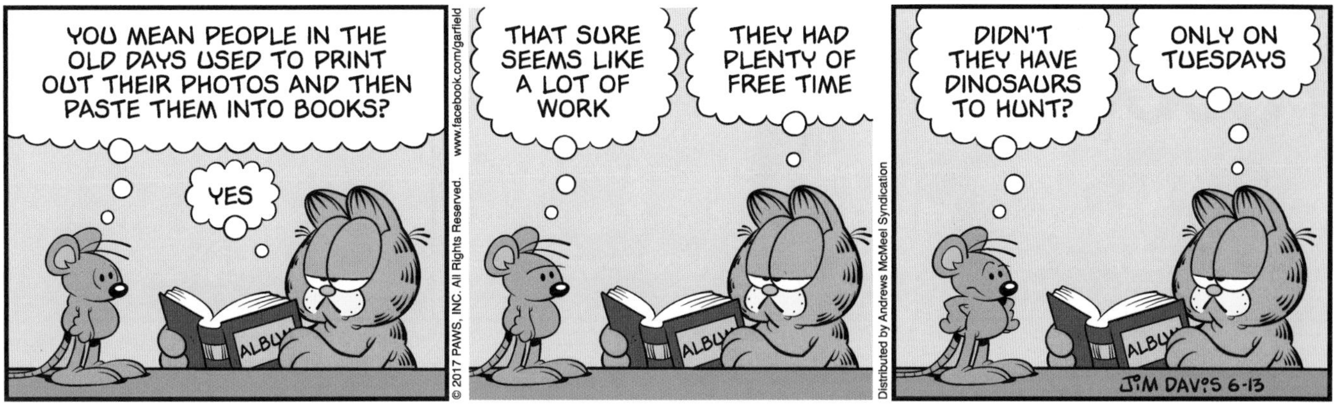
YOU MEAN PEOPLE IN THE OLD DAYS USED TO PRINT OUT THEIR PHOTOS AND THEN PASTE THEM INTO BOOKS?
YES
THAT SURE SEEMS LIKE A LOT OF WORK
THEY HAD PLENTY OF FREE TIME
DIDN'T THEY HAVE DINOSAURS TO HUNT?
ONLY ON TUESDAYS
JIM DAVIS 6-13
© 2017 PAWS, INC. All Rights Reserved. www.facebook.com/garfield
Distributed by Andrews McMeel Syndication

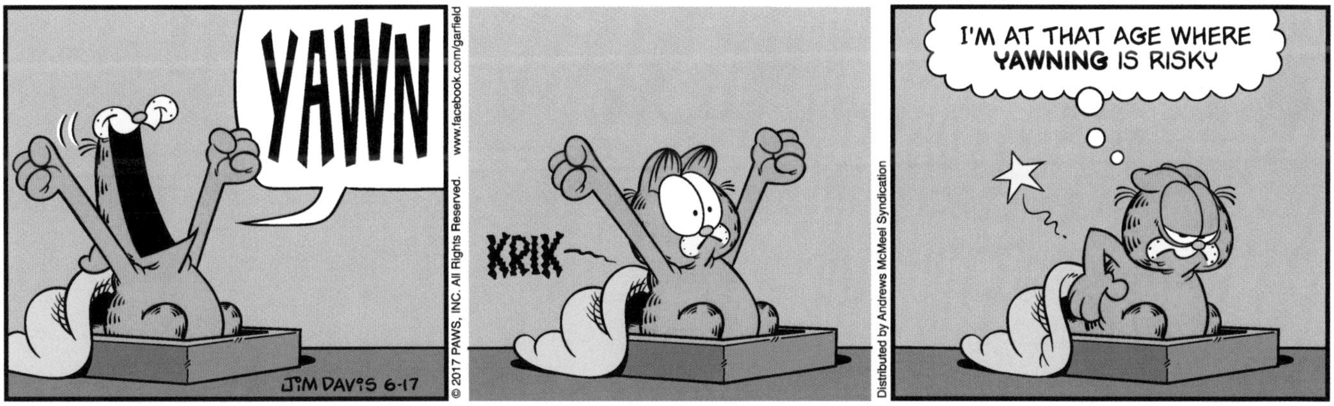
YAWN
KRIK
I'M AT THAT AGE WHERE **YAWNING** IS RISKY
JIM DAVIS 6-17
© 2017 PAWS, INC. All Rights Reserved. www.facebook.com/garfield
Distributed by Andrews McMeel Syndication

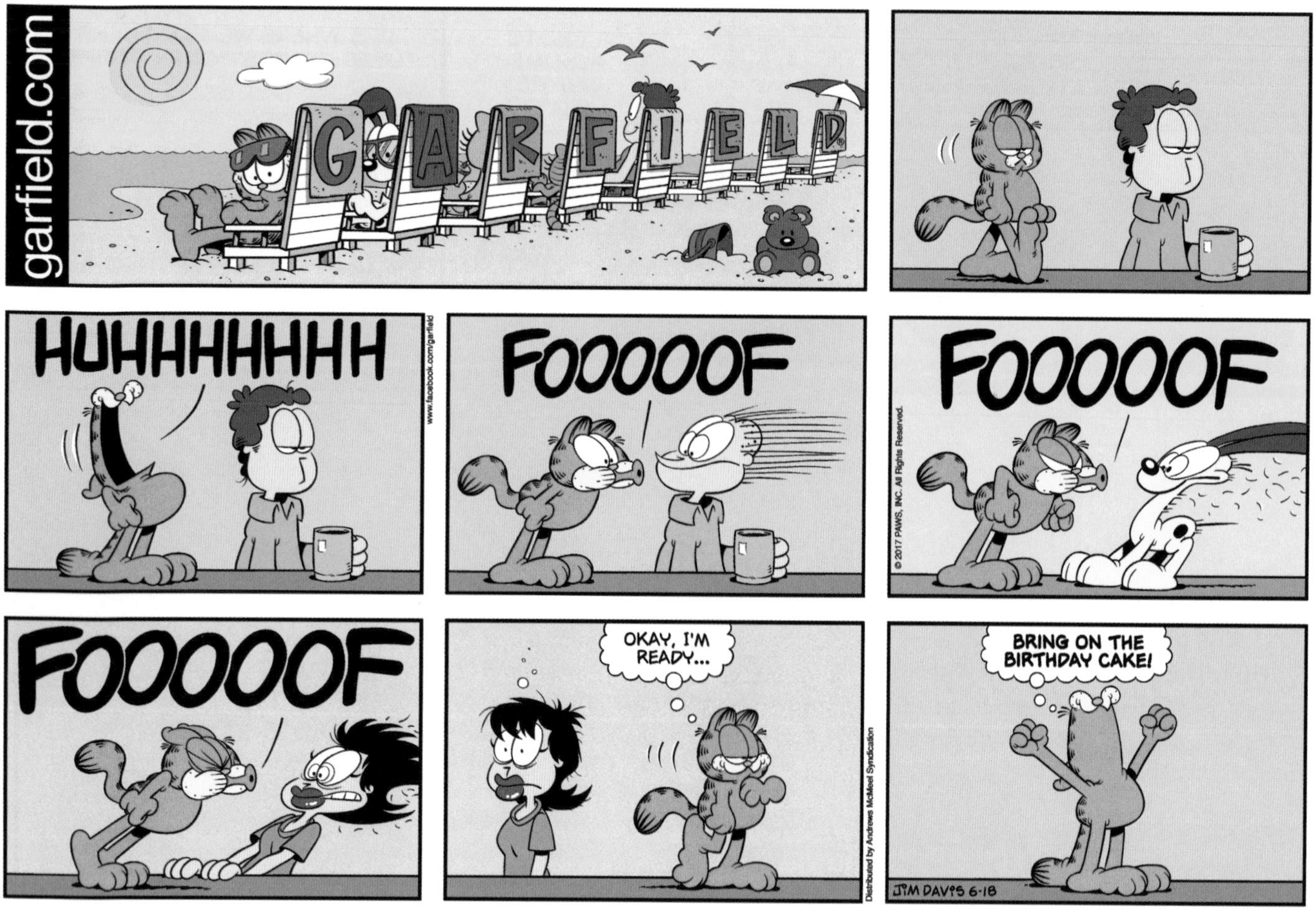
garfield.com
GARFIELD
HUHHHHHHH
www.facebook.com/garfield
FOOOOOF
© 2017 PAWS, INC. All Rights Reserved.
FOOOOOF
FOOOOOF
OKAY, I'M READY...
Distributed by Andrews McMeel Syndication
BRING ON THE BIRTHDAY CAKE!
JIM DAVIS 6-18

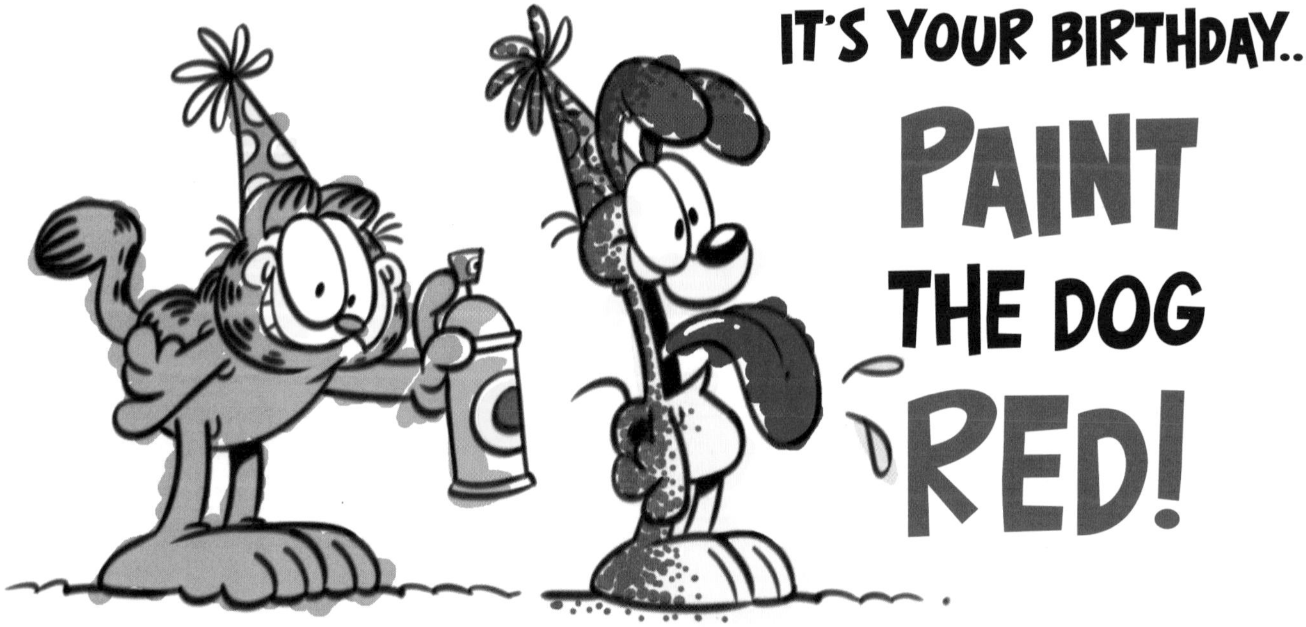
IT'S YOUR BIRTHDAY...
PAINT
THE DOG
RED!

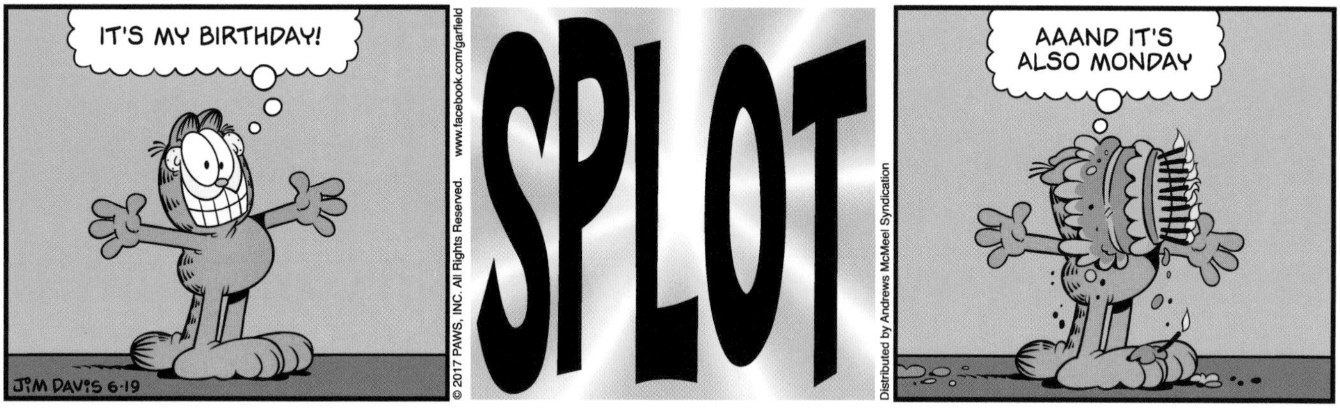
IT'S MY BIRTHDAY!
JIM DAVIS 6-19
© 2017 PAWS, INC. All Rights Reserved. www.facebook.com/garfield
SPLOT
Distributed by Andrews McMeel Syndication
AAAND IT'S ALSO MONDAY

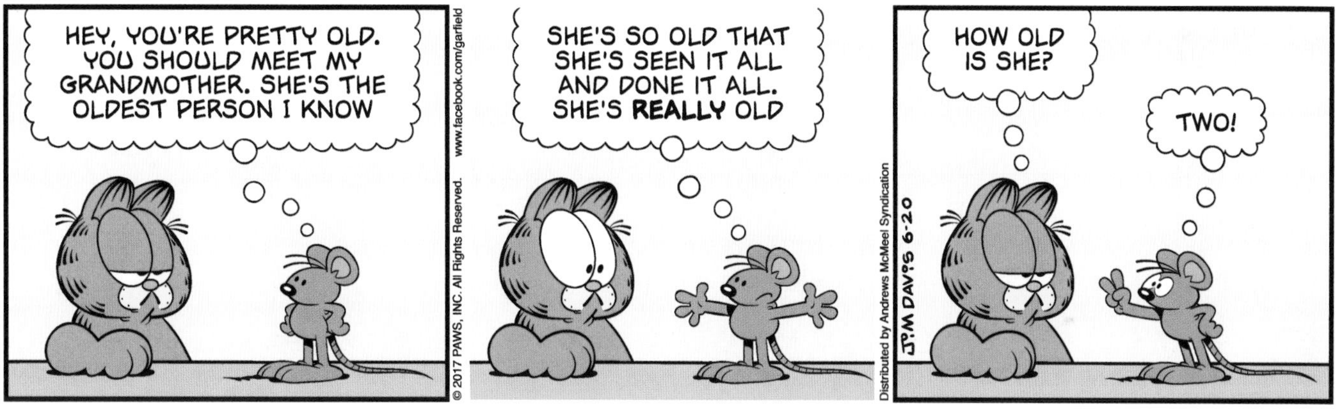
HEY, YOU'RE PRETTY OLD. YOU SHOULD MEET MY GRANDMOTHER. SHE'S THE OLDEST PERSON I KNOW
© 2017 PAWS, INC. All Rights Reserved. www.facebook.com/garfield
SHE'S SO OLD THAT SHE'S SEEN IT ALL AND DONE IT ALL. SHE'S REALLY OLD
Distributed by Andrews McMeel Syndication
JIM DAVIS 6-20
HOW OLD IS SHE?
TWO!

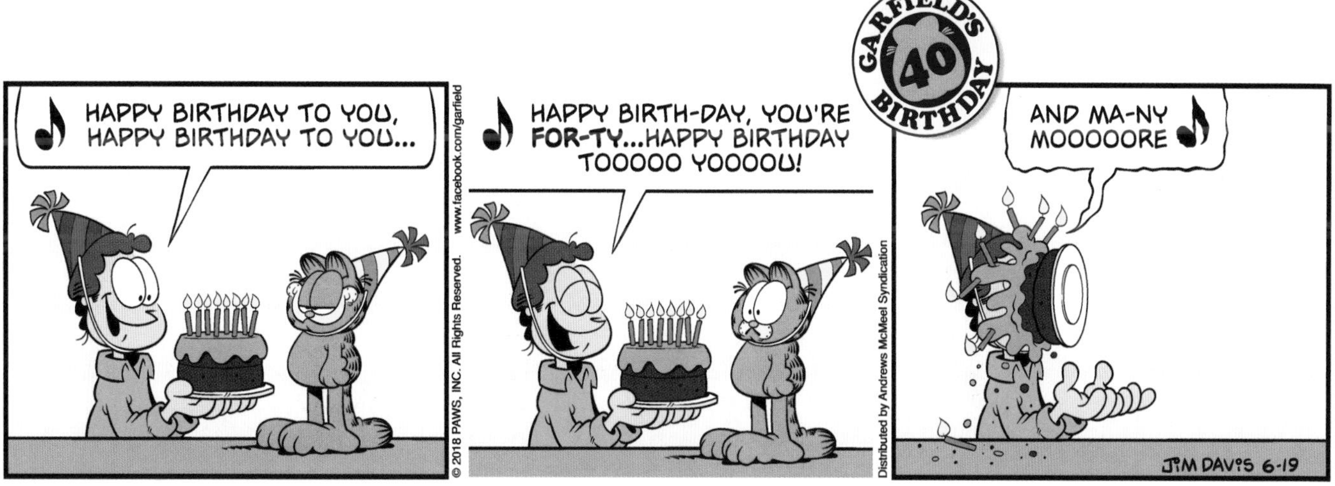
HAPPY BIRTHDAY TO YOU, HAPPY BIRTHDAY TO YOU...
© 2018 PAWS, INC. All Rights Reserved. www.facebook.com/garfield
HAPPY BIRTH-DAY, YOU'RE FOR-TY...HAPPY BIRTHDAY TOOOOO YOOOOU!
GARFIELD'S 40 BIRTHDAY
Distributed by Andrews McMeel Syndication
AND MA-NY MOOOOORE
JIM DAVIS 6-19

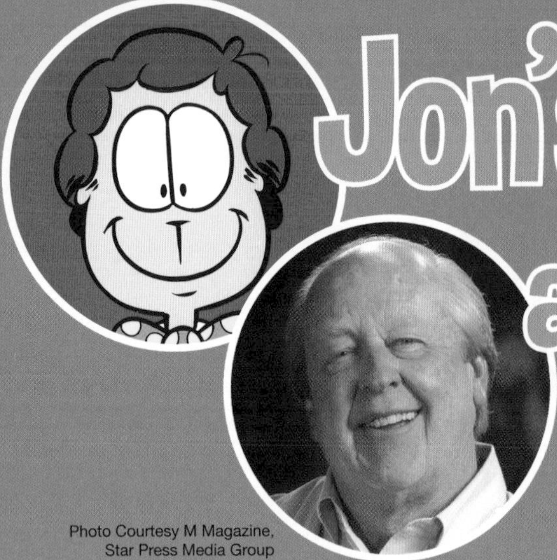

Photo Courtesy M Magazine,
Star Press Media Group

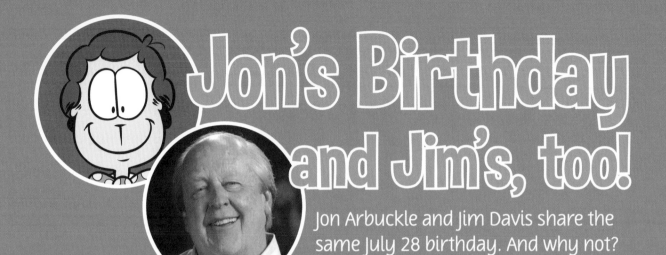

Jon's Birthday and Jim's, too!

Jon Arbuckle and Jim Davis share the same July 28 birthday. And why not? Nerds of a feather celebrate together!

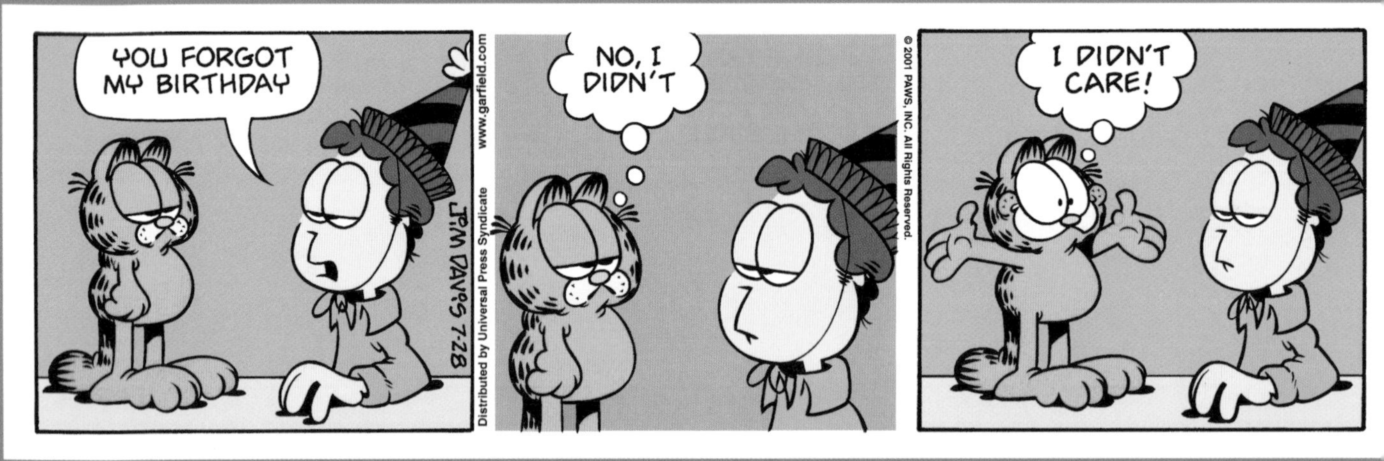
YOU FORGOT MY BIRTHDAY
www.garfield.com
Distributed by Universal Press Syndicate
JIM DAVIS 7-28
NO, I DIDN'T
© 2001 PAWS, INC. All Rights Reserved.
I DIDN'T CARE!

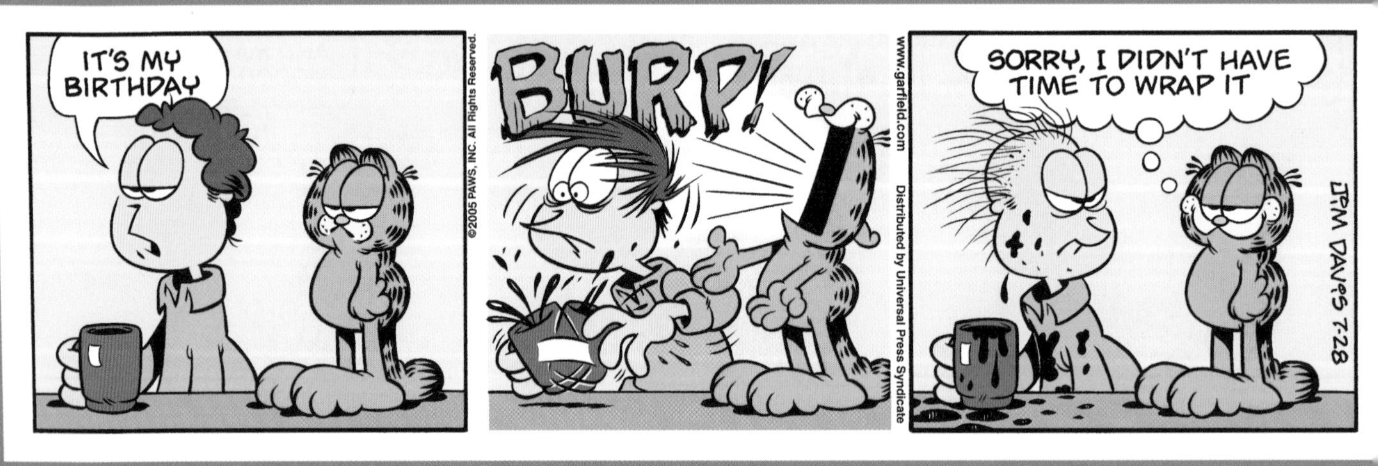
IT'S MY BIRTHDAY
©2005 PAWS, INC. All Rights Reserved.
BURP!
www.garfield.com
Distributed by Universal Press Syndicate
SORRY, I DIDN'T HAVE TIME TO WRAP IT
JIM DAVIS 7-28

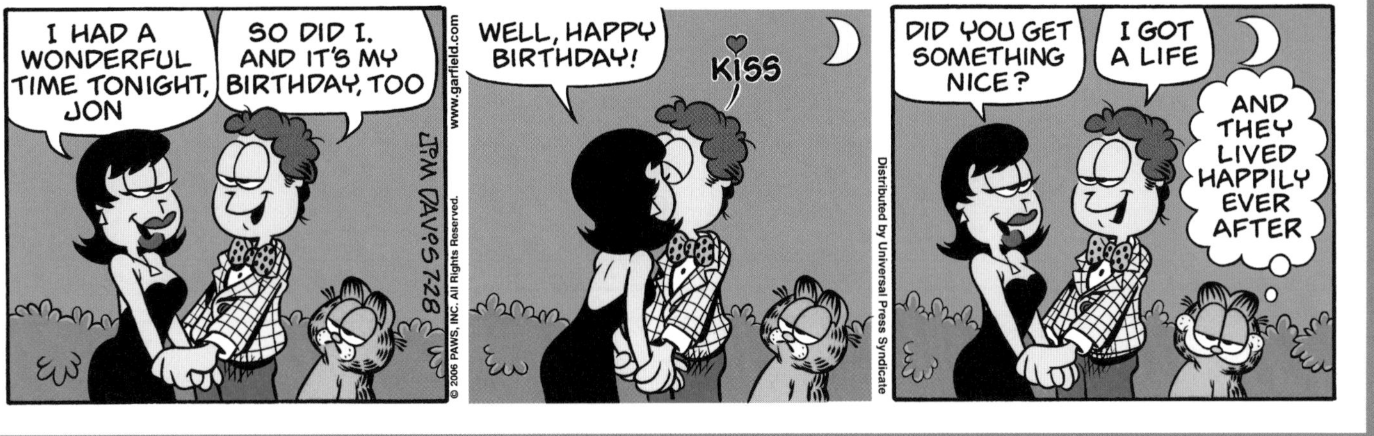
I HAD A WONDERFUL TIME TONIGHT, JON
SO DID I. AND IT'S MY BIRTHDAY, TOO
JIM DAVIS 7-28
© 2006 PAWS, INC. All Rights Reserved.
www.garfield.com
WELL, HAPPY BIRTHDAY!
KISS
Distributed by Universal Press Syndicate
DID YOU GET SOMETHING NICE?
I GOT A LIFE
AND THEY LIVED HAPPILY EVER AFTER

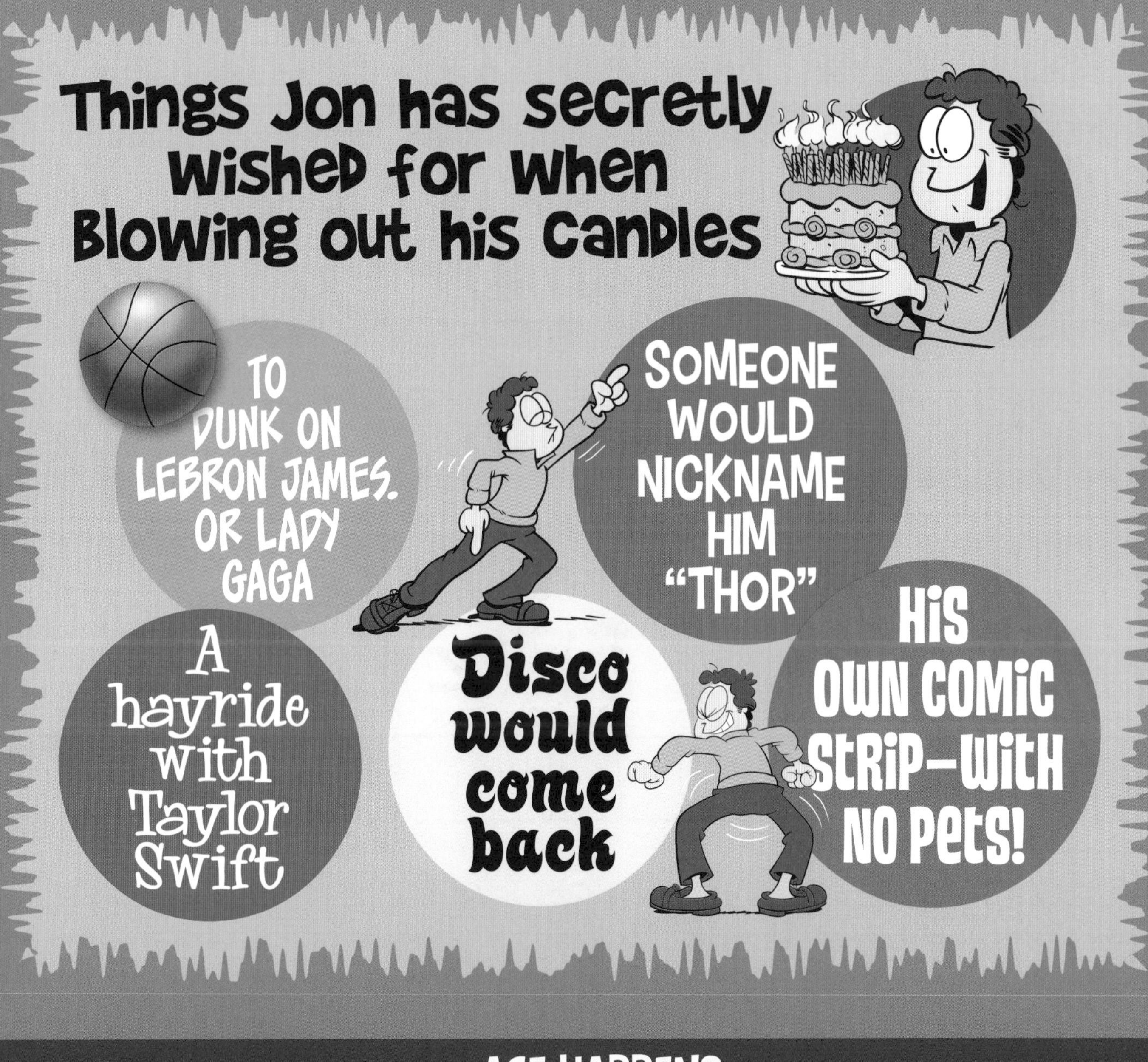
Things Jon has secretly wished for when Blowing out his candles
TO DUNK ON LEBRON JAMES. OR LADY GAGA
SOMEONE WOULD NICKNAME HIM "THOR"
A hayride with Taylor Swift
Disco would come back
His own comic strip—with no pets!

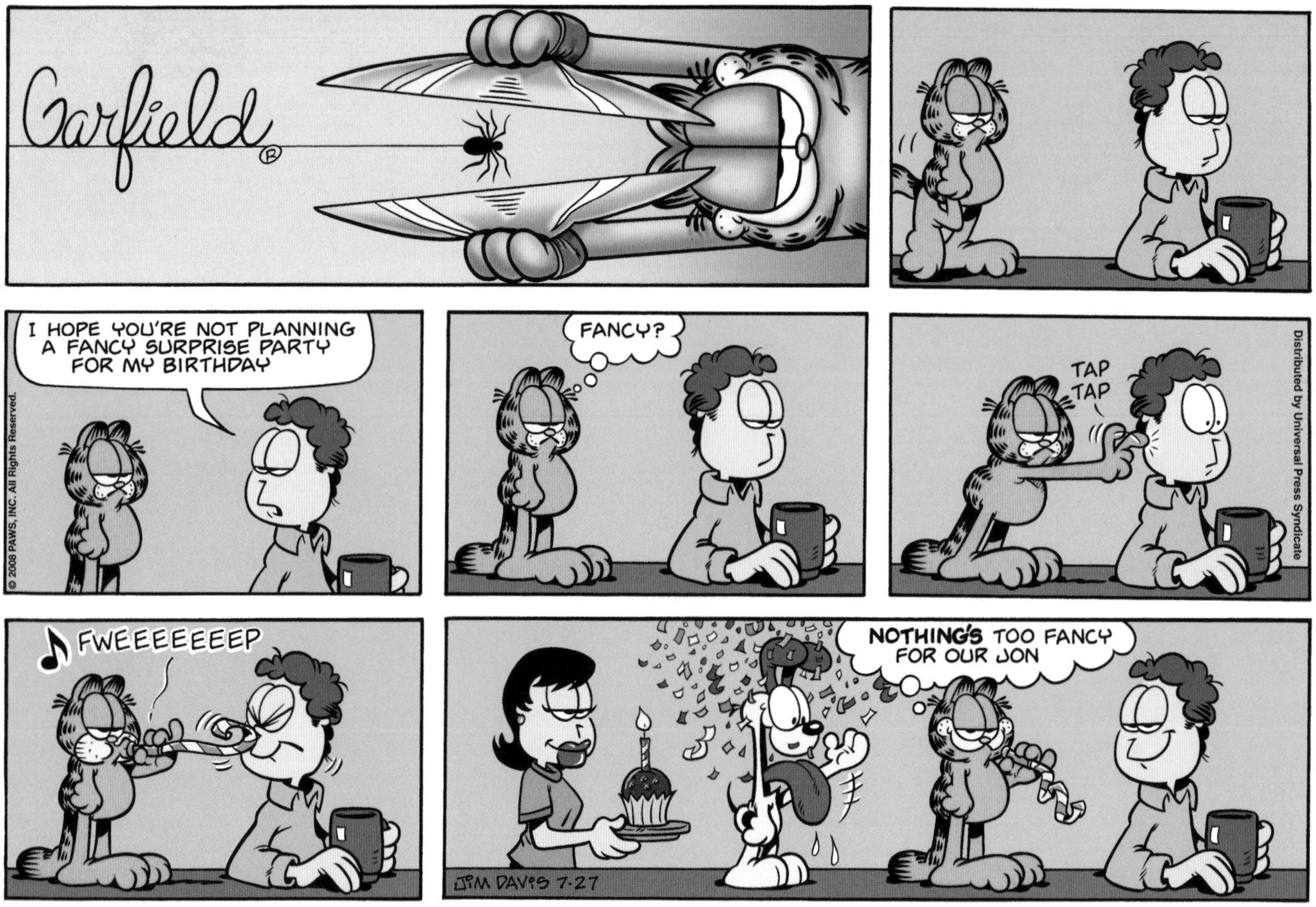
Garfield
I HOPE YOU'RE NOT PLANNING A FANCY SURPRISE PARTY FOR MY BIRTHDAY
FANCY?
TAP TAP
FWEEEEEEEP
NOTHING'S TOO FANCY FOR OUR JON
JIM DAVIS 7-27
© 2008 PAWS, INC. All Rights Reserved.
Distributed by Universal Press Syndicate

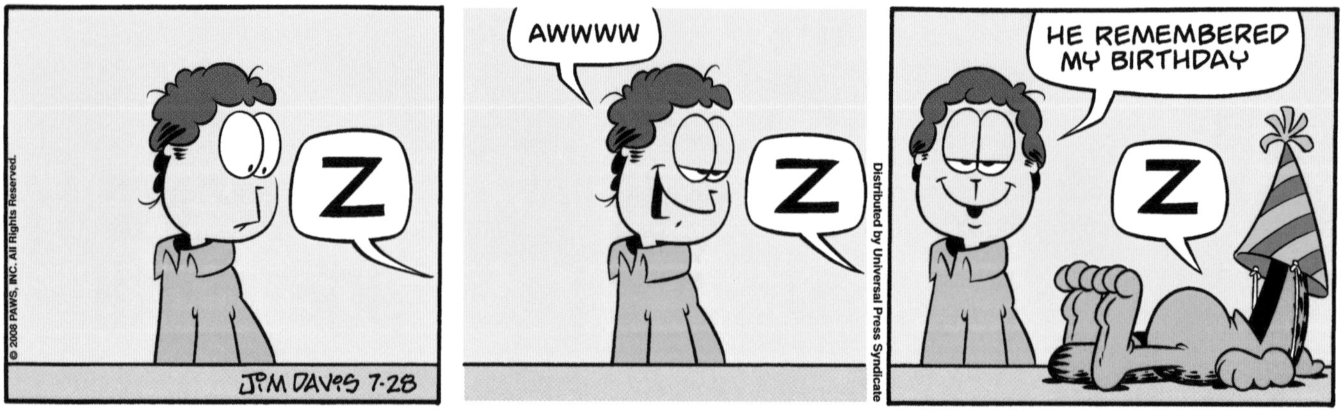
Z
AWWWW
Z
HE REMEMBERED MY BIRTHDAY
Z
JIM DAVIS 7-28
© 2008 PAWS, INC. All Rights Reserved.
Distributed by Universal Press Syndicate

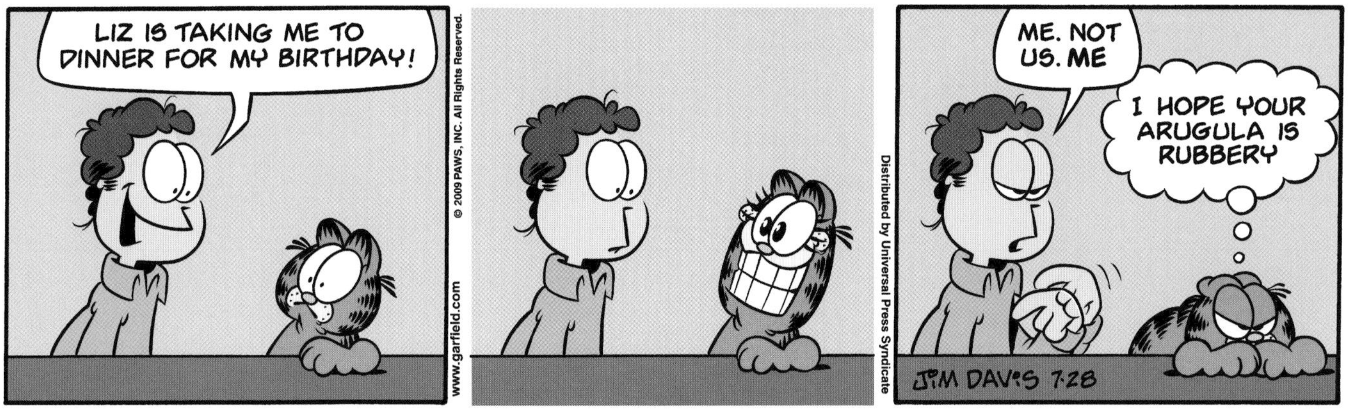
LIZ IS TAKING ME TO DINNER FOR MY BIRTHDAY!
www.garfield.com
© 2009 PAWS, INC. All Rights Reserved.
Distributed by Universal Press Syndicate
ME. NOT US. ME
I HOPE YOUR ARUGULA IS RUBBERY
JIM DAVIS 7·28

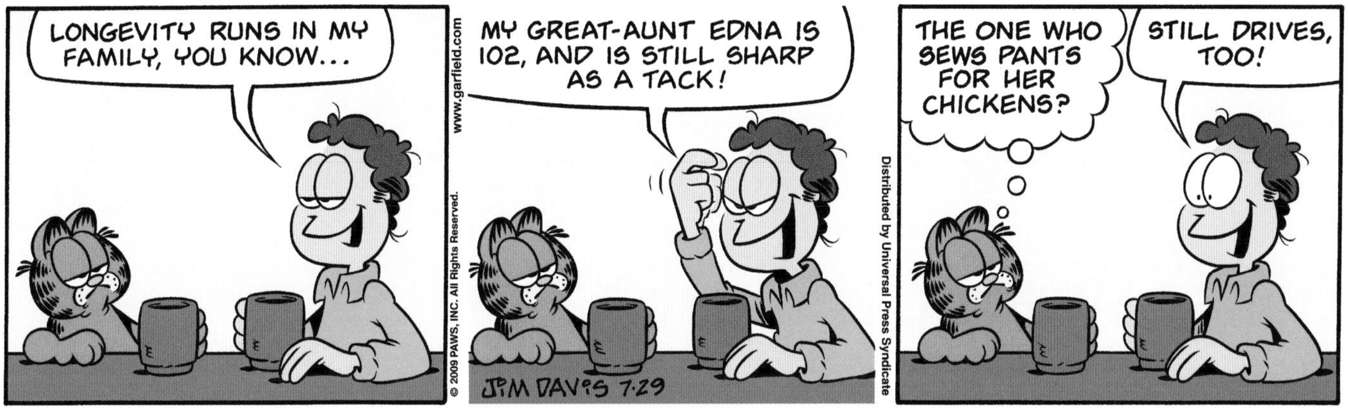
LONGEVITY RUNS IN MY FAMILY, YOU KNOW...
www.garfield.com
© 2009 PAWS, INC. All Rights Reserved.
MY GREAT-AUNT EDNA IS 102, AND IS STILL SHARP AS A TACK!
JIM DAVIS 7·29
Distributed by Universal Press Syndicate
THE ONE WHO SEWS PANTS FOR HER CHICKENS?
STILL DRIVES, TOO!

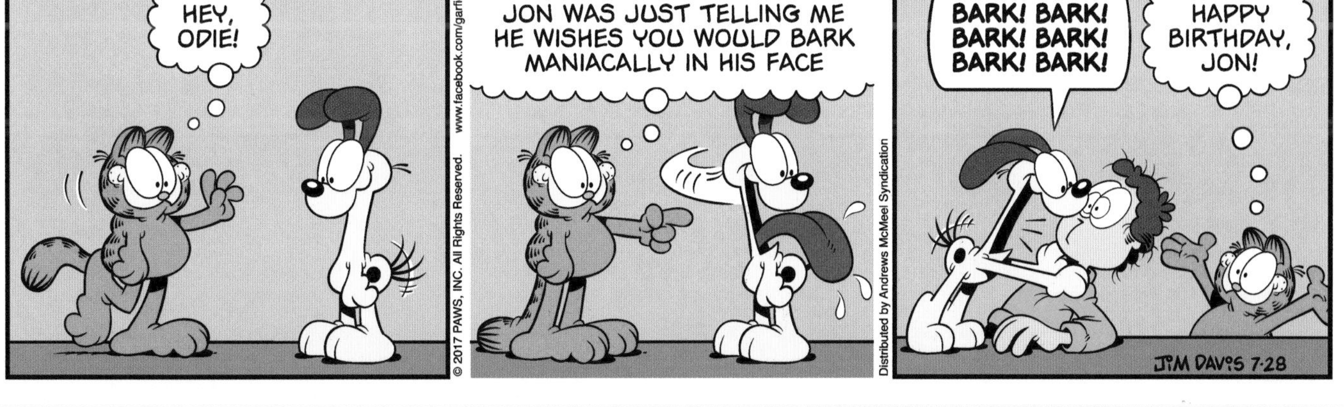
HEY, ODIE!
© 2017 PAWS, INC. All Rights Reserved.
www.facebook.com/garfield
JON WAS JUST TELLING ME HE WISHES YOU WOULD BARK MANIACALLY IN HIS FACE
Distributed by Andrews McMeel Syndication
BARK! BARK! BARK! BARK! BARK! BARK!
HAPPY BIRTHDAY, JON!
JIM DAVIS 7·28

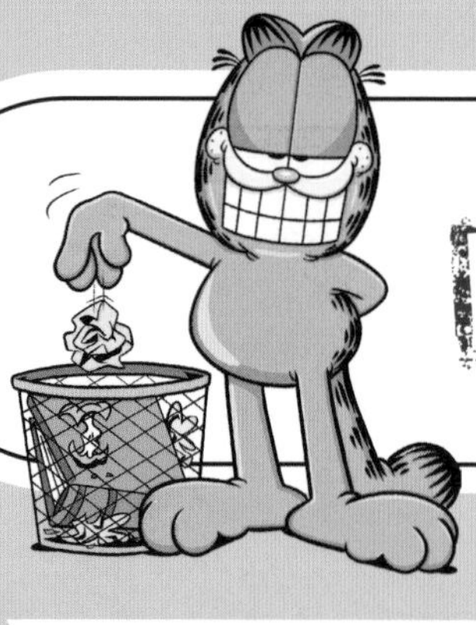

TOP TEN REJECTED TITLES FOR THIS BOOK

10. *The Cat with the Wrinkled Tattoo*

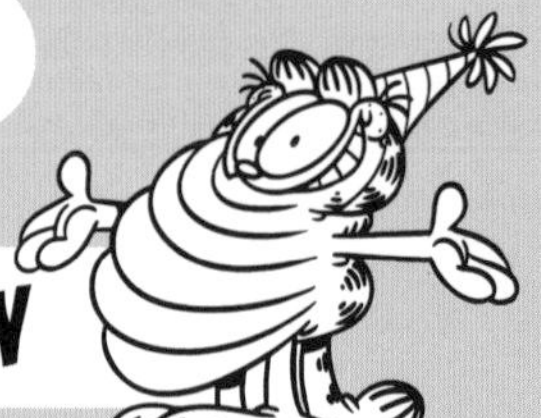

9. ANOTHER YEAR, ANOTHER CHIN
8. ORANGE IS THE NEW GRAY
7. A Brief History of Hairballs
6. WRINKLES ON MY TEETH

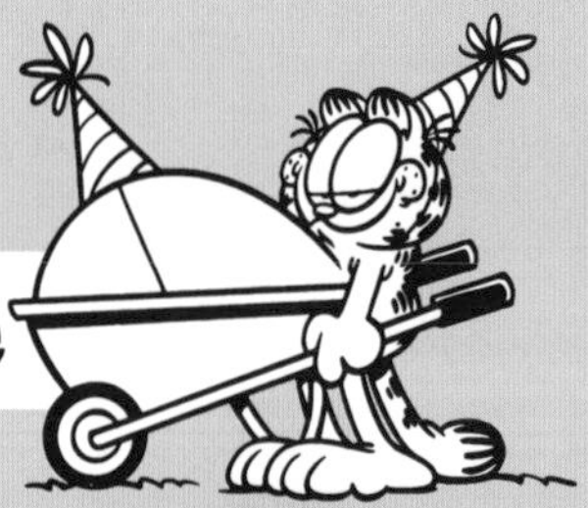

5. **Forty Years of Fattitude**
4. EAT, PRAY, LOVE, BURP

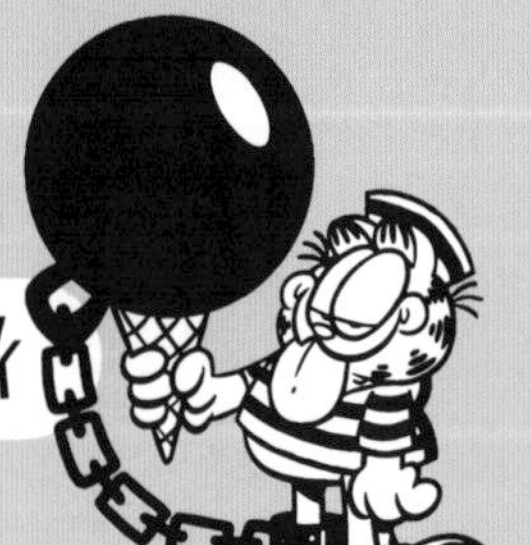

3. *Forty Years for Hijacking an Ice Cream Truck*
2. *Wake Up and Smell the Nursing Home*
1. FORTY YEARS AND DAVIS STILL WON'T LET ME RETIRE

YOU KIDS

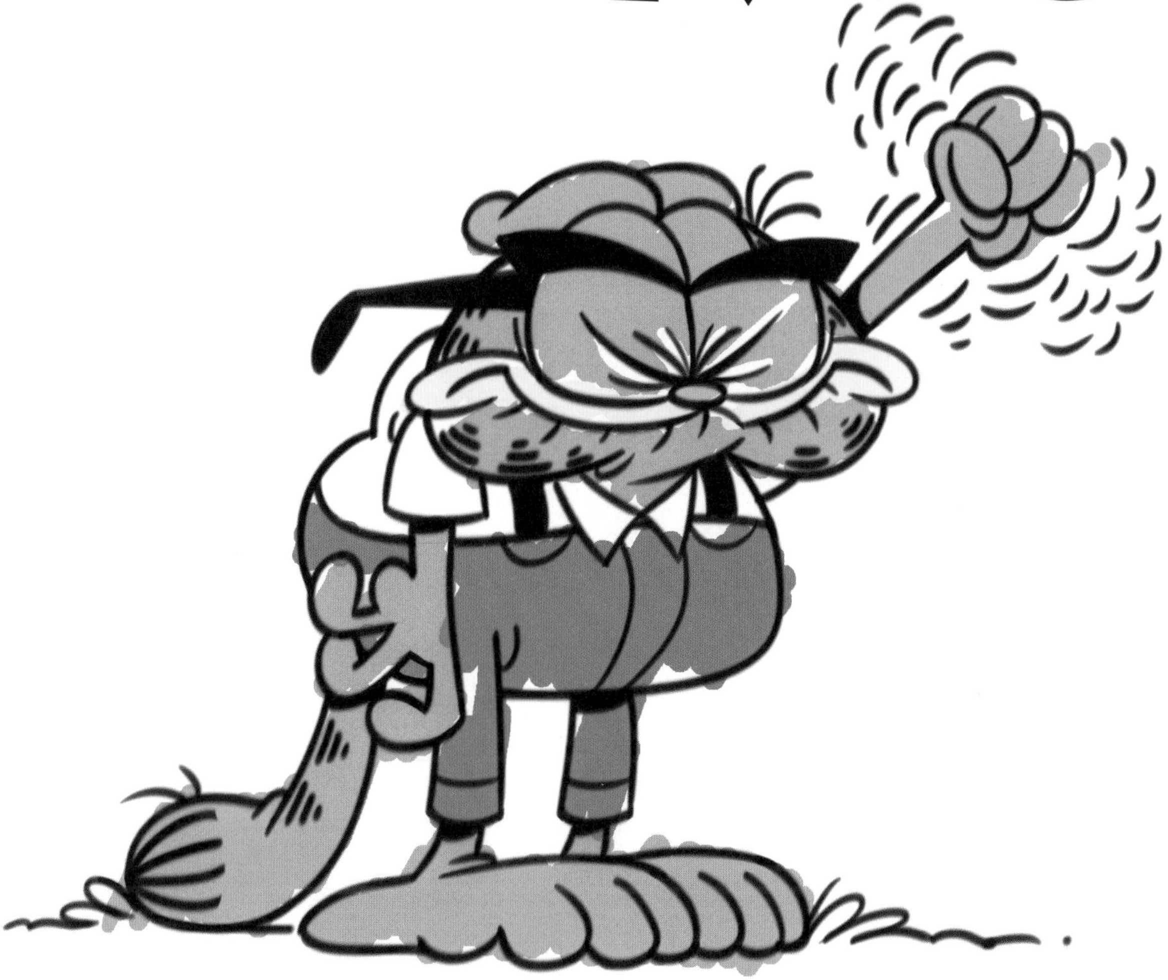

GET OFF MY LAWN

Jim ("Jimmy") Davis
on his sixth birthday, July 28, 1951

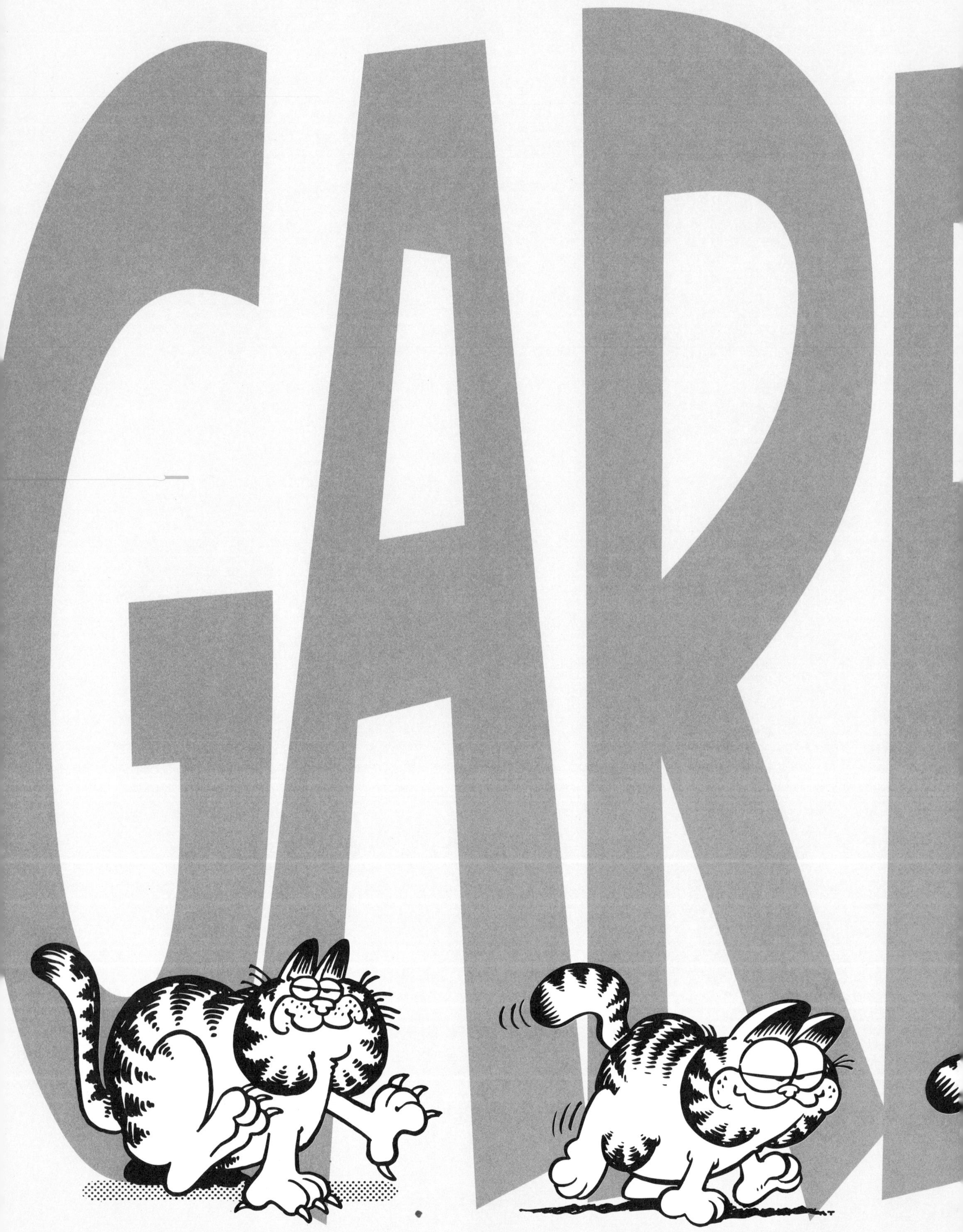
GAR